COMPUTER ARCHITECTURE
A MODERN SYNTHESIS

VOLUME 2: ADVANCED TOPICS

COMPUTER ARCHITECTURE
A MODERN SYNTHESIS

VOLUME 2: ADVANCED TOPICS

Subrata Dasgupta
Edmiston Professor of Computer Science
University of Southwestern Louisiana
Lafayette, Louisiana

WILEY
John Wiley & Sons
New York   Chichester   Brisbane   Toronto   Singapore

Library of Congress Cataloging-in-Publication Data:

Dasgupta, Subrata.
  Computer architecture.
    References : v. 1, p. 331–366; v. 2, p. 365–400
    Includes indexes.
    Contents: v. 1. Foundations.—v. 2. Advanced topics.
    1. Computer architecture. I. Title.
QA76.9.A73D35 1989   004.2′2   87-37188
ISBN 0-471-82310-4 (v. 1)
ISBN 0-471-60152-7 (v. 2)

87-37188
CIP

Printed in the United States of America

10 9 8 7 6 5 4 3 2 1

To
Jaideep
and
Monish

PREFACE

The casual reader turning the pages of a comprehensive text or survey article on computers will be struck by the *diversity* of computers that have emerged over the past four decades.

This diversity manifests itself across several dimensions. One of these is the *technological* dimension—that is, the physical basis for their construction and implementation. Most strikingly, however, other sources of computer diversity lie in their *functional* characteristics—their externally observable behavior, properties, and capabilities—and in their *internal structure and organization*. Collectively, these essentially abstract properties define what has come to be known as *computer architecture* and constitute the architectural dimensions of computer diversity.

Thus, one view of computer architecture sees it as the study of such abstract characteristics of computers and their interrelationships that have led to the "evolution" and proliferation of computer species. The analogy between computer architecture and the anatomical and evolutionary studies in biology is, in some sense, evident.

Unlike organisms, however, computers are designed and built entities; they are *artifacts*. Thus, from another viewpoint computer architecture is seen as a *design discipline* concerned with the design, development, description, and verification of computer *architectures*. Here the appropriate analogy is perhaps with *building architecture*. Indeed, in the latter context we use the term "architecture" both in the declarative sense as defining some set of abstract properties, plan, or theme that a building exhibits as well as in the procedural sense of a design discipline concerned with the process of producing these abstract properties.

The analogy between computer architecture and building architecture is really striking in this respect: they are both concerned with abstract properties that ultimately depend on appropriate technologies for their effective implementation; yet each has its own autonomous vocabulary, heuristic rules, and scientific principles—constituting a universe of discourse—that are distinct from the vocabulary, rules and principles of its underlying technology; the efficacy of both architectural disciplines and principles are ultimately tested in social (i.e., human) environments; and finally, they are both, again as disciplines, preoccupied with the problem of organization.

However, this text and its companion volume are not about these analogies, fascinating though they are. In these two volumes I have attempted to deal simultaneously with the two faces of computer architecture—its compendium of architectural *principles* and the issues related to architectural *design*. The first is concerned with parts or subsystems viewed in convenient isolation. The second with the design of the whole. The "synthesis" in the title refers, first, to the unification of these two facets and, second, to my attempt to organize the diversity of architectural principles within a single integrated framework.

The two texts are intended to form a coherent whole. However, they have been written and organized so that each volume can be read, studied, and used independently of the other. The present volume, *Advanced Topics,* is written to serve as a graduate-level text for a one-semester graduate course in computer architecture. Its companion volume, *Foundations,* is intended for senior level undergraduate students. There are, however, two aspects common to the two books: shared references and an identical first chapter, which establishes a common framework and terminology for both *Foundations* and *Advanced Topics.*

Volume 2 is organized into three parts. Part I deals with some of the issues pertaining to computer architecture as a whole. In particular, Chapter 1 introduces the important idea of *architectural levels* and establishes the connections between architecture on the one hand and design methodology, compilers, microprogramming, software technology and implementation technology on the other. Chapter 2 discusses the fascinating (but difficult) problem of establishing a taxonomy for architectures, an issue that brings to mind once more the analogy between computer systems and biological systems.

Part II is devoted to a relatively new topic—the development of tools for the design and description of architectures. Chapter 3 discusses the general issues pertinent to the design of architecture description languages (ADLs) and their applications; Chapter 4 presents the structure of two recently developed, but rather different, ADLs. Finally, Chapter 5 surveys the development of firmware engineering—which is concerned with tools and techniques for the design, verification, and automatic implementation of firmware.

Part III of this book concentrates on various facets of parallel processing. Parallelism can, of course, be manifested at many levels of "granularity" and abstraction. Chapter 6 is, thus, concerned with the parallelism between (or overlap of) instruction executions in pipelined uniprocessors; Chapter 7 presents the principles of parallel processing as it is found in vector computers. Pipelining is manifested in a slightly different manner in these machines. Chapter 8 discusses the multiprocessor, which might be viewed as forming the basis for the most general type of parallel processing activity. Finally, the relatively distinctive principles of dataflow computing are presented in Chapter 9.

In concluding, I would like to note an important feature of the problem sets at the end of each chapter: and that is (in keeping with the view of computer architecture as a design discipline), the emphasis on *design problems.* Some of these are suitable for solution as normal "assignments" whereas others are more in the nature of "projects" that can be pursued in the course of an entire semester.

Lafayette, Louisiana
July 31, 1987   Subrata Dasgupta

ACKNOWLEDGMENTS

A project of this kind can only be conducted in an atmosphere in which one's research, teaching, and writing can be carried out in symbiotic harmony and where one is relatively free of administrative duties. I have been fortunate in enjoying, for several years, precisely such a climate at the Center for Advanced Computer Studies of the University of Southwestern Louisiana. Its Director, Terry Walker, has had much to do with this pleasant state of affairs. I thank him for the environment and his support.

I also must thank the National Science Foundation for supporting my recent studies of computer architecture as a design discipline. The fruits of these studies have advertently and inadvertently influenced several parts of this book. These same researches formed the basis of continuing discussions of many aspects of architecture with my students (and collaborators), notably, Philip Wilsey, Ulises Aguero, Alan Hooton, Cy Ardoin, and Sukhesh Patel. My ideas were also formed under the influence of an ongoing transatlantic dialogue (stretching over six years) with Werner Damm, formerly of Aachen Technical University, and now with the University of Oldenburg, West Germany. I thank them all for the pleasure of their intellectual company.

A part of this work was done while I was a visiting fellow at Wolfson College, Oxford, and the Oxford University Computing Laboratory in the summer of 1986. I am very grateful to Professor C. A. R. Hoare and to Sir Raymond Hoffenberg, President of Wolfson College, for providing me the facilities and an enchanting physical environment in which to work.

Several persons were kind enough to read and review selected chapters from the two volumes. I thank, in particular, Laxmi Bhuyan, Dipak Ghosal, John Gurd, Steven Landry, and Robert Mueller for their many helpful comments. I also thank William M. Lively and James L. Beug who provided very useful reviews of the manuscripts. For any residual errors that may be found in the text, may I say, in the time-honored tradition: *mea culpa*!

In the course of this work I received enormous logistical help from several persons. In particular:

Cathy Pomier, who typed the manuscripts and undertook their many revisions with invariable and sustained good humor. For her, the adjective "unflappable" is truly apt.

Nancy Pellegran, who typed the problem sets and the index and helped put the finishing touches to the manuscript.

Philip Wilsey and Ulises Aguero who exercised their computational ingenuity in producing the computer generated diagrams that appear in the text, and who assisted me in innumerable ways.

Richard Bonacci, my original editor at Wiley, who warmly supported this project.

Gene Davenport, Senior Editor at Wiley, who provided firm, wise, and invaluable advice during the later, crucial stages of my writing.

Joe Dougherty, Editor, Gilda Stahl, Senior Copy Editor, and Dawn Reitz, Senior Production Supervisor at Wiley, for their assistance during the physical production of this book.

I am grateful to each one of these persons for their help.

My thanks to Steven Vegdahl, Robert Mueller, Werner Damm, Gert Dohmen, the Institute of Electrical and Electronic Engineers, Intermetrics, Inc., the Association for Computing Machinery, Digital Equipment Corporation, John Wiley & Sons, Academic Press, McGraw-Hill, and MIT Press for granting me permission to reproduce diagrams and excerpts from their publications. I also thank George Spix and Linda Turpin of Cray Research for providing information on some recent Cray systems.

Finally, a note of gratitude to my wife, Sarmistha, and sons, Jaideep and Monish, for living patiently with this, seemingly interminable, project and for their love and support.

CONTENTS

COMPUTER ARCHITECTURE
A MODERN SYNTHESIS

VOLUME 2: ADVANCED TOPICS

PART ONE

INTRODUCTION AND BACKGROUND

CHAPTER 1

THE SCOPE OF COMPUTER ARCHITECTURE

In this book the term *computer architecture* will be used in two complementary ways. It will refer to certain *logical* and *abstract properties* of computers, the nature of which will be described herein. The term will also be used to denote the art, craft, and science — or more generally, the discipline — involved in *designing* these same logical and abstract properties. Thus, computer architecture (or more simply, when there is no room for ambiguity, architecture) refers both to certain characteristics of computers and to the design methods used in realizing these characteristics.

1.1 EXO-ARCHITECTURE

What are these logical and abstract properties that are of interest to the computer architect? There are first the *functional* characteristics of computers: their externally observable behavior, properties, and capabilities that are of fundamental interest to a certain group of users. These users include, in particular, system programmers responsible for the construction of operating systems and compilers for a given computer and the applications programmers involved in writing programs in the computer's assembly language.

The collection of externally observable behavior, properties, and capabilities goes by several names in the architectural literature, including, simply, computer *architecture* (Myers, 1982), the *instruction set processor* (ISP) level (Siewiorek, Bell, and Newell, 1982), the *conventional machine level* (Tanenbaum, 1984), and *exo-architecture* (Dasgupta, 1984). I will employ this last term in this book to remind you that these properties reflect the *external* functional and logical features of computers.

The primary components of a computer's exo-architecture are

1. The organization of programmable storage.
2. Data types and data structures, their encoding and representation.
3. Instruction formats.
4. The instruction (or operation code) set.
5. The modes of addressing and accessing data items and instructions.
6. Exception conditions.

3

A computer's exo-architecture represents a particular abstraction level at which we may choose to view it. An *abstraction* is a simplified or selective description of a system that highlights some of the system properties while suppressing others. In the case of complex systems, we may need to perform *different kinds* of abstraction depending on the purpose at hand. Furthermore, these different kinds of abstractions may be so selected as to form a hierarchic relationship with one another. In that case, we talk of the existence of different *abstraction levels.*

The abstraction level of a computer that we call exo-architecture defines the interface between the physical machine and any software that may be superimposed on it (Fig. 1.1). Indeed, the establishment of such user interface is the *purpose* of this abstraction level. The "users" of this interface are the operating system and compiler writers and, generally, those who wish to program in assembly language.

It is important to note that abstractions and abstraction levels are *artifacts.* We invent them so that we have a means for organizing and understanding complex phenomena, but there is nothing sacrosanct about them. Thus, two different designers of an exo-architecture may choose and define two very distinct sets of functional capabilities, depending on what they consider to be useful for the "user."

Example 1.1

For most conventional single-processor systems the exo-architecture will consist of the features cited earlier; namely, the instruction set, operand addressing modes, the word length, the number of words (or bytes) of available main memory, the number and types of high-speed programmable registers, and so on. The user may never need to know such "internal' details as the precise mechanisms by which instructions are interpreted by the hardware or whether, for example, instructions are "pipelined."

In contrast, the user of a *vector processor* may well have to know some details of its internal processor organization in order to effectively exploit the potential parallelism that such processors offer. The exo-architecture of these machines may then be defined to reveal such details rather than to hide them as in conventional processors.   ■

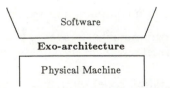

FIGURE 1.1   Exo-architecture: The interface between software and physical machine.

1.2 ENDO-ARCHITECTURE

An exo-architecture is realized by mechanisms implemented in hardware and microcode (or firmware). We can, in fact, describe these mechanisms and their interactions at various levels—for example, the circuit, logic (gate), or register transfer levels. However, important as these levels are, for many purposes they are too detailed—they contain too much information. To understand how the hardware/firmware complex realizes an exo-architecture may require us to abstract from the details of logic or even register transfer levels. This abstraction of the hardware/firmware details has been given several names in the literature, including *processor architecture* (Myers, 1982), *computer organization* (Hayes, 1978), and *endo-architecture* (Dasgupta, 1984). I will use this last term in this book to emphasize that these characteristics constitute a description of a computer's *internal* organization.

Basically, a computer's endo-architecture consists of the following descriptions.

1. The capabilities and performance characteristics of its principal functional components.
2. The ways in which these components are interconnected.
3. The nature of information flow between components.
4. The logic and means by which such information flow is controlled.

It is important to realize that the purpose of this abstraction level is really to aid *understandability*. This abstraction is necessary not only for the "reader" of the design but also for the designer so that he or she need not have to manage and master too many "low-level" details.

The relationship between exo-architecture, endo-architecture, and the next lower (e.g., register-transfer) level representation of the circuits that interpret and realize these architectural levels is illustrated in Figure 1.2.

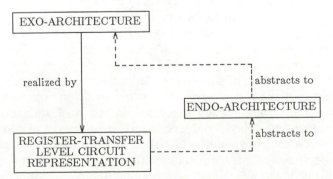

FIGURE 1.2 The relationships between exo-architecture, endo-architecture, and the register-transfer level.

1.3 MICRO-ARCHITECTURE

As described in the foregoing sections, a processor's endo-architecture is an abstracted view of its internal hardware organization. However, architects in practice may exercise considerable freedom in deciding how detailed the endo-architectural design and description should be. A very special situation arises in the cases of *microprogrammed* and *user microprogrammable* computers because, for these machine classes, the architect specifies the endo-architecture at a level of detail necessary for the microprogrammer to write and implement the microcode for such machines.

I will reserve the term *micro-architecture* to denote the internal architecture —the logical structure and functional capabilities—of a computer as seen by the microprogrammer.

Remarks

Several points about micro-architecture are worth noting.

1. The *purpose* of micro-architecture as a distinct abstraction level is to establish and define *the interface between the hardware* and the *superimposed* firmware (microcode). Thus, micro-architecture is to the microprogrammer what exo-architecture is to the (assembly language) programmer.
2. Extending this parallel, and given the recent trend toward the use of high-level microprogramming languages (HLMLs) and their compilers, the micro-architecture of a processor defines those aspects of the hardware system required either by the microprogrammer or by the HLML compiler writer.
3. Although a micro-architecture may be viewed as a special version of a machine's endo-architecture, it is important to keep in mind that the latter may be defined independent of (a) whether microprogramming or hardwired logic is used to implement the processor or (b) the precise style, logic, and organization of the control unit. In other words, a given computer may be designed and described meaningfully in terms of its exo-architecture, its micro-architecture on which the microprogram is run so as to realize the exo-architecture, and an endo-architecture that is an abstraction of the micro-architecture/microprogram complex. The relationship between these levels is shown in Figure 1.3.
4. The micro-architecture of a processor, depending on how detailed it is, may or may not coincide with the *register-transfer level* description. At the latter level, computer structures are described in terms of such primitives as terminals, registers, delays, counters, clocks, memories, and combinational circuits. The primitives from which such a description is composed bear obvious one-to-one correspondences with common medium-scale integration (MSI) logic circuits. Generally speaking, the register-transfer level description will contain more information than the microprogrammer needs to know, hence the micro-architecture abstracts somewhat from this level (Fig. 1.3).

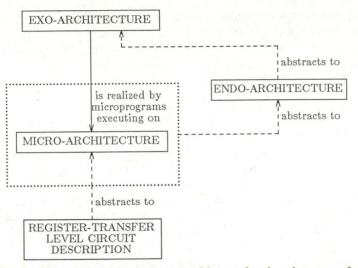

FIGURE 1.3 **The relationships between architectural and register-transfer levels.**

5. Finally, note that the foregoing "definition" of micro-architecture and its relationship to endo-architecture as depicted in Figure 1.3 is universally valid only for *single processors*. In the case of a *multiprocessor* system, you may refer to the endo-architecture of the system as a whole—that is, to the collective, internal structure of the whole, integrated complex. However, it does not usually make sense to talk of the micro-architecture of the multiprocessor. The individual processors comprising the system—if microprogrammed—will, of course, have their own, local micro-architectures.

1.4 EXAMPLES OF ARCHITECTURAL LEVELS: THE VAX FAMILY

I will illustrate the typical characteristics of, and the distinctions between, architectural levels using as an example, Digital Equipment Corporation's VAX family of 32-bit processors (Digital, 1981a, 1981b). There are several members of this family, including the VLSI VAX microcomputer (Brown and Sites, 1984), the VAX-11/750 and VAX-11/780 systems (Digital, 1981b), and, most recently, the VAX 8600 (Digital, 1985).

1.4.1 Exo-architecture

The VAX family of processors was designed to share a common exo-architecture, which is described in the *VAX Architecture Handbook* (Digital, 1981a).[1]

---

[1]As we have noted earlier, various names are used to designate what has been called exo-architecture here. In the VAX literature, this is simply referred to as the "architecture" of the VAX family. See the Bibliographic and Historical Notes at the end of this chapter for further remarks on this matter.

The commonality of exo-architecture assures *compatibility* among the individual family members—that is, it ensures that software originally intended for execution on one member-processor may be transported for execution on some other member-processor with a minimum of reprogramming.

The VAX exo-architecture contains the following features.

1. A 4 gigabyte (2^{32} bytes) virtual address space.
2. A set of numeric data types for the representation, storage, and manipulation of 8, 16, 32, 64, and 128 bit integers; 32, 64, and 128 bit floating-point numbers; data types representing packed decimal strings up to 16 bytes long with two digits packed per byte; unpacked numeric strings up to 31 bytes with one digit per byte; character strings; and queue data types allowing the representation and manipulation of circular, doubly linked lists.
3. A high-speed register space consisting of 16 32-bit registers of which some have special roles such as the program counter, stack pointer, and stack frame pointer.
4. A repertoire of operand addressing modes—that is, means for specifying (either directly or indirectly) operands located in either main memory, the registers, or within the instruction stream itself.
5. The VAX exo-architecture also provides several mechanisms for supporting multiprogramming. However, such features are not part of the "user-visible" exo-architecture. Rather, they are part of the more general interface visible to the systems programmer. Thus, for instance, context switching between processes may be performed by the operating system, using such special instructions as *save process context* and *load process context.*
6. A variable-length instruction format consisting of a 1 or 2 byte opcode field followed by 0 to 6 operand specifiers whose number and type depend on the opcode.
7. A general instruction set for the manipulation of the various numeric and nonnumeric data types, a repertoire of control instructions, special instructions for manipulating special data types such as addresses and queues, and a privileged instruction set available only to the systems programmer.
8. Specification of various exceptions and interrupts. In the VAX terminology, *exceptions* are unusual events that may occur in the context of the "currently" executing process. These include, for example, various arithmetic overflow and underflow conditions. *Interrupts* are events that may have been generated on a systematic basis or outside the context of the currently executing process. These include, for example, interrupts induced by device errors or a device completion condition.

1.4.2 Endo-architecture

Figure 1.4 shows the principal endo-architectural components of the VAX-11/780 processor and their interconnections. The *data cache* is an 8K byte, two-way set associative memory (see Chapter 8, Volume 1) that is used for all information coming from main memory, including data, addresses, and instructions.

The *address translation buffer* (TB) is a cache containing 128 virtual-to-physi-

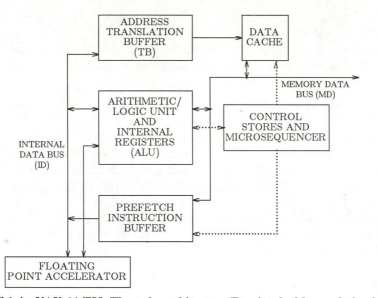

FIGURE 1.4 **VAX-11/780: The endo-architecture (Reprinted with permission from** *The VAX Hardware Handbook* © **Digital Press/Digital Equipment Corporation, Bedford, Mass, 1981).**

cal page address translations that is used to reduce the time required for dynamic address translation.

The *prefetch instruction buffer* (PIB) is 8 bytes long and is used to improve the performance of the central processing unit (CPU) by prefetching instructions. The control logic continuously fetches data from memory to keep the buffer full.

In addition, the (optional) floating-point accelerator executes arithmetic operations on single-and double-precision floating-point data, while the control unit includes a 96-bit wide, 4K word read-only memory holding the principle microprogram implementing the VAX-11 instruction set, a 1K 96-bit word writable diagnostic control store holding diagnostic microroutines, and an optional 1K 96-bit word user writable control store.

The distinction between exo- and endo-architecture, and the idea that the former is an abstraction of the latter, can be more clearly appreciated when we examine the dynamics of instructions execution. Consider as a specific example the interpretation of the VAX-11

CLRL R0

instruction, assuming it is stored at virtual address V. At the exo-architectural level, the meaning of this instruction is simply given by the equations

$$\left.\begin{array}{l} \text{reg.R0}' = 0 \\ N' = 0 \\ Z' = 1 \\ V' = 0 \\ C' = C \end{array}\right\} \ \textbf{Condition codes} \qquad\qquad (1.1)$$

where the symbol X′ indicates the *new* value of X whereas the unprimed symbol denotes its old value.

However, when we look at the interpretation of this same instruction at the endo-architectural level, several events take place involving the functional components shown in Figure 1.4.

1. The virtual address V is converted to a physical address P by the translation buffer TB.
2. The data cache is queried to see if it contains P.
3. Assuming this is not so, a block of bytes beginning at P in main memory is fetched and the addresses and contents are loaded into the cache.
4. The first few of these same bytes are also loaded into the prefetch instruction buffer.
5. Finally, the relevant instruction is read from the buffer, decoded, and executed by the arithmetic and logic unit (ALU), resulting in the effects shown in Equation (1.1).

Remarks

1. Note, in this example, that for a complete understanding of the endo-architecture and how it supports the execution of the (CLRL) instruction, it is necessary to understand the *functional behavior* of such components as the data cache, the translation buffer, and the prefetch instruction buffer as well as how information is transferred between these components.
2. On completion of the instruction execution the state of the machine at the exo-architectural level is identical to that prior to its execution except for the changes shown by Equation (1.1). On the other hand, the state change of the same machine at the endo-architectural level will include, in addition to those shown by Equation (1.1), changes to the states of the two caches and the instruction buffer in addition to those of register RO and the condition code flags. The exo-architectural state of the machine is, thus, an abstraction of the endo-architectural machine state — that is, there is, in general, a many-to-one mapping from the latter state space to the former state space (Fig. 1.5).
3. Finally, note that the foregoing description of instruction execution remains valid regardless of whether or not the processor is microprogrammed.

1.4.3 Micro-architecture

Finally, when we move down to the micro-architecture of the VAX-11/780 processor,[2] the state space is further enlarged since many additional components are visible at this level. Most importantly, the microprogrammer must have precise knowledge of the internal organization of the control unit, including the microinstruction word format, the semantics of each of the micro-operations that may be encoded within a microinstruction, and the mechanism used by the microsequencer to generate the successive addresses of microinstructions. An-

[2] Also called the KA780 central processing unit in the VAX literature (Digital, 1979).

Exo-architectural state space

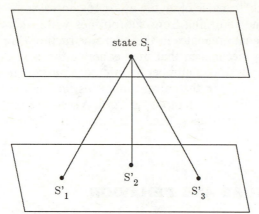

Endo-architectural state space

FIGURE 1.5 Mapping between exo-architectural and endo-architectural state spaces.

other important component of the micro-architecture is the clocking (or timing) system that guides the synchronized execution of micro-operations, microinstructions, and the sequencing logic. This information was factored out at the endo-architectural level.

A highly selective view of the VAX-11/780 micro-architecture contains the following components.

1. A 96-bit wide ("horizontal") control store with a single microinstruction format containing some 30 fields. These fields enable the microprogrammer to encode concurrently executable micro-operations, including a variety of 8-, 16- and 32-bit arithmetic, logical, and shift operations (Fig. 1.6).

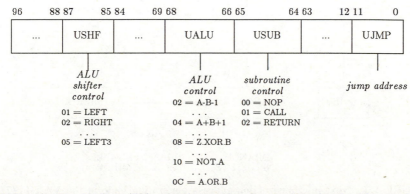

FIGURE 1.6 The VAX-11/780 microinstruction format (Reprinted with permission from *KA780 Central Processor Technical Description*. © Digital Equipment Corporation, Maynard, Mass, 1979).

2. A 200 ns, four-phase system clock, each phase being 50 ns long.
3. A "microstack" capable of saving up to 16 control store addresses and used for calling and returning from subroutines within a microprogram. The call/return signal originates in the microinstruction (Fig. 1.6).
4. A sequencing mechanism that may generate the next executable microinstruction address from a number of different sources. The normal source is a 13-bit "jump" field in the current microinstruction logically added to special 3-, 4- or 5-bit "branch input" entities. A second address source is the top element of the microstack, used when control returns from a (micro)subroutine (Fig. 1.7).

1.5 STRUCTURE AND BEHAVIOR

Every architectural level contains both structural and behavioral components. By *structure* we mean the set of important static (time invariant) components of

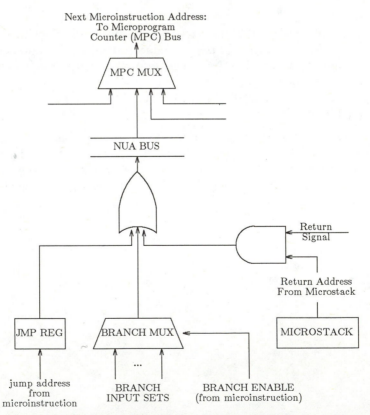

FIGURE 1.7 Next microinstruction address generation logic in the VAX-11/780 microarchitecture (Reprinted with permission from *KA780 Central Processor Technical Description*. © Digital Equipment Corporation, Maynard, Mass, 1979).

the architecture and their static (time invariant) relationship. Because of their nature, structural aspects of an architecture can be easily described and even be represented diagrammatically.

Thus, the data types, data structures, and instruction formats in an exo-architecture, or the microinstruction format in a micro-architecture — that is, its internal organization and the names and encodings of their constituent operations (Fig. 1.6) — are often pictorially represented. The "block diagram" form, as shown in Figure 1.4, is a common representation of the structural aspect of endo-architectures, whereas Figure 1.7 is a hybrid diagram consisting of functional blocks (the NUA bus, microstack), register-transfer-level elements (the JMP register, and the two multiplexers) and gate level elements (the OR and AND gates). The components in both diagrams are connected by lines denoting data and control paths.

The structural aspect of an architecture establishes the basis for formulating how it should behave. By *behavior* we mean the dynamics of the abstract machine that the architecture represents: what the functions of its components are and how information and control actually flow between the components.

In an exo-architecture, it is therefore necessary to know not only how an instruction is represented and encoded but what the *meaning* of an instruction is: the mapping it performs between its input and output storage elements. Similarly, the name of an operand addressing mode (e.g., "autoincrement" in the VAX-11) and its encoding in an instruction is a structural feature; the corresponding computation performed by the machine hardware/firmware to generate the effective real address is a behavioral component.

Behavior becomes particularly crucial in endo- and micro-architectures since the source of complexity at these levels lies in their behavior. The problem of designing or analyzing the endo-architecture of the VAX-11/780, for instance, lies in one's ability to comprehend the dynamic relationships between the components depicted in Figure 1.4. Questions are, typically, of the form:

- What is the mapping performed by the address translation buffer?
- How is this unit activated and which of the other components have the power to activate it?
- Can two or more of the components shown become active concurrently?
- What if one needs the result of the other — how are they synchronized to exchange information at the right time?

Concurrency and synchronization are, thus, notable factors contributing to the behavioral complexity of architectures.

1.6 COMPUTER ARCHITECTURE AS A DESIGN DISCIPLINE

In the preceding sections I described those properties of computers that fall within the scope of computer architecture. A major part of research, development, and innovations in this field is concerned with the identification, development, refinement, and implementation of such architectural properties at one or more of the architectural levels. The totality of our knowledge of these properties at any particular time constitute what might be termed architectural *principles.*

However, computers and their properties are artifacts; architects must, therefore, also deal with how an appropriate subset of these principles are selected, composed, and integrated during the *design* of a particular architecture. The subject of computer architecture, then, deals not only with the description, analysis, and understanding of architectural principles; it is also a *design discipline* concerned with how the *total architecture* of a computer may be derived.

A *discipline* means, among other things, "a system of rules of conduct."[3] This meaning is particularly relevant to our context: A discipline of computer architecture design may be defined as *a system of rules and procedures governing the design of computer architectures.*

Interest, among theorists and practitioners, in formulating such a discipline — a rational, formal, "scientific" basis for architectural design — is of relatively recent origin (Dasgupta, 1984). At the time of this writing, it is not yet a major movement, although there are signs that the movement as such is steadily gaining momentum.[4] It is, therefore, important to examine the causes of this newly emergent interest in a discipline of computer architecture.

The first and probably the most vital of these causes is technology. The development of very large scale integration (VLSI) semiconductor technology has resulted in a potential for processor chips of enormous circuit density. On the one hand, this has led to entire processors being embedded on a single chip or a few chips. On the other, the atoms from which larger, more powerful computer systems may be built are no longer simple circuits but entire (micro)processors. Thus, whether they are designing and building single-chip processors or multichip multiprocessor systems, computer architects are having to grapple with design issues and the problems of "complexity management" that are quite different from those of a decade or so ago.

Taking their cue from other fields — in particular, software technology (Wegner, 1979) — many architectural theorists and practitioners have turned their attention to a more careful examination of the design process in the conviction that only the development of highly ordered, disciplined, and logical methods of design can control and solve these newly emergent problems of complexity (Mead and Conway 1980; Dasgupta 1984).

Second, substantial parts of the computer design process have been fully or partially automated. Much of *design automation* has traditionally been concerned with the low-level or physical aspects of computer design, such as the

---

[3]J. B. Sykes (ed.): *Concise Oxford Dictionary, 6th ed.* Oxford: Clarendon Press, 1976.

[4]One such sign is of an institutional nature: the ninth (1982) and tenth (1983) International Symposia on Computer Architecture — the premier international conference on the subject — had entire sessions on design methods. The "call for papers" for the eleventh and twelfth symposia (1984 and 1985, respectively) identified "methods for the design and description of architectures" as one of the selected topics of interest.

design, simulation, and testing of logic level and electrical circuits and the solution of chip layout problems (Breuer, 1975; Rabbat, 1983). More recently, efforts have been directed to the more difficult, high-level stages of the design process, including the synthesis of register-transfer-level systems (Parker, 1984), and microcode and micro-architecture synthesis (Dasgupta and Shriver, 1985; Mueller and Varghese, 1985; Nagle, Cloutier, and Parker, 1982).

Finally, as observed by Dasgupta (1984), the ad-hoc, informal and intuitive nature of conventional architecture design has proved to be highly unsatisfactory for a number of reasons. In particular, because architects have, by and large, ignored the use of formal methods of modeling, describing, and documenting their designs, it has proved difficult to demonstrate design correctness and accurately predict the performance of an architecture without actually implementing it in the form of a physical system.

Thus, much interest has recently been shown, and some progress made, in the construction of unified, theoretical frameworks within which one may systematically and formally design, describe, model, verify, and evaluate computer architectures prior to undertaking the costly endeavor of physically realizing such systems. Note that this program of research and development rests on its own merit quite independent of any desire to automate the design process.

1.7 THE INTERACTION OF COMPUTER ARCHITECTURES AND COMPILERS

The task of a compiler is to transform a program written in some high-level, machine-independent language into an efficient, functionally equivalent representation in the target machine's instruction set.[5] Thus, there is an obvious interaction between the design of a computer's exo-architecture and the design of compilers intended to generate code for that computer. In particular, the complexity of the compiler itself, the difficulty of writing it, the ease and efficiency with which the compiler generates code, and the efficiency (in both time and space) of the executable code are all profoundly influenced by the nature of the target exo-architecture as well as by the harmonious relationship between the exo-architecture and the source (high-level) programming language.

1.7.1 The RISC Philosophy

A widely discussed architectural topic in recent years is the philosophy of the reduced instruction set computer (RISC) (Patterson and Ditzel, 1980; Patterson, 1985), which not only illustrates how technology influences architecture design

---

[5]In the compiler literature, the machine that will execute the compiled code is referred to as the *target* machine. In contrast, in microprogramming terminology, the machine that executes the microcode is called the *host* machine whereas that which the microprogram emulates is referred to as the target.

(see Section 1.9) but also demonstrates how compiler-related issues may influence architecture. It puts forth a view of exo- and endo-architecture designs intended to both ease the compilation process and enhance the efficiency of the compiled code.

RISC architectures are discussed in some detail in Chapter 7, (Volume 1), but we can summarize the issue in relation to compilers as follows:

Basically, it has been observed that for various reasons exo-architectures have evolved over the years toward greater complexity—as manifested in larger instruction sets and more complex ("powerful") instructions. Because of the widespread replacement of assembly languages by high-level programming languages the burden of using such instruction sets falls on the compiler, which very often is unable to exploit the more complex instructions.

The result is that only a small subset of the instruction repertoire is actually used by the compiler. Empirical observations of this phenomenon have been reported by several investigators. For example, in their study of the XPL compiler for the IBM System/360, Alexander and Wortman (1975) found that only 10 instructions accounted for 80% of the instructions executed and 99% of executed instructions were accounted for by 30 instructions.

Thus, the proponents of the RISC philosophy suggest that rather than design architectures with large instruction sets, most of which are ignored by the compiler, one should strive to select a small (or "reduced") set of instructions that are sufficiently simple to be exploited fully by the compiler.

1.7.2 Architectural Ideals from a Compiler Writer's Perspective

The design of a small number of relatively simple instructions is, in fact, one of a number of exo-architectural features that influences compilers and the compilation process. A more comprehensive set of issues from the compiler writer's perspective was discussed by Wulf (1981). He identified a collection of "ideal" characteristics or principles that should guide the definition of exo-architectures.

1. **Regularity**   If a particular feature is realized in a certain way in one part of the architecture, then it should be realized in the same way in all parts.

Example 1.2

There should only be one way of encoding or representing a particular operand address in an instruction, regardless of the instruction type or format.

As another example, if a set of programmable general purpose registers are defined for a machine, these registers should indeed be usable in a general, uniform way by all instructions. It should not be the case, for instance, that certain instructions can only reference certain registers and not others, or that one or more of these "general purpose" registers have special roles.   ■

2. **Orthogonality**   This is also referred to as the "separation of concerns" principle. The overall architecture should be partitionable into a number of independent features, each of which can be defined separately.

Example 1.3

The definitions of opcode (instruction) set and the set of operand addressing modes should be mutually independent — that is, orthogonal — issues. ■

3. **Composability** By virtue of the two foregoing principles, it should be possible to compose the separate, orthogonal features in arbitrary ways.

Example 1.4

Given that the instruction (opcode) set and operand addressing modes are regular and orthogonal, the compiler would be able to combine any opcode with any addressing mode. ■

4. **The one or all principle** From the compiler's point of view, there should be either only one way to do some something or all ways should be possible.

Example 1.5

For generating conditional branching code if the only available branch instructions are ones for testing "equality" and "less than," then the compiler has only one way to generate each of the six possible relations; or if all six test relations are defined in the exo-architecture, there is, again, only one method of generating code for these relations. The problem arises when some *arbitrary* subsct of thc relations are defined in the architecture, in which case the compiler has a nontrivial analysis on hand to determine how to implement one of the undefined or "nonprimitive" relations. ■

5. **Provide primitives not solutions** This ideal has a bearing on the interaction of architectures with both compilers and programming languages. The point is, that from the compiler's point of view it is better for the architecture to provide good "primitive" features that can be used efficiently by the compiler to solve code generation problems than for the architecture itself to provide these solutions.

   This principle is, in fact, the cornerstone of the RISC philosophy (see Section 1.7.1). Its validity rests on the observation that certain "powerful" instructions — solutions — are often available in a machine to support a particular high-level language construct. Precisely because of this, however, such instructions represent solutions to *particular* code generation problems and may not be usable to solve even slightly deviating problems.

Example 1.6

1. Subroutine call instructions that support only some parameter passing mechanism.
2. Looping instructions that support only a certain type of high-level language iteration construct. ■

   It is preferable for the compiler to have access to more primitive general features that can be used to support all programming language constructs rather than a subset.

The point of this set of ideals is that the code generation and optimization phases of a compiler essentially involve an enormous *case analysis,* the objective of which is to extract and use information from both program and architecture to generate the most efficient possible code in the best possible way. It is because of this case analysis that the foregoing principles are so important: Any deviation constitutes a special case to be analyzed separately in a possibly ad-hoc manner. The greater the number of such deviations, the larger the number of special case analyses that must be done by the compiler.

1.7.3 Microcode Compilers and Micro-architectures

Since the relationship between compilers and exo-architectures directly affects the performance of both system and application software, the nature of this interaction has been widely discussed. A far less appreciated fact is that one of the very real obstacles that has hitherto prevented the widespread development and acceptance of compilers for *high level microprogramming languages* (HLMLs) is the inherently complex, and frequently convoluted, nature of micro-architectures for which such compilers are supposed to generate microcode.

The crucial problem is that a microcode compiler *must* generate microcode that compares favorably with conventional hand-produced and assembled microprograms. Furthermore, most micro-architectures support horizontal micro-instruction formats that can encode and store several primitive micro-operations intended for execution in parallel. Thus, a microcode compiler must have the capacity to generate sequential code, optimize it, detect which operations can be done in parallel, and, based on this analysis, *compact* the sequential code into a sequence of horizontal micro-instructions. Figures 1.8 and 1.9 contrast the compilation processes for conventional single-processor exo-architectures and horizontal micro-architectures.[6]

Research into high-level microprogramming languages began only in the early 1970s (Dasgupta and Shriver, 1985), and the full-scale development of microcode compilers is of even more recent vintage. At the time of this writing, only a few compilers capable of producing good quality microcode have actually been completed (Baba and Hagiwara, 1981; Ma and Lewis, 1981; Sheraga and Gieser, 1983). There is no doubt that *one* of the major reasons for the paucity of such systems is the sheer difficulty of coping with the idiosyncrasies of micro-archi-

---

[6]Note that Figures 1.8 and 1.9 depict in a very general way the structure of these two types of compilers. One can also point to exceptions. Thus, there is a class of exo-architectures (vector processors) for which compilers must incorporate compaction techniques in order to produce acceptable executable code. Likewise, there are some micro-architectures that may not necessitate compaction at all.

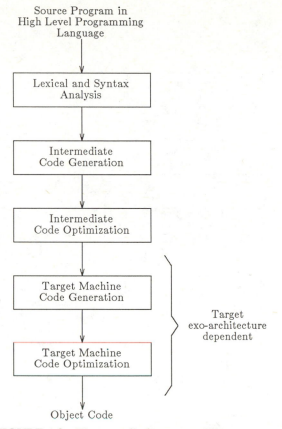

FIGURE 1.8 **The compilation process for programs.**

tectures. Because of the relative youthfulness of microcode compiler technology, very little exists in the way of a careful analysis and documentation of how micro-architectures could be changed to help the compilation process. Instead, firmware engineers[7] have been content to construct progressively more powerful *models* of micro-architectures, hoping that these would allow them to represent larger classes of host machines. These models then form the basis for the code-generation and compaction phases of the compiler.

[7]*Firmware engineering* is the discipline concerned with the identification of scientific principles underlying microprogramming and the application of these principles to the firmware development process (Dasgupta and Shriver, 1985). The firmware engineer is, then, typically interested in constructing tools and techniques to support the various phases of the firmware life cycle, that is, functional specification, design, verification, implementation, and maintenance of microcode. Refer to Chapter 5, for further details.

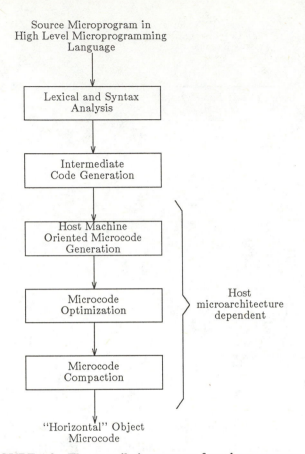

FIGURE 1.9   The compilation process for microprograms.

1.8   THE INFLUENCE OF SOFTWARE TECHNOLOGY ON ARCHITECTURES

As I have noted in Section 1.1, an exo-architecture provides the interface between the computer's *inner environment*—its internal structure—and its *outer environment* (the terms are from Simon, 1981). One of the main reasons why the design of exo-architectures poses difficulties for the architect is because the outer environment is often wide ranging and not predictable to any degree of precision.

The architect has traditionally dealt with this problem by assuming an arbitrary environment and designing exo-architectures that are adapted to this "virtual" environment. The result of this is the now well known *semantic gap* (Myers, 1982) between real and virtual outer environments (Fig. 1.10). The task of bridging this gap is then delegated to compilers and operating systems.

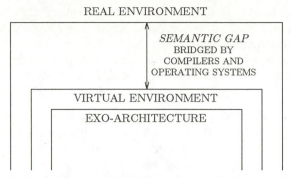

FIGURE 1.10 **The semantic gap (Dasgupta 1984; © 1984, John Wiley & Sons; reprinted with permission).**

Fortunately, this situation has been changing (albeit slowly) over time. From 1961 onward, the Burroughs Corporation has developed and marketed the B5000/B5500/B6500/B6700/B7700 series of general-purpose computers, largely dedicated to the direct architectural support of Algol-like programming languages (Lonergan and King, 1961; Barton, 1961; Organick, 1973; Doran, 1979). In the United Kingdom, beginning in 1968, International Computers Limited initiated the design and production of the ICL 2900 series intended to support efficiently a range of common programming languages (Buckle, 1978). Many of the ideas embodied in this series of machines were first developed by Iliffe (1968) in his Basic Language Machine and by the designers of the Manchester University MU5 (Kilburn *et al.*, 1969; Morris and Ibbett, 1979). Other, more contemporary systems embody similar principles.

To emphasize this relatively new direction in which the real outer environment provides the springboard for designing exo-architectures, such phrases as *software-directed, high-level language,* and *language-directed* are used to describe these architectures. In this book, I will use the last-named term and contrast such language-directed architectures with the more *conventional* exo-architectural styles.

The sources of the mismatch between real and assumed outer environments in conventional machines are many, but they all ultimately appear to originate in the fact that conventional architectures—even contemporary ones—are, largely, evolutionary offsprings and close descendents of the original, so-called *von Neumann computer model* of the 1940s.[8] As Myers (1982) has pointed out, most of these architectural features were more or less identified in the early 1950s—that is, in an era when the programming craft was scarcely understood, operating systems were primitive, and high-level programming languages had yet to be invented. The semantic gap in its present form came into being because exo-architecture design has evolved *much* more slowly than software technology.

---

[8]For an explanation of this term and a brief account of the controversy surrounding it, see Section 1.10, "Bibliographic and Historical Notes," at the end of this chapter.

Thus, the conventional exo-architectures contain features that have little or no direct bearing on how computations are actually conceived, designed, and described by programmers.

The issue of language-directed architectures are dealt with further, in Chapters 6 and 7 of Volume 1. However, it may be useful to state briefly here the principal causes of the semantic gap. These have been identified by Myers (1982) as

1. *Language-related causes.* Programming languages embody many concepts that are not directly reflected in the underlying architecture. Examples include (a) the explicit separation of data and executional statements (instructions) in high-level language programs; (b) the definition of data types as a set of values together with a set of operations that may be applied to these values; (c) a concept of storage that is intrinsically nonlinear and nonmonolithic; and (d) the notion and use of multidimensional and nonregular data structures.
2. *Operating system-related causes.* Modern operating systems provide several functions. These include (a) utility services such as storage and other resource allocation functions, process synchronization, and interprocess communication; (b) the creation of abstract virtual machines and memories; and (c) the enforcement of both information sharing and protection.

Again, some very critical aspects of these operating systems functions are poorly supported by conventional machines. For example, Denning (1978) has pointed out that while the working-set concept (see Volume 1, Chapter 8) is crucial in paged virtual memory mechanisms, there are no contemporary architectures in which this concept is implemented in hardware—although studies (Morris, 1972) have demonstrated its economic feasibility. Myers (1982) has also noted that the long-established and central notion of the *process* as the basic unit of parallel execution and owner of resources has no support in conventional architectures.

1.9   IMPLEMENTATION TECHNOLOGY AND COMPUTER ARCHITECTURE

Regardless of the extent to which compilers, programming languages, and computational issues exert their influence, the dominant force on architecture and computer design has, and will continue to be, the implementation technology prevalent at a given time. It is the technology that determines the potential performance and the cost of a computer and the latter's form and function are inevitably dictated by, and the result of, these technology-determinant parameters. We may illustrate the nature of the interaction between technology and architecture through several examples.

Example 1.7

In a sense, the most celebrated instance of this interaction—and how implementation technology may influence the success or failure of an architectural proposal — is Charles Babbage's work on the Difference and Analytical Engines, the former occupying him between 1822 and 1833 and the latter for the rest of his life till he died in 1871.

The Difference Engine — in modern terms, a special-purpose processor — was intended to generate successive values of algebraic functions by means of the method of finite difference. However, it was Babbage's conception of the Analytical Engine that was more remarkable since in the course of its design, Babbage discovered most of the key principles of a programmable general-purpose computing device consisting of a store, an arithmetic unit, punched card input/output, and a card-controlled sequencing mechanism that allowed for both iteration and conditional branching (Randell, 1975, Chapters 1 and 2; Wilkes, 1977). In fact, it has been pointed out by Wilkes (1977) that Babbage was essentially dealing with what we now call problems of logical design and architecture.

The reason why Babbage failed to complete the construction of these two machines is complex and diffuse. Certainly, it must have had something to do with whether the ethos of the time was receptive to his ideas on computing engines. But it is equally clear that a *major* factor was that the successful construction and operation of these machines *lay beyond the available technology of the day.* In the case of the Difference Engine, in fact, a master machine-tool builder, Joseph Clement, was hired to work on the project; Randell (1975, Chapter 1) has pointed out that the engineering demands exerted by the Difference Engine actually resulted in significant improvements in machine-tool technology.

As for the Analytical Engine, a committee appointed in 1878 by the British Association for the Advancement of Science to advise it on the construction of the Analytical Engine, although recommending highly its conceptual design, voiced its scepticism concerning the physical realizability of the machine.

Herein lies the essential tension between the vision and concepts of an architect and the hard reality of the technology available at the given time.   ∎

Example 1.8

Jumping forward some 150 years to the present, the way in which technology may influence architecture is most dramatically illustrated by developments in very large scale integration (VLSI).

The essential point about VLSI is that while it offers the enormous benefits of low-cost fabrication and high chip density, it also imposes significant constraints, one of which is that if VLSI is to be used effectively, then systems must be of an *orderly, regular,* and *repeatable* form. Thus, the technology places the very real constraint of regularity on VLSI-based endo-architectures (Mead and Conway, 1980; Snyder, 1984) whether that architecture is realized on a single chip or through multiple chips.

As a good example of such architectures, Kung and coworkers (Kung and Lieserson, 1980; Foster and Kung, 1980; Fisher and Kung, 1983) have developed a whole class of structures called *systolic* systems that are particularly suited for VLSI implementation. The basic idea is to use a highly regular

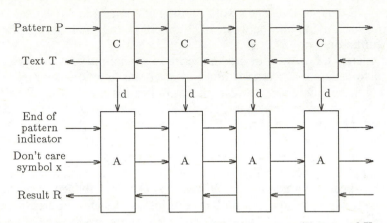

FIGURE 1.11 Structure of a systolic pattern matching system (Foster and Kung 1980; © 1980, IEEE; reprinted with permission).

configuration of identical cells that realizes a particular function in the form of a special purpose processor.

Figure 1.11 depicts the general architecture for a systolic pattern matching system. It consists of a one-dimensional array of two types of cells. The *comparator* cell (C) receives a single character from a pattern P and from a text string T flowing in opposite directions. It compares them and passes the text character to the left adjacent cell and the pattern character to the right adjacent cell. The result of the comparison is a match signal d that passes down to the *accumulator* cell (A).

Inputs to an accumulator cell are an end-of-pattern indicator λ and a "don't care" symbol x, entering from the left; the match signal d entering from the top; and the intermediate result signal R flowing from right to left. The accumulator cell maintains a temporary result T, and at the end of the pattern it uses T to replace the result R according to the computation

$$\lambda_{out} := \lambda_{in}$$
$$x_{out} := x_{in}$$

If λ_{in} then $R_{out} := T$; T := TRUE
else $R_{out} := R_{in}$; T := T $\wedge$ (x_{in} v d)

It is interesting to note that the idea of using highly ordered structures of identical cells was formulated almost 20 years ago under the name of *cellular logic* (Minnick, 1967; Kautz, 1971; Mukhopadhay and Stone, 1971), in anticipation of large-scale integration (LSI) technology. Systolic arrays represent a modern reincarnation largely driven by the arrival of the necessary technology. ∎

Example 1.9

Finally, we return once more to the Berkeley RISC machines, which exemplify in a different way how VLSI technology may influence architectural design. We have already noted (see Section 1.7) that one of the objectives of the reduced instruction set philosophy was to ease the task of efficient compilation. A second major objective was to effectively use "scarce" silicon area to implement a single-chip processor comparable in performance to more complex processors such as the VAX-11/780 (Patterson and Sequin, 1981; Patterson, 1985).

These two objectives matched one another well. By analyzing the frequency of various types of instructions generated by compilers the RISC architects identified a set of 31 instructions. Implementing such a small set resulted in a substantial saving in control logic—from about 50% of the chip area on typical microprocessors to about 6% in RISC-I (Patterson, 1985). The saved area was then used to hold a large set of internal registers [138 in the case of RISC-I (Patterson and Sequin, 1981)], which, in turn, was used to implement a scheme called *overlapping register windows* for improving procedure calls and returns.

The net result was a distinctive architectural style (spanning both exo- and endo-levels) that achieved a performance comparable (in some ways) to that of the so-called "complex" instruction set computers. ∎

1.10 BIBLIOGRAPHIC AND HISTORICAL NOTES

The word "architecture" appears to have been used for the first time in the early 1960s by the designers of the IBM System/360 series (Amdahl, Blaauw, and Brooks, 1964). They used this word to denote the attributes of the machine as seen by the programmer, that is, the conceptual structure and functional behavior of the machine as distinct from the organization of the data flow or the logical and physical design. This definition has since been adopted by other authorities, for example by Fuller and associates (1977a) in their work on the computer family architecture (CFA) project, Myers (1982), and the VAX designers (Digital, 1981a).

Unfortunately, there has never been any consistency in the use of this word, either in the published literature or in the institutional setting in which computer architects practice their craft. An inspection of the actual topics that are the subject of their research, writing, and discussion reveals that architects are as much interested in internal structure and behavior of processors as in their external characteristics. For instance, a very active area of investigation is the design of interconnection networks—a quintessential characteristic of the internal structure of a system. Moreover, some architects, for example, those designing single-chip processors, are interested in the relatively low-level structure of machines as seen at the microprogramming level.

These inconsistencies with respect to the original definition have, in fact, been recognized by several authors, for example, Baer (1980), and Dennis and co-workers (1979). The terms "exo-architecture" and "endo-architecture" were coined by Dasgupta (1981) largely to reflect this social reality and was used widely in Dasgupta (1984).

"Micro-architecture" has been in reasonably common use, especially in the microprogramming literature (Salisbury, 1976). For another viewpoint on the concept of architecture, refer to Zemanek (1980).

The name of the Hungarian born mathematician John von Neumann (1903–1957) has become permanently associated with the style that has dominated computer design since the mid-1940s. At the heart of the so-called *von Neumann machine model* is the stored program idea. The question of who originated this fundamental concept has generated controversy that remains unabated almost to this day.

The key figures in the earliest development of the electronic computer were J. Presper Eckert (b. 1919) and John W. Mauchly (1907–1980) on the one hand, and von Neumann on the other. Eckert and Mauchly were the principle designers of the ENIAC, the very first electronic computer, built at the Moore School, University of Pennsylvania, between 1942 and 1946 (Randell, 1975, Chapter 2; Stern, 1981). This was not a stored program computer—the program was manually loaded through external pluggable cables and switches.

Very soon after the ENIAC design had been frozen (in 1944), von Neumann became associated with the Moore School group as a consultant, and the planning of a new computer named EDVAC soon followed. The basic design of this machine was outlined in a memorandum authored by von Neumann (1945). This widely distributed report contained, apparently for the first time, the description of the role of a memory "organ," including its need to hold instructions. Furthermore—and this is significant—the report noted that although the "different parts" of the memory were to perform different functions (e.g., holding input data, intermediate results, instructions, tables), it should be conceived as a single organ with the different parts being "interchangeable." Thus was born the stored-program computer concept with a homogenous multifunctional memory.

As Stern (1980) has pointed out, because this report was authored only by von Neumann, and contained neither references to, nor acknowledgements of, any other contributor, the stored program principle was widely believed to have been invented by von Neumann. A later, more detailed, report on the stored program computer by Burks, Goldstine, and von Neumann (1946) that, over the years, has been widely reprinted in various anthologies (Randell, 1975; Bell and Newell 1971; Swartzlander, 1976) further helped to strengthen this general belief.

However, according to several other participants of the ENIAC and other projects that followed, the stored-program concept had emerged within the ENIAC group consisting of Eckert, Mauchly, von Neumann, and others in the course of their many discussions at the time (Stern 1980). Both Wilkes (1968) and Metropolis and Worlton (1980) state very clearly that Eckert and Mauchly had *conceived* the stored-program idea during the ENIAC development period —that is, before von Neumann became associated with the Moore School.

For further discussion of the stored-program controversy, refer to Randell (1975, Chapter 8); Stern (1980); Metropolis and Worlton (1980); and Goldstine (1972, Part 2).

Quite apart from the debate it generated over the stored-program concept, one very important aspect of the initial EDVAC report (von Neumann, 1945) must be noted. And that is, its remarkable focus on the *logical* principles and organization of computers in contrast to the electrical/electronic means of realizing these principles; in other words, in the modern history of the computer, the EDVAC report appears to have been the first to make a clear distinction between what we now call the architecture and the technology of computers.

PROBLEMS

1.1   The adoption of the term *computer architecture* seems to imply an analogy of some sort between computers and buildings. However, scientists also talk about the *architecture of matter,* the *architecture of the brain,* and so on. Thus, the word "architecture" seems to be used to designate some set of *shared properties* present in very dissimilar objects.

Using these and other relevant objects as examples, identify exactly what these common properties are that justify the use of the word "architecture" in the context of such diverse objects as computers, buildings, matter, and brains.

1.2   One of the hallmarks of a complex system — whether natural or made by humans — is that it can be described at several different *abstraction levels* such that each abstraction level serves a specific purpose that is not served by any of the other levels. Furthermore, the different abstraction levels are related to one another in some fashion.

Consider an arbitrary computer program P.

(a)   Identify at least three distinct levels at which P may be meaningfully designed (or described). Also describe the purpose of each of these abstraction levels.

(b)   Explain how these different levels are related to one another. [*Hint*: It might be helpful to answer this question by considering a specific program that you have written or are familiar with.]

1.3   The exo-architecture of a pocket calculator may be defined as the structure and behavior of the calculator that need to be known by the "user." Write a concise but complete description of your pocket calculator's exo-architecture. Keep in mind that from your description it should be possible for others to learn to use your calculator correctly.

1.4   Consider the "exo-architecture" of an automobile. As with all architectural descriptions, this will consist of a structural component and a behavioral component.

(a)   Characterize the structure of an automobile at the exo-architectural level.

(b)   Characterize the behavior of an automobile at the exo-architectural level.

1.5 Is it possible to define the structure of a system without any reference to the system's behavior? Justify your answer.

1.6 Is it possible to describe the behavior of a system without any reference to the system's structure? Justify your answer. [*Hint*: It might be helpful to answer both 1.5 and 1.6 by referring to a specific system.]

1.7 We talk about a particular person being the *architect* of a plan or a policy. We also say that a person has *engineered* some particular event. Using these figures of speech as clues, explain what you think is the real distinction to be made (if any) between the disciplines of computer architecture and computer engineering.

1.8 Consider a vending machine that will dispense three types of soft drinks, one priced 40 cents, the second 45 cents, and the third 50 cents. For each of these services the machine will accept only exact amounts as combinations of quarters, dimes, and nickels. After inserting the coins, the consumer presses one of three buttons corresponding to the three types of drinks, and, if the correct coinage has been inserted, the machine responds by dispensing the drink. Otherwise an error light comes on.

Prior to actually building the vending machine, it is required to implement a program that will *simulate* the device.

(a) Design the *exo-architecture* of the simulated machine.

(b) Design an *endo-architecture* for the simulated machine such that your exo-architecture design is a correct abstraction of the endo-architecture.

(c) *Implement* the endo-architecture in the form of a fully executable computer program.

1.9 Given the experience gained from solving 1.8, what conclusions do you reach regarding the role of architecture in the design and implementation of a system and the distinctions (if any) between "architecture" and "implementation"?

1.10 The basic premise behind the design of RISC architectures (see Section 1.7.1) is that for "typical" computers only a very small subset of the instruction set is actually used by the compiler during code generation. Based on your experience in programming in high-level languages such as FORTRAN, Pascal or C, identify what in your opinion are likely to be the 10 most important instructions that a computer must contain as part of its exo-architecture. Justify each of your choices.

CHAPTER 2

CLASSIFICATION AND TAXONOMY

2.1 BASIC TERMS

Whenever a discipline has a large number of diverse objects as its domain of study, the problem of classification arises. The most well-known example of this is biology, in which the development of classification schemes has a long history going back to the Greeks of the sixth and seventh centuries B.C. (Ross, 1974). However, one encounters this instinct to classify in many other disciplines, including those within the "Sciences of the Artificial" (Simon, 1981) — building architecture, for example (Steadman, 1979, Chapter 3).

By *classification*, we mean the ordering of objects into categories on the basis of their relationships. A *taxonomic system* (or, synonymously, a *classification scheme*) is a system of rules that allows us to classify in a particular way. The word *taxonomy* is sometimes (loosely) used as a synonym for "classification," but more often it refers to the theory, practice, and science of classification. In this book I will use the word in this latter sense.

Thus, taxonomy (with respect to a particular discipline) may, in general, embrace a number of taxonomic systems, each of which leads to the objects being classified in a certain manner.

A related though somewhat broader word (encountered especially in biology) is *systematics*, which refers to the scientific study of the diversity and distribution of objects (in biology, organisms).

The simplest of taxonomic systems will at least consist of two components: the set of fundamental *objects*, the very diversity of which prompts one to investigate their classification, and a set of *taxa* within which we attempt to partition the set of objects. A *taxon* is a named group of objects that are sufficiently distinct (with respect to a specific set of properties) from the objects belonging to some other taxon. The set of such taxa constitute a *category* (Ruse, 1973).

In more comprehensive classification schemes several categories of taxa may be identified and these may, possibly, be ranked in a hierarchy. Each object would appear in exactly one taxon in each category.

Finally, once a classification has been achieved, it becomes necessary to be able to refer to the categories and taxa. Thus, one needs a convenient and meaningful method of *nomenclature*.

Example 2.1

Flynn (1966) proposed a simple scheme for classifying computers. This involved a single category ("computers") consisting of four taxa called "single-instruction, single-data streams" (SISD), "single-instruction, multiple-data streams" (SIMD), "multiple-instruction, single-data streams" (MISD), and "multiple-instruction, multiple-data streams" (MIMD). ∎

Example 2.2

In the Linnaean classification system established in biology by Carolus Linnaeus in the eighteenth century, there are seven categories called (and ranked in ascending order) Species, Genus, Family, Order, Class, Phylum, and Kingdom. Within the lowest category (Species), a wolf belongs to the taxon *lupus*, a honeybee to the taxon *mellifera*, and a wasp to the taxon *vulgaris*. At the next higher category rank (Genus), a wolf is in the taxon *Canis*, the honeybee in *Apis*, and the wasp in *Vespula*. The honeybee and the wasp, though belonging to distinct categories in the lowest three ranks (Species, Genus, and Family), fall into the same taxon (Hymenoptera) in the next higher category (Order). Finally, all three organisms fall within the Animalia taxon in the highest (Kingdom) category. Thus, the Linnean system is hierarchical in nature. ∎

2.2 THE PURPOSE OF CLASSIFICATION

There are several reasons why one would want to establish a classification scheme for computer architectures. The first and least contentious reason is that it provides a basis for *information ordering*: A classification of computer architectures in some order, say within a filing system, is useful for efficient storage and retrieval of information. This has the most obvious utility in cataloging documents on computer architectures in a library or in organizing architectural descriptions in a textbook.

A far more scientifically interesting purpose is that classification provides a basis for *predicting* properties of an architecture. That is, given a taxonomic system, and a statement that a particular machine falls in a particular category/taxon, we should be able to predict properties of the architecture from our knowledge of the taxonomic system.

Example 2.3

As a very simple example, suppose we have a classification scheme that includes a taxon named "32-bit processer"; then, the announcement of a new "32-bit machine x" should immediately allow us to infer a number of important properties about x, based on the properties associated with this taxon. ∎

The third, and by far the most ambitious, purpose of classification is that it provides a basis for *explanation*. That is, a classification scheme reflects, in some sense, a scientific theory of computer architecture—the scheme has a scientific basis in other words—such that it may be used to explain *why* a particular group of architectures are in a particular category/taxon.

Note the distinction between the predictive and the explanatory goals of classification. The former allows us to merely state that if a set of objects x_1, x_2, . . . , x_n belong to a certain taxon they possess such and such properties (and vice versa). The latter additionally tells us what are the *causes* for x_1, x_2, . . . , x_n to share these properties. One easily sees that constructing a taxonomic system with such explanatory power is a considerably more difficult task than devising a scheme with only predictive power.

Example 2.4

Suppose we devise a classification scheme that has a category containing the taxon "reduced instruction set computers" (RISC). This taxon is characterized by the following architectural properties.

1. Only LOAD and STORE instructions access main memory. All other instructions access registers only.
2. All instructions, except LOAD and STORE, are executed in a single machine cycle.
3. Instructions, except the procedure CALL and RETURN, are very primitive in their power.
4. The instruction set is very small (say of the order of ≤ 32).
5. Computers within the RISC taxon are single-chip processors.
6. There are a large number (say ≥ 100) high-speed programmable registers.

This taxonomic system has predictive power of the following kind: Given that we know that computer x falls in this taxon, we can "predict" (if not told already) one or more of the listed properties. Note, however, that the foregoing description gives only a few clues as to the significance of these properties and how they are connected. (We can, of course, make some inferences; for example, that (2) and (3) are related, that (1) and (2) are related—though which is the cause and which the effect cannot be known—and that because of (1), (2), and (3), most instructions will be quite fast).

In contrast, we may design a different taxonomic system with the following characteristics: The RISC taxon is defined such that not only does it reflect the properties listed herein but also by the fact that these properties are the *consequences of the following causes*.

1. To conserve scarce chip area, the proportion of area given to control logic is reduced to the minimum by reducing both the number and complexity of the instructions.
2. Because of reduction in the number and complexity of instructions, much greater care goes into their design. The instructions are defined by carefully analyzing the frequency of execution of high-level language statement types

and selecting operators that reflect the most common types of high-level language operations. The relatively powerful CALL and RETURN instructions are the consequences of the disproportionately high time spent by programs in doing procedure calls and returns.

3. To speed up execution time, all instructions (except LOAD and STORE) need to access only high-speed registers. Also, efficient implementations of the relatively time-consuming and complex CALL and RETURN should use registers to pass parameters and hold local variables. Both these goals are met if the chip area "released" by the reduced control logic can be allocated to a large bank of high-speed registers.

Although the characterization of this particular taxon is cumbersome, it has considerable explanatory value. The architectural features (1) through (6) are the consequences of the design decisions (1) through (3). The taxon, in other words, captures the *development logic* underlying this particular class of machines. We can *explain* that computers x and y belong to the RISC taxon because their design decisions were along similar lines.   ■

An important consequence of a taxonomic system with this kind of explanatory power is that it provides the architect with a *design tool*. Architects — whether experienced or not — rarely embark on a new design starting from first principles. Rather, they draw on their knowledge of, or experience with, previously developed designs, architectural categories, or styles and adopt those most suited to their design goals with appropriate modification or enhancement. Even the most radically distinct architecture will have a lot in common with established styles.

Thus, assuming that the classification scheme reflects not only the properties of "completed" architectures (what biologists call "morphological" features) but also their development logic and history, the architect planning a new architecture should be able to identify rather quickly the category/taxon nearest to his or her design goals and use that as the basis for the design. The architect would also be able to determine the extent to which the new design may adopt established, well-tested, architectural features or whether it has to incorporate properties either genuinely new or borrowed from machines belonging to other categories or taxa. By implication, the precise location of the new design in the existing classification scheme will become evident; that is, whether it falls in an established category/taxon, as a new point in the taxonomic space, or as the progenitor of a new evolutionary pathway.

2.3 TWO PHILOSOPHIES OF TAXONOMY

There are broadly two taxonomic philosophies. In the first, architectures are classified according to the features they exhibit in the "finished" form, that is, after their designs are completed. I will call this the *morphological* approach insofar as classifications based on this philosophy rely on the *forms* that architectures take.[1]

Clearly, morphological taxonomy is, in an obvious sense, related to the predictive goal of classification as formerly described. It should also be noted that, on the basis of one's experience and knowledge of architectural principles, and the relationship of form and function, a morphological classification scheme may also allow one to *infer* certain underlying causes of architectural features; thus, depending on the precise features selected, and the number of such features, morphological classification schemes may, at least implicitly, exhibit some explanatory power.

Example 2.5

Consider a class of machines with the dominant architectural feature of a data-cum-control stack, which is a morphologic feature of this machine group. However, anyone conversant with stack-based architectures will be in a position to infer the underlying goals and functions of these machines, namely, that they are intended to provide run-time support for block-structured language programs. ∎

In the second philosophy, the emphasis is on how the past influences architectural forms. I call this the *evolutionary* approach. It, in turn, involves two different kinds of historical factors:

1. Where a given architecture is a member of an architectural family that has evolved over a period of time. That is, the architecture in question has a clearly identifiable and deliberately designed "pedigree." Examples of such families abound in computer architecture; for example, the Burroughs B5500, B5700, B6700, B7700 series (Doran, 1979), the PDP-11 series (Bell and Mudge, 1978), and the IBM System/360, System/370, 3030, 4300 series (Siewiorek, Bell, and Newell, 1982). I call such factors *phylogenic* since they reflect the way the architecture has been derived from its ancestors.[2]
2. The architecture reflects design decisions and goals established and evolved during the course of the architectural design itself, independent of its phylogenic background. That is, such factors reflect the development or unfolding of the architecture. I call such features *ontogenic*.[3]

---

[1]In biology, *morphology* is the "study of the form of animals and plants" (*Concise Oxford Dictionary*, 6th ed., 1976; J. B. Sykes, Ed.). See Mayr (1982, pp. 455–469) for an extended discussion of the history of morphology, which he defines as the "science of animal and plant form."

[2]This is, again, a word borrowed from biology; phylogeny: (a) the "(history of) evolution of animals or plant type" (*Concise Oxford Dictionary*, 6th ed., 1976; J. B. Sykes, Ed.); (b) "An animal's pedigree in terms of evolutionary descent" (*Fontana Dictionary of Modern Thought*, 1977; A. Bullock and O. Stallybrass, Eds.).

[3]Ontogeny: "The course of growth within the lifetime of a single member of the species." (*Fontana Dictionary of Modern Thought*, 1977; A. Bullock and O. Stallybrass, Eds.).

Of course, every machine architecture is a product of its immediate design past. However, not every taxonomic system takes this fact into account explicitly.

Example 2.6

As a first example, consider once more, the RISC type of architecture discussed earlier, where the goals related to both implementation technology and support of high-level languages played dominant roles in the architecture design.

As a second example, consider the architecture of a target machine T intended for emulation on a given microprogrammable host machine H. In this case, the micro-architecture of H will shape in a very significant way the development of T's architecture (Dasgupta, 1984, Chapter 15). ■

Clearly, just as morphological taxonomy provides for predictive power, evolutionary taxonomy supports classification schemes that allow for causal explanation and deeper understanding.

This does not necessarily imply that the evolutionary approach is "better" than the morphological type. Indeed, I tend to agree with Ruse (1973) that the goodness of a classification scheme or taxonomic philosophy is entirely context-dependent: *One constructs or selects a scheme that is most appropriate to the needs of the classifier.* The strengths and weaknesses of any particular scheme must therefore be assessed by examining the extent to which it satisfies such stated needs. I will use this context-dependency factor as the basis for discussing various architectural taxonomic systems.

2.4 FLYNN'S CLASSIFICATION SCHEME

Probably the earliest and certainly most frequently cited classification scheme is that of Flynn (1966). This scheme relies on six *taxonomic characters* (TCs), that is, architectural features used to establish the taxonomic system:

1. Instruction memory (IM).
2. Data memory (DM).
3. Control (or instruction handling) unit (CU).
4. Processing (or instruction execution) unit (PU).
5. Instruction stream (IS).
6. Data stream (DS).

The distinction between *instruction* and *data memories* is simply to establish explicitly the sources of instructions and data. It is, thus, a logical distinction and does not imply that instructions and data reside in physically distinct memory modules.

A *control unit* denotes the entire complex of hardware required to generate an instruction address, fetch and decode instructions, and generate operand addresses. The CU, in other words, accepts instructions from IM and prepares instructions for execution.

Flynn defines an *instruction stream* simply as "the sequence of instructions performed by the machine" (Flynn, 1966). However, an implied assumption appears to be that an instruction stream denotes an ordered set of instructions under the control of a single program counter—and therefore, a single CU (Fig. 2.1).

A *processing unit* denotes the complex of hardware required to execute *all* the arithmetic, logical, and data-transfer instructions of the computer.[4] A PU may, therefore, include several more specialized, functional units such as adders, multipliers, and shifters.

Precisely what is meant by *data stream* poses some problems. Flynn (1966) defines this term as "the sequence of data called for by the instruction stream (including input and partial or temporary results)," which, at first, seems to imply that a data stream contains *all* the data required by a single instruction stream. Evidently, this is not what is meant, as the classification scheme to be given here will make clear. Indeed, Flynn completely decouples the two concepts of instruction stream and data stream. One unambiguous interpretation we may give, then, is that a data stream denotes the data traffic exchanged between a single data memory and a single processing unit (Fig. 2.2).

Flynn's scheme is nonhierarchic: It consists of a single category ("computer") composed of four taxa, the names of which are

- SISD (single-instruction stream, single-data stream).
- SIMD (single-instruction stream, multiple-data stream).
- MISD (multiple-instruction stream, single-data stream).
- MIMD (multiple-instruction stream, multiple-data stream).

Each taxon denotes a particular structuring of one or more copies of the six TCs; more specifically, each taxon is composed of copies of the elemental structures described in Figures 2.1 and 2.2. The four taxa are shown in Figures 2.3 through 2.6; Table 2.1 lists some of the machines within each taxon. Note the absence of examples from the MISD taxon.

2.4.1   A Critique

The most obvious feature of Flynn's taxonomic system is that it classifies *endo-architectures* expressed in a very abstract way. As the TCs together with the

---

[4]Or what Flynn (1974) has also called functional- (F-) type and move- (M-) type instructions.

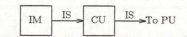

FIGURE 2.1   A single instruction stream.

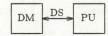

FIGURE 2.2   A single data stream.

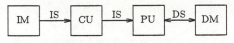

FIGURE 2.3   The SISD taxon.

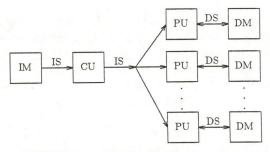

FIGURE 2.4   The SIMD taxon.

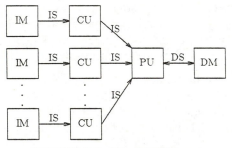

FIGURE 2.5   The MISD taxon.

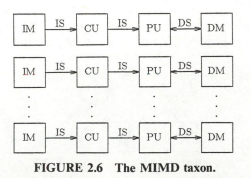

FIGURE 2.6   The MIMD taxon.

TABLE 2.1 **Flynn's Classification with Examples**

Taxon	Members
SISD	Intel 8080, Intel 8086, DEC VAX 11/780, IBM System 360/91, CDC 6600, Cray-1, CDC Cyber 205, IBM System 370/168 (Uniprocessor)
SIMD	ILLIAC IV, Burroughs Scientific Processor (BSP), Goodyear Aerospace MPP, Goodyear Aerospace STARAN, The Connection Machine
MISD	—
MIMD	Cm*, IBM System 370/168 (Multiprocessor), Denelcor HEP, Cray XMP, C.mmp, Multimax

four taxa clearly indicate, this is essentially a scheme for classifying the *structural relations* at what Bell and Newell (1971) termed the processor-memory-switch (PMS) level. All other aspects of architecture are ignored.

Furthermore, because the classification is based only on these six TCs, it is very much a morphologic scheme: Given that two computers, C_1, C_2, fall within a particular category, the classification tells us nothing about their evolutionary (phylogenic) histories (which may, indeed, be very different) or about their ontogeny.

As regards predictive power, at first it would seem that one would be able to make some qualitative comments concerning gross relative performance. For instance, given our knowledge that, with the same technology, multiple instruction streams imply higher instruction bandwidth[5] than what would be obtained in a single instruction stream system, and that a multiple data stream signifies relatively higher operand fetch and execution bandwidths, one could infer that a computer in the MIMD taxon will have higher performance than a machine in the SISD taxon.

However, as Table 2.1 suggests, the SISD taxon spans a rather wide range of computers from 8-bit microprocessors (e.g., Intel 8080), through 32-bit "super minis" (e.g., the VAX-11/780), to high performance 64-bit machines such as the Cray-1. Thus, one cannot sensibly say anything reasonable about the performance of machines in the SISD *taxon* as a whole. Nor, indeed, can one make any reasonably accurate general statement about the relative performances of SIMD and MIMD machines.

Finally, a well-known troublesome aspect of this classification is the MISD taxon, which seems to describe no existing von Neumann machine adequately. For this reason, some commentators have chosen to ignore MIMD as a member of Flynn's taxonomic system (e.g., Hwang and Briggs, 1984).

---

[5]The general term *bandwidth* refers to the rate of occurrence of an event. Thus, *instruction bandwidth* refers to the rate of retrieval of instructions from IM (expressed as instructions or words per second, say); *operand fetch bandwidth* refers to the rate of retrieval of operands from DM; and *execution bandwidth* refers to the rate of execution of instructions by the PU.

2.4.2 The Hwang-Briggs Modification to Flynn's Classification Scheme

In partial response to some of the weaknesses just discussed, Hwang and Briggs (1984) suggested a modification to Flynn's classification. Its main features are

1. Elimination of the MISD taxon.
2. Refinement of the original SISD taxon into two taxa: the class of processors with *single functional units* (SISD-S) and the class of machines with *multiple functional units* (SISD-M).
3. Refinement of the original SIMD taxon into two taxa: the class of machines that feature *word-slice processing* (SIMD-W) and those that are characterized by *bit-slice processing* (SIMD-B). Word-slice processors are systems that operate on entire words in parallel in contrast to bit-slice processors, which operate on the same bit of several words in parallel (Fig. 2.7).[6]
4. Refinement of the original MIMD taxon into two taxa: the class of *loosely coupled processors* (MIMD-L) and the class of *tightly coupled processors* (MIMD-T). These qualifying terms are, themselves, very loosely defined: If the degree of interaction among the PUs is high, then the machine falls within the MIMD-T taxon, otherwise it is placed in the MIMD-L taxon.

---

[6]Word-slice processing is also referred to as "bit-parallel" processing, which, of course, is the case with the vast majority of processors, SIMD or otherwise. The need to explicate this becomes necessary only to distinguish it from bit-slice processing, which is also referred to as "word parallel" or *associative* processing (Thurber, 1976).

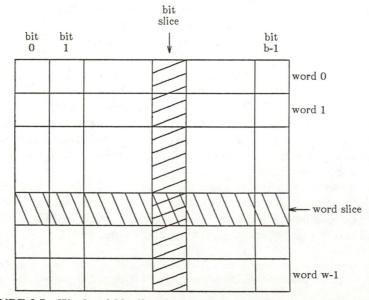

FIGURE 2.7 Word and bit slices in a b bits/word and w word memory array.

From a theoretical standpoint, it is worth noting that the Hwang-Briggs refinement does *not* lead to a two-rank hierarchical classification scheme as depicted in Table 2.2. The main properties of such a hierarchical system are that

1. Every computer would fall in one and *only* one taxon in each ranked category.
2. The taxa in the lower-ranked category form disjoint sets, each of which would be subsumed in exactly one taxon of the higher-ranked category.

Although property 2. does indeed hold, property 1. may easily be violated. For example, a given computer may be both tightly coupled and contain multiple functional units. Indeed, in a logical sense, such characteristics as "multiple functional unit" and "word-slice processing" are totally independent of one another. The Hwang-Briggs scheme is hierarchical, but only in a "top-down" sense. In order to classify a machine within this system, one must first select the higher-level category (see Fig. 2.8) and then decide which of its constituent descendant taxa is the appropriate one.

The Hwang-Briggs modification enhances the predictive power of the original scheme to the extent that the SISD-M taxon will, in general, have higher performance than those in the SISD-S taxon. However, no such general inference can be made for the SIMD-B and SIMD-W taxa; for example, using the *maximum degree of potential parallelism* as a performance measure according to the data presented by Hwang and Briggs (1984, Chapter 1, Section 1.4), we may place the following four machines in ascending order of performance:

STARAN	(SIMD-B)
ILLIAC IV	(SIMD-W)
PEPE	(SIMD-W)
MPP	(SIMD-B)

Thus, bit-slice machines perform both better and worse than word-slice machines.

Finally, the two new MIMD taxon provide us with the following kinds of information: Whether a machine is in the tightly or loosely coupled MIMD taxon tells us whether it uses a shared (common) or disjoint main memory. In the case of a tightly coupled system, expanding the system degrades performance owing to increased memory conflicts. This does not, in general, happen in the case of a loosely coupled system.

TABLE 2.2

Category	Taxa
2 (higher level)	SISD, SIMD, MIMD
1 (lower level)	Single functional unit, multiple functional units, word-slice processing, bit-slice processing, tightly coupled, loosely coupled

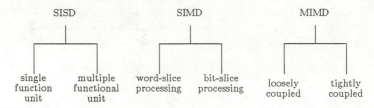

FIGURE 2.8   The Hwang-Briggs modification to Flynn's classification.

2.5   THE ERLANGEN CLASSIFICATION SYSTEM

The Erlangen classification system (ECS) was developed at the Friedrich Alexander University of Erlangen-Nürnberg by Händler (1977, 1981). As in Flynn's scheme, the domain is the endo-architectural level. However, the approach is very different.

The Erlangen system begins by distinguishing between three levels of processing hardware.

1. The *program control unit* (PCU), which interprets the instructions of a program. The PCU thus corresponds to the control unit in Flynn's system.
2. The *arithmetic logic unit* (ALU), which executes the operations specified via control signals issued by the PCU. The ALU is simply the processing unit in Flynn's scheme.
3. The *elementary logic circuit* (ELC), which is the circuitry within the ALU dedicated to the processing of a single bit of data.

In general, a given computer consists of one or more PCUs; each PCU controls one or more ALUs; an ALU in turn consists of as many ELCs as there are bits in the ALU data path. The number of ELCs/ALU is, of course, the word length of the machine.

In the Erlangen system, a minimal description of a computer c is given as a 3-tuple

$$t(c) = (k, d, w)$$

where k is the number of PCUs, d, the number of ALUs/PCU, and w is the number of ELCs/ALU.

Example 2.7

$$t(\text{IBM } 701) = (1, 1, 36)$$
$$t(\text{ILLIAC IV}) = (1, 64, 64)$$
$$t(\text{C.mmp}) = (16, 1, 16)$$

■

Each of the foregoing descriptions quantifies collectively the potential parallelism across three levels of processing hardware. In order to take into account *pipelining*, the 3-tuple form is further expanded as follows.[7]

Händler postulates that pipelines may exist at all three levels of processing hardware.

1. At the ELC level, each ALU may be pipelined internally, in which case w, the number of ELCs/ALU, may be multiplied by w', the number of *pipeline stages* per ALU. Notationally, this is shown as

$$w \times w'$$

2. At the ALU level, there may be several functional units within a single ALU, all of which can potentially execute instructions simultaneously. This is denoted as

$$d \times d'$$

where d is the number of ALUs and d' is the number of functional units per ALU.

Note, first, that the introduction of the integer d' quantifies and unifies the Hwang-Briggs concepts of single and multiple functional units. On the other hand, this interpretation of d' seems to imply that an instruction pipeline invariably involves multiple functional units, which is not necessarily the case.

In an *instruction pipeline* the various stages of instruction processing are organized into a sequence of stages such that several instructions may be simultaneously in the pipeline. Figure 2.9 shows, for example, a 5-stage instruction pipeline that at its highest point of use is processing five consecutive instructions I_0, I_1, I_2, I_3, and I_4 from the same instruction stream. Since a functional unit is actually required only for the final stage (i.e., execution), it is possible to realize an instruction pipeline with only *one* functional unit. The rest of the pipeline is contained in the PCU.

A more precise interpretation of d' is that it reflects the condition when several instructions are simultaneously *executed*. This may indeed occur in a pipeline architecture, but not necessarily so: Instructions may, instead, be *prefetched*, made ready for execution and then allocated to different functional units whenever they are available. This is sometimes called *instruction lookahead*. The distinction between lookahead and pipelining is often obscured, as it appears to have been in the Erlangen scheme.

---

[7]*Pipelining* refers to a mode of processing a task in which the processing unit is segmented into several successive stages. A given task passes through these consecutive stages sequentially, occupying each stage for some period of time. At any given time then, several tasks may be in the pipeline simultaneously, each occupying a distinct stage of the pipeline. Thus, although a single task will be processed in time identical to that performed by a nonpipelined processor, the overall *throughput* (the number of tasks processed per unit time) will be greatly increased. Theoretically, if the pipeline contains s stages, each requiring t time units for execution, a given task will require st time units; however, in a pipelined unit s tasks will be processed in this same time period. See Chapter 6 for a thorough discussion of pipelining.

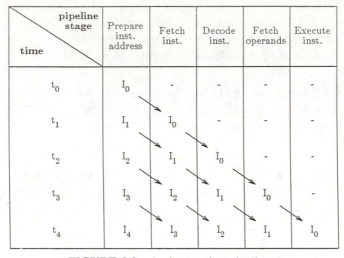

pipeline stage / time	Prepare inst. address	Fetch inst.	Decode inst.	Fetch operands	Execute inst.
t_0	I_0	-	-	-	-
t_1	I_1	I_0	-	-	-
t_2	I_2	I_1	I_0	-	-
t_3	I_3	I_2	I_1	I_0	-
t_4	I_4	I_3	I_2	I_1	I_0

FIGURE 2.9   An instruction pipeline.

3. At the PCU level, two or more PCUs may be coupled to form a pipeline through which a single data stream flows. Händler (1981) refers to this as a *macro-pipeline*. In this case k is multiplied by k′, the number of PCUs that form a macro-pipeline.

$$k \times k'$$

Thus, taking into account both multilevel parallelism and multilevel pipelining, a computer c is described by a 6-tuple:

$$t(c) = \langle k \times k', d \times d', w \times w' \rangle.$$

Whenever k′, d′, or w′ is equal to 1, it may simply be omitted. Thus, for example, $\langle k \times 1, d \times 1, w \times w' \rangle$ can be abbreviated to $\langle k, d, w \times w' \rangle$.

Example 2.8

Consider the central processing unit of the CDC 6600 (Thornton, 1964). This has an ALU consisting of 10 specialized functional units that may execute concurrently. The functional units operate on 60-bit words. Thus, it may be denoted as

$$\langle 1, 1 \times 10, 60 \rangle \qquad \blacksquare$$

The Erlangen system notation also includes two "operators" x and v, which may connect the basic 6- or 3-tuples in order to designate more complex structures. Thus, the notation

$$t(c) = \langle k \times k', d \times d', w \times w' \rangle \times \langle k_0 \times k_0', d_0 \times d_0', w_0 \times w_0' \rangle$$

describes a computer c with two computational subcomponents, one of which may, for instance, be of a special-purpose nature.

In contrast, the v (or alternative) operator is used to designate distinct configurations of a given computer structure. That is,

$$t(c) = <k \times k', d \times d', w \times w'> v <k_0 \times k_0', d_0 \times d_0', w_0 \times w_0'>$$

expresses the fact that the computer c may be configured (and therefore classified) in the form of the first 6-tuple or the second.

Example 2.9

1. In the case of the CDC 6600, in addition to a CPU as described herein, there are 10 peripheral processors—each with 12-bit word lengths—that can execute simultaneously. The complete structure can therefore be described as

$$<1, 1 \times 10, 60> \times <10, 1, 12>.$$

2. The 16-bit C.mmp multiprocessor (Wulf and Bell, 1972; Wulf, Levin, and Harbison, 1980) developed at Carnegie-Mellon University in the early 1970s could, at least in theory, have been configured in a number of different ways. In its "normal" MIMD mode, it consists of 16 PCUs (all PDP-11s) with 1 ALU/PCU:

$$<16, 1, 16>.$$

If, however, all 16 PDP-11s are synchronized and placed under the control of a master processor, the former become individual ALUs as in SIMD machines:

$$<1, 16, 16>.$$

Finally, the 16 processors could have been configured to form a macropipeline:

$$<1 \times 16, 1, 16>.$$

Thus the overall description of the C.mmp would be

$$<16, 1, 16> v <1, 16, 16> v <1 \times 16, 1, 16>. \qquad \blacksquare$$

In summary, the Erlangen system is morphological and assigns a "metric" to endo-architectures based on some key structural features. A major limitation is that it provides no basis for naming, in any meaningful way, groups of "similar" computers; nor, indeed, does it give us any idea as to how "similarity" may be defined in this system. Its main utility is that it provides us with some idea about the *structural complexity* of endo-architectures, taking into account parallelism and pipelining at distinct levels of hardware abstraction.

2.6 GILOI'S CLASSIFICATION SCHEME

Giloi (1983) proposed a classification scheme in which architectures are described in terms of a kind of *formal grammar*. Using the standard representation, such a grammar, G, is given as a 4-tuple

$$G = <V_N, V_T, P, S>$$

where: V_N, the set of nonterminal symbols (names), denotes certain complex or higher level architectural features.

V_T, the set of terminal symbols (names), denotes elementary, undefined, or "axiomatic" architectural characteristics.

P, the set of production or rewrite rules, of the form A ::= α, where A ϵ V_N and α is a string, denotes the composition of each complex architectural feature in terms of other (elementary or complex) features.

S, is the sentential symbol "computer architecture."

Figure 2.10 specifies the first few rules in P. In this notation, a rule of the form

    <A> ::= (<B>, <C>, <D>)

states that the architectural feature A is an ordered triple consisting of the architectural features B, C, and D. The notation < . . . > denotes a nonterminal symbol, that is, a complex architectural feature. A rule of the form

    <A> ::= <B>|<C>|<D>|

states that the feature A denotes the features B or C or D.

Ultimately, a complex architectural feature will be composed of primitive or undefined features. Thus, for example, given the following production rules

    <resource_allocation> ::= (<processor_allocation>, <memory_management>)
    <processor_allocation> ::= TASK_ALLOCATION|TASK_ATTRACTION

the feature <processor_allocation> is either of the primitive features TASK_ALLOCATION or TASK_ATTRACTION. The latter two are assumed to be sufficiently well-understood in Giloi's scheme to not need further elaboration — and are, therefore, terminal symbols.

Using this grammar, a particular architecture may be completely described by a *parse tree*. For example, Figure 2.11 shows the partial parse tree describing the architecture of the STARLET machine (Giloi and Gueth, 1982).

The main characteristics of Giloi's scheme may be summarized as follows:

1. It takes a morphological approach.
2. It assumes a reasonably comprehensive view of architecture, in particular exo-architecture. Unlike the systems discussed earlier, Giloi takes into account not only structural features, but also representational issues and control and behavioral features.

< computer_architecture > ::= (< operational_principle >,
                               < hardware_structure >)
< operational_principle > ::= (< information_structure >,
                               < control_structure >)
< hardware_structure >::= (< mhr_structure >,
                           < interconnection_structure >,
                           {< cooperation_rules >}$^+$
< information_structure > ::= {< machine_data_type >}$^+$
< control_structure > ::= (< resource_management >,
                           < execution_control >, < data_control >)
< mhr_structure > ::= (< processor_structure >, < memory_structure >)
< interconnection_structure >::= < multidrop_bus >|
                                 < memory_sharing > |
                                 < message_buffer > |
                                 < message_switching_bus > |
                                 < interconnection_networks > |
                                 < interrupt_structure >
< cooperation_rule > ::= < synchronous_cooperation > |
                         < asynchronous_cooperation >
< machine_data_type >::= (< object_class >, < function_set >,
                          < object_representation >)
< resource_management > ::= (< resource_allocation >,
                             < inter_resource_communication >)
< execution_control > ::= < program_flow_control > |
                          < data_driven_control > |
                          < demand_driven_control >

FIGURE 2.10 **A partial description of Giloi's classification. The notation {x}$^+$ denotes a set of one or more instances of x. (Based on Giloi, 1983).**

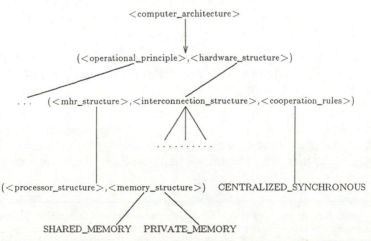

FIGURE 2.11 **Partial description of the STARLET architecture (based on Giloi, 1983).**

3. It appears to be sufficiently general and flexible in that any arbitrary architecture or architectural feature may be incorporated into the scheme. For example, certain features that are given as primitives may be redefined as complex features simply by adding production rules.
4. Similarities between architectures would be expressed in terms of similarities between their respective parse trees.
5. It appears that the classification scheme may be fruitfully applied during the architecture design process.

All these characteristics seem to make Giloi's scheme very attractive. Unfortunately, its major disadvantage is also a very serious one and that is, it is not clear as to how one would actually use this scheme as a taxonomic system. It appears particularly unsuitable for information ordering; and the lack of an appropriate nomenclature makes it less than useful for predictive purposes since it gives us no sense of architectural taxa or categories.

The overall strength of Giloi's proposal, then, lies not in that it is useful for classifying whole architectures; it provides a classification of architectural *features* and suggests, along the way, an approach or *method* that may be useful for constructing a classification scheme for complete architectures. That is, it suggests that in order to construct a comprehensive scheme it is first necessary to classify architectural features (in the manner shown here) and then to establish different categories and taxa within categories in which architectures would be placed, depending on their particular set of features. In this sense, Giloi's scheme is an incomplete though promising proposal.

2.7 ARCHITECTURAL STYLES

As noted in Section 2.1, the problem of classification has been studied in many other disciplines and not always with the intention of formulating a rigid taxonomic system. For example, artifacts are often described in terms of their *style*, a term that was defined by Dasgupta (1984, p. 174) as:

> A set of characteristics, features or attributes that may set one group of artifacts apart from another—artifacts that otherwise are functionally equivalent (or at least serve some common purpose).

The concept of style is closely related to that of a taxonomic system. It provides, however, a looser, less rigorous way of grouping artifacts than may be expected from a taxonomic system.[8] This is precisely where the concept has its advantages. Styles may meet and mingle in a particular design, leading, possibly,

---

[8]Style is inherently an aspect of the "artificial"—that which is designed or created by humans or machine—rather than of the natural. Thus, although biologists talk as a matter of course about biological categories or taxa relative to some classification scheme, they do not describe "biological styles." Nor do chemists speak of distinctive "chemical styles" when discussing the chemical elements, although the periodic *classification* scheme is part of our basic chemical knowledge.

to the emergence of a new style. Furthermore, just as an artifact may be the meeting point of two or more styles, different styles may have features in common. Thus, a style is not only a loosely structured set of attributes that "stands out" among lesser attributes; it may very easily evolve and mutate.

The issue of style in computer architecture is discussed at length in Dasgupta (1984, Chapter 12), which is largely an exploration in a specific context of more general ideas first put forward by Simon (1975).

Style in computer architecture may arise essentially in three distinct ways.

1. By the presence of some common set of structural or behavioral features shared by a set of computer systems. That is, a style is manifested by virtue of morphological features that dominate in some obvious way the design of a group of computers. I will denote this simply as *architectural style*.

2. Styles may also arise from, or be associated with, the process by which architectures are implemented or "manufactured." The method of implementation either influences the design itself, the thinking that goes into the design act, or, more directly, leaves its imprint in the final architectural form. Thus, when we talk of "VLSI-based architectures" or "the influence of VLSI technology on architecture," we are really talking about an *implementation style*.

3. Finally, we may associate style with the *design process*: The design process itself is of sufficient distinction to influence the final architecture. Although such *design styles* are well known in software engineering, they are only just beginning to emerge in the arena of architecture and hardware design, largely because of the very recent and still embryonic developments in design automation and synthesis.

As suggested herein, both design and implementation styles may strongly influence, indeed determine, architectural styles. An excellent example of this is how systolic arrays have emerged as a viable mode of information processing largely driven by VLSI technology (see Chapter 1, Section 1.9). Thus, an architectural style, though expressing some dominant structural or behavioral feature, may well reflect, at least implicitly, its design or implementation history. The identification of such styles, then, may be of considerable explanatory advantage.

Example 2.10

Exo-architectures may be conveniently described in terms of a number of reasonably well-delineated styles. We single out, for example, *stack-oriented* architectures (see Volume 1, Chapter 6) exemplified by the Burroughs B6700/B7700 series (Doran, 1979) and *object-oriented* architectures represented by the Intel iAPX/432 (Intel Corporation, 1981).

In the B6700/B7700 series the exo-architecture design is dominated by a central theme: The use of a *stack* as a unified medium for executing instructions, controlling run-time environments, and managing storage for block-structured programs.

In the Intel 432, exo-architectural entities are structured into one or another type of *objects* (also known to programmers and software engineers as abstract data types). An object encapsulates in a single logical entity a primitive or composite data item together with a set of operations such that the only way of manipulating the data item is through the defined operations. An example is the "process" object in the Intel 432, which consists of a data structure describing the state of a schedulable piece of software along with a set of operators (e.g., READ PROCESS CLOCK, GET STATE INFORMATION, SAVE STATE INFORMATION). The notion of objects is a central theme in the 432 exo-architecture. ∎

Example 2.11

At the endo-architectural level, *pipelining* represents a major style (see Chapter 6). Recall, from footnote 7, that the basic characteristic of a pipelined system is that it is composed of distinct, dedicated subprocesses or "stages" that can concurrently execute different stages of distinct processes. Any particular process, however, goes through several of, sometimes all, the stages of the pipeline in sequential fashion (Fig. 2.9). ∎

Example 2.12

Over the past two decades it has become common to talk about *horizontal* machines. Historically, this term denotes a style relevant to micro-architectures (see Volume 1, Chapter 5; also Sections 1.3 and 1.4 of Chapter 1) and, in particular, to microinstruction word organizations that possess one or more of the following characteristics:

1. They enable different functional units to be controlled and activated independently from the same microinstruction.
2. They have relatively large word lengths (of the order of 75 to 360 bits).
3. They allow the exercise of very low level control; that is, the operators encodable within a single microinstruction are functionally very primitive.

In recent years the horizontal machine style has also come to embrace certain exo-architectures. That is, machines that present to the programming/compiling universe interfaces that have the characteristics listed above. Instances of such machines are the so-called attached array processors such as the AP-120b and the FPS-164 marketed by Floating Point Systems (Charlesworth, 1981; Touzeau, 1984) and the ELI-512 (Fisher, 1983). ∎

2.8 SUMMARY

In this chapter we first established a general set of objectives that taxonomic systems should meet. The two main philosophies of classification, namely the evolutionary and the morphological, were also identified.

We then examined several taxonomic systems that have been devised for the purpose of classifying computers in general. These include Flynn's classification, the Hwang-Briggs extension to this, the Erlangen system, and Giloi's scheme.

However, none of these proposals lead to a truly satisfactory taxonomic system with the rigor, power, completeness, and the availability of an elegant nomenclature that we would desire. The taxonomy of computer architecture as a discipline and a science is still very much virgin territory.

An alternative manner of classifying computers is to identify different styles. The concept of styles provides an informal, intuitively appealing and flexible framework in which to discuss computer classes. It also allows us to understand the evolutionary (phylogenic, see Section 2.3) history of a machine—that is, how it has emerged from previous styles.

2.9 BIBLIOGRAPHIC AND HISTORICAL REMARKS

By far the most mature taxonomy is that of biological systems, which has (as already mentioned) a history reaching back to classical times. For general discussions of traditional biological taxonomy, refer to Mayr (1969) and Ross (1974). Some of the philosophical issues surrounding the classification problem are discussed in Ruse (1973). The classic monograph on the "new" (mathematical or numerical) taxonomy is Sokal and Sneath (1963); a shorter and more recent treatment of this subject is Dunn and Everitt (1982).

As noted in Section 2.1, the problem of classification has been studied in many other disciplines. An example *par excellence* of a scheme with great predictive and explanatory power in a natural science other than biology is, of course, Mendeleev's periodic classification of the chemical elements. Steadman (1979) presents a fascinating discussion of how certain theorists in (building) architecture attempted to establish a "typology" of buildings.

More generally, building architectures are frequently classified in terms of their styles. Thus, Pevsner (1963), in his classic survey of European architecture, describes such styles as the Romanesque, the early and classic Gothic, the late Gothic, Renaissance and Mannerism, the Baroque, and so on, and associates specific historical periods with these styles. Of course, it is not the period that determines style; rather, it is that the particular complex of morphological features and philosophical spirit that determines or characterizes a style may dominate a particular historical period. The great example of this in the present century is the so-called Modern or International Style (Banham, 1982; Pevsner, 1963, Chapter 9; Wolfe, 1981).

Style in computer architecture was discussed in length by Dasgupta (1984, Chapter 12). An earlier, more general discussion of style in the design process — the role of style in the "Sciences of the Artificial" — was presented by Simon (1975).

The different architectural classification schemes described here are by no means exhaustive. Additional proposals at the level of general architecture have been made by Kavi and Cragon (1983) and Hockney (1981). Baer (1983) also discusses some problems in the context of the *ACM Computing Reviews* classification of topics in architecture.

Many more taxonomic systems have been proposed for restricted aspects or classes of architectures. These include the classification of data-flow and data-driven machines by Treleavan, Brownbridge, and Hopkins (1982) (see Chapter 9), several schemes for interconnection networks (Anderson and Jensen, 1975; Enslow, 1977; Feng, 1981; Hwang and Briggs, 1984) (see Chapter 8), and the classification of fault-tolerant attributes (Avizienis, 1983).

PROBLEMS

2.1 A classification scheme is meaningful only in the context of some particular use to which it will be put. Consider, in particular, the problem of classifying *exo-architectures*.

Discuss the different *purposes* for which we might want to construct exo-architectural classification schemes.

2.2 Recall from Section 2.1 that in devising even the simplest of taxonomic schemes for a set of objects, the taxonomist must establish a number of different taxa among which the objects must be partitioned. A set of such mutually exclusive taxa constitutes a *category*. Establishing a particular category of taxa is usually based on the identification of a set of *taxonomic characters* (TCs) (see Section 2.4).

In describing *exo-architectures* (see, e.g., Volume 1, chapter 4) we often find it convenient to use the following *exo-architectural components* as a basis for discussion.

Storage organization

Data types

Addressing modes

Instruction set

Instruction formats

Word length

Analyze and discuss the usefulness (or otherwise) of these components as possible TCs for the purpose of constructing classification schemes for exo-architectures.

[*Hint*: Answering this question requires, first, the identification of the particular purpose envisioned for a classification scheme — see Problem 2.1].

2.3 [Continuation of Problem 2.2.] If your argument, in response to Problem 2.2, is that these are not useful as TCs, then

(a) Identify a set of TCs that *will* serve as a basis for classifying exo-architectures.

(b) What role would the abovementioned exo-architectural components serve (if any), in the classification of exo-architectures?

2.4 One very common way of classifying computers is by referring to their *word lengths*. Within the formal terminology of taxonomy, the term "word length" denotes a category consisting of a (potentially unlimited) collection of taxa with names such as "8-bit machine," "32-bit machine," "64-bit machine."

Discuss the effectiveness of the word length as a basis for classifying architectures. [*Hint*: Consider its descriptive, predictive, or explanatory power].

2.5 In their book, Siewiorek, Bell, and Newell (1982) proposed a classification scheme in which the taxa are called *computer classes*. The principal classes named there were the following.

Monolithic (i.e., single chip) microcomputers

Microcomputers

Minicomputers

Maxicomputers

Recently, Bell (1985) introduced a new class, which he has named "Multi-microprocessors" (or "Multis" for short).

Based on our shared knowledge of computers and computer architectures, we certainly have an *intuitive* understanding of what these taxa represent. Indeed, we do not hesitate in assigning computers to particular classes—the Intel 8086 to the microcomputer class, the PDP-11/70 to the minicomputer class, the IBM System/370 series to the maxicomputer class, and so on.

However when we try to characterize these classes formally, it is another matter! Consider, then, the problem of developing a precise taxonomic system based on computer classes.

(a) What are the taxonomic characters (TCs) that should be used in establishing such a system?

(b) Based on these TCs, give a defining characteristics of each of the aforementioned computer classes and any additional classes that may be identified.

(c) What are your conclusions concerning classes as a good classification scheme?

[*Note*: Siewiorek, Bell, and Newell (1982) have identified a set of "metrics," which, they claim, correlate well with the different computer classes. These include *price*, the *physical space*, and the size of the *real memory address space*. However, there are problems (which may become apparent to you) in using these metrics as TCs for the purpose of identifying classes.]

2.6 **(a)** Using the Erlangen classification scheme (ECS), describe the following machines:

(i) The Intel 8080
(ii) The Intel 8086
(iii) The Intel 80286
(iv) The PDP-11/45
(v) The PDP-11/70
(vi) The VAX-11/750
(vii) The VAX-11/780
(viii) The IBM System/360 Model 91
(ix) The IBM System/370 Model 145
(x) The IBM System/370 Model 168

(b) Based on part (a), what are your conclusions regarding the advantages and disadvantages of ECS?

2.7 [A taxonomical project.] Construct a comprehensive taxonomic system for *micro-architectures* (i.e., the architectural level as seen by the micropro-grammer). Your system should at least have predictive power. That is, given your taxonomy, and given the assertion that the micro-architecture of some particular computer has a particular place in your taxonomy, one should at least be able to predict the significant properties of that particular micro-architecture.

2.8 [A research project.] In Section 2.3 we defined an *evolutionary* taxonomic system as one that allows objects to be classified into taxa/category according to evolutionary factors. Taking the classic example of biological classification, the Linnean system (see also, Example 2.2) recognizes several *categories*, called (and ranked in ascending order): species, genus, family, order, class, phylum, and kingdom. There may also be intermediate level categories, for example, superfamily (between family and order), and subfamily (between genus and family). In the Linnean system, taxonomists have established that

(i) The species called *Homo sapiens* also belongs to the genus called *Homo* (Man) and to the family called *Hominidae*.
(ii) The (now extinct) genus called *Ramapithecus* (Early Ape Man) also belongs to the family *Hominidae*.
(iii) The (now extinct) genus called *Australopithecus* (Ape Man) also belongs to the family *Hominidae*.
(iv) Any member of the family *Hominidae* is also a member of the super-family *Hominoidea* (Apes and Men) and to the order *Primate*.

The three genera, *Homo*, *Ramapithecus*, and *Australopithecus* are morphologically distinguished according to anatomic features. However, the fact that they are all rooted in the same family strongly indicate that man and ape man have either a common ancestor or man is an evolutionary descendent of ape man. And, further [from (iv)], at an earlier age apes, ape men, and men have a common heritage. The Linnean system is, thus, an evolutionary scheme.

Unfortunately, computer scientists are nowhere near establishing an architectural taxonomy that even remotely approaches the scheme developed over centuries by biological taxonomists.

One way by which we might fruitfully begin such an ambitious enterprise is to examine particular, well-documented *computer families* and analyze in detail their comparative morphologies and their evolutionary histories. Only when we have carried out such analysis in painstaking detail will we begin to imagine what an evolutionary taxonomic system for computer architectures might look like.

(a) Select any well-documented computer family that has a relatively long line of historical development in terms of the number of distinct architectures. Conduct a detailed analysis of the similarities and distinctions between members of your chosen family and examine closely how successive architectures evolved.

(b) Based on this study, construct an evolutionary taxonomic system for *this particular family*. The system should have considerable explanatory power. That is, it should be such that (1) not only should we be able to predict a significant set of properties of any given architecture said to occupy a particular place (i.e., category/taxa) in your system from our knowledge of the system; but also (2) we should be able to explain *why* and *how* an architecture occupies a particular place in your taxonomy.

PART TWO

TOOLS FOR DESIGN AND DESCRIPTION

CHAPTER 3

DESCRIPTION OF COMPUTER ARCHITECTURES: CLASSIFICATION AND APPLICATIONS

3.1 INTRODUCTION

Perhaps few intellectual disciplines have been so preoccupied with the problem of *precise description* as has computer science. For instance, although notation and the use of formal language have always been integral to the mathematical sciences and technologies, computer science is on its own in that the *design* of notation or description languages constitute a substantial part of its research program. One gets paid, so to speak, to invent notation.

The origins of this concern are reasonably obvious: In the early days of computing the first primitive programming languages (assembly languages such as the IBM 1401 Autocode) were conceived primarily as a means for the problem solver to communicate algorithms to the machine. Ease of machine execution was the key issue, and thus, in a very real sense, programs written in such languages resembled *code* in their terseness and rigidity of form.

It soon became evident to some, however, that the real issue in programming language design is not so much one of communicating with the computer as one of *describing or specifying computations in the most exact and appropriate manner possible independent of any particular computer.* It is then the computer system's responsibility to do what it can to understand such specifications and execute them as efficiently as possible (Dijkstra, 1976). Programming and the languages for describing programs were, as a result of this philosophical stance, liberated from the machine's bondage.

Indeed, in the area of programming one can go as far as to state that the power of languages transcends the mere ability to *describe* ideas. Some languages have imposed their own imprint on how the problem solver views the computational universe; they have helped create, in other words, distinct programming paradigms (Floyd, 1979).[1]

---

[1]We use the word "paradigm" here and elsewhere in this book to mean, loosely, a set of organizing principles or a model that governs one's perception of some particular universe. One talks, for example, of the "artificial intelligence (AI) paradigm." Our use of the word is, thus, very much in the sense that Kuhn (1970) made famous in his epoch-making book.

Since the late 1960s or so, further impetus for research into language principles, their design, and their applications has been provided by the growth of interest in the methodology of design—that is, in the intellectual, social, and computational mechanisms underlying the design process.

The main reason for this explicit interest in the design process was the conviction on the part of many that, given the rapidly increasing complexity of computing systems—in particular, software systems—the organization and management of such system complexity demands a "structuring" of the design process itself. Concommitantly, growing awareness of the need to demonstrate a priori the reliability and correctness of a system's design (see Volume 1, Chapter 3, and Chapter 5 and the Appendix, this volume) helped focus interest on design methods that were, in some sense, conducive to correct design.[2]

Many of these early—and at the time, revolutionary—ideas at the core of software engineering were owed to a small group of programmers, theorists, and language designers, most notably, Dijkstra (1972), Mills (1972), Floyd (1967), Hoare (1969), Zurcher and Randell (1968), Parnas (1972), and Wirth (1971).

The relevant point to note is that an essential requirement for disciplined design is the availability of the "right" design language. In the case of particularly complex systems, the design process may be segmented into distinct stages, each of which creates a particular level of abstraction; in such cases, several languages may be required.

Although the central position of language in software design is obvious, its role in *hardware design* is much less apparent; and it is this latter role that is the concern of this and the following chapter. More specifically, these two chapters cover the principles, design, and applications of a class of languages that may be used for the design and description of computer architectures. We call these *architecture description languages* (ADLs); they are members of a larger family of *computer hardware description languages* (CHDLs).

CHDLs are languages designed and implemented specifically for the description of computer hardware systems. However, as I have noted before, hardware systems may be described at several distinct levels of abstraction, sometimes with very distinct sets of characteristics. Thus, different classes of such languages have sprung into existence, each specialized to a particular view of computer hardware. ADLs form one such class of languages. Section 3.2 discusses these different classes of CHDLs more fully.

It must be noted that developments or interest in CHDLs are not a particularly recent phenomenon. Dietmeyer and Duley (1975), for instance, have traced their origins back to the work of I. S. Reed in the 1950s. However, it was really in the mid-1960s that the first systematic designs of CHDLs were reported (Iverson, 1962; Falkoff *et al.*, 1964; Chu, 1965; Schlaeppi, 1964; Parnas and

---

[2]1968 is generally regarded as a watershed year in this regard. In that year a NATO-sponsored conference on software engineering was held. This, the first such conference, provided the forum at which the "crisis" of large-scale software design and management was first publicly and explicitly acknowledged. Thus was born a discipline and an industry.

Darringer, 1967; Duley and Dietmeyer, 1968). Since then, the number of CHDLs have steadily continued to increase (Barbacci and Uehara, 1985).

Unfortunately, unlike the case for software systems, the role of CHDLs in the computer design process was, until recently, never held to be very important. A vast majority of such languages were developed in universities either as "basic" research investigations or as pedagogic tools and, thus, remained "laboratory curiosities" as far as the design community was concerned.

This situation has changed somewhat in the last half a dozen years. The development of CHDLs and their applications is now being pursued in both academic and industrial laboratories; CHDLs are beginning to be used as "front ends" in design automation systems and to support systematic, even formal, design procedures (see Sections 3.2 and 3.3 of this chapter and also Chapter 4). There are several reasons for this change, the most obvious of which are the following.

1. As a result of developments in LSI and VLSI technologies, processor chips of unprecedented *circuit complexity* are now becoming available (see Volume 1, Chapter 2). The design, modeling, and implementation of such LSI- and VLSI-based processors have placed demands on highly structured and rigorous design methods as a means for mastering and managing this complexity.

2. These same technological developments have enhanced the feasibility of cost-effective distributed systems, networks, and highly concurrent multiple processors. Thus, computer hardware systems of enormous *organizational complexity* are being designed, built, and studied. Again, as in reason (1), the need for structuring both the design process and design descriptions seems imperative if designers are to produce well-behaved, understandable, and intellectually manageable systems. These are by no means the only reasons, although they are the ones most publicly recognized. There are other, more subtle influences that have motivated recent developments in CHDLs. In the specific context of ADLs, we will consider these other issues later in this chapter. However, it is fair to say that many of these other factors are, in one way or another, consequences of the growth in circuit and organizational complexities largely brought about by technological developments.

Along with all such recently perceived practical needs for CHDLs, there is also a rather basic theoretical pressure. Thus, as a third significant reason we state:

3. The desire on the part of many designers of CHDLs to comprehend the essential, formal, mathematical nature of hardware structures—especially at abstraction levels above the logic design level. It is only when we have such an understanding that we can hope to establish a sound and rigorous basis for designing and implementing hardware systems. The development of formal models of hardware, firmware, and architectures, the definition of the formal semantics of CHDLs, and the construction of techniques for proving the correctness of hardware and firmware design are all part of this more theoretical research program surrounding CHDLs.

3.2 DIMENSIONS OF THE HARDWARE DESCRIPTION SPACE

To make some sense of the universe of hardware description languages we must take recourse (as always, in these matters) to some sort of classification scheme. For this purpose we may identify a number of key, high-level "dimensions" that collectively form a *hardware description space* (Dasgupta, 1984, 1985). A given CHDL may then be viewed as a "point" in this multidimensional space according to its specific characteristics. One may also view combinations of these dimensions as constituting specific *styles of description* (see also Chapter 2, Section 2.7, for a brief discussion of "style").

The dimensions of principal interest are:

1. The *levels of hardware abstraction* for which a given language is designed.
2. Whether the CHDL allows for *operational descriptions*.
3. Whether hardware may be specified in *functional terms*.
4. The rule(s) governing *how control flows* through a hardware description.
5. Whether the CHDL allows for the description of hardware system *structure*, hardware *behavior*, or both.

3.2.1 Levels of Abstraction

I have noted before that the design of a computer involves several stages, each responsible for a level of abstraction. The output of each such stage is a representation of the design that must capture the characteristics of the related abstraction level. Furthermore, since each level has one or more *roles* to play, the design representation must be *useful* for these roles to be played out.

Example 3.1

As I will further elaborate in Section 3.3, the description of a machine's exo-architecture may be required by a retargetable compiler to generate code for the machine in question. The representation of the exo-architecture should, ideally, be such as to enhance the efficacy and efficiency of such compilers. ■

CHDLs may, thus, be characterized by which level or levels of abstraction they are intended or best suited to describe.

Table 3.1 recapitulates the significant abstraction levels relevant to the logical design of computers (note that I have omitted the physical design aspects, since they are somewhat removed from the domains of primary interest to us, namely, the architectural levels). Alongside each level, the table lists examples of representative CHDLs. Before we proceed further, some cautionary observations must be made.

1. The CHDLs appearing in this table are only a small subset of the many that have been described in the literature. Unlike the situation in programming languages, where some languages have become more "important" because of their technical merits or because of their industrial or governmental

TABLE 3.1 Hardware Abstraction Levels and CHDL Examples per Level

Levels of Abstraction	Examples of Languages
Architectural	
Exo-architecture	SLIDE S*A ISPS MIT/ADL HISDL PADL SARA
Endo-architecture	MIDL AADL
Micro-architecture	S*M
Microprogramming	
Machine-independent	MARBLE S* u-C VMPL Ada MIMOLA VHDL CONLAN
Machine-dependent	STRUM Ohne YALLL
Register-transfer	DDL CDL AHPL ZEUS SARA
Logic design	

Sources:

SLIDE: Parker and Wallace (1981)
MIDL: Sint (1981)
S*A: Dasgupta (1981, 1984)
S*M: Dasgupta, Wilsey, and Heinanen (1986)
AADL: Damm (1985), Damm et al. (1986)
MIT/ADL: Leung (1979, 1981)
ISPS: Barbacci et al. (1978); Barbacci (1981)
HISDL: Lim (1982) [PADL: Lim and Leung (1983)]
MARBLE: Davidson and Shriver (1980)
STRUM: Patterson (1976, 1981)
S*: Dasgupta (1980, 1984)
Ohne: Wagnon and Maine (1983)

AHPL: Hill and Peterson (1978)
μ-C: Hopkins, Horton, and Arnold (1985)
YALLL: Patterson, Lew and Tuck (1979)
SARA: Estrin (1978, 1985a, 1985b); Vernon and Estrin (1985)
CDL: Chu (1965, 1972)
DDL: Duley and Dietmeyer (1968); Dietmeyer and Duley (1975)
VMPL: Lewis, Malik, and Ma (1980)
MIMOLA: Marwedel (1984, 1985)
VHDL: Shahdad et al. (1985)
CONLAN: Piloty et al. (1983)
Ada: Barbacci et al. (1985)
ZEUS: German and Lieberherr (1985); Lieberherr (1984).

Note: Ada is a registered trademark of the U.S. Government ADA Joint Program Office

support, no real consensus has yet emerged from either a technical or a commercial perspective as to what languages are "important." Thus, the selection of these examples is to a great extent arbitrary and reflect my familiarity with these specific languages. One should also note that with the exception of VHDL (Shadad *et al.*, 1985), Ohne (Wagnon and Maine, 1983), and Zeus (Lieberherr, 1984; German and Lieberherr, 1985) all the languages mentioned here were developed, implemented, and nurtured at universities. Probably because of this, they have been better documented in the open scientific literature.

2. Not all observers may agree with the way that one or more of the CHDLs have been assigned to a particular level or range of levels. Each assignment is based on either the structure of the language or the explicit goals proclaimed by the language designers. In some cases, languages have been stated as supporting multilevel representations, in which case vertical dark arrows delineate the span. In other cases, the span is extended by dashed arrows to signify that the language in question appears to have the capability to support additional levels but that this conjecture remains (at this time of writing) to be tested.

The earliest CHDLs, designed and implemented in the 1960s, were *register-transfer languages* (RTLs). As the name suggests, languages in this category are primarily intended to describe digital systems at the register-transfer level of abstraction. It is interesting to speculate as to why the initial interest in formal hardware descriptions was focused on the register-transfer level in particular. One can identify at least two reasons for this.

First, having been trained in, and being familiar with, the logic design level for which a rigorous, well-established theory of design was already in place, the hardware designer would naturally seek a formalization of the next higher level in the abstraction hierarchy: the register-transfer level. In the absence of an algebra or a calculus for the latter, the symbolic computational approach was an obvious choice, particularly since the advent of the early high-level programming languages [such as Algol 60 (Naur, 1963) and APL (Iverson, 1962)] had already demonstrated the potential elegance and conciseness of such descriptive mechanisms.

Second, one of the principal purposes of formal descriptions of hardware is to serve as an input to a design automation system. The latter would translate the input description to some appropriate lower-level representation, either for purposes of simulation, logic-level synthesis, or other computer-aided design (CAD) purposes (Fig. 3.1). When one reflects on the form of input descriptions to such systems, the register-transfer level represents a "happy mean" between the very abstract and the unduly detailed.

The fundamental characteristic of the register-transfer-level is that a given digital system is composed from entities that are functionally similar to MSI logic circuits (see Volume 1, Chapter 2). Typical segments of a register-transfer-level description would characterize structural entities such as registers, terminals, clocks, buses, and multiplexers and would specify the overall behavior in

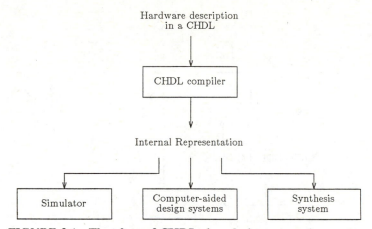

FIGURE 3.1   The place of CHDLs in a design automation system.

terms of operations that invoke the combinational circuits or cause transfers between registers.

As Table 3.1 shows, two of the earliest RTLs were CDL (Chu, 1965, 1972) and DDL (Duley and Dietmeyer, 1968; Dietmeyer and Duley, 1975). Despite its relative age, DDL is still a living language, since it provides the descriptive basis for a formal hardware verification system developed at the Fujitsu Laboratories in Japan (Uehara *et al.*, 1983; Maruyama and Fujita, 1985). AHPL is a slightly later RTL and was conceived, implemented, and continues to be improved and used at the University of Arizona (Hill and Peterson, 1978).

Example 3.2

As an example of a register-transfer level description, consider a partial CPU as diagrammed in Figure 3.2. The opcode portion of the instruction register (IREG) is input to a decoder, which generates one of eight possible signals. The control unit accepts signals from the decoder output and a four-phase clock and generates, in turn, control signals.

Figure 3.3 shows a partial CDL description of this CPU. The elements shown in the upper part are declarations of relevant structural elements whereas the lower part of the description specifies the behavior in terms of either simple register-to-register transfers or actions involving (implied) functional units such as an ALU or a counter. Thus, for example, in the instruction fetch segment, the register-transfer operation

  MAR←——PC

is executed both when a signal is received on the FETCH output line of DE-CODER [i.e., line S(7)] *and* when the clock P is in phase 1. Instruction fetch, thus, shows the sequence of register-to-register actions taking place in each of the four clock phases. ∎

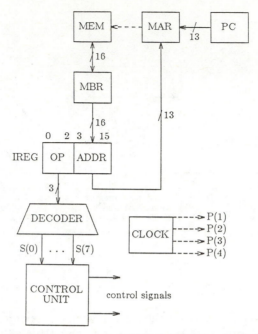

FIGURE 3.2 A partial CPU [Dasgupta (1982) © 1982, Academic Press, Inc.; Reprinted with permission].

Note that RTLs may well be suited for describing *microprograms*; indeed, the control sequences shown in Figure 3.3 are very-low-level symbolic micropro-gram routines involving primitive micro-operations. However, the *microprogramming level*—that is, the level of description visible to the microprogrammer—may vary considerably, depending what language is available to the microprogrammer. It ranges from the register-transfer level—as depicted in Figure 3.3, in which the microcode is specified in terms of very primitive micro-operations and the precise conditions under which a micro-operation is executed (e.g., the conjunction of a signal appearing on one of the decoder output lines and one of the four clock-phase signals)—through more abstract but still machine-dependent representations, to still more abstract and totally machine-independent forms.

Example 3.3

Figure 3.4 is a description of the same segment shown in Figure 3.3, this time expressed in a version of the microprogramming language S* (Dasguage, 1980, 1984). For present purposes, the details are not too important. What you should note about this description are:

1. The variables declared and used are still representations of (are bound to) the storage elements shown in Figure 3.2 but are now defined as instances of

```
REGISTER, MBR(0-15), IREG(0-15), ACC(0-15),
          MAR(0-12), PC(0-12),
. . . . . .
SUBREGISTER, IREG(OP) = IREG(0-2), IREG(ADDR) = IREG(3-15),
MEMORY, MEM(MAR) = MEM(0-8191,0-15),
DECODER, S(0-7) = IREG(OP),
TERMINAL, AND = S(0),
          TAD = S(1),
          . . . . . .
          JMP = S(6).
          FETCH = S(7),
CLOCK,    P(1-4)  $four-phase clock

Comment Instruction fetch
/FETCH * P(1)/ MAR< —PC,
/FETCH * P(2)/MBR < —MEM(MAR),
/FETCH * P(3)/ IREG < —MBR,PC countup PC
/FETCH * P(4)/ MAR < —IREG(ADDR),

comment 'and' operation
/AND * P(1)/ MBR < —MEM(MAR),
/AND * P(2)/ ACC < —ACC∧MBR, IREG(OP) < —7
. . . . . .

Comment 'jump'
/JMP * P(1)/ PC < —IREG(ADDR), IREG(OP) < —7
. . . . . .
```

FIGURE 3.3 Partial description of CPU in CDL [Dasgupta (1982) © 1982, Academic Press, Inc.; Reprinted with permission].

the abstract types *sequence* and *array*. The archetypal register-transfer level concepts of "register" and "memory" have disappeared.

2. A higher-level control structure—the *while* statement—is used to capture the overall flow of control through the microprogram. There is no obvious way in which you may infer how the loop is actually implemented by the control unit: such machine-specific detail has been (deliberately) suppressed.

3. The use of the *cocycle* statement; the meaning of this construct is that its component statements are all executed in a single microcycle either sequentially (indicated by the ";" operator) or in parallel (indicated by the "□" operator). Thus, although the specifics of the controlling clock phases so explicit in Figure 3.3 have been omitted, the microprogrammer must still be aware of them in order to write a *cocycle* statement correctly, although you need not know these specifics. Furthermore, in order for the *cocycle* statement to be valid, its component statements must correspond to the primitive micro-operations used in Figure 3.3.

In short, the description of Figure 3.4 is part machine-specific (at the register-transfer level of abstraction) and part machine independent. ∎

```
type addr_width = seq[12..0] bit;
type data_width = seq[15..0] bit;

var mem : array [0..8191] of data_width;
var mbr, acc, ireg : data_width;
var mar, pc : addr_width;

syn op = ireg[15..13],
    addr = ireg[12..0];

/* instruction_fetch */
while true do
    cocycle
        mar := pc;
        mbr := mem[mar];
        do ireg := mbr ☐ pc := pc + 1 od
        mar := addr
    coend;
/* instruction execution */
    case op of
        0: cocycle          /* AND inst. */
            mbr := mem[mar];
            acc := acc ∧ mbr
        coend
        . . . . . .
        6: pc := addr   /* JMP inst. */
    endcase
od /* end of while statement */
```

FIGURE 3.4   Partial description of CPU in S*.

Because of the importance and ubiquity of microprogramming in computer design, the microprogramming level has, over the past decade or so, been of enormous interest in its own right and a vast literature has sprung up on the issues surrounding the design and implementation of *microprogramming languages*. This topic is discussed in greater detail in Chapter 5.

From a historical perspective, languages designed explicitly as *architecture description languages* (ADLs)—see Table 3.1—are mostly products of the late 1970s and early 1980s. This seems to suggest an emerging awareness of a need for formal descriptions at the more abstract levels of the computer design process.

Again, as in the case of the microprogramming level, ADLs vary considerably in form and philosophy; languages such as MIDL (Sint, 1981), AADL (Damm, 1985; Damm *et al.*, 1986), and S*M (Dasgupta, Wilsey, and Heinanen, 1986) intended specifically for micro-architecture descriptions are, in some ways at least, very similar to RTLs. ADLs such as ISPS (Barbacci *et al.*, 1978; Barbacci, 1981), S*A (Dasgupta, 1981, 1984), SLIDE (Parker and Wallace, 1981), and MIT/ADL (Leung, 1979, 1981) intended primarily for the description of exo- and endo-architectures are far nearer to programming languages in their structure, semantics, and style of usage. Their common hallmark is the deliberate intent to suppress specific hardware interpretations for the language constructs and an attendant emphasis on logical properties.

An obvious issue that will occur to you is the thorny problem of how a design may be transformed across several abstraction levels. One can imagine three distinct solutions to this problem:

1. In the first, the design is expressed at the highest possible level and automatically *translated* down to the target level through various intermediate representation forms. The problem of using hardware description languages for these intermediate levels is simply removed. This, of course, is the basis for much of the current research on design synthesis and automation in the realms of hardware and firmware (see Chapter 5).

2. In the absence of the most satisfactory automatic techniques, an alternative approach is to conceive of a *family of languages*, different members of which could be used for the various abstraction levels. By designing languages that, although oriented to specific abstraction levels, are relatively "close" to one another (i.e., bear "kinship"), the transformation from one level to the next may be made relatively painless and intellectually manageable.

    This technique was demonstrated by Dasgupta and Olafsson (1982), who used the ADL S*A and the closely related microprogramming language S* to develop the formal description of an exo-architecture and the microprogram to emulate the architecture on the Nanodata QM-1 (see also Dasgupta, 1984).

3. The third approach is exemplified by the recent trend in CHDL design toward *multilevel languages*—that is, a single language that may be used for specifying hardware structure and behavior at different abstraction levels. MIMOLA (Marwedel, 1984, 1985), CONLAN (Piloty *et al.*, 1983), and SARA (Estrin, 1978, 1985a, 1985b; Vernon and Estrin, 1985) are examples of this approach, but the most recent effort in this direction is VHDL (Shahdad *et al.*, 1985) which is receiving considerable industrial attention because of its support from the U.S. Department of Defense.

Later (in chapter 4) we will look more closely at ADLs. I will present the desirable characteristics of such languages and describe both languages designed specifically for architecture descriptions and those intended for multilevel representation, including architectural levels.

3.2.2 Operational Descriptions

A language is said to support an *operational* mode of description when its user can define the behavior of a system in terms of a program or algorithm.[3]

---

[3]The use of the word operational originates in the notion of the *operational semantics* of programming languages (Wegner, 1972a, 1972b) in which the meaning of a language construct is defined in terms of an observable sequence of state transformations that result from the execution of some abstract "computer" interpreting the construct. This operational viewpoint, in turn, has its roots in the philosophy of science called *operationalism*, expounded by the physicist P. W. Bridgeman (1927), in which a scientific concept is defined solely in terms of some experimental procedure. For example, the notion of "length" is defined in terms of operations by which length is measured. For more on operational and other forms of prescribing behavior or meaning, see Section 3.2.3 and the Appendix.

Consider, as a simple example, the operational description of an ADD micro-operation of the kind that may be typically defined as part of a machine's micro-architecture. Figure 3.5 specifies this operation in a slightly simplified version of S*A (Dasgupta, 1981, 1984).

The important point to note about this example is that the "meaning" of this operation is specified by an *explicitly* ordered set of actions that must be more primitive than the ADD. Sequential ordering is denoted by ";" and parallel execution by "☐". Furthermore, since at the *micro-architectural* level — the level being defined — the ADD itself is considered to be a "primitive"; this implies that the actions specified in Figure 3.5 (the assignments, and the **call**, **case**, and **if** statements) represent events at least at the register-transfer level.

Such assumptions about the nature, existence, or availability of primitive register-transfer level actions and their ordering may of course be entirely pre-

```
var ir :
        tuple
            opcode: seq[1..0] bit;
            src: seq[2..0] bit;
            dest: seq[2..0] bit;
        endtup;
var acc, buffer: seq[7..0] bit;
var local_store: array[0..7] of seq[9..7] bit;
var alu_out: seq[8..0] bit;
var psw:
        tuple
            sign, zero, parity, carry: bit
        endtup

proc ADD
    case ir.src of
        0..5: buffer := local_store[ir.src];
        6..7: buffer := acc
    endcase;
    alu_out := acc + buffer;
    do call SETCC ☐ acc := alu_out[7..0] od
endproc

proc SETCC
    do psw.carry := alu_out[8]
    ☐ psw.sign := alu_out[7]
    ☐ psw.parity :=
            (alu_out[7] ⊕ alu_out[6] ⊕ alu_out[5] ⊕
            alu_out[4] ⊕ alu_out[3] ⊕ alu_out[2] ⊕
            alu_out[1] ⊕ alu_out[0])
    ☐ if alu_out[7..0] = 0 --> psw.zero := 1
        || else --> psw.zero := 0
      fi
    od
endproc
```

FIGURE 3.5 Operational description of a microoperation [Dasgupta (1985) © 1985 IEEE; Reprinted with permission].

sumptuous unless we know how the ALU actually carries out its operations. That is, we may be totally ignorant of how the ADD is actually performed and yet Figure 3.5 prescribes a mechanism, a register-transfer level "program," in fact, that seems to indicate "how" the operation takes place.

There are, of course, some compelling advantages to having operational descriptions, not the least of which is that such descriptions being "program-like" are familiar and may be readily understood. Furthermore, there are many other situations in which they are needed or justified; in fact, whenever the CHDL user describes a system involving explicit flow of control that is known to be true — that has actually been designed — an operational description is the natural choice.

Perhaps largely because of the "familiarity argument," most CHDLs are operational in nature. In the case of ADLs (see Table 3.1) all but AADL and S*M are primarily operational languages or at least support, in part, operational descriptions.

3.2.3 Functional Descriptions

Operational descriptions, of course, directly mirror the familiar, orderly, step-by-step execution of programs in von Neumann style machines. *Functional descriptions* represent a radically different style in that the behavior of the system being described is specified in terms of a mapping from the set of system inputs to the set of system outputs without, however, revealing how the system does the mapping. More ordinarily stated, functional descriptions treat the system as a "black box," the behavior of which is defined *only* in terms of inputs to and outputs of the system (Fig. 3.6).[4]

The need for functional descriptions arises in many areas of computer systems design and it does so for two basic reasons.

---

[4]If operational descriptions relate to Bridgeman's operationalism philosophy of science, functional descriptions bring to mind the school of psychology called *behaviorism* associated with J. B. Watson and I. Pavlov in the early years of this century and, in more recent times, B. F. Skinner (1972). The basic tenet of behaviorism is that psychological attributes of organisms can be studied purely in terms of observable behavior, that is, how the organism *responds* to *stimuli*.

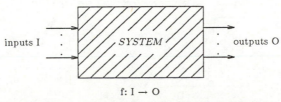

inputs I   SYSTEM   outputs O

f: I → O

FIGURE 3.6   Schematic of functional descriptions.

The Design of Abstractions

One of the applications of formal description languages is to support the systematic, controlled design of a system. Given an initial conception of the design — that is, given an *informal design* (Dasgupta, 1984) — one should be able to represent and document the design in a formal fashion down to a level sufficiently detailed as to be adequate for implementation.

However, there may be a substantial gap between informal design and formal description; the problem is to provide the means to bridge this gap in an effective manner.

One technique advocated for this is that of *abstraction*; that is, a simplified or selective description of a system that emphasizes some of its properties while suppressing others. Thus, for instance, a *procedural abstraction* describes the intended behavior of an algorithm or procedure while deliberately ignoring the details of how this behavior is realized (Liskov, 1980). A *data abstraction* defines the "behavior" of a data object purely in terms of the operations (which in turn are specified as procedural abstractions) that can act on or manipulate the object while ignoring the internal structure or representation of the object.

In the design method known as *stepwise refinement*, key steps in each stage of the refinement include the identification of distinct modules and the creation of abstractions for these modules. The abstraction serves two roles: a *use* role, which characterizes all that needs to be known about a module in order to use it as a component in the overall system; and a *requirements* role, which identifies the properties of the module that *must* be preserved or satisfied when the module is refined to the next level of detail (Fig. 3.7). For both these needs, it is the functional characteristics of the module that are important. Thus, a language used during stepwise refinement, say, should have the capability to support the design of such abstractions.

Confession of Ignorance

In contrast to the foregoing, which is a case of pretending ignorance, there are situations in which we actually do *not* know the internal workings of a system or

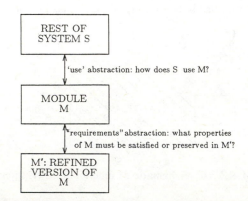

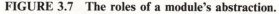

FIGURE 3.7 The roles of a module's abstraction.

a system component and, equally important, we do not particularly care. This situation was illustrated earlier in the example of the ADD micro-operation shown in Figure 3.5. More generally, consider the case where an exo-architecture (or a micro-architecture) is to be formally described in order to serve as input to a retargetable code (or microcode) generation system (Fig. 3.8; this, as we will see in Section 3.3, is one of the principal applications of an architecture description language).

The basis for formulating such a specification is usually an informal description provided in a "Principles of Operation" manual, an "Architecture Handbook" or a "Microprogramming Handbook." All that such documents usually describe is the state transformational behavior of instructions, microinstructions, or micro-operations (as the case may be) without any indication as to how the underlying firmware or hardware actually effects these state transformations. Thus, in developing a formal description of the architecture, although it is certainly possible to provide an operational description, this could entail making unwarranted assumptions about the underlying mechanism; it is wiser, more natural, and more truthful to confess ignorance and simply specify the architectural characteristics in functional terms.

There are several styles of functional description languages. One of these, termed the *axiomatic* style (Dasgupta, Wilsey, and Heinanen, 1986) is illustrated by the example of Figure 3.9. This specifies the same ADD micro-operation defined operationally in Figure 3.5.

The main characteristic of an axiomatic description language is that the behavior of a system is expressed in terms of assertions in some axiomatic or deductive system.[5] Consider, for instance, a system module M that computes a function f_M from a set of inputs I onto a set of outputs O (Fig. 3.6). Then the essence of an axiomatic description is to specify the function

$$f_M : I \longrightarrow O$$

in terms of an assertion PRE (called the *precondition*) and an assertion POST

---

[5]For the moment, I will not attempt to define rigorously what an assertion is. It suffices to note for now that an assertion is a statement (involving certain variables as arguments) that is either true or false.

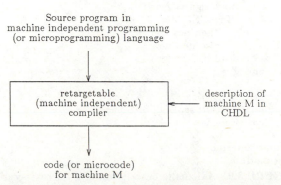

FIGURE 3.8   **The role of a CHDL in a retargetable code (microcode) generation system.**

(called the *postcondition*) such that if PRE is true, the behavior of M is given by POST. Note that how M actually works in order to effect the transformation from PRE to POST is not specified nor is it stated what happens if PRE is not true.[6]

The precise manner in which PRE, POST, and the inputs to and outputs from the module are expressed will differ from one language to another. Referring to Fig. 3.9 in particular, the <PRE, POST> pair is expressed under the **effects** keyword in the form

[6]In a certain sense, then, the assertions PRE and POST together capture the "meaning" of the module M. There is, thus, a natural analogy between the way system behavior or meaning is defined here and the *axiomatic semantics of programming languages* originally invented by Hoare (1969) (see Gries, 1981; de Bakker, 1980), where the meaning of language constructs are also defined in terms of assertions or formulas in a deductive system. It is because of this parallel that the term *axiomatic descriptions* was used by Dasgupta, Wilsey, and Heinanen (1986). Referring also to the discussion of operational languages, there is a nice symmetry between the two parallels: operational languages being analogous to operational semantics and axiomatic languages being analogous to axiomatic semantics.

```
module add
    inport ir:
        record
            opcode: seq[1..0] of bit;
            src: seq[2..0] of bit;
            dest: seq[2..0] of bit
        end record;
    inport local_store: array[0..7] of seq[7..0] of bit;
    inport mir: microinstruction;
    inport acc: seq[7..0] of bit;
    outport acc: seq[7..0] of bit;
    outport sign, zero, parity, carry: bit;
    . . . . . .
    effects /* specifies the behavior of the module */
        if mir.add = 1    /* precondition */
            then          /* postcondition */
                new acc = result[7..0] & new carry = result[8] &
                new parity = result[7] xor result[6] xor result[5]
                        xor result[4] xor result[3] xor result[2]
                        xor result[1] xor result[0] &
                new sign = result[7] &
                if result[7..0] = 0
                    then new zero = 1
                    else new zero = 0
                end if
        end if

    /* private function */
    function result: seq[8..0] of bit =
        case ir.src is
        . . . . . .
    end function
end module
```

FIGURE 3.9   Axiomatic description of a micro-operation.

if PRE
  then POST
end if

Thus, if the predicate mir.add $= 1$ is true (the precondition) when the add module is activated, then its function is defined by the conjunction of several predicates:[7]

new acc $=$ result [7..0]
new carry $=$ result [8]
  . . . .
etc.

where the notation "**new** x" (with x being declared an output port) denotes the state of x that will be observed when the module terminates its activity. When the postcondition refers to an "old" value of a port (i.e., to the state of a port when the module is activated), then the prefix **new** is omitted.

Note also, in order to enhance readability, the postcondition has been made as "program-like" as possible—although it is *not* a program—with such artifices as *if then else* statements and the use of additional abstractions such as private *function* modules.

Two additional remarks about axiomatic descriptions may be made:

1. Consider a system S of modules M_1, M_2, . . . , M_n with the behavior of each M_i specified in the form of a $<PRE_i, POST_i>$ pair. Then the behavior of S as a whole will be deduced from those of M_1, M_2, . . . ,M_n using appropriate *rules of inference*. Typically, an inference (or proof rule) is expressed in the notation

$$\frac{H_1, H_2, \ldots, H_n}{H}$$

which states that if the premises (or antecedents) H_1, H_2, . . . , H_n are valid (known to be true), then the conclusion (or consequence) H is also valid.

Example 3.4

As an elementary example, given M_1 defined by $<PRE_1, POST_1>$ and M_2 defined by $<PRE_2, POST_2>$ such that M_1, M_2 involve totally distinct sets of input and output variables, then the behavior of a system S in which M_1 and M_2 may be active in parallel will be determined by an inference rule of the form

$$\frac{M_1 : <PRE_1, POST_1>, M_2 : <PRE_2, POST_2>}{S : <PRE_1 \text{ \& } PRE_2, POST_1 \text{ \& } POST_2>}$$

In other words, if we know that the respective behaviors of M_1 and M_2 are

---

[7]Recall that a predicate P over a domain D is a function that takes arguments from D and returns either the value *true* or the value *false*:

P:D $\longrightarrow$ (**true, false**)

defined by the pre- and postconditions shown as premises, then the behavior of S as a whole is given by the pre- and postconditions shown in the conclusions.
∎

Inference rules will be part of the language definition itself and their precise nature will depend on how modules will be composed together and be activated.

2. Since axiomatic descriptions suppress how the mappings from inputs to outputs are realized, they can serve to formally define the *specification* of a system yet to be implemented — that is, to define formally the *functional requirements* of a system prior to the start of its design or implementation. Figure 3.9, for example, may be viewed as the specification of the ADD micro-operation that is given to the ALU designer whose task is to implement the logic design of the ALU.

    Indeed, the roots of axiomatic description as presented here go back to Parnas's early work on software module specification (Parnas, 1972), which later formed the basis for the software specification language Special developed at SRI International (Robinson, Levitt, Neumann, *et al.* 1977; Melliar-Smith, 1979).
∎

Referring back to Table 3.1, S*M and AADL are both examples of axiomatic ADLs whereas VHDL and CONLAN have some capability for functional descriptions.

3.2.4 Flow of Control: Procedural and Nonprocedural Descriptions

Yet another important axis of the hardware description space is concerned with the rule(s) governing the flow of control through a hardware description — or more precisely, the rule(s) by which actions specified in a description would be selected for activation if the description was to be executed by a simulator or was to be directly realized in hardware. The important distinction to be made here is between *procedural* and *nonprocedural* descriptions.

In a *procedural* description, the order of activation of statements (or operations or whatever is the unit of activation) is determined essentially by the textual structure of the description. The typical form of a procedural description is a statement sequence

$$S_1; S_2; \ldots ; S_n$$

such that, except when a branch appears to cause an explicit change in the flow of control, S_i will execute before S_j if $i < j$. Associated with a procedural description is an "invisible" program counter that in the course of execution is automatically incremented except when a branch occurs (Fig. 3.10).

In the case of procedural descriptions admitting concurrency, the most general form may be depicted as

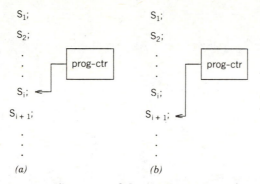

FIGURE 3.10 Two consecutive states of the program counter in executing a sequential procedural description.

$$P_1;$$
$$\textbf{cobegin } P_2 \parallel P_3 \parallel \ldots P_n \textbf{ coend;}$$
$$P_{n+1}$$

where the P_i's are themselves sequential or concurrent processes, ";" denotes sequential composition in the usual sense, and "$\parallel$" denotes parallel composition. In this case, the flow of control is explained by associating with each distinct sequential process a program counter and, when a new concurrent process (e.g., **cobegin** $P_2 \parallel \ldots \parallel P_n$ **coend**) is entered, creating "new" program counters for each additional component within the concurrent process (Fig. 3.11).

Most of the well-known programming languages are, of course, procedural; this is a natural reflection of the flow of control through programs in the archetypal "von Neumann" machine. Following this lead, many of the CHDLs are also essentially of a procedural nature, including S*A, SLIDE, and ISPS among ADLs and all the microprogramming languages listed in Table 3.1.

There are, however, many types and levels of information processing where computation proceeds in a *nonprocedural* fashion. That is, if such systems were to be described in a formal language, the ordering of the statements would not be of any particular significance. Instead, an action within a nonprocedural system would be selected for execution when some particular condition was true. Thus, one may model a nonprocedural description by a set of condition-action pairs:

$$\text{cond}_1 \Rightarrow \text{action}_1$$
$$\text{cond}_2 \Rightarrow \text{action}_2$$
$$\ldots \ldots \ldots \ldots$$
$$\text{cond}_n \Rightarrow \text{action}_n$$

such that whenever cond_i is true, action_i would execute, causing a change of state of the variables involved in this action. This may then make cond_j true, in which case action_j would next be selected for execution, and so on. In a system admitting concurrency, it may be possible for two or more noncontradictory

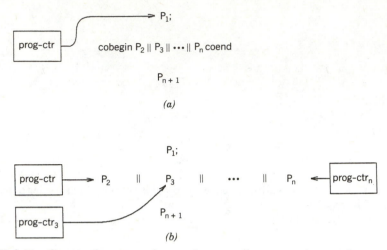

FIGURE 3.11   Consecutive generations and states of program counters in executing a parallel procedural description.

conditions to be true at any given time, in which case several actions would execute in parallel.[8]

Nonprocedural systems crop up in a variety of situations. In the specific context of hardware descriptions they are of particular interest since digital systems are widely conceived and designed as nonprocedural *state machines*— that is, when the system is in state S_i a certain set of actions will take place and the system state changes to S_j. This causes another set of actions to take place accompanied by a further change of state, and so on.

Thus, there exists many register-transfer level CHDLs that are nonprocedural in style, including DDL and CDL. Consider, for example, the CDL fragment shown in Figure 3.3. Here, the rule that governs the flow of control through the description is simply that whenever a condition denoted by

/ . . . . . /

is true the corresponding action is selected for execution.

Indeed, this example illustrates very clearly that the behavior of micro-architectures, especially the way in which micro-operations are selected for execution, are particularly well represented by nonprocedural descriptions.

Example 3.5

As a further instance, we may complete the specification of the ADD micro-operation shown in Figure 3.9 as follows: Suppose we have defined a single-

---

[8]The word "nonprocedural" is also used in the literature on CHDLs in other ways. For example, Dudani and Stabler (1983) use the word to mean what I call "structural" descriptions in Section 3.2.5.

phase clock C such that the ADD is executed under the control of this clock. Then the (nonprocedural) rule governing the selection and execution of this micro-operation is simply that C must be active and the precondition "mir.add = 1" is true. Whenever both these conditions are met, ADD will execute such that when it terminates the postcondition is satisfied. Note that the predicate "mir.add = 1" simply asserts that the "current" microinstruction (contained in the microinstruction register, mir) should encode in the appropriate bits (corresponding to "add") the fact that ADD is to be executed. ∎

Going further up the abstraction ladder, in the past decade or so, a class of computers called *dataflow* machines has become a focus of considerable interest (Dennis, 1980; Treleavan, Brownbridge, and Hopkins, 1982; Watson and Gurd, 1982). This is perhaps the most obvious class of machines that exhibits nonprocedural characteristics particularly at the exo-architectural level (see Chapter 9). Basically, and simplifying matters somewhat for the present, an instruction in a dataflow computer is selected for execution when all its operands are "available" to the instruction. That is, the availability of all operands to an instruction is the condition for the instruction to execute. Thus, an ADL intended for the description and simulation of dataflow architectures should obviously be nonprocedural in nature.

3.2.5 Structure and Behavior

Another aspect of the hardware description space has to do with the distinction between structure and behavior: A given CHDL may be characterized by whether it is capable of describing structure only, behavior only, or both.

In the context of CHDLs, *structure* refers to the nature of the communication paths within a system; the structure of the hardware system is described in terms of its "primitive" functional and storage components and the manner in which they are interconnected. Because of their static nature, structures have traditionally been described pictorially: At the logic level, structure is shown by *logic diagrams* in which gates and flip-flops are the primitive components; at the register-transfer, micro-architectural, and endo-architectural levels, structural descriptions traditionally take the form of *block diagrams* (see Figs. 1.4, 1.5, or 3.2) with the primitives that are interconnected becoming more powerful in their storage or functional capabilities with increasing levels of abstraction.

In contrast to the foregoing, *behavior* denotes the dynamic aspects of a system — what the system does. Our entire discussion of the hardware description space up to now was concerned with hardware system behavior.

It is important to note that even a "purely" behavioral description contains some amount of structural information, just as the purest of structural descriptions must include some behavioral component. For example, functional (i.e., behavioral) specifications must at least include the input and output ports (Fig. 3.6) — and these are structural components. What is ignored or only implied are the internal structural characteristics of the system and the precise nature of the communication paths between the system and its input/output ports.

Conversely, consider the simple structure shown in Figure 3.12, consisting of two primitive components C_1, C_2 communicating through a link L. A description of this structure, in order to be complete, must at least provide a specification of the behavior of the components C_1 and C_2. Indeed, strictly speaking, it should also incorporate a description of the link's behavior. If the link has a reasonably standard and very simple behavior—for example, it simply transmits a word of information from C_1 to C_2—then this may not be necessary. However, if the link is as complex as the PDP-11 Unibus (Digital, 1978), then its behavioral specification is obviously necessary.

It is because of this inevitable need to include some behavioral information in a structural description, and the fact that most forms of structural diagrams are rarely formal or unambiguous in their meaning, that block diagrams are so limited in their usefulness.

Clearly, there are certain contexts of hardware description in which structure is of enormous importance, whereas in other contexts it either is irrelevant or can safely be ignored. An ADL concerned with the specification of exo-architectures in which structure plays a relatively small role can be designed as a behavioral language. Even in the description of endo-architectures to be used for simulation or as front-ends to design automation systems (Fig. 3.1), structural characteristics—in particular, communication paths—can often be ignored. S*A and ISPS are instances of ADLs used for such purposes.

In contrast, when a dominant aspect of the architecture or the hardware system is the nature and topology of the communication paths, the CHDL must have the ability to describe structure, often in very great detail. A chip layout is dominated by the topology of the wires, and layout languages are about the purest of structural languages one can conceive. In general, languages used for logic level design and register-transfer level design (and not merely for their description) must necessarily have some structural capabilities. In essence, this would include a construct for describing the structure and behavior of the individual components and a construct for describing the connection between components. Several of the multilevel CHDLs listed in Table 3.1, intended as they are for spanning the logic, register-transfer, and micro-architectural levels and for use as design languages, include constructs for specifying structure. These include VHDL, CONLAN, SARA, and Ada.

Finally, moving up to the endo-architectural level, languages intended to describe multiprocessor and packet communication system architectures will also need to have powerful structural capabilities. The languages ADL, HISDL, and PADL developed at MIT for describing dataflow systems are all of this class.

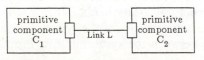

FIGURE 3.12 A simple structure.

3.3   THE USES OF ARCHITECTURE DESCRIPTION LANGUAGES

Within the framework of the foregoing discussion we can now discuss ADLs in more detail. One of the first issues that is important to understand is the nature and range of their applications.

Although Falkoff, Iverson, and Sussenguth (1964) were probably the first to develop the full description of an architecture in a formal language—the definition of the IBM System/360 in APL—it was only with the appearance of the ISP notation in Bell and Newell (1971) that the idea of an *architectural* description language (in contrast, that is, to register-transfer languages) took explicit shape. Thus, ISP may be legitimately regarded as the first notational system developed expressly for architectural description, specifically, the description of exo-architectural behavior.[9] This notation formed the basis for what eventually became ISPS, designed and implemented by Barbacci and colleagues in the late 1970s (Barbacci *et al.* 1978; Barbacci and Northcutt, 1980; Barbacci, 1981; Barbacci and Siewiorek, 1982). ISPS is undoubtedly the most important of the *first-generation* ADLs in that it was implemented as a machine-executable language, formed the basis for a wide variety of computer-aided design tools (see later, this section), and is one of the very few ADLs that developed a user base outside the immediate locus of its invention (e.g., Djordjevic, Ibbet, and Barbacci, 1980; Patterson, 1976; Crocker, Marcus, and van Mierop, 1980). It also served as the base for further language evolution, as exemplified by the I/O description language SLIDE (Parker and Wallace, 1981).

When Bell and Newell (1971) first presented ISP, their main objective was to provide an algorithmic notation that could be used to describe certain aspects of a computer's exo-architecture in a precise, clean fashion. However, the role of architecture description has itself undergone very significant changes since the early 1970s. Many designers and users of ADLs no longer see these languages as mere instruments of *recording* architectural attributes. Instead, ADLs are increasingly being regarded as vital, active components in the *design and implementation* of digital systems at several levels of abstraction. The most important of these applications of ADLs are identified and discussed in the following sections.

3.3.1   Modeling and Simulating Architectures

The ability to experiment with a *representation* of an artifact rather than the artifact itself, and to be able to predict and evaluate the performance and

---

[9]In the same publication, Bell and Newell (1971) also introduced the graphic notation PMS for describing structures in which the primitives are such components as "processors," "memories," "switches," "links," "controls," "transducers," and "data operations." In a sense, PMS may be viewed as a notation for specifying rather high-level endo-architectural structures. However, in the absence of (a) a rigorous definition of these primitives types, (b) the ability to specify the behavior of primitives, and (c) the lack of precise rules by which such primitives may be composed into legal PMS descriptions, one can hardly view PMS as a formal language. It is perhaps best regarded as a concise way of drawing block diagrams. For an updated discussion of PMS, see Siewiorek, Bell, and Newell (1982).

functioning of the artifact from such experiments, is often viewed as a mark of the maturity of a design discipline (Dasgupta, 1984, especially, Chapters 2 and 3). Such "experiments" may be of a highly formal nature, as when we represent the artifact by a set of parameterized mathematical equations and solve the equations for various values of the parameters.

In other situations, where mathematical modeling is difficult or impossible to apply, the designer may create *simulation models* of the artifact and conduct experiments with the simulated representation.

Computer architectures—at all levels—exhibit a kind of complexity that demands the use of *computer simulation* as a means of experimenting with the design.[10] In the different applications of architectural simulation that follow, the architecture to be simulated is described in an ADL. It is this latter description that is executed by the simulator.

Example 3.6

Figure 3.13 shows the general structure of a *simulation testbed* that may be used to evaluate the performance of an architecture. The architecture x (which may

---

[10]One is apt to forget in this age of computers that there are also *physical* modes of simulation—for example, the use of scale models, as has been done in the past in civil and structural engineering; wind tunnels in aeronautics; and pilot plants in chemical and metallurgical engineering. The equivalent of the pilot plant in computer design is the "prototype."

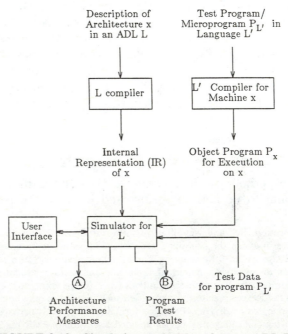

FIGURE 3.13 Simulation testbed based on an ADL L.

be at any level of abstraction) is rigorously specified in an ADL L and translated by a compiler into an internal representation (IR), which is then executed (interpreted) by a simulator—a real or virtual machine designed and implemented specifically to interpret this internal representation. The architect interacts with the simulator through a user interface, essentially a command language and its interpreter.

Using the simulator and the interface, the architect may conduct appropriate experiments on the architecture x under investigation. Such experiments will be particularly useful in evaluating design choices during the design of a new architecture or to assess the performance effects of modifying an existing architecture. This was done, for example, by Djordjevic and colleagues, who used the ISPS simulation facility at Carnegie-Mellon University to study the effects of modifying certain features of the MU5 architecture (Djordjevic, Ibbett, and Barbacci, 1980).

Another application of such a simulation testbed in architecture performance evaluation is illustrated by the Computer Family Architecture (CFA) project (Barbacci and Parker, 1980; Fuller *et al.*, 1977a) in which the ISPS facility was used to evaluate a set of candidate exo-architectures against a standard set of benchmark programs (see the right side of Fig. 3.13) in order to select the most appropriate exo-architecture as a military standard. ∎

Example 3.7

When a computer is in the process of being built, a simulated version of its exo-architecture can serve as a basis for testing and debugging the machine's system software so that the latter's development is not held up till the physical machine is available.

Similarly, a simulated version of a machine's micro-architecture can be used as a virtual micro-machine to test and debug the machine's microcode in the absence of the real machine. In fact, when the microcode is to be committed to read-only memory or PLA, it makes sense to use a simulator for its testing and debugging.

The testbed of Figure 3.13 can thus be used for such purposes also when the right side is integrated with the left side of the system. ∎

Several architectural simulation testbeds based on an ADL have been implemented. Perhaps the most mature of these are the ISPS and N.mPC facilities, both developed during the late 1970s.

The ISPS architecture research facility was developed at Carnegie-Mellon University by Barbacci and colleagues (Barbacci, 1981; Barbacci *et al.*, 1978) to serve as part of a multipurpose design automation system. At the heart of this system is the simulator, which runs on a PDP-10 and executes code generated from ISPS descriptions of architectures.

N.mPC was developed at Case Western Reserve University by Rose and colleagues (Parke, 1979; Rose, Ordy, and Drongowski, 1984) and uses ISP' as the source ADL. The simulator executes on a PDP-11 running under UNIX.[11]

---

[11]UNIX is a registered trademark of AT&T Bell Laboratories.

Examples of simulation testbeds intended primarily for the study of micro-architectures are the S*M and AADL/S* systems. Both are characterized by the fact that the ADLs involved are axiomatic description languages. The former system was recently designed and implemented by Dasgupta and colleagues at the University of Southwestern Louisiana (Dasgupta, Wilsey, and Heinanen, 1986; Wilsey, 1985) and is based on the nonprocedural, axiomatic ADL called S*M. The simulator runs on a VAX 11/780-based UNIX system. The AADL/S* system has been developed at the Technische Hochschule Aachen by Damm and colleagues (Damm, 1985, 1986) and uses a combination of a language called AADL and S* (Dasgupta, 1980, 1984) for the specification of micro-architectures.

Example 3.8

A third example of the use of ADL-based simulation is for the purpose of hardware *fault simulation and testing.*

As the term suggests, fault simulation involves the specification of the target system in an appropriate language, insertion of faults into the description, and the simulation of the system behavior under such faulted conditions. Fault simulation, which can be contrasted to *physical fault insertion*, provides all the advantages that experimenting with the representation of a physical system entails: One can study the fault tolerance and reliability properties of a hardware system even before the latter is built; furthermore — and this is probably even more important — modern scales of integration (see Volume 1, Chapter 2) make it increasingly more difficult to insert faults at points inside an integrated circuit.

The abstraction level at which the system is simulated and faults inserted is very important since it affects the cost of simulation: the higher the level, the less the system complexity and the lower the simulation cost. Furthermore, a fault inserted at a higher abstraction level itself serves as an abstraction for many lower-level factors that may have caused the fault. To cite an example given by Barbacci (1981), a fault such as "the sign bit of register 5 is always 0 (i.e., is a stuck-at-0 fault)" inserted in an ISPS description of the system may, when interpreted in terms of lower-level phenomena, involve several details such as pin positions, electrical properties, and gate delays that vary from one physical implementation to another. At the ISPS level, in contrast, the fault is precisely defined.

Thus, an ADL description, say at the micro-architectural level, the insertion of faults into such a description, and the simulation of the effects of such faults on system behavior is a most elegant method of conducting fault analysis and testing.

The ISPS fault simulation facility has been applied in several ways. For example, faults were inserted into an ISPS simulation of the PDP-11/70 to assess the correctness and effectiveness of its various built-in test modules. In another study, faults were inserted into an ISPS description of the Honeywell Modular Missile Borne Computer to determine how the system behaved in the presence of faults. ∎

3.3.2 Retargetable Code-Generation Systems

A machine's exo-architecture is, by definition, what the compiler needs to know about the machine to generate code for it to execute. A formal description of the exo-architecture in an appropriate ADL can thus provide the compiler writer with a rigorous specification of the target machine for which code is to be produced by the compiler (Fig. 1.8). Similarly, a formal definition of a computer's micro-architecture serves as a precise, unambiguous document that may be profitably used for the development of microcode compilers (Fig. 1.9).

The natural extension of this application is the use of formal machine descriptions in the development of retargetable code or microcode generators (Fig. 3.8). The global objective is to minimize, for a given programming language, the cost of producing a compiler—specifically, its code generation part—for each distinct target architecture.

Although there has been substantial work done on retargetable code generation in the past decade or so—see the survey by Ganapathi, Fischer, and Hennessy (1982)—the pioneering effort in applying a general purpose ADL to this problem was the work done by Cattell (1980) using ISPS.

Similarly, there has been vigorous progress in the development of retargetable microcode-generation systems. The reasons for this more specialized activity will be explained in detail in Chapter 5, it being sufficient to note for the present that this interest was motivated by the general realization on the part of many that if microcode production is to be routinely mechanized, the tools and systems for this purpose must be retargetable. As a result, many theoretical, practical, and implementation aspects of microcode retargetability have been investigated and several systems have been implemented (Ma and Lewis, 1980; Baba and Hagiwara, 1981; Sheraga and Gieser, 1983; Marwedel, 1984; Damm, *et al.*, 1986; Dasgupta, 1985). Again, it is only very recently—in the 1980s—that the application of general purpose ADLs to this problem is being investigated (Dasgupta, Wilsey, and Heinanen, 1986; Marwedel, 1984).

Example 3.9

In Cattell's (1980) system, the generation of object code for a given target architecture involves two phases.

In the "compiler-compile-time" phase, executed once for each target architecture, a functional representation of the target machine, termed MD, is extracted from an ISPS description. In this representation, instructions are specified in the form of a set of *input/output assertions* (similar to the precondition/postcondition pairs discussed in Section 3.2.3) along with specifications of other relevant architectural features. The extraction of assertions from the ISPS description can be performed automatically, using a symbolic execution method developed specifically for ISPS by Oakley (1979).

The MD representation then becomes the source for the derivation of *production rules* (or templates) that collectively form a set of machine-description tables, MT, and the code generator is driven by these tables.[12] The production rules are of the form

pattern ⇒ action to be performed

and is used in the manner described below.

The "compile-time" phase is executed once for each program to run on the target machine. The source program is translated into an intermediate parse-tree type of representation called TCOL by a machine-independent compiler front end. The code generator "walks" the TCOL tree and matches each node in the tree against the pattern on the left side of the production rules in MT. When a match takes place, the right side of the production specifies what action is to be taken: whether to generate code or to perform further matches recursively or to perform other compiler actions such as register allocation.

As a simple example, a production such as

R ⟵ R + E ⇒ ADD R, E

might be used by the code generator to emit code for the TCOL representation

X ⟵ X + L

where the pair X, R, and the pair L, E, respectively, are recognized by the code generator to belong to the same operand classes. ∎

Example 3.10

As already noted, several retargetable microcode generation systems have been developed (Ma & Lewis, 1980; Baba & Hagiwara, 1981; Sheraga and Gieser, 1983; Marwedel, 1984). Among these, however, only Marwedel's system uses a general purpose ADL (or in this case a multilevel CHDL) — the MIMOLA language — to specify the host micro-architecture (see footnote 5, Chapter 1, regarding the terminological convention regarding "hosts" and "targets)." It is only very recently, in fact, that a systematic connection has been established between the design and implementation of ADLs and the development of microprogramming systems (Dasgupta, 1985).[13]

Figure 3.14 shows the general structure of a retargetable microcode-generation system. This is representative of several systems both built (Marwedel, 1984) and, at the time of this writing, under development (Dasgupta, 1985; Dasgupta, Wilsey, and Heinanen, 1986; Damm et al., 1986; Mueller and Varghese, 1985). ∎

---

[12]Thus, Cattell's scheme is an example of *table-driven code generation*. For more on this, see Ganapathi, Fischer, and Hennessy (1982).

[13]By *microprogramming system* I mean any integrated set of software tools and techniques that can be used in the firmware design and implementation process.

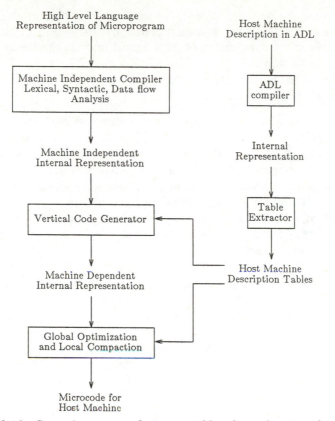

FIGURE 3.14   General structure of a retargetable microcode generation system.

3.3.3 Formal Design of Architectures

Perhaps the strongest similarity in the uses of ADLs and programming languages is when an ADL supports the formal, systematic design and implementation of machine architectures. Yet this has been, till very recently, the most neglected application area of ADLs—paradoxical though this may seem—and certainly the most neglected aspect of the discipline of computer architecture.

The first systematic and extensive treatment of the formal design of computer architectures is Dasgupta (1984). Here, an architectural design process is "defined" to be *formal* if it satisfies all the following characteristics:

1.   There exists a formal method of describing the design.
2.   There exists formal principles for validating the design for correctness against well-defined correctness criteria without the need to implement the physical system.

3. The design can be manipulated and evaluated for its performance characteristics without the need to construct the physical system. (This characteristic clearly falls in the realm of experiment and simulation discussed previously in Section 3.3.1).
4. There exists a communicable (and therefore teachable) set of methods and models of the design process.

At the heart of formal design, then, is the ability to *describe* the design in a precise, formal fashion. Depending on the complexity of the design problem, it may, in fact, be necessary to summon into use *several* modes of description — the specification of structure or of behavior, functional description at one level of abstraction, operational description at another, and so on. The use of ADLs and the pursuit of formal design, then, go hand in hand.

A second important characteristic of formal design is that it must include the capability of demonstrating or deducing that the design is *correct* with respect to a given set of functional requirements.

More specifically, the task of formal verification (or synonymously, proof of correctness) of a system (be it an architecture, a logic circuit, a program, or a microprogram) rests on the availability of an independent *specification*, Spec, of the desired behavior of the system, and a *formal description*, Desc, of the system itself. Verification then involves a demonstration that the system as described by Desc does indeed behave in the manner prescribed by Spec. This requires, in turn, the availability of a precisely defined *semantics* Sem(Lang) for the description language Lang. Thus, formal verification involves the 3-tuple

< Spec, Desc, Sem(Lang) >

in the sense that Sem(Lang) is used to infer (i.e., logically deduce) the correctness of Desc (expressed in language Lang) with respect to Spec.

In the present context, Desc would be the formal description of the architecture design in an ADL, Spec a specification of the functional behavior the architecture is intended to meet, and Sem(Lang) the semantics of the ADL used to demonstrate that the design is correct.

In a very real sense, the whole idea of formal design is to *objectify* the design process, that is, to remove it from the realm of private or personal knowledge and place it in the public domain. The use of formal language to describe the design at its successive stages of development, the use of objective procedures to prove its correctness, and the application of the experimental method (such as simulation) to critically test the performance of the design are all aspects of this desire to make design an objective, public process — in other words, to make design *scientific*.[14]

---

[14]The relationships between objective or public knowledge, criticism, and the scientific method have been explored for the past 60 years or so by many philosophers of science, the most notable of whom are Karl Popper (1965, 1968, 1972) and Thomas Kuhn (1970). Some aspects of these relationships, as they touch on the topic of design, are discussed in Volume 1, Chapter 3.

The last of the characteristics just listed — that there is associated with formal design a set of methods and models that may be communicated between designers — is yet one further (and certainly the most difficult) step toward the goal of objectifying the design process.

This characteristic states that in going about the design of a system, despite all the highly personal, idiosyncratic, and creative thinking that goes on in each individual designer's mind, it is possible to identify and abstract out a set of invariant, objective principles of design; and that these principles can be couched in sufficiently precise terms so as to be transmitted from one person to another and be documented; and that, finally, these principles once crystalized and constituted into a set of design methods can be used explicitly as tools to guide the thinking process.

Example 3.11

Stepwise refinement is an example of such a design method; it emerged essentially from introspective analysis by some designers, was formulated in fairly precise language, thus became a design principle or method, and is now taught to neophyte designers who then use it as an explicit and objective tool.[15] ∎

The concept of a design method — that is, an objective intellectual tool that may be used to guide the designer's thought processes — poses many problems. For example, although formal design is an obviously laudable goal, we know from experience that even with an entire armory of descriptive and other tools one does not rush into the use of formalisms in the initial stages of design. Rather, there is an initial phase during which the designer, faced with a problem, draws on past familiarity with similar problems and his or her knowledge of the problem domain to make a few key decisions and formulate a "sketch" or initial "shape" of the overall form. This process was termed *informal design* by Dasgupta (1984, see especially Chapter 2, Section 3.3, and Chapter 12). The presence of this kind of mental activity gives rise to questions of the following kind: What is the relationship between informal and formal design? What are the limits to formal design?

In addition, there are some very thorny problems even within the restricted domain of formal design: How should proofs of correctness be integrated with a design method? How do we combine the complimentary activities of (experimental) simulation and mathematical (theoretical) verification in a design procedure?

Chapter 3 of Volume 1 discusses these and other issues to do with the design process, particularly as they relate to architecture. I conclude the present section with a few examples of how ADLs can be used in formal (or semiformal) design.

---

[15]Although countless designers and programmers must have realized through their own experiences the heuristic value of stepwise refinement, the scientists whose names are most closely connected with this idea are Dijkstra (1972); Mills (1972); and Wirth (1971), since they appear to have been the first to have crystallized stepwise refinement into a communicable design method.

Example 3.12

The use of the ADL S*A in the formal verification of architectures has been described by Dasgupta (1983, 1984). In one example, (see Dasgupta, 1984, Chapters 4 and 5) part of an asynchronous instruction pipeline is considered (Fig. 3.15).

Instruction packets of 8 16-bit instructions each are received from an external process (SAC) by an INPUT process (or "mechanism," in S*A terminology) and placed in an INPUT-BUFFER; an UNPACK mechanism unpacks the instructions one by one and queues them in an OUTPUT-BUFFER. In the process of unpacking, it also determines, by sending an appropriate request signal to another external mechanism, STORE-REQ, and receiving the appropriate response signal, whether the instruction most recently transferred to OUTPUT-BUFFER is a branch or not. If so, then the remaining instructions in the packet (still in INPUT-BUFFER) are locked out from the pipeline and are prevented from being transferred to OUTPUT-BUFFER. Finally, an OUTPUT mechanism transmits the instruction at the head of the OUTPUT-BUFFER queue to an external mechanism called PROP.

The three mechanisms, INPUT, UNPACK, and OUTPUT are conceived as concurrently executing, asynchronous entities that communicate with one another through shared variables and semaphore-like synchronization primitives.

For this particular problem, a formal S*A description of the mechanisms and their interactions was first developed. Verification was then performed on the resulting S*A description. This procedure first proved that each of the individual mechanisms, INPUT, UNPACK, and BUFFER was correct, independent of its interactions with other mechanisms; it then showed that the interaction of the mechanisms did not in any way interfere with the proof of correctness of the individual mechanisms. The formal basis for the verification procedure was the Floyd-Hoare axiomatic technique for sequential processes (Floyd, 1967; Hoare, 1969; de Bakker, 1980; Gries, 1981) extended by Owicki and Gries (1976) to proofs of parallel processes. An overview of these techniques is given in the Appendix. ■

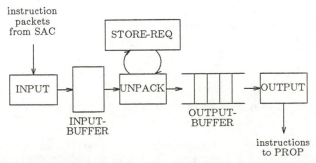

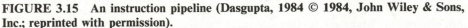

FIGURE 3.15 An instruction pipeline (Dasgupta, 1984 © 1984, John Wiley & Sons, Inc.; reprinted with permission).

In the foregoing discussion the description of an architecture and its verification was taken to be the formal design task. However, just as architectural descriptions serve as a basis for retargetable microcode generation (Section 3.3.2), it can also be used in the formal development, synthesis, and verification of microprograms intended for execution on a given host machine.

Example 3.13

Figure 3.16 depicts in simplified form, an automated host machine-independent microprogram verification system being developed by Damm and colleagues at the Technische Hochschule Aachen (Damm 1984, 1985; Damm *et al.*, 1986). The source program is written in a high-level microprogramming language (HLML) consisting of high-level machine-independent and low-level machine-specific statements. The semantics of the former is provided as a set of machine-independent axioms and proof rules. The machine-specific constructs and their semantics are supplied separately through a description of the host machine in an ADL.[16] ∎

Example 3.14

The Aachen S*-system is also being used for the rigorous stepwise *design* of microprograms (Damm, 1985; Damm and Doehmen, 1985). Figure 3.17 schematizes the overall approach.

The design method begins with a specification of both the target exo-architecture T and the host micro-architecture H in the same ADL. The designer's task is to develop a microprogram M that will realize T on H. This objective is carried out in a rigorous top-down fashion by constructing one or more *intermediate* architectures $I_n, I_{n-1}, \ldots, I_1$ $(n \geq 1)$ such that

$$T = I_{n+1} > I_n > I_{n-1} > \ldots > I_1 > I_0 = H$$

where ">" stands for the relation "more abstract than" and the I_j's are all specified in the same ADL.

[16]The system briefly introduced here is based on the high-level microprogramming language schema S* (Dasgupta, 1980, 1984; see also Example 3.3). Both S* and the Aachen S*-system are discussed in further detail in Chapter 5.

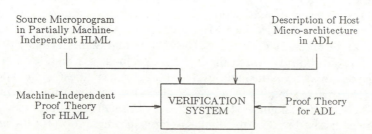

Source Microprogram
in Partially Machine-
Independent HLML

Description of Host
Micro-architecture
in ADL

Machine-Independent
Proof Theory
for HLML

VERIFICATION
SYSTEM

Proof Theory
for ADL

FIGURE 3.16   Host machine — independent microprogram verification system.

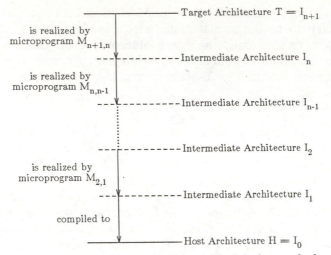

FIGURE 3.17   The Aachen hierarchical design method.

Each successive design step, then, creates a microprogram in a partially machine-independent HLML (see Example 3.13) that implements I_{j+1} on I_j ($n \geq j \geq 1$). The final version of the microprogram, executable on the virtual host I_1, is then compiled, optimized, and compacted onto the real host I_0. This design method is, thus, an adaptation to the architectural and firmware domain of the hierarchical design method (HDM) developed at SRI International for software design (Levitt, Robinson, and Silverberg, 1979).

The microprogram $M_{j+1,j}$ refines the data structures and operations of the higher-level architecture I_{j+1} using the data structures and operations of I_j. At the same time, the verification system described in Example 3.13 is used to prove that the microprogram is correct. Thus, the entire Aachen S*-system revolves around the use of the ADL for architecture specification, microprogramming, and design verification.   ■

3.3.4   Design Automation

In recent years, some experimental systems have emerged in which formal machine descriptions serve as the starting point for the automatic synthesis of designs at low levels of abstraction. The output representation may be at the register-transfer level as in the CMU-DA system (Director *et al.*, 1981; Nagle, Cloutier, and Parker, 1982) or the MIMOLA system (Zimmerman, 1980; Marwedel, 1985), in both of which the input is specified in a high-level behavioral language; or it may be at the logic level as in the logic synthesis system developed at IBM (Darringer, 1985; Darringer *et al.*, 1984) where the input specification is in a register-transfer language. Thus, in such systems the ADL or the RTL (as the case may be) is used to describe digital systems in preparation for the automatic production of a lower level, functionally equivalent specification. The parallel with programming languages and their compilers is obvious.   ■

Example 3.15

The synthesis steps undertaken by the CMU-DA system (Director *et al.*, 1981) are shown in broad outline in Figure 3.18. The input to the synthesis process is an ISPS description of the target system. This is then compiled into an intermediate flowgraph representation called the *value trace* (VT) somewhat similar to the directed acyclic graph representations generated by programming language compilers; the VT is then subject to various optimizing transformations similar to those performed by optimizing compilers.

The optimized VT becomes the actual input to the synthesis subsystem, which consists of two sequential phases that produce, respectively, the data path part and the control unit part of the target machine. Each of these phases involves, in turn, two steps: In the *allocation* step, an unbound register-transfer level structure of the data path (or control unit) is synthesized; in the *module binding* step, the components of the unbound structure are bound to physical technology-specific modules. Thus, the allocation and binding steps are analogous to those for

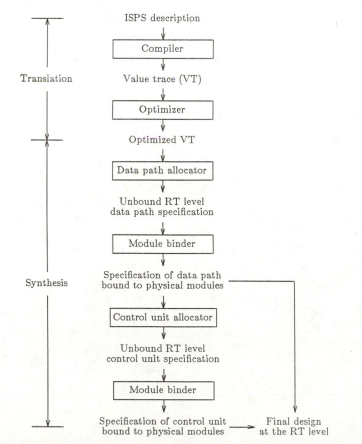

FIGURE 3.18 Design synthesis using the CMU-DA system (Based on Director *et al,* 1981. © 1981, IEEE).

generating machine-independent and machine-specific code, respectively, in programming or microprogramming language compilers. ∎

Example 3.16

In the MIMOLA system (Marwedel, 1985), synthesis begins with a set of *application programs* expressed in a "high-level version" of the MIMOLA language (Fig. 3.19). The semantics of this language is only defined at the register-transfer level ("RT-level MIMOLA"), hence the semantics of high-level MIMOLA is specified by a set of macros or *substitution rules* that define mappings from the high-level version to RT-level MIMOLA.

To provide the synthesis system with additional information as to which programs are worth optimizing during synthesis, *estimated usage frequencies* of the programs may be optionally provided. The input specification is completed by supplying a set of *boundary conditions* that place constraints on the synthesis procedure. These may state, for example, the number and types of different resources to be used, cost constraints, or bounds on chip area, and so forth.

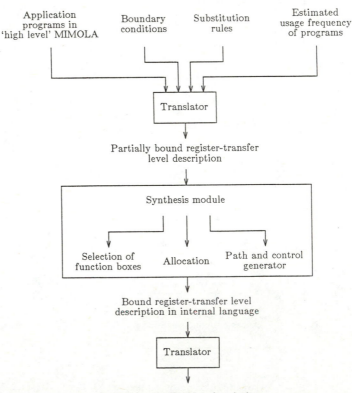

FIGURE 3.19   Synthesis using MIMOLA (Based on Marwedel, 1985).

The *translator* accepts these inputs and produces a partially bound register-transfer level description. The *synthesis* module then takes this description and generates a complete, bound specification of the target machine at the register-transfer level. The actual synthesis phase consists of a number of key components, including the selection of the number and types of functional units, the allocation of hardware resources to operations and variables (in the original programs), and the generation of data and control paths. The output of synthesis, expressed in an internal representation language, may then be translated for documentation purposes into RT-level MIMOLA. ∎

3.3.5 Application Classes and the Operational/Functional Issue

In summary, then, there are four broad classes of applications for ADLs: as a means for simulating the behavior of an architecture; to provide a basis for generating code or microcode; as a descriptive tool in the formal design and verification of architectures; and as a component for the automated synthesis of hardware and firmware systems. We thus see that, in addition to its location in the hardware description space, a given ADL may well be characterized by the application classes for which it is intended.

An additional point of some importance is that the intended application classes for a given ADL may well dictate some of the dimensional characteristics of the language—in particular, whether the ADL should be functional, operational, or both.

Thus, for example, if an ADL is intended for simulation purposes, it is sufficient (though not necessary) for it to be operational. In contrast, when an architecture is being formally described to provide information for code or microcode generators, a functional form of description is the most appropriate choice; indeed, as noted in Section 3.2.3 in attempting to describe architectures for such purposes in an operational form, we may be either guilty of distorting the real state of affairs or of providing more information than is necessary.

For the purpose of formal design, both functional and operational languages may be necessary: The initial specification of the architecture-to-be, by its very nature, should be expressed in functional form, whereas the realization of this functional specification will, in general, necessitate an operational mode of description. Furthermore, as pointed out in Section 3.3.3, the objective of formal verification is to demonstrate that the operational description is correct with respect to the functional specification.

Finally, when we consider using an ADL in design automation, it would seem that both operational and functional descriptions may be used. In both examples cited in Section 3.3.4 the input descriptions are operational. However, as Director and colleagues (1981) have pointed out in their discussion of the CMU-DA system, the operational aspects of an input ISPS description—in particular, the specification of control flow—if adhered to during subsequent synthesis may have adverse consequences on performance and cost, since it constitutes a form of "early binding" of the intended design to physical resources. The VT representation, thus, must undo the effects of the original ISPS operational descriptions.

Thus, it would seem that a DA system is better served by functional modes of descriptions. Similarly, as we will see in Chapter 5, automatic *microcode synthesis* systems are being built that require as little commitment to a priori operational biases as possible in order to maximize the efficacy of the synthesis procedure. Again, functional modes of description are strongly suggested.

PROBLEMS

3.1 Every computer language (whether for programming, microprogramming, or hardware description) contains a set of *primitive* and a set of *structured data types*. Define precisely, and give arguments for, an appropriate set of such data types for the definition of hardware "data" at each of the following abstraction levels.

    (a) Logic design
    (b) Register transfer
    (c) Micro-architecture
    (d) Exo-architecture

3.2 Consider the use of your favorite programming language ("FPL") as a hardware description language, in particular, as an ADL for describing *micro-architectures*. Some of the more important components of a micro-architecture are

    (i) The storage organization (i.e., the main memory, local store, and other registers visible at this level).
    (ii) The syntax and semantics of the micro-operations.
    (iii) The microinstruction formats.
    (iv) The timing characteristics of the micromachine.

    (a) Analyze and discuss the ease or difficulty of using FPL to describe each of these types of components. Use examples of descriptions to support your arguments.
    (b) Based on this experience, what are your overall conclusions concerning the suitability of FPL as a micro-architecture description language?

    [*Note*: Any meaningful response to this question must take into account the uses to which the micro-architecture description are to be put.]

3.3 Consider, this time, your favorite programming language ("FPL") as an *exo-architecture* description language. Recall that some of the main components of an exo-architecture are

    (i) Storage organization
    (ii) Data types
    (iii) Addressing modes
    (iv) The instruction set

(v)   Instruction formats

(a)   Analyze and discuss the ease or difficulty of using FPL to describe each of these components. Use example descriptions to illustrate your analysis.

(b)   Based on this exercise, what are your overall conclusions concerning the appropriateness of FPL as an exo-architecture description language?

[*Note*: In answering this question, you should take into account the uses to which an exo-architectural description will be put.]

3.4   In section 3.2.3, the characteristics and uses of *functional* modes of description were discussed. It was also pointed out that a functional description serves as an interface between the user and the implementer (Fig. 3.7).

The programming language Ada contains as one of its most important constructs, the *package specification*. To what extent can this construct be used or adopted for the purpose of functional descriptions (of architecture or firmware)? Justify your answer and use examples to support your argument.

3.5   Show with examples how any procedural mode of description can always be converted into (or simulated by) a nonprocedural mode of description.

3.6   Is the converse true? That is, can a nonprocedural mode of description be simulated by (or converted into) a procedural mode of description? Justify your answer.

3.7   Consider the simple system shown in Figure 3.12. Invent a mini-language and show how you can use this language to describe the system:
(a)   In purely behavioral terms.
(b)   In such a way that the structure of the system is revealed explicitly by the description.

[*Note*: To answer this question you may have to make some "reasonable" assumptions concerning this system. Keep your assumptions to a minimum, and state them explicitly.]

3.8   Consider the register-transfer-level block diagram shown in Figure 3.2. The partial description (in CDL) given in Figure 3.3 is almost a "pure" behavioral description in the sense that the data paths between the various functional and storage components are only *implied* by the behavioral specification in the lower half of Figure 3.3.

If we wanted to *simulate the overall behavior* of this particular system, then such a description is adequate. However, suppose we want to refine this down to a *structural description* in which the data paths are shown explicitly as in Figure 3.2. Furthermore, we wish to simulate the operation or behavior of this structural description.

Invent a mini-language (or augment the CDL notation shown in Fig. 3.3) so that (a) the structure shown pictorially in Figure 3.2 can be textually described; and (b) this description will allow us to understand the operation and behavior of the system.

3.9 A major government agency has decided to establish a particular exo-architecture (call it X) as its *standard*. That is, every computer that the agency buys in the future must support and implement X. By standardizing its exo-architecture the agency hopes to establish a single agency-wide interface for its software: Programs developed for execution on one of its computer installations can be transported and executed on *any* of its other installations.

X can, of course, be implemented in many different ways with different cost/performance characteristics. This allows different computer manufacturers to compete for the agency's numerous contracts.

However, one of the preconditions for the agency's award of a contract to a potential vendor is a certification that the contractor's system defines the exo-architecture X *exactly*. This certification can be done by a special unit of the agency.

Assuming that you have been appointed a consultant to the agency on this matter, suggest a standard procedure (based on the use of ADLs) that could be followed by the agency's certification unit and its potential contractors to meet this precondition.

3.10 Undoubtedly, one of the most problematic aspects of describing computer hardware and architecture is the handling of *time*. The issue, here, is that any CHDL designed to specify the structure and/or functional behavior of systems at a particular abstraction level must be capable of capturing the *temporal* behavior of the system at that level. Furthermore, what counts as significant temporal behavior may differ from one abstraction level to another.

Consider, in particular, the following levels:

(i) Exo-architecture

(ii) Micro-architecture

(iii) Logic design

(a) Analyze and describe the temporal characteristics of each of these abstraction levels from the perspective of designing a CHDL (or a set of CHDLs) for the specification or description of these levels.

(b) Based on your analysis, what are your opinions about the feasibility of capturing the temporal behavior of all three abstraction levels in a *single* CHDL?

3.11 [A term project.] In this chapter, CHDLs have been discussed within the framework of a set of "dimensions" that collectively constituted a "hardware description space" (see Section 3.2). Useful though this framework is, it is not really a comprehensive *taxonomic system* for CHDLs (in the sense in which this term is used in Chapter 2).

Develop a formal, comprehensive taxonomic system for CHDLs along the following lines:

(a) Identify the principal *taxonomic characteristics* (TCs) that should be used for this purpose.
(b) Establish the *categories* (there may be more than one) of your system and the relationship (hierarchical or otherwise) between the categories.
(c) For each category, define its consistuent *taxa*.
(d) Discuss the descriptive/predictive/explanatory power of your scheme.

CHAPTER 4

ARCHITECTURE DESCRIPTION LANGUAGES: CASE STUDIES

4.1 SELECTION OF LANGUAGES

In this chapter, I will give detailed examples of two selected ADLs. My objective here is to illustrate how the issues discussed in Chapter 3 are encountered in some representative languages; at the same time, I will present two languages in sufficient detail so that the specific nature of such ADLs will become reasonably clear to you.

The selection of ADLs as case studies poses some problems because, as Table 3.1 suggests, we are faced with an embarrassment of riches. Many of these ADLs exhibit features that are interesting in one or another respect and are, therefore, worthy of discussion. Yet limitations of space restrict the extent to which the variety of languages may be included.

Accordingly, the choice of ADLs for the present discussion has been restricted to two: VHDL and S*M. The reasons for this selection are

1. Partly in reaction to the proliferation of CHDLs and partly because of its own needs, the U.S. Department of Defense (DoD) initiated as part of its Very High Speed Integrated Circuits (VHSIC) program the development of a DoD-wide standard CHDL, much as Ada was developed as a standard programming language. The language called VHDL (i.e., VHSIC hardware description language) is the result of this program (Shahdad *et al.*, 1985). Although VHDL is still under development, it is sufficiently mature in its structure to merit discussion here. The choice of VHDL as one of the case studies stems at least in part from its obvious significance as a potential CHDL standard. But there is more to it than that: VHDL is designed for the specification of hardware across the entire range of hardware abstraction levels and is intended for interfacing with a variety of design automation tools. It is, thus, an excellent example of a *multilevel, multipurpose* CHDL.

2. In Chapter 3, Section 3.3, we saw that functional descriptions are appropriate in a surprisingly large range of applications; yet very few ADLs possess such descriptive capabilities. ISPS and Ada, for instance are both wholly operational languages whereas VHDL has very limited capabilities for functional specifications. To illustrate the nature and style of functional specifi-

cations, the axiomatic ADL S*M (Dasgupta, Wilsey, and Heinanen, 1986) has been selected as the second language example. S*M is, in fact, a *nonprocedural* axiomatic language that, along with AADL (Damm, 1985; Damm *et al.*, 1986), addresses a part of the hardware description space and application classes not readily covered by such languages as ISPS or VHDL. S*M is a more specialized HDL than, say, VHDL.

Before starting our discussion of these two languages, however, I offer the following remarks about ISPS. Although ISPS does not embody many of what are now thought to be the most desirable principles of language design (see Chapter 3, Section 3.2), its pioneering role in the development of ADLs and their applications is beyond question. ISPS occupies a special place in the history of ADLs: It provides an exemplar of "first generation" ADLs. However, the details of this language have been very well documented not only in the research literature (Barbacci *et al.*, 1978; Directer *et al.*, 1981; Barbacci and Parker, 1980; Dasgupta, 1982) but also in several textbooks (Baer, 1980; Siewiorek, Bell, and Newell, 1982; Barbacci and Siewiorek, 1982). Thus, the interested reader is referred to these sources for details of ISPS. I will not discuss this language any further here.

4.2 VHDL

As I have noted previously, the overall objective of the VHDL effort was to construct a single language that will support the design, description, and simulation of hardware structures at abstraction levels ranging from the architectural to logic. The language was designed to be independent of any specific technology, design environment, or design methods, and, consequently, it should be possible to integrate it into any combination of environment, technology, and methodology. VHDL is intended to become the standard CHDL in all DoD hardware design projects.[1]

In the context of the hardware description space discussed in Chapter 3 (Section 3.2), VHDL is a *multilevel* language, capable of both *structural* and *behavioral* descriptions. Behavior is specified *operationally*, and the flow of control through such descriptions may be both *procedural* and *nonprocedural*. Finally, note that many of the concepts present in the programming language Ada (U.S. Department of Defense, 1981) have been adopted in the design of VHDL.

In illustrating the important features of VHDL, I will use as a running example, the description of a four bit adder. A diagram of this is shown in Figure 4.1. The inputs to this device are two 4-bit quantities A and B, and the 1-bit carry in while its outputs are the 4-bit sum and the 1-bit carry out. The four bit

[1]This discussion of VHDL is based on Shahdad and colleagues (1985) and Intermetrics (1984b).

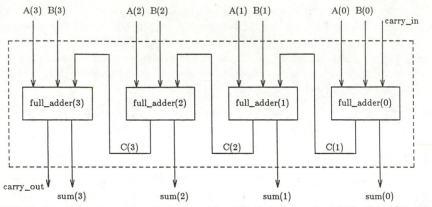

FIGURE 4.1 Structure of a four-bit adder (Shahdad *et al.*, 1985. © 1985 IEEE; reprinted with permission).

adder consists of four instances of a full adder, which is shown in "black-box" form in Figure 4.2.

4.2.1 Entities

The smallest complete executable hardware description in VHDL is called an *entity*, which is composed of two segments, an *interface* and a collection of one or more *bodies*. The interface defines the entity's externally observable features whereas the body defines an implementation of the entity that is not visible to the entity's environment. When several bodies are associated with a single interface, each body describes an alternative implementation of the entity characterized by the common interface.

4.2.2 Interfaces

Figure 4.3 is a partial definition of the interface for the entity called four_bit adder. It begins with a *context clause*

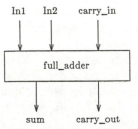

FIGURE 4.2 Input-output Ports for a full adder (Shahdad *et al.*, 1985. © 1985 IEEE; adapted with permission).

```
with adder_resources: use adder_resources;
entity four_bit_adder
    -- ports
    (A, B : in bit_vector (3..0); -- input operands
     carry_in : in_bit;
     carry_out: out_bit;
     sum : out bit_vector (3..0)) is -- output
    -- other declarations
        . . . . . .
end four_bit_adder;
```

FIGURE 4.3   Skeleton of the interface definition (Shahdad *et al.*, 1985. © 1985 IEEE; reprinted with permission).

with adder_resources; **use** adder_resources;

which names a VHDL *package* called adder_resources in the context of which the entity is to be compiled. Packages are described later; for the present, it is sufficient to note that a package is a means of encapsulating a collection of declarations into a single module. Thus, the context clause states that the declarations in adder_resources are visible within, and needed by, the entity four_bit_adder. The **with** and **use** clauses will shortly be explained.

Data Types

The *ports* of an interface are the only means by which an entity can exchange data with other entities. As Figure 4.3 shows, port declarations include a *mode* (such as **in**, **out**, or **inout**) and the *data type*. Both *bit* and *bit vector* are predefined types, the former being a primitive (or "scalar" in VHDL terminology) and the latter a composite type. Other predefined scalars available in VHDL include *integer, real, Boolean,* and *character*. The user may also define an *enumeration* type, so called because they are defined by enumerating the values of the type, or a *physical type* whereby quantities associated with physical units of measurement may be specified. Examples of these will be given later.

Composite data types are, in the usual fashion, constructed out of elements that are either scalars or other composites. The two principal classes of composites are *arrays* and *records*. VHDL includes, as predefined array types, *bit vector*, the elements of which are of type *bit*, and *string*, which consists of elements of type *character*.

Variables, Constants, and Signals

The ports declared in a design entity are always *signals*, which constitute one of three kinds of data objects in VHDL. The others are *constants* and *variables*. A constant, of course, carries its usual meaning in that it is assigned a value when created and retains this value thereafter. Variables and signals share the common property that their values may change over time; however, they differ in a rather fundamental way as follows. Values assigned to variables (by means of *variable assignment statements*) result in an "immediate" change of value as, for example, in the statement

sum := In1 **xor** In2 **xor** carry_in

Thus, the only concept of time associated with a variable is that of "now," which is when a value is assigned to it. Another characteristic of variables is that they are used to represent data objects in relatively abstract descriptions of entities called *behavioral bodies* (see Section 4.2.3).

A signal, on the other hand, is viewed as holding a *sequence of values* over time. At any particular time, this sequence consists of two parts: the "past and present" part and the "future." The former represents, so to speak, the history of the signal — that is, values that are visible but cannot be changed — whereas the latter denotes values that can be altered but are not visible. Values are assigned to a signal through the *signal assignment statement*, and this assignment may be delayed in time. Thus, for example, the signal assignment

S ⇐ sum **after** 5ns

causes the "present" (or "now") value of sum to be assigned to S at time "now" + 5 nsec.

A signal may also be assigned a sequence of values with associated times. Such an assignment could represent a wave form. For example, given a declaration (with an initialization value of 0):

signal x : **bit** := 0

the assignment

x ⇐ '1' **after** 2ns, '0' **after** 4ns, '1' **after** 6ns

causes the value of x to change according to the timing diagram of Figure 4.4.

Signals, in general, are intended to be used to denote wires, buses or storage elements of a digital system.

In addition to ports, the interface of a design entity may (optionally) contain other declarations and assertions that are common to all bodies of the design entity. We illustrate these features by completing the description of the four_bit_adder interface as shown in Figure 4.5.

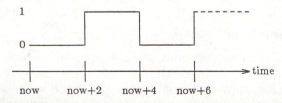

FIGURE 4.4   Timing diagram for the signal x (based on Intermetrics, 1984b. Copyright © Intermetrics, Inc. 1987).

```
with adder_resources; use adder_resources;
entity four_bit_adder
    -- ports
    (A, B : in bit_vector (3..0);   -- input operand
     carry_in : in bit;
     carry_out: out bit;
     sum : out bit_vector (3..0)) is   -- output
    -- parameter
    generic
        (delay : time := 36ns);
    attribute
        four_bit_adder' entity_level is logic_group
    -- assertions to be satisfied by all alternative bodies
    assertion
        delay > 36ns;
        sum' fanout ⇐ max_fanout
end four_bit_adder
```

FIGURE 4.5 Complete specification of the four-bit adder interface (Shahdad *et al.*, 1985. © 1985 IEEE; reprinted with permission).

Generic Parameters

Declarations may include *generic parameters*, which allow other referencing design entities to specify values to be used as constants within the entity. For instance, such parameters may be used to describe delay or power characteristics of the design entity. In Figure 4.5, the generic declaration defines a parameter delay of type time. The latter is a predefined (i.e., part of the predefined VHDL environment) physical type as defined in Figure 4.6, which first states that the basic unit of time is femtosecond with the specified range and then defines other units of time.

Each time the design entity four_bit_adder is instantiated (see section 4.2.4), a value will be assigned to delay. In the absence of a value, a default value of 36 nsec as shown in the generic declaration will be assigned.

```
type time is range 0..1E18
    units
        fs;                              --femtosecond
        ps    =    1000 fs;              --picosecond
        ns    =    1000 ps;              --nanosecond
        ms    =    1000 ns;              --millisecond
        s     =    1000 ms;             --second
        min   =    60 s;                --minute
        hr    =    60 min;              --hour
    end units
```

FIGURE 4.6 Definition of the physical type time (Shahdad *et al.*, 1985. © 1985 IEEE; adapted with permission).

Attributes

Other declarations that may appear inside an interface include definitions of data types, constants, and attributes. An *attribute* is a value associated with an item (such as a signal, a variable, a port, or a design entity) the purpose of which is to provide some additional information about the item. This information may be referenced within the VHDL description or it may be used by one of the design tools that process the description. In Figure 4.5, the attribute section states that the value of an attribute called entity_level is logic_group. The definition of entity_level is actually given in the package called adder_resources (to be defined in section 4.2.3). Intuitively, this attribute declaration establishes the abstraction level at which the design entity four_bit_adder is being described.

Assertions

Finally, an interface may include one or more *assertions*, which specify predicates that the design as a whole must satisfy when it is executed (simulated). In our particular example, constraints are imposed on the values of the generic parameter delay and an attribute called fan_out for the output port sum. Fan_out is, in fact, a predefined attribute of signals (and, by implication, ports). The quantity max_fanout is also defined within the package adder_resources.

4.2.3 Packages

The VHDL *package* mechanism is a means for creating and encapsulating a collection of declarations such as types, subtypes, attributes, and functions that may then be acquired by a design entity or shared by different design entities. Although several kinds of declarations may appear within a package, signals and variables may *not*; this forces the VHDL user to explicitly specify signals and variables in the descriptions to which they actually belong.

A package, once defined, may be referenced by other descriptions provided a *context clause* at the head of a description names the package (see Fig. 4.3; also below). Subsequently, all the declarations appearing in the package are visible within the description. A number of standard packages are provided with every VHDL installation.

Figure 4.7 is a description of a package called "adder_resources;" it consists of an enumeration type declaration called "levels," two attribute definitions, and the specification of a function named "computed_delay." We can now explain the context clause

with adder_resources; **use** adder_resources

at the head of four_bit_adder's interface definition (Fig. 4.5)—the *with* clause allows the scope of declarations in the package adder_resources to extend to the end of the design entity four_bit_adder—including, that is, each body (yet to be described) associated with the interface definition. The presence of the *use* clause

```
package adder_resources is
   -- type declaration
   type levels is (gate, logic, logic_group, board, subsystem, system);
   -- attribute definitions
   attribute entity_level of entity is levels;
   attribute max_fanout of signal, port := 10
   -- function definition

   function computed_delay (nominal_delay: time, actual_power: power)
      return time is
         constant nominal_power: power := 5mW

   begin
      return (nominal_delay * (nominal_power / actual_power));
   end computed_delay;
```

FIGURE 4.7   Definition of the package adder resources (based on Intermetrics, 1984b. Copyright © Intermetrics, Inc. 1987).

causes declarations in the package adder_resources to become directly visible within the entity—including, again, the bodies associated with the interface. Thus, the objects described in adder_resources may be referenced by their names without the need to qualify it each time with that of the package.

4.2.4   Bodies

A body within a design entity describes an "implementation" of the entity that is not visible to the entity's environment. In general, several bodies may be specified to describe alternative implementations, all of which conform to a common interface definition. For example, Figure 4.8 outlines the structure of a design entity called "x" consisting of an interface specification followed by the description of two alternative but functionally equivalent bodies called, respectively, "A" and "B."

Bodies are of two types: behavioral and architectural. A *behavioral* body is a construct for describing a component's behavior in an operational, procedural

```
entity x(...) is
   . . . .
end x;

behavioral body A of x is
   . . . .
end A

architectural body B of x is
   . . . .
end B
```

FIGURE 4.8   An interface with two associated bodies.

fashion. That is, a behavioral body is similar to the specification of a computation in a high-level programming language. The only kinds of data objects that may be declared within a behavioral body are constants and variables. Thus, signals may not appear as declarations inside a behavioral body, although, of course, signals representing ports may be referenced through signal assignment statements.

The VHDL user will construct a behavioral body when the intention is to specify the operational behavior of a component at an abstract level without indicating the internal structure of the component.

Figure 4.9 shows a behavioral body called "behavior" for the entity four_bit adder. It can be seen that this description has an Ada-like flavor. Basically, the behavioral body contains declarations of types, variables, and local functions; other types of declarations such as constants or attributes may also appear in a

```
behavioral body behavior of four_bit_adder is
    type sum_range is_range 0..31;
    variable t : sum_range;

    -- following function  converts binary to integer
    function int(input : bit_vector) return integer is
        variable sum: sum_range := 0;   -- initialized to zero
        variable multiplier: sum_range := 1 -- initialized to one
        begin
            for i := input'right to input'left loop
                sum := sum + bit'pos(input(i)) * multiplier;
                multiplier := multiplier * 2;
            end loop;
            return sum;  -- returns integer value of bit_vector
    end int;

    -- following function converts integer to binary
    function bin(input : sum_range) return bit_vector is
        variable output: bit_vector (4..0);
        variable temp: sum_range;
        begin
            temp := input;
            for i := output'right to output'left loop
                output(i) := bit'val (temp rem 2);
                temp := temp / 2;
            end loop;
            return output; -- returns bit_vector value of integer
    end bin;

    -- main behavioral description
    begin
        t := int(A) + int(B) + int(carry_in);
        carry_out & sum <== bin(t) after delay;
    end
end behavior;
```

FIGURE 4.9   Behavioral body for four-bit adder.

behavioral body. The description of behavior is given by the last *begin . . . end* block.

The one feature of this particular body that concedes to the fact that it is a description of hardware is the signal assignment statement at the end, which transmits the result of adder's operation to the output ports (the notation "carry_out & sum" symbolizes the concatenation of the two ports carry_out and sum). Apart from the assignment to signals, all other computations are assumed to happen in "zero time."

In contrast to behavioral bodies, an *architectural body* describes a design entity in terms that more accurately reflect its actual structure or behavior. An architectural body may be a specification of an entity's structure only, its behavior only, or it may describe both aspects of the entity.

When an architectural body specifies *behavior* only, it will consist of a set of actions—primarily signal assignment statements—that collectively define the entity's behavior. Such an architectural body is, thus, a more concrete expression of behavior than is allowed through a behavioral body. Furthermore, executional statements in an architectural body may be executed in parallel and in a nonprocedural fashion.

When an architectural body specifies *structure* only, it will consist of a set of *component declarations* and a set of *instantiations*—that is, statements that define instances of the components and their interconnections. The "behavior" of the structure can only be deduced if the behavior of the components have themselves been defined elsewhere.

We can illustrate these two extreme forms of architectural bodies by considering *full adder*, the main component of the four_bit_adder (Fig. 4.1). Figure 4.10 shows the interface for a design entity called "full_adder" while Figure 4.11 defines two different forms of architectural bodies: (*a*) a description of its behavior only, and (*b*) a description of its structure.

In Figure 4.11(*a*) the signal sum will take the value of the expression on the right side of the statement—obtained on the basis of the values of In1, In2, and carry_in at time "now"—at time "now" + 24 nsec. A similar interpretation holds for the second signal assignment. When the design entity is simulated, the two statements will execute in parallel.

Figure 4.11(*b*) first declares three components with input and output parame-

```
with adder_resources; use adder_resources;
entity full_adder(In1, In2, carry_in: in bit);
                    sum, carry_out: out bit) is
    attribute
        full_adder'entity_level is logic;
    end full_adder;

-- followed by definitions of bodies
```

FIGURE 4.10   Interface description of full_adder (based on Intermetrics, 1984b. Copyright © Intermetrics, Inc. 1987).

```
architectural body pure_behavior of full_adder is
begin
    sum ⇐ In1 xor In2 xor carry_in after 24ns;
    carry_out ⇐
        (In1 and In2) or ((In1 xor In2) and carry_in) after 26ns;
end pure_behavior;
```

(a)

```
architectural body pure_structure of full_adder is
    component and_gate(a, b: in bit; c: out bit);
    component xor_gate(a, b: in bit; c: out bit);
    component or_gate(a, b: in bit; c: out bit);

    -internal signals
    signal S1,S2,S3 : bit;

begin
    x1: xor_gate(In1, In2, S1);
    x2: xor_gate(S1, carry_in, sum);
    a1: and_gate(carry_in, S1, S2);
    a2: and_gate(In1, In2, S3);
    or1: or_gate(S2, S3, carry_out);
end pure_structure;
```

(b)

FIGURE 4.11 Alternative forms of an architectural body for full_adder (Shahdad *et al.*, 1985. © 1985 IEEE; reprinted with permission).

ters and three signals S1, S2, S3, representing internal wires or connections. The statement block defines named instances of the components, including identifiers of the actual parameters.[2] Instantiation results not only in defining the components of the structure but also in the specification of their interconnections. The resulting structure can be pictorially represented by Figure 4.12.

An architectural body can also provide a mixture of behavioral and structural information, a capability that will be useful during the design process since it allows the designer to make some structural decisions (i.e., what components to use and how they should be connected) while postponing others. In the latter case, the subsystem may simply be described (temporarily) in behavioral terms.

Returning to the specification of four_bit_adder, let us consider its structure (Fig. 4.1). Although this may be described by a set of four instantiations of component full_adder in the manner of Figure 4.11, regular structures of this kind—which may, in general, involve a very large number of identical components—are more concisely depicted using a *generate* statement.

---

[2]Thus, the named components and_gate, xor_gate, and or_gate are, strictly speaking, component *types*, analogous to data types.

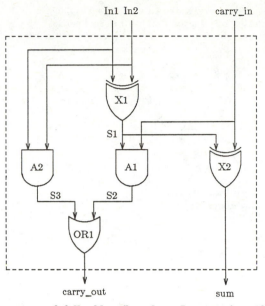

**FIGURE 4.12 Structure of full_adder (based on Intermetrics, 1984b. Copyright ©
Intermetrics, Inc. 1987).**

Figure 4.13 uses such a statement in specifying four_bit adder's structure.
Since the connection patterns of the low-order, the two middle, and the high-
order stages differ, the instantiations reflect this.[3] Thus, there are two forms of
the generate statement. The *iterative generate* form contains a discrete range of
values that the generate parameter (i in Fig. 4.13) assumes and that will determine the number of times the body of the iterative generate will be expanded.
The *conditional generate* form, on the other hand, will only expand its body if
the specified Boolean condition evaluates to true.

A complete description of four_bit_adder will then have the outline shown in
Figure 4.14. It is assumed that the components (the and-, or-, and exclusive-or-
gates) of full_adder are predefined and are available in a design library.

4.2.5 The VHDL Support Environment

Figure 4.15 shows the basic processing steps through which a VHDL description
will pass and the associated support environment. The source description is
analyzed and translated by a compiler (termed the *Analyzer*) into an internal,
intermediate representation. The smallest unit of compilation—called a *design
unit*—may be a design entity interface, a (behavioral or architectural) body, a

---

[3]Some of the parameters in the component declaration (of full_adder) have the same names as the
corresponding actual arguments in the instantiation statements. This is because the ports of full
adder and those of four_bit_adder have several names in common (compare Fig. 4.10 and Fig. 4.5).

```
architectural body structure of four_bit_adder is
    signal c: bit_vector (3..1); -- internal carries
    component full_adder (In1, In2, carry_in : in bit
                                    sum, carry_out :out bit);
begin
    for i in 3..0 generate
        if i = 0 generate                  -- connect first stage
            full_adder(A(i), B(i), carry_in, sum(i), c(i+1));
        end generate;
        if i > 0 and i < 3 generate  -- connect middle stages
            full_adder(A(i), B(i), C(i), sum(i), c(i+1));
        end generate;
        if i = 3 generate                  -- connect last stage
            full_adder(A(i), B(i), C(i), sum(i), carry_out));
        end generate;
    end generate;
end structure;
```

FIGURE 4.13 **Structural description of four-bit adder (Shahdad *et al.*, 1985. © 1985 IEEE; adapted with permission).**

```
package adder_resources is
    . . . .
end adder_resources;

-- full_adder definition follows
-- full_adder interface
with adder_resources; use adder_resources;
entity full_adder
    . . . .
end full_adder
-- full_adder body
architectural body pure_structure of full_adder is
    . . . .
end pure_structure;
-- full_adder body
architectural body pure_behavior of full_adder is
    . . . .
end pure_behavior;

-- four_bit_adder description follows
-- four_bit_adder interface
with adder_resources; use adder_resources;
entity four_bit_adder;
    . . . .
end four_bit_adder;
-- four_bit_adder behavior definition
behavioral body behavior of four_bit_adder is
    . . . .
end behavior;
-- four_bit_adder structure definition
architectural body structure of four_bit_adder is
    . . . .
end structure;
```

FIGURE 4.14 **Outline of complete four-bit adder description.**

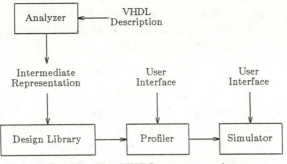

FIGURE 4.15   The VHDL support environment.

function, or a package. The basic precedence rules for analysis are that a body cannot be analyzed prior to its interface and that a package referenced by some other unit must be analyzed before the referencing unit. A complete design description will be contained in one or more *design files*.

The output produced by the Analyzer is stored in a central *Design Library*, which is sharable by all users of the VHDL support environment. These descriptions can then be extracted and integrated by the *Profiler* and prepared for execution by the *Simulator*. Both these components can be controlled interactively through user interfaces.

4.2.6   Discussion

To summarize, VHDL has several very distinctive features that appear to make it attractive as a multilevel hardware description language. The more notable of these are

1.   Separation of the description of a design entity into an interface and a body, each of which can be separately compiled; the former presents the entity's externally observable characteristics whereas the latter specifies how it is actually realized. This particular feature is, of course, taken from the way Ada packages are organized.

2.   The ability on the part of the VHDL user to specify alternative forms of bodies. This should facilitate the application of stepwise refinement during design, since the designer can specify the behavior of a component in abstract terms (by using a behavioral body), later refine the description to a more detailed specification of behavior by transforming the behavioral body into an architectural body, and, finally, transforming this description into an equivalent structural form using, again, an architectural body.

3.   The ability to define attributes and assertions. An attribute is some property about an item such as a signal, a variable, a port, or a design entity that may be referenced in a useful way within the VHDL description. While the language includes several predefined attributes (e.g., "fanin" and "fanout," associated with signals), others may be constructed by the user inside a package (e.g., "entity_level" defined in Fig. 4.7 and referenced in the inter-

face of Fig. 4.5). Similarly, an assertion is some global invariant predicate that must be satisfied by the design entity at all times and may refer to attributes as, for example, in the assertion

$$\text{sum' fanout} \Leftarrow \text{max\_fanout}$$

which appears in the interface of Figure 4.5.

4. As a design progresses toward physical realization, the flow of control will become more nonprocedural. In VHDL the flow of control within a behavioral body is procedural, in keeping with the abstract, algorithmic nature of this construct. However, the flow of control within an architectural body is nonprocedural and, consequently, allows concurrency among the statements. The basic (behavioral) statement in an architectural body is, of course, the signal assignment; such a statement is executed when it receives stimuli (i.e., changes of values) on its inputs. Thus, for example, in the architectural body of Figure 4.11(*a*) the signal assignment statement

$$\text{sum} \Leftarrow \text{In1 } \textbf{xor } \text{In2 } \textbf{xor } \text{carry\_in } \textbf{after } 24\text{ns}$$

executes whenever a "new" value is received on one of the signals on the right side of this assignment. The outcome is that the signal sum will assume a new value after a time interval "now" + 24 nsec. If sum is the input to some other statement or is the input port to an entity, then once the value of sum is defined it will trigger the activation of the concerned statement or entity. Architectural bodies and the statements within are, thus, executed in an event-driven fashion.

5. In actual fact, the semantics of architectural statements are a bit more complicated. Consider a signal assignment statement S:

$$x \Leftarrow e(x_1,\ldots,x_n) \textbf{ after } \text{tns}$$

where $x, x_1, \ldots, x_n$ are signals and e denotes an expression over $x_1, \ldots, x_n$. Then this statement has associated with it exactly one *guard*, which is a Boolean expression. This guard is the logical conjunction of the predicate TRUE and the value of the guard of any statement that encloses S. (If there is no enclosing statement then the guard is simply the predicate TRUE.)

A signal assignment statement is executed when its guard is true and one of its input values changes.

Guards may be stated explicitly in architectural *if* and *case* statements.[4] Consider, for example, the architectural *if* statement

```
if c₁ then a ⇐ b₁ after 10ns;
  elseif c₂ then a ⇐ b₂ after 10ns;
  else a ⇐ b₃ after 6ns;
endif
```

---

[4]*if* and *case* statements may also appear in behavioral bodies as in usual procedural languages. These are then called behavioral *if* and *case* statements.

Then the guards on the signal assignment statements

$$a \Leftarrow b_1 \ldots$$
$$a \Leftarrow b_2 \ldots$$
$$a \Leftarrow b_3 \ldots$$

are, respectively "c_1," "*not c_1 and c_2*" and "*not c_1 and not c_2*." In the architectural **case** statement

```
case E is
    when v₁ ⇒ a ⇐ b₁ after 10ns;
    when v₂ ⇒ a ⇐ b₂ after 10ns;
    when v₃ ⇒ a ⇐ b₃ after 6ns;
end case
```

where the expression E evaluates to an enumeration or integer type value, the guards for the three signal assignments are, respectively,

$$E = v_1, \quad E = v_2, \quad \text{and } E = v_3$$

Finally, we note that since VHDL is (at the time of writing) a very new language, it is too premature to assess its capabilities and limitations as a multilevel hardware description language and, in the particular context of our interest here, as an architecture description language. There are several dimensions across which the language needs to be empirically evaluated, of which the following seem particularly important.

1. VHDLs descriptive capability at a given level of abstraction.
2. The ease with which it facilitates transformations across abstraction levels.
3. Its ability to incorporate design tools or be integrated into a given design environment.
4. The extent to which it facilitates formal design verification.

4.3 S*M

The design of S*M was motivated by the following interpretation of the role of computer architecture in the design and implementation of hardware systems: The principal architectural levels—exo-, endo-, and micro-architectures—are collectively related to physically realized hardware systems as abstract specifications are related to executable software systems. In other words, just as in the software development process specifications are intended to serve as a precise, implementation-independent description of desired program behavior (Gehani and McGettrick, 1986), in the hardware development process an architectural description serves as a specification of the desired behavior of the digital system.

In this view, then, *architectures serve as abstract specifications of computer hardware systems.* An exo-architecture characterizes the behavior of a digital system as a whole—as seen by the users of the system—whereas its endo-architecture specifies the functional behavior of the principal components of the digital system and the ways in which the components are allowed to interact. A micro-architecture specifies the behavior of a digital system from the perspective of the microprogrammer.

Now, the key to the development of a specification is that it is intended to define a system's (or a component's) behavior only; furthermore:

1. This behavior must be so defined as to reveal only as much of it to the environment as is needed for the system (or component) to be *used* by other systems (or components) in the environment.
2. The specification should suppress or hide to the greatest extent possible information as to how the behavior is, should be, or may have been, implemented.

This second property is desirable for reasons discussed in Section 3.2.3, namely, that

(a) If the system is yet to be built, then the specification should not *unnecessarily* bias the implementer toward any particular implementation.[5]
(b) If the system has already been built, then we may not, in fact, know how components are implemented, and any assumptions to the contrary would be presumptuous or, worse, grossly inaccurate.

It is clear then that a language for describing computer architectures viewed as specifications should be *functional* in nature (see Section 3.2.3). S*M (Dasgupta, Wilsey, and Heinanen, 1986; Wilsey, 1985) is an example of a functional ADL based, specifically, on the *axiomatic* style of specifying behavior — that is, the behavior of a system is expressed in terms of assertions (pre- and postconditions) in some axiomatic or deductive systems (Section 3.2.3).

S*M is also a nonprocedural language (Section 3.2.4) in that its basic components, called *modules*, become active whenever one of a specified set of conditions or *guards* associated with each such module is true. Since each module may be associated with distinct and disjoint guards, and since at a given time these guards may possibly all be true, modules may be executed in parallel.

4.3.1 Informal Description of a Shifter

As in the case of VHDL, I will use an example to illustrate the important features of S*M. The discussion that follows is based on Dasgupta, Wilsey, and Heinanen (1985).

Figure 4.16 is a block diagram of the ALU/shifter part of a 32-bit data path.

---

[5]Note the emphasis on the word "unnecessarily"; as I pointed out in Chapter 1, certain key implementation decisions (e.g., concerning the technology to be used) may have been made so early in the design of a system as to influence the specification (i.e., the architecture) itself. We assume that when such implementation-related decisions are made during architecture development they are made for sound reasons; that is, they are necessary for the development of the architecture and, therefore, for specification development. For a brief but cogent argument as to how specifications and implementations may be "intertwined," refer to Swartout and Balzer (1982).

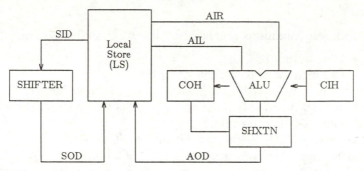

**FIGURE 4.16 Partial view of a data path (Dasgupta, Wilsey, and Heinanen, 1986. ©
1986, IEEE; reprinted with permission).**

This diagram, then, represents part of a machine's micro-architecture and is
based, loosely, on the architecture of the Nanodata QM-1 [Nanodata, 1979].

The Shifter

Consider, in particular, the *shifter*. This unit can perform different shift operations upon the data present on the SID bus. The result is transmitted to the SOD
bus from which it may, under the control of a particular micro-operation, be
gated to a local store register.

The following types of *single-shifts* can be performed by the shifter:

1. **Left and right logical**   Zeros shifted in at one end, bits shifted off the other
   end.
2. **Right arithmetic**   Sign bit extended rightward, bits shifted off the right end.
3. **Left and right circular**   Rotations of the 32-bit quantity.

Each of these operations can perform shifts of 0 through 32 positions without
any time penalty associated with the shift amount.

Double-shifts can be performed by the shifter and the shifter extension,
SHXTN, operating together as a logically single unit. This unit accepts the ALU
output and the value on SID as the high- and low-order halves, respectively, of a
65-bit quantity. The corresponding halves of the 64-bit double-shift output
appear on the AOD and SOD buses, respectively. The types of double-shift
operations are identical to the single-shift operations except that the *left* and
right logical operations accept a 65-bit quantity (the carry is included) whereas
the *right arithmetic* and the *left* and *right* circular shifts operate on 64-bit
quantities.

Double shifts of 0 through 65 bits can be done in parallel. The microprogrammer specifies a particular shift operation through two fields in the microinstruction: one is a 7-bit *shift amount* field whereas the other, 5-bits long, specifies the
shift control; the latter has subfields for the shift type (circular, logical, arithmetic), mode (single, double), and direction (left, right).

Test Conditions

There are six test conditions generated by the ALU/shifter system.

1. **Carry**   The output of COH.
2. **Sign**   The high-order bit on the AOD bus.
3. **Result**   The bitwise "or" of the low-order 31 bits on the AOD bus.
4. **Overflow**   Set if and only if the carry-in to the sign bit and to the carry out positions are of opposite values.
5. **Shifter high bit**   The high-order bit on the SOD bus.
6. **Shifter low bit**   The low-order bit on the SOD bus.

Timing

The machine is controlled by a 3-phase clock cycle (or microcycle). The first and third phases are both 25 nsec whereas the second phase is 50 nsec long. The timing scheme is so defined that a pair of operands can be gated from local store to the ALU or shifter, an arithmetic/logical/shift operation performed, and the result written back to local store in one microcycle. The shifter and shifter extension operate in the second phase of the clock. Test conditions are generated at the end of the second phase and remain stable for the duration of the last phase.

4.3.2   Formal Specification of the Shifter

The following S*M specification characterizes the shifting capabilities of the machine as a whole. That is, we suppress the fact that the shifter and the shifter extension are physically distinct entities viewing this as an aspect

1. Not needed to be known by the "user" of the shifter specification.
2. That is essentially an implementation issue.

Note that this is a kind of decision (about what to include in the specification) that may well be found to be wrong at a later stage (when the specification is used for whatever purpose at hand); in which case, the specification may have to be revised.

A first, skeletal version of the shifter is depicted in Figure 4.17. Here, we have definitions of two data types: a collection of stores that are instances of predefined or the declared data types, and a clock. The definitions are global, that is, they may be referenced throughout the system description.

Data Types and Stores

The primitive data type in S*M is the *bit*, whereas structured data types are built using the constructors *sequence*, *array*, and *record*. In this particular example, all the stores are instances of either the primitive data type *bit* or the structured types "microinst" and "bus." A point to note in the definition of stores is the declaration

```
system micro_machine
    . . . .
type microinst is record . . . end record
type bus is seq[31..0] of bit;
store
    mir: microinst;
    sid, aod, sod: bus;
    cih, coh: bit;
    pseudo psign, presult, povflo,
            pshb, pslb: bit transient after (25ns);
    . . . .
clock clk
    aligned with tk = 0ns
    dur 100ns
    subclock
        ph1 : dur 25ns;
        ph2 : dur 50ns;
        ph3 : dur 25ns;
end clock
    . . . .
module shifter . . . end module
    . . . .
end system
```

FIGURE 4.17 A skeletal description of the shifter (Dasgupta, Wilsey, and Heinanen, 1986. © 1986, IEEE; reprinted with permission).

pseudo psign, presult, . . . , pslb: **bit transient after** (25ns);

The stores psign, . . . , pslb are instances of what in S*M are called *pseudo stores*. Pseudo stores are used in an S*M description to designate *variables* that have not been bound (or allocated to) an actual store at specification time. Pseudo stores become necessary in two situations: (1) If the system being described is yet to be implemented, then by defining a pseudo store the specifier defers the decision to bind this object to actual hardware to implementation time; (2) if the description is of a system that has already been implemented, then the specifier may not know of how a particular variable has been implemented—in which case he or she may declare it as a pseudo store. For instance, the informal shifter description simply states that six testable "conditions" are generated by ALU/shifter operations. Where these conditions are held is left unspecified.

Another idiosyncratic feature of micro-architectures is that certain stores may retain the most recently written values for only a specified period of time after which the state of the store is reset to some standard default or is undefined. We therefore need to distinguish between such transient stores and the more common static stores. The pseudo stores psign, presult, . . . , pslb are instances of such transient stores, and their declaration states that their values (which, as will be seen later, are actually set in the second phase of the clock clk) are retained only for a duration of 25 nsec—that is, for the duration of the third phase of clk; the value becomes undefined hereafter until it is subsequently reset. Had there been a default value, such as 0 for these transient stores, then the last part of the declaration would have indicated this fact.

. . . **bit transient after** (25ns,0)

Clocks

The clock clk is synchronized with the initial value of a global timekeeper (tk), which is simply a counter that increments itself after a predefined unit interval — in this example, a nanosecond. In contrast to tk, which keeps "linear" time, a clock declaration allows us to describe periodic events or cycles. The clock definition simply states that it cycles through three phases or states ph1, ph2, and ph3 of durations 25, 50, and 25 nsec, respectively, and that the clock begins its cyclic behavior when synchronized with the initial value of tk = 0.

For the description of the shifter system, a single clock definition suffices. In general, though, different architectural components may exhibit different timing characteristics, in which case several clocks would be declared, each synchronized with some particular value of the timekeeper and designating a particular set of periodic events in the target architecture. For example, a machine description may require the clock declarations shown in Figure 4.18. The timing diagram corresponding to these declarations is given in Figure 4.19.

In more complex situations, the duration of a particular clock may be "stretched," depending on some condition being true. This situation is illustrated in Figure 4.20, which is part of a VAX 11/780 micro-architecture description in S*M. Here, C2 is a single-phase clock with two inputs (designated as *inports*) to it, the (previously declared) stores mir and interrupt. Under "normal" conditions, the duration of C2 is 50 nsec. However, when the value of the (*bit* type) store "interrupt" is 1, the clock duration extends to 8 times the normal duration, that is, to 400 nsec. When interrupt = 0 but mir.kmx ≥ 8, the duration

```
clock clk1
    aligned with tk = 0ns
    dur 100ns
    subclock
        ph1 : dur 50ns;
        ph2 : dur 50ns
end clock

clock clk2
    aligned with tk = 50ns
    dur 75ns
    subclock
        ph1 : dur 25ns;
        ph2 : dur 25ns;
        ph3 : dur 25ns
end clock
```

FIGURE 4.18 Definition of a two-clock system (Dasgupta, Wilsey, and Heinanen, 1986. © 1986, IEEE; reprinted with permission).

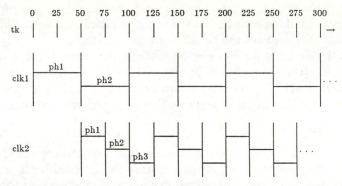

FIGURE 4.19 Timing diagram for the two-clock system (Dasgupta, Wilsey, and Heinanen, 1986. © 1986, IEEE; reprinted with permission).

of the clock doubles. When a clock duration is stretched, the duration of its constituent phases are also stretched by the same factor.

It is important to note that the admission of an arbitrary number of clock definitions in an S*M description does not imply the presence of an equal number of "physical" clocks in the real machine. The description is intended to reflect accurately the overall timing behavior of a target micro-architecture and not the means by which the behavior is realized.

Modules

Consider now the definition of the module named shifter. Our intention is to define this in terms of

1. Its interface with the environment; that is, the means by which data passes to and from the module and the means by which the module may be activated.
2. Its timing characteristic.
3. What the meanings of the constituent operations of the module are.

Leaving aside for the moment the last of these items, the shifter module can be characterized according to Figure 4.21. Basically, this defines the shifter as a data

```
clock C2
    inport
        mir.kmx;
        interrupt
    aligned with tk = 0ns
    dur 50ns
    stretch
        {(not interrupt) and (mir.kmx >= 8), 2}
        {interrupt, 8}
    end clock
```

FIGURE 4.20 A stretched, one-phase clock (Dasgupta, Wilsey, and Heinanen, 1986. © 1986, IEEE; reprinted with permission).

abstraction consisting of a set of input and output ports that provides the module's data interface with its environment, a guard (see following), and an effects section that specifies the behavior of this module.

The port declarations refer to one or more of the stores previously declared globally (as, for example, shown in Fig. 4.17). Although not shown in this example, it is possible for an input/output port to be bound to a module for the entire duration of the module's activity. For example, the declaration

inport sid **bound**

causes the store sid to be dedicated as a port to shifter; no other active module can use sid as either an input or an output port during the time shifter is active.

A module may also contain private declarations of stores and store types. Obviously, such declarations are referenced only within the module and are inaccessible to its environment.

A guard is of the form

{Boolean condition, clock (or subclock) identifier}

and denotes the fact that if the Boolean condition is true then the timing behavior of the module as a whole is defined by the clock (or subclock) specifier. In general, a module may be controlled by several mutually exclusive guards, although in the example here only one guard is given. Each of the operations depicted within the effects section of Figure 4.21, thus, can be activated at the beginning of the clock phase clk.ph2 and, very importantly, is guaranteed to terminate at the end of the phase.

```
module shifter
    inport sid; mir; alu
    outport sod; psign; presult; povflow; pshb; pslb
    inoutport cih; coh
      . . .
    guard {true, clk.ph2}
    effects
        case mir.f34[3..0] is
            when 2#0100# => . . ./* single left logical */
            when 2#0101# => . . ./* single right logical */
            when 2#1100# => . . ./* single left circular */
            when 2#1101# => . . ./* single right circular */
            when 2#1001# => . . ./* single right arithmetic */
            when 2#0110# => . . ./* double left logical */
            when 2#0111# => . . ./* double right logical */
            when 2#1110# => . . ./* double left circular */
            when 2#1111# => . . ./* double right circular */
            when 2#1011# => . . ./* double right arithmetic */
        end case
    end module
```

FIGURE 4.21 **Overview of the shifter module specification (Dasgupta, Wilsey, and Heinanen, 1986. © 1986, IEEE; reprinted with permission).**

Consider now the specification of module behavior—for example, the effects of the "single right arithmetic" shift operation. The semantics of this operation is described in terms of pre- and postconditions. Taken in conjunction with the guard definition, such a declaration states that if the precondition is true at the beginning of the guard clock period then the result of the operation satisfies the postcondition that will hold at the end of the guard clock period. In S*M, we therefore activate operators nonprocedurally; that is, not by explicit calls but by the fact that some particular condition holds. This aspect is further discussed in the next section.

Although we are eschewing operational descriptions for the semantics of operators, we would, for obvious reasons, like to make the axiomatic specifications as "program-like" as possible; hence, such considerations as modularization, structuring, and understandability must prevail. Figure 4.22 is, thus, a specification of the "single right arithmetic" operation in "structured" form that uses a private function called "sra." Note that "sra," in turn, uses primitive language defined operators *shr* and *shr1*. These denote, respectively, operations that perform a right shift with zero's inserted at the high-order end and a right shift with one's inserted at the high-order end. Note also that "sra" is defined as a generic function in the sense that its formal parameter "n" is bound to an integer constant at compile time.

The precondition for the "single right arithmetic" operation is defined by conjunction of the *when* and *if* clauses and states the values that fields f34 and f35 of mir (the microinstruction register) must satisfy. If this precondition holds, then the "behavior" of the operation is given by the rest of the specification. The notation "**new** x," where x identifies an output port, denotes the "new" value of x—that is, the state of the port x existing at the termination of the (sub) clock guarding the operator. When the postcondition contains a reference to an "old" value of a port, then the prefix *new* is omitted.

Consider now the specification of a double shift operator, say "double right logical." In the case of double shifts, the input and output ports are "virtual" 64-

```
function sra(x: seq[6..0]of bit; y: seq[n..0]of bit): seq[n..0]of bit =
    if y[n]
        then shr(x,y)
        else shrl(x,y)
    end if
end function
    . . . .
when 2#1001# => /* single right arithmetic */
    if mir.f35 <= 32 then
        new sod = sra(mir.f35,sid) &
        new pshb = new sod[31] &
        new pslb = new sod[0]
    end if
    . . . .
```

FIGURE 4.22 **Definition of a private function (Dasgupta, Wilsey, and Heinanen, 1986.** © 1986, IEEE; reprinted with permission).

or 65-bit entities as indicated in the informal description. We thus declare the following synonyms:

syn
    double_sid_with_carryin:**seq**[64..0]**of bit** = alu@sid@cih
    double_sod_with_carryin:**seq**[64..0]**of bit** = alu@sod@coh

which create two virtual 65-bit sequences that are concatenations of previously defined data objects and assign identifiers to these entities. Figure 4.23 describes the "double right logical" operation. Its postcondition refers to a private function "cond_presult," which, in turn, depends on a private recursive function "bit or."

The rest of the shifter module can be specified in a similar manner. The complete module is given in Figure 4.24.

In the case of the shifter example, a specific module has been defined. It is also possible, in S*M, to define a module type and declare instances of this type. Consider, for example, a micro-architecture that has two functionally identical ALUs. We may in this case define an ALU module type (Fig. 4.25) and create two instances of this type as shown in Figure 4.26. The instantiation, in fact, creates two copies of the ALU module with input and output ports as defined by the substitutions in the respective parameter lists.

```
function bit_or(x: array(0..m)of bit; n: seq[5..0]of bit): bit=
    if n = 1
        then x(1) or x(0)
        else x(n) or bit_or(x, n-1)
    end if
end function

function cond_presult(x, y: seq[31..0] of bit): bit =
    if mir.f34[5] or mir.f34[4]
        then bit_or(x[30..0] @ y, 61)
        else bit_or(x, 31)
    end if
end function
    . . . .

when 2#0111#  => /*double right logical*/
    if mir.f35 <= 64 then
        new double_sod_with_carryin =
            shr(mir.f35, double_sid_with_carryin) &
        new psign = new double_sod_with_carryin[64] &
        new presult = cond_presult(aod, sid) &
        new pshb = new sod[31] &
        new pslb = new sod[0]
    end if
    . . . .
```

FIGURE 4.23 Specification of a "double right logical" shift operation (Dasgupta, Wilsey, and Heinanen, 1986. © 1986, IEEE; reprinted with permission).

```
module shifter
/* port declarations */
inport sid: bus; mir: microinst; cih:bit;
    pseudo alu: bus
outport sod, aod: bus; cih, coh: bit;
    pseudo psign, presult, povflo, pshb, pslb: bit transient after 25ns
/* synonym declarations */
syn double_sid: seq[63..0] of bit = alu @ sid;
    double_sod: seq[63..0] of bit = alu @ sod;
    double_sid_with_carryin: seq[64..0] of bit = alu @ sid @ cih;
    double_sod_with_carryin: seq[64..0] of bit = alu @ sod @ coh


/* guard definition */
guard {true, clk.ph2_3}


/* private functions */
function sra(x: seq[6. .0]of bit; y: seq[n..0]of bit): seq[n..0]of bit=
    if y[n] = 0 then shr(x,y)
    else shrl(x,y)
    end if
end function


function bit_or(x: array(0.m) of bit; n: seq(5..0) of bit): bit=
    if n = 1 then x(1) or x(0)
    else x(n) or bit_or(x, n-1)
    end if
end function


function cond_presult(x, y: seq[31..0] of bit): bit=
    if mir.f34[5] or mir.f34[4]then bit_or(x[30..0] @ y, 62)
    else bit_or(x, 31)
    end if
end function


effects
    case mir.f34[3..0] is
    when 2#0100# => /* single left logical */
        if mir.f35 <= 32 then
            new sod = shl(mir.f35,sid) &
            new pshb = new sod[31] &
            new pslb = new sod[0]
        end if
    when 2#0101# => /* single right logical */
        if mir.f35 <= 32 then
            new sod = shr(mir.f35, sid) &
            new pshb = new sod[31] &
            new pslb = new sod[0]
        end if
```

FIGURE 4.24   Complete S*M specification of shifter module.

```
when 2#1100# => /* single left circular */
   if mir.f35 <= 32 then
      new sod = slc(mir.f35, sid) &
      new pshb = new sod[31] &
      new pslb = new sod[0]
   end if
when 2#1101# => /* single right circular */
   if mir.f35 <= 32 then
      new sod = src(mir.f35, sid) &
      new pshb = new sod[31] &
      new pslb = new sod[0]
   end if
when 2#1001# => /* single right arithmetic */
   if mir.f35 <= 32 then
      new sod = sra(mir.f35, sid) &
      new pshb = new sod[31] &
      new pslb = new sod[0]
   end if
when 2#0110# => /* double left logical */
   if mir.f35 <= 64 then
      new double_sod_with_carryin =
         shl(mir.f35, double_sid_with_carryin) &
      new psign = new double_sod_with_carryin[64] &
      new presult = cond_presult(aod, sid) &
      new pshb = new sod[31] &
      new pslb = new sod[0]
   end if
when 2#0111# => /* double right logical */
   if mir.f35 <= 64 then
      new double_sod_with_carryin =
         shr(mir.f35, double_sid_with_carrying) &
      new psign = new double_sod_with_carryin[64] &
      new presult = cond_presult(aod, sid) &
      new pshb = new sod[31] &
      new pslb = new sod[0]
   end if
when 2#1110# => /* double left circular */
   if mir.f35 <= 64 then
      new double_sod = slc(mir.f35,double_sid) &
      new psign = new double_sod[63] &
      new presult = cond_presult(aod,sid) &
      new pshb = new sod[31] &
      new pslb = new sod[0]
   end if
when 2#1111# => /* double right circular */
   if mir.f35 <= 64 then
      new double_sod = src(mir.f35, double_sid) &
      new psign = new double_sod[63] &
```

FIGURE 4.24 (Part 2 of 3)

```
              new presult = cond_result(aod,sid) &
              new pshb = new sod[31] &
              new pslb = new sod[0]
          end if
      when 2#1011# => /* double right arithmetic */
          if mir.f35 <= 64 then
              new double_sod = sra(mir.f35, double_sid) &
              new psign = new double_sod[63] &
              new presult = cond_presult(aod, sid) &
              new pshb = new sod[31] &
              new pslb = new sod[0]
          end if
      end case
  end module
```

FIGURE 4.24 (Part 3 of 3)

Nonprocedural Interaction of Modules

As previously noted, modules in S*M are activated not through explicit calls as in a procedural description, but nonprocedurally; that is, they are activated by one or more conditions being true at the beginning of a clock period. More specifically, the activation of a module is determined by the following conditions.

1. The module is not active.
2. One or more of the clocks in the guard list associated with the module is entering a period of activity in the "current" unit interval of the timekeeper. We refer to these as "rising" clocks.
3. One and only one of the Boolean expressions in the guard list associated with a rising clock is true.

```
module type ALU
    inport ail; air; ctl
    outport aod

    guard {ctl <> 0, cl.ph3}
    effects
        new aod =
            case ctl is
                when 0 => ail + air
                when 1 => ail + air + 1
                when 2 => ail - air
                when 3 => ail - air -1
                . . .
            end case
end module
```

FIGURE 4.25 ALU module type declaration (Wilsey, 1985).

```
system S1
    module type ALU
        /* as defined in Fig. 4.25 */
        . . .
    end module

    . . .
    inst
        ALU(ail=amx1_l, air=amx1_r, ctl=mir.alu_1, aod=aod1);
        ALU(ail=amx2_l, air=amx2_r, ctl=mir.alu_2, aod=aod2)
end system
```

FIGURE 4.26   Instantiation of module type ALU (Wilsey, 1985).

Under these conditions, the module becomes active and the rising clock associated with the Boolean expression that is true becomes the controlling clock for the module. At the fall of the controlling clock:

4. The postconditions associated with whichever precondition was true at the rise of the controlling clock will hold.

If conditions (1) through (3) hold but none of the preconditions in the *effects* section are true, then the effect is the equivalent of a "no-op" (i.e., time passes, a clock cycle is consumed, but no state change takes place).

We can further illustrate the nature of nonprocedural activations by showing the interaction between the shifter module (Fig. 4.24) and a module called "fetch," the intent of which is to fetch a microinstruction from control store and place it in the microinstruction register. However, the precise outcome of this fetch process depends on the "current" state of the microinstruction register — for example, whether the latter encodes a branch microinstruction or not. A specification of a portion of "fetch" is given in Figure 4.27. Note the presence of private stores in this module; the *init* clause in the declaration of "mpc" indicates that mpc is initialized to some constant value.

This module should be read in conjunction with the description of shifter. Since the durations of fetch and shifter overlap in time and it is possible for preconditions in both modules to be simultaneously true, the modules may be activated in parallel.

One must therefore ensure that concurrent activations of these two modules do not interfere with one another. Specifically, in this case, the value of mir at the beginning of clk's activity should not be destroyed (by the *new* value resulting from fetch's activation) prior to the fall of clk.ph2 (i.e., prior to the time at which shifter terminates). The semantics of S*M guarantees this since the postcondition for the fetch module is said to hold only when the module terminates; prior to that time mir holds the same value as at the beginning of clk's activation.[6]

---

[6]In this entire discussion "time" refers to the values of the timekeeper.

```
module fetch
  inoutport mir
  store
    cs: array(0..8196) of microinst;
    mpc: seq[12..0] of bit init(. . .)
  guard {true, clk}
  effects
    if mir.f26 then /*sequence to next*/
      new mir = cs(mpc) &
      new mpc = mpc +1
    else   /*branch to next*/
      new mpc = mir.branch &
      new mir = cs(mpc)
    end if
end module
```

FIGURE 4.27 A microinstruction fetch module (Dasgupta, Wilsey, and Heinanen, 1986. © 1986, IEEE; reprinted with permission).

In general, it will be up to the S*M user describing some architectural system to formally demonstrate that certain global properties (resulting from the interaction of its constituent modules) are satisfied — that the system is deadlock free, for example, or that it is interference free, or that the specification as a whole is consistent.

Since the behavior of the modules are in the form of pre/postconditions one does not have to prove anything about these descriptions: The axiomatically defined behavior are taken as given. These assertions are then used in essentially three ways: (1) as functional specifications for subsequent (possibly operational) implementations of the modules — either through systematic manual design procedures or automated synthesis; (2) as functional specifications of the target architecture that can be used in code/microcode generation, synthesis, and verification; and (3) as axioms of module behavior that are used for proving global properties of the system as a whole.

4.4 BIBLIOGRAPHIC REMARKS

The ISPS language is completely defined in Barbacci and associates (1978). A comprehensive review of the various applications to which ISPS has been put is contained in Barbacci (1981). Barbacci and Siewiorek (1982) presents ISPS descriptions of a variety of exo-architectures, including those of the PDP-11, the IBM System/370, and the CDC 6600. For another perspective of ISPS, refer to the critique by Parker and associates (1979).

The entire VHDL design is recorded in a series of reports. These include a document on the language requirements (Intermetrics, 1984a); three volumes of the user's manual (Intermetrics, 1984b); and the language reference manual (Intermetrics, 1984c).

VHDL includes several features present in the programming language Ada.

This brings to mind the question often asked as to whether CHDLs are at all necessary. Could we not, it is asked, use an available programming language for the description of hardware systems? One project currently under way is attempting to address precisely this question: It involves a study of using Ada as a multilevel CHDL. Some preliminary results of this investigation are reported by Barbacci and coworkers (1985).

The evolution of the design of S*M has been documented in Dasgupta (1985) and Dasgupta, Wilsey, and Heinanen (1986). The full language definition is presented in Wilsey (1985).

S*M is the most recent member of the S* family of languages developed since 1978 for the formal description and verification of architectures and microprograms. Other members of the family include the microprogramming language schema S* (Dasgupta, 1980) and the operational and procedural ADL S*A (Dasgupta, 1984). The schema S* and its applications are discussed in Chapter 5.

The role and nature of software specification languages and techniques have been discussed in many publications. Several of the key papers have been assembled by Gehani and McGettrick (1986). Of special note in this anthology are Liskov and Berzins (1979), Balzer and Goldman (1979), Swartout and Balzer (1982), Guttag (1979), Parnas (1972), Guttag and Horning (1980), and Burstall and Goguen (1981). In addition to this collection, Parnas' (1977) paper and reports on the Larch family of specification languages (Guttag, Horning, and Wing, 1982, 1985) are recommended.

PROBLEMS

4.1   **(a)**   Construct a VHDL interface specification of an 8-input, 1-bit multiplexer.

(b)   Implement this specification (at the logic design level) with a VHDL behavioral body.

(c)   Implement the interface specification (at the logic design level) with a VHDL architectural body showing behavior only.

(d)   Implement the interface specification (at the logic design level) with a VHDL architectural body showing structure only.

[*Note*: Include whatever package definitions are necessary for your VHDL descriptions. Also, assume that gate definitions are primitive components in VHDL.]

4.2   [Continuation of Problems 4.1.] Using the description of the 8-input, 1-bit multiplexer, develop a VHDL description of an 8-input, 8-bit multiplexer. Your description should consist of

(a)   An interface specification.

(b)   A behavioral body.

(c)   An architectural body showing structure only.

4.3   [Continuation of Problem 4.1.] With respect to your solution to Problem

4.1, discuss in detail how, using testing, formal verification and/or stepwise refinement, you would demonstrate

(a) The *equivalence* of the behavioral body (4.1b) and the architectural body showing behavior (4.1c). (Alternatively, that the behavior-architectural body is a *correct refinement* of the behavioral body.)

(b) That the structure-architectural body (4.1*d*) is a *correct structural implementation* of the behavior-architectural body (4.1*c*).

4.4 VHDL (and some other CHDLs) specify timing behavior by associating a timing delay with an assignment statement. The general form for such an assignment is

$$X \Leftarrow E \text{ after } T$$

where X denotes a store, E is some expression, and T denotes a time period. When such an assignment is "executed," the current value of E is placed in X T time units from "now."

(a) What is (are) the advantage (advantages) of this approach to timing?

(b) Contrast this approach to the timing semantics of modules in S*M. How are they similar or different?

4.5 Consider the partial data path depicted in Figure 3.2 (Chapter 3) and the corresponding CDL description of its behavior (Fig. 3.3). You are required to formally capture, in VHDL, the structure and behavior of the subsystem responsible for *instruction fetch* (see Fig. 3.3).

(a) Develop an interface specification for this subsystem.

(b) Implement this specification (at the register-transfer level) with a behavioral body.

(c) Implement the specification (at the register-transfer level) with a behavior-architectural body.

(d) Describe the structure of the data path by means of a structure-architectural body.

[*Note*: State explicitly any assumptions that you have to make.]

4.6 Consider the two-clock system depicted in Figure 4.19. (Its S*M description is shown in Fig. 4.18). How would you specify this in VHDL? Based on this exercise, what are your conclusions regarding VHDL's ability to deal with such timing characteristics?

4.7 Consider the stretched one-phase clock specified in S*M in Figure 4.20. How would you define this clock in VHDL?

4.8 In a particular micromachine, a 32-bit register, IR, is used to hold instructions (fetched from main memory) with two different formats. In format 1, the high-order 8 bits constitute one field, the next 12 bits constitute a second field, and the remaining (low order) 12 bits make up a third field. In format 2, the high-order 8 bits constitute one field, the next 4 bits constitute a second field, the next 12 bits a third field, the next 4 bits a fourth field, and the remaining (low-order) 4 bits constitute a fifth field.

Thus, at the micro-architectural level, there are three distinct "views" of IR: as a 32-bit register, when an instruction is loaded into IR during instruction fetch; as a format 1 register when the instruction it contains is of format 1 and it has to be decoded in preparation for execution; and as a format 2 register when it holds a format 2 instruction.

Devise a language construct that could be built into VHDL (or any other CHDL) by means of which one can describe IR so as to make all three views visible. Characterize the semantics of this construct.

4.9　(a)　Develop a complete VHDL description of the shifter module described (in S*M) in Section 4.3.2 (see, in particular, Fig. 4.24). Keep in mind that you do not know how the module has been implemented. Your specification should capture the timing behavior of the module as well as its functional behavior.

　　　(b)　Comparing your VHDL description with the S*M specification, comment on the comparative advantages of the two languages, at least with respect to this particular example.

4.10　Consider two *asynchronous, concurrently executing* modules called PRODUCER and CONSUMER. The former does some computations (of no real interest to us) and places a 32-bit data packet into a register, called BUFFER—providing, of course, that BUFFER is empty or has been emptied of its previous contents. (Otherwise, PRODUCER waits.) CONSUMER takes a 32-bit packet from BUFFER (providing that BUFFER has been filled with a new packet since the last time it was accessed by CONSUMER) and does something with it (of no interest to us).

PRODUCER and CONSUMER operate in parallel, at their own speeds. There are no global clocks controlling their operations. Nor, when the system was being designed, could the designer make any assumptions regarding their relative speeds.

　　　(a)　Specify this concurrent, asynchronous system in S*M.

　　　(b)　What are your conclusions regarding S*M's capability to handle asynchronous concurrency?

4.11　[This problem was originally posed by P. A. Wilsey.] The timing behavior of a micromachine (call it MM) is described in MM's "Microprogramming Manual" as follows.

MM uses a 4-phase clock that controls the execution time of microinstructions. The phases are related to each other in the following way: the first and second phases occur in succession, with phase 2 beginning when phase 1 ends. Phase 3 starts 20 nsec after the beginning of phase 2, and phase 4 begins 20 nsec after the start of phase 3.

Each phase has a "normal" duration of 40 nsec (and so, phase 3 overlaps with phase 2, and phase 4 with phase 3). However, the phase durations can be *conditionally stretched* to take two or three times longer. Thus, a phase can have a duration of 40, 80, or 120 nsec under the conditions described as follows.

Five fields in the "current" microinstruction (i.e., the microinstruction residing in the microinstruction register) control the clock stretch conditions. Call these fields, F1, F2, . . . , F5. The microinstruction duration is doubled when *any* of the fields F1–F4 are nonzero. This type of stretching is called an *implicit* stretch. The other field, F5, is used to *explicitly* define a stretch in the microinstruction execution time. The duration is doubled when F5 is nonzero.

If an implicit and an explicit stretch *both* occur, the duration of each clock phase is tripled.

Develop an S*M specification of this timing scheme.

[*Hint*: Keep in mind that the S*M user attempts to capture the functional and timing *behavior* of a system. Thus, there does not *have* to be a structural one-to-one correspondence between entities in the S*M description and the entities in the system being described.]

4.12 [P.A. Wilsey.] Consider the store multiple instruction (STM) in the IBM System/370. This instruction stores the contents of a set of general purpose registers in main memory. Assume that the registers R1, R3, B2, and D2 contain, respectively, the following values: the first register number to be stored, the last register number to be stored, the number of the base address register, and the displacement from the base address.

An operational description of the STM instruction is

```
    mm-ptr := reg [B2] + D2;
    i := R2;
L:  main-mem [mm-ptr] := reg [i];
    mm-ptr := mm-ptr + 1;
    i := i + 1
    if i ≤ R3 then goto L
```

Devise an appropriate *nonoperational iterative* construct (that is consistent with the axiomatic nature of S*M) which can be used to axiomatically specify the STM instruction.

4.13 A local store in a processor (call the store, LS) consists of 1K words. Each word is 64 bits long and consists of a 10-bit *tag* field and a 54-bit *value* associated with that tag. LS is accessed by matching the contents of a 10-bit register, R, against the tags in LS. Whenever a match is found, the associated value is loaded into a register, called G. If no match is found, a flag, F, is set.

Devise a *nonoperational iterative* construct (that is consistent with the axiomatic nature of S*M) which can be used to axiomatically specify the *functional behavior* of this subsystem.

4.14 [A small project.] Taking cues from S*M (or any other relevant language, for that matter) develop language constructs that could either enhance or replace the VHDL interface construct so that the functional and temporal behavior of an entity can be completely and autonomously specified by the interface.

[*Note*: If necessary, changes may also have to be made to the VHDL 'body' constructs to maintain coherence with the new 'interface' that you develop.]

4.15 [A research problem.] Investigate the problems of the *formal verification* of VHDL descriptions. That is, develop a formal theory (i) for after-the-fact verification of VHDL descriptions; or (ii) that can be used during the development of a VHDL description to verify the description incrementally.

4.16 [A project.] Much of the burden of assessing the "goodness" of a language is placed on the user. Such assessment is essentially of an empirical nature involving, possibly, long periods of time during which the user "discovers" the limits or capabilities of the language.

However, the language designer or specialist may also approach this issue of assessment in the following way. As in all design activities, every language is designed to satisfy certain goals or requirements. Thus, even before the language is tested empirically "in the field," it should be possible to carry out at least a theoretical assessment by investigating whether, how, and the extent to which, the language meets its stated goals.

Apply this principle to VHDL as an *architecture description language.*

(a) Establish the requirements that should be met by any CHDL that claims to be suitable for describing computer architectures (at the exo-, endo-, and micro-architectural levels).

(b) Demonstrate (with examples or logic) the extent to which VHDL meets these requirements.

CHAPTER 5

FIRMWARE ENGINEERING

5.1 INTRODUCTION

In Volume 1, Chapter 5, I noted that microprogramming was originally conceived by Wilkes (1951) as a systematic method for implementing the circuits of the control unit. This might be called the "classical" (hardware) interpretation of microprogramming.

On the other hand, some view microprogramming as a method for programming one machine — the host — so that it behaves like (or emulates) another — the target (see Volume 1, Chapter 5, Section 5.4). Furthermore, the target is more abstract than the host. Thus, in the general version of this interpretation, microprogramming is a method of programming a machine at one level of abstraction (at the micro-architectural level, in fact) to create a machine at a higher abstraction level. To emphasize the role of the microprogramming level relative to those more familiar to software and hardware designers. Opler (1967) suggested the word *firmware* as a synonym for "microcode."

One may, then, label this the "software" interpretation of microprogramming; the adoption of this view naturally raises the question as to whether one can aspire for tools and techniques for the design and implementation of firmware that are of the same order of sophistication as are available for software.

This view and the questions it led to have yielded rich dividends. The development of firmware became an object of enquiry in its own right and resulted in the emergence of a discipline of *firmware engineering* (Shriver, 1978). Broadly speaking, firmware engineering is occupied with the discovery of the scientific principles and logic governing microprogramming and their applications to the problem of producing firmware (Dasgupta and Shriver, 1985).

Most of the developments in this field have, in fact, been concerned with the way programming theory, methodology, languages, and systems can be applied to the design and implementation of firmware. The issues of principal interest in this domain are

1. The design, implementation, and use of high-level microprogramming languages.
2. Automatic methods for generating, optimizing, and compacting microcode.
3. Systematic and formal methods for firmware design.
4. The formal verification of firmware.

In this chapter I will discuss some of these aspects of firmware engineering. I will begin by identifying some of the specific characteristics of firmware (Section 5.2). High-level microprogramming is then discussed (Section 5.3). In Section 5.4 I describe developments in microcode optimization and compaction. The problems and issues of firmware verification are considered in Section 5.5. Finally, in Section 5.6, the issue of retargetability is described.

5.2 CHARACTERISTICS OF FIRMWARE

To understand the basic problems in firmware engineering, it is necessary to comprehend the characteristics of firmware and how they differ from the properties attending software. For this purpose we will consider the following issues: (1) the machine-specificity of firmware; (2) the concern for efficiency; (3) the place of firmware development in the computer design process; and (4) the nature of firmware complexity. In following the discussion of these issues, it may be convenient to refer back to Volume 1, Chapter 5, in particular, Section 5.3 where the architectural aspects of microprogramming are discussed more concretely.

5.2.1 Machine Specificity

Regardless of how one chooses to view microprogramming, the one indubitable fact is that a microprogram controls the actions of a *particular machine's hardware devices.* Moreover, the nature of this control is direct in the sense that once a micro-instruction has been fetched from control memory into the micro-instruction register there is usually only some decoding logic separating the micro-instruction from the devices that they control.[1]

Thus, microprograms, no matter how abstractly one chooses to specify them are, by their very nature, *machine specific.* For instance, the variables and operations appearing in a microprogram must designate *actual* hardware resources (registers, arithmetic units, buses, etc.) in a *specific* machine—the host that is being microprogrammed.

This can be contrasted with the modern view of programming where one abstracts as far as possible from the actual hardware. As Dijkstra (1976) has pointed out, programs specify computations on abstract machines, and it becomes the "real" computer's task to execute such programs as efficiently as possible.

5.2.2 Efficiency

The concern for efficiency surfaces for three reasons. First, the modern computer system is a multilayered, hierarchical structure in which a combination of

---

[1]The one exception to this assertion is the idea of two-level control stores (see Volume 1, Chapter 5, Section 5.3.3).

hardware, firmware, and (possibly several layers of) software creates the abstract machine that the "typical" user sees (Fig. 5.1). Since firmware realizes one of the lowest of these layers, which is then used directly or indirectly to create all the higher layers, the speed of microcode execution will have a direct bearing on the efficiency of the higher machine levels.

Second, the design of highly efficient firmware is important since microprograms must compete with hardwired (random) logic as an alternative option for implementing the control unit.

Third, reimplementing functions and tasks previously implemented in software, in the form of firmware, has emerged as an attractive means for improving a computer system's performance. This technique has come to be known as *vertical migration* (Winner and Carter, 1986; Stankovic, 1981). Clearly, the reimplemented microded function must significantly outperform the equivalent software in order to justify the development cost of vertical migration.

5.2.3 The Place of Microprogramming in the Design Cycle

In Volume I, Chapter 5 (Section 5.4), I described how the availability of writable control stores has made it possible for the systems or the applications programmer to create new architectures on a user-microprogrammable host machine. Such hosts may be "universal," such as the QM-1, or more specialized, such as the VAX-11/780 micro-architecture.

Despite this, most of the microcode that is actually produced is stored in the

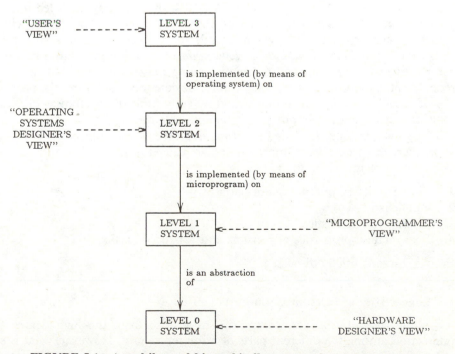

FIGURE 5.1   A multilayered hierarchically structured computer system.

control memory of *microprogrammed* computers. In such situations, firmware development proceeds hand-in-hand with processor and control-unit developments (Tredennick, 1982). The microcode will almost never be written *after* the computer has been built, as in the case of user-microprogrammable machines.

This fact may have a significant impact on the effectiveness of a given firmware engineering technique. For example, to use a high-level microprogramming language, a compiler for that language must be available. If, however, for every new computer design project a new microcode compiler is required, the heavy investment of time and money in compiler development may simply be unacceptable. Davidson (1986) has suggested that this could be one of the reasons for the lack of acceptance by manufacturers of high-level microprogramming languages.

5.2.4   The Complexity of Firmware

In the past two decades much has been written on the issue of software complexity (Wegner, 1979). It is now widely agreed that software systems become complex as the result of many reasons, including program size, the variety of environments in which they are required to function properly, and the amount of interaction and interdependencies that may exist among program modules.

One may regard the complexity issues surrounding software as issues of *macroscopic* complexity in the sense that in order to understand and cope with software design issues, the localized low-level properties of the underlying hardware are suppressed.

In contrast, firmware engineers have to deal with what may be called *microscopic* complexity, the ultimate source of which is the inherent machine-specificity of a microprogram. On the one hand, the firmware engineer strives to construct a *general, machine-independent model* of the microprogramming environment so that the tools and techniques being devised are universal in their scope. On the other hand, the model cannot deviate too much from the properties of "real" machines since that would severely limit the usefulness of these tools and/or techniques in any particular machine demain.

While machine-specificity is the ultimate source of the complexity of firmware, there are a number of more immediate causes of which the most important and problematic are the following:

1. Connectivity of microprogram parts.
2. Parallelism.
3. Timing characteristics.
4. Idiosyncratic properties of registers and functional units.

Each of these is briefly discussed.

1.   Connectivity of Microprogram Parts

As in the case of software, complexity may arise from the high degree of interaction among the different parts of a microprogram. However, what is so characteristic of firmware is that this interaction is an inherent consequence of the micro-architectures with which microprograms must deal. At the micro-architectural level there is usually a small set of stores, buses, and functional units. These are constantly used and reused by different segments of a microprogram for different purposes. In other words, a small, bounded set of resources are shared between different firmware modules.

For this reason, some of the techniques widely advocated by software engineers for controlling intermodule connectivity are seldom applicable in the firmware domain. Examples of such techniques include the idea of *thin interfaces* (Dijkstra, 1976) in which modules communicate through a small and rigorously controlled set of ports; the principle of *information hiding* (Parnas, 1972), which suggests that each module of a program should contain within it some key piece of information that cannot be accessed or even "known" by other modules; and the notion of *abstract data types,* where one encapsulates storage objects together with a set of procedures defined on these objects (Liskov, 1980).

In practical terms, a microprogram expressed in a high-level language, say, would more likely possess the structure shown in Figure 5.2 than the more desirable structure of Figure 5.3.

2. Rules of Parallelism

Horizontal host machines are characterized by the fact that several micro-operations encoded in appropriate fields within a micro-instruction may be executed in parallel. To understand the nature of this *microparallelism,* let us consider a number of possible situations.

Let M_i, M_j be two micro-operations, and let $SOURCE_i$, $SOURCE_j$ denote the *data source* sets of M_i, M_j, respectively. Similarly, $DEST_i$, $DEST_j$ denote the *result destination* sets of M_i, M_j, respectively. Finally, let $UNIT_i$, $UNIT_j$ denote the sets of *functional units* required to execute M_i, M_j, respectively.

Then the simplest set of conditions under which M_i, M_j may execute in parallel can be stated as

[RULE 1] $(SOURCE_i \cap DEST_j = \emptyset)$ and $(DEST_i \cap SOURCE_j = \emptyset)$ and $(DEST_i \cap DEST_j = \emptyset) \land (UNIT_i \cap UNIT_j = \emptyset)$

where $\emptyset$ is the empty set.[2]

_____

[2]See also the conditions for hazard formation in pipelined processors discussed in Chapter 6, Section 6 3.2.

```
microprogram M1;

    <global declaration of all data objects>;

    proc P1 <procedure body> endproc;
    proc P2 <procedure body> endproc;
    . . . . . . . . . . . . . . . .
    proc Pn <procedure body> endproc;

endprogram
```

FIGURE 5.2   Procedures interfacing through a common set of data objects.

```
microprogram M1';

    <global declaration of a few data objects>;

proc P1' (<input/output parameters>);
    <local data object declarations>
    <procedure body>
endproc;
. . . . . . . . . . . . . .
proc Pn' (<input/output parameters>);
    <local data object declarations>
    <procedure body>
endproc;

endprogram
```

FIGURE 5.3   Desirable structure of a microprogram.

Unfortunately, microparallelism does not simply consist of the issue of whether two or more micro-operations can execute "simultaneously," as is implied in RULE 1. Rather, the relevant question is

What conditions would have to be satisfied in order for two or more micro-operations to be allocated to the same micro-instruction?

Clearly, some additional parameters must be considered in order to accommodate this revised view of microparallelism.

First, we note that in order for micro-operations to be executed from a micro-instruction they must be encoded in fields of the micro-instruction. Let $FIELDS_i$ denote the *set of fields* of the micro-instruction that encode for a given micro-operation M_i. In general, a micro-operation may require one or more fields for its complete specification.

Clearly, assuming that the field encodings are not identical, a necessary condition for placing two micro-operations in the same micro-instruction is that they do not require the same set (or subset) of fields. That is

$$FIELDS_i \cap FIELDS_j = \emptyset$$

Second, micro-operations appearing together in a micro-instruction do not all necessarily execute "at the same time." More specifically, a micro-instruction will *usually* execute in a fixed period of time called the *microcycle;* a few micro-operations (such as main memory read or write) may require two or more microcycles, in which case the micro-instruction containing them will execute in the corresponding number of cycles; but otherwise the time to execute micro-operations may be much shorter than the microcycle, in which case different micro-operations may be executed in different *phases* of a *polyphase* microcycle.

In general, let $TIME_i$, $TIME_j$ denote the timing attributes of micro-operations M_i, M_j, respectively. If there is no overlap of $TIME_i$, $TIME_j$, it is possible for M_i, M_j to be encoded in and executed from the same microinstruction even though their data and functional unit resources may not satisfy RULE 1. On the other hand, if there is an overlap in their timing attributes, RULE 1 must be satisfied. These considerations lead us to the following revised rule of parallelism:[3]

[RULE 2] $(FIELDS_i \cap FIELDS_j = \emptyset)$ and $(TIME_i \cap TIME_j = \emptyset)$

or

$(FIELDS_i \cap FIELDS_j = \emptyset)$ and $(TIME_i \cap TIME_j \neq \emptyset)$ and [RULE 1]

These appear to be reasonably general conditions for microparallelism. Yet there are situations in which this rule may not suffice.

Example 5.1

Consider the following two micro-operations:

M1: mbr := mem[pc]
M2: pc := pc + 1

for which the resources and timing attributes are as follows:

$SOURCE_1 = \{mem, pc\}$	$SOURCE_2 = \{pc, "1"\}$
$DEST_1 \quad = \{mbr\}$	$DEST_2 \quad = \{pc\}$
$UNIT_1 \quad = \{mem.unit\}$	$UNIT_2 \quad = \{incrementer\}$
$FIELDS_1 = \{f_1, f_2\}$	$FIELDS_2 = \{f_3\}$
$TIME_1 \quad = \{clock\_C\}$	$TIME_2 \quad = \{clock\_C.phase2\}$

where clock_C is a two-phase microcycle. The duration of M1's execution is the entire microcycle, whereas M2 is executed in the second phase of the microcycle. It is observed that

1. $SOURCE_1 \cap DEST_2 \neq \emptyset$
2. $TIME_1 \cap TIME_2 \neq \emptyset$

Hence, according to RULE 2, M1 and M2 cannot be placed in the same micro-instruction. However, suppose that during M1's execution pc is "released" at the end of clock_C.phase1. Since M2 only needs pc during clock C.phase2, these two micro-operations could legitimately be executed from the same micro-instruction. ∎

In other words, the (potential) microparallelism between micro-operations may require a deeper analysis of the pattern of resource request and release using a *finer grain of time* than is given by the timing attributes of the micro-operations. Later, in Section 5.5, I will describe an analysis of this problem by Damm and colleagues. In passing, it should be noted that this example is not hypothetical; it is based on the characteristics of a number of machines (Varian, 1975; Shriver and Kornerup, 1980).

---

[3]RULE 2 (as also RULE 1) merely stipulates the *potential* for parallelism based on the characteristics of the microoperations. Whether two microoperations can *actually* be placed in the same micro-instruction depends on other factors, as will be seen in Section 5.4.

3. Temporal Issues

From a consideration of the various aspects of micro-architecture (see Volume 1, Chapter 5, in particular Sections 5.3.2 – 5.3.4) and the foregoing discussion, it should be obvious that the treatment of *time* constitutes one of the most problematic features in firmware engineering. There are not only wide variations in the temporal characteristics of different micro-architectures; but also within a micro-architecture. Thus:

1. Micro-instructions may execute in monophase or polyphase mode.
2. Certain micro-instructions may require several microcycles if they encode micro-operations that require several microcycles for their complete execution.
3. The duration of a particular micro-operation M_j (say) may extend beyond the duration of the micro-instruction I_k containing it. However, the execution of the "next" micro-instruction I_{k+1} will not be delayed unless M_j also appears in I_{k+1}.
4. There may be different schemes for sequencing the phases of the micro-instruction fetch/decode/execute cycle. This may range from a strictly serial scheme to a pipelined mode.
5. Within the duration of a micro-operation's execution, resources may be required and released at different points of time.

Thus, the firmware engineer is posed the problem of constructing a powerful, general *model of time* that allows as many of these variations to be captured in order that the tools and techniques that are developed are independent of the temporal features of a given micro-architecture.

4. Idiosyncratic Features of Host Machines

The complexity of firmware is further manifested in terms of the various idiosyncrasies that micro-architectures exhibit. The most prominent of these are

1. The presence of *transient* stores. In general, stores such as registers retain their value unless a new value is explicitly written to the store through the execution of some micro-operation. Such stores may be termed *static*. In contrast, a transient store is one whose value can change either through an explicit operation or implicitly *after the elapse of a specified period of time*.

Example 5.2

Consider the output latch of an arithmetic/logic unit (ALU). This may hold the result of the most recent ALU operation for a specific time period after which it is reset to zero. ∎

Example 5.3

Condition code flags are often transient and must be tested within a definite interval from when they are set. ∎

The problem with transient stores, then, is that if such a store is the destination of a micro-operation then any other micro-operation requiring this store value as an input must be executed before the value disappears. Transient stores appearing as variables in microprograms may, therefore, have to be treated as special cases in both microcode optimization and compaction and microcode verification.

2. The presence of *residual control* (see Volume 1, Chapter 5, Section 5.3.3). In such schemes control information may be placed in special (residual control) registers and even in special fields of the micro-instruction register *during the execution of the microprogram.* It turns out that many of the host machine models used in firmware design tools and techniques assume that all control information is localized in the micro-operations and that all resources required by these operations can be determined prior to the execution of the microprogram. Residual control and its implications are thus ignored.

3. The occurrence of *side effects.* Side effects may result from the execution of even the most innocuous-looking micro-operations. These include, for example, the setting of condition codes as a result of executing ALU operations or buses being set to certain (possibly transient) values when register-to-register transfers (*via* these buses) are done.

    The occurrence of such side effects is an example of the distinction that can be made between programs and microprograms in certain contexts, as, for instance, in verification.

Example 5.4

In the *axiomatic approach* to program verification, the "standard" axiom of the assignment statement

$$X := E$$

is given as

$$\{P[X/E]\}\ X := E\ \{P\}$$

where if P is an assertion (the postcondition) that is true after execution of the assignment, then P[X/E] (i.e., P with all free occurrences of X replaced by E) is the assertion (the precondition) that is true prior to its execution.[4] If an assignment statement appears in a microprogram, however, and this statement represents a micro-operation with side effects, then this axiom would not be appropriate. Thus, a micro-operation

$$AOUT := AIL + AIR$$

which, in addition to performing the operations explicitly stated, generates as

---

[4]Axiomatic semantics is discussed in the Appendix, Section A.3. The axiomatic approach to program verification is explained in Section A.5.

"side effects" condition code values. Suppose the postcondition for this statement is

AOUT = 20 ∧ OVERFLOW = 1

then applying the axiom of assignment "backward" produces as a precondition

AIL + AIR = 20 ∧ OVERFLOW = 1

However, the condition OVERFLOW = 1 is produced as a *result* of the add operation and should not have been propagated back into the precondition. The axiom of assignment in its standard form is clearly not sufficient for characterizing the behavior of certain microoperations. ∎

In concluding this section on the characteristics of firmware (and how they resemble or differ from software) some remarks need to be made about the *sizes* of microprograms. Compared to many system or application programs, microprograms are generally small in terms of the number of control store words that they typically occupy. Thus, one cannot refer to firmware as an example of "large-scale" systems in the sense that this term is used in the context of software.[5] Size, as such, is not a significant factor contributing to the complexity of firmware. Furthermore, the sizes of microprograms are affected in an obvious way by the precise trade-offs used between hardware, software, and firmware in implementing a processor. Thus, the real complexity of firmware stems from the other factors discussed herein, namely, connectivity issues, parallelism, temporal properties, and the idiosyncrasies of host machines in general, coupled with the need for efficiency.

5.3 HIGH-LEVEL MICROPROGRAMMING

Perhaps the first and most important goal of firmware engineering has been the design and implementation of *high-level microprogramming languages* (HLMLs). The reasons are fairly obvious: As in many other aspects of computer systems design, the objective here was to create an abstract view of the host machine so as to facilitate the design, description, and comprehension of reliable firmware.

Systematic research on HLMLs may be said to have begun with Eckhouse's (1971) Ph.D. dissertation.[6] Stated simply, the initial research goal was one of

---

[5]For example, the PDP-11/60, which had significantly more microcode than other members of the PDP-11 series, used 2410 words of 48 bits/word control store (Snow and Siewiorek, 1978). The VAX-11/780 required a total of 5K words of 99 bits/word control store (Digital, 1979). Further data on these and other computers are summarized in Dasgupta and Shriver (1985).

One must point out, though, that in very recent times, systems have emerged with much larger control stores. For example, some modern microcoded graphics processors have 64K–256K words of control stores with 60–125 bits/word (R. A. Mueller, personal communication).

[6]There were, however, several interesting earlier discussions of the possibility of high-level microprogramming. See the section on Historical Remarks at the end of this chapter.

technology transfer—that is, to apply the techniques and principles of programming language design to the microprogramming domain. It was thought that given such a language the microprogrammer would be able to concentrate on characterizing the structure and behavior of the target machine (e.g., the exo-architecture being implemented) rather than be concerned with the problem of mapping the target machine on to the host micro-architecture. The task of producing this mapping would be delegated to a *microcode compiler.*

In reality, of course, this ideal had to be modified somewhat because of the issues described in Section 5.2—notably, the machine-specificity of microprograms. Thus research on high-level microprogramming has advanced on a number of different fronts; and as a result, a number of languages based on different design philosophies have been proposed since about 1970.

5.3.1   A Classification of Microprogramming Languages

It is convenient to describe the different approaches to microprogramming language design in terms of a general classification scheme suggested by Davidson (1986).[7] This scheme is based on two criteria: the *level* of the language, and whether or not the language is *host machine dependent.*

Language Level

The level of a language characterizes how similar the features of the language are to typical features of a host machine's micro-architecture.

Generally speaking, a *low-level* microprogramming language typically contains

1. Operators that can be mapped onto single micro-operations or, possibly, single micro-instructions.
2. The capability to use host machine storage resources directly as the variables of a microprogram.
3. A rather primitive set of control statements that mirror the common sequencing logic in host machines.

A *high-level* language, in contrast, will usually

1. Contain operators that are functionally more powerful than those that are typically encodable in a single micro-operation or even a single micro-instruction. Such operators will generally have to be compiled into an ordered set of host machine operations.
2. Allow the microprogrammer to define *virtual* stores (i.e., "variables" in the programming languages sense). Thus, at least some amount of register and storage allocation will have to be performed by a microcode compiler.

---

[7]While on the question of taxonomy, you may also refer back to Chapter 3 (Section 3.2) where a classification of hardware description languages (HDLs) based on abstraction levels is presented. There, microprogramming languages are considered as a subclass of the class of HDLs (see also, Table 3.1). However, as will be seen in this chapter, the development of microprogramming languages has mostly been influenced by the principles of programming languages rather than HDLs.

3. Contain a set of control statements that are typically more powerful than those available in host machines.

Machine Dependence

A (host) *machine dependent* microprogramming language is one in which the operators, storage elements, and control statements are specific to a particular host architecture. That is, the problem of *binding* (or mapping) the variables and operators appearing in a program written in the microprogramming language to the storage and functional resources of a host machine is resolved at the language-definition level. In the case of a *machine-independent* language, it is the job of the compiler to perform this binding: The microprogrammer's ability to define variables, construct expressions using the language-defined operators, and use control statements are not dictated by any particular micro-architecture.

Thus, in simplest terms, the extent to which a language is independent of particular host machines is determined by the nature and extent to which the burden of binding is assigned to the microcode compiler.

Using these two criteria, most of the proposed microprogramming languages appear to fall into one of the following categories.

1. Low-level machine-dependent (LLMD) languages. For example, GMPL (Guffin, 1982).
2. Low-level machine-independent (LLMI) languages. An example is YALLL (Patterson, Lew, and Tuck, 1979).
3. High-level machine-dependent (HLMD) languages. Examples include MPL (Eckhouse, 1971) and STRUM (Patterson, 1976).
4. High-level, partially machine-independent (HLPMI) languages. For example, Marble (Davidson and Shriver, 1980), S* (Dasgupta, 1980), and Ohne (Wagnon and Maine, 1983).
5. High-level machine-independent (HLMI) languages. Examples include VMPL (Lewis, Malik, and Ma, 1980) and various microprogramming-level versions of C—the so-called "Micro-C" languages (Gurd, 1983; Duda and Mueller, 1984; Hopkins, Horton, and Arnold, 1985).

These categories and their constituent languages have been recently surveyed by Dasgupta and Shriver (1985) and Davidson (1986). These, together with slightly older reviews by Sint (1980), Dasgupta (1980), and Davidson and Shriver (1980) provide a comprehensive picture of the developments in HLML design and philosophy.

Thus, in this chapter, rather than consider the entire space of HLMLs, I will describe a few specific languages from the HLPMI and HLMI categories since these appear to address best the most ambitious goals of HLML design: How to create firmware development systems that are applicable across a reasonably wide range of host machine architectures.

5.3.2 S* and Its Extensions

An example of a high-level partially machine-independent (HLPMI) language is S* (Dasgupta, 1980, 1984). The assumptions underlying the design of S* were the following:

1. The idiosyncratic characteristics of host micro-architectures (see the last part of Section 5.2.4) make themselves most felt at the micro-operation level. These operations correspond to such language constructs as assignment statements, arithmetic, logical, and shift expressions, and relational expressions. Thus, the syntax and semantics of these constructs should, from a pragmatic viewpoint, be bound to individual host machines rather than be defined in machine-independent terms.
2. In contrast, the rules of composition for microprograms appear to be common across micro-architectures. Thus, the syntax and semantics of composite statements can be formulated in a machine-independent manner.
3. Although automatic optimization and compaction of microcode (by a microcode compiler) is highly desirable, there are limits to which this can be achieved by purely mechanical means. Thus, it would be desirable for the microprogrammer to have the choice of optimizing the code at the source language level itself—say, in the case of time-critical or heavily used segments of the microprogram. For less critical segments, optimization may be delegated to the compiler.
4. A great deal of the complexity of writing low-level microprograms stems from the (often) baroque organization of microinstructions and the need for the microprogrammer to be aware of these organizations. It is, thus, desirable to free the microprogrammer from having to be concerned with such matters that are internal to the control unit architecture.

A language satisfying these issues cannot be wholly machine-independent. It would rather be a partially machine-independent language—a language *schema,* in fact—that with some augmentation could be used for specific host machines. S* was proposed as such a schema. It actually denotes a *family of microprogramming languages* such that for a given micro-architecture A (say), a particular language S*(A) is obtained by completing the (inherently) incomplete syntax and semantics of S* based on the idiosyncrasies of A. S* is then said to be *instantiated* to a particular language S*(A).[8]

An Overview of S*

The only primitive *data type* in S* is the *bit,* which consists of the values {0,1}. Instances of type *bit* may be structured into an ordered *sequence* or into the higher-order types *array, stack,* and *tuple* (which is similar to the Pascal *record*

---

[8]An instantiation of S* for the von Neumann machine, called S* (VN), was informally introduced and used in Volume 1, Chapter 5, Section 5.2.4, for describing the microprogram for the von Neumann machine.

type). Since an instantiation, S*(A) (say), is a machine-*dependent* language, the microprogrammer cannot freely create data objects as and when required. The only data objects available to the programmer are those defined in the instantiated language, which in turn are determined by the stores available in the host machine A. All such data objects are, however, instances of S* data types. Furthermore, programmer-defined names may be assigned to data objects using *synonym* declarations.

Example 5.5

```
/* data objects in the Microdata 1600 **/
    type register = seq [7..0] bit;

    var   md_reg, out_reg, t_reg, u_reg : register;
    var   regfile: array [1..30] of register;
    var   mar : tuple
                    m = seq [7..0] bit
                    n = seq [7..0] bit
                endtup
    syn   index_reg1 = regfile [1],
          index_reg2 = regfile [2],
          stack_ptr = regfile [3];                                    ∎
```

The general form for the *assignment* statement in S* is

$$X_1, X_2, \ldots, X_n := E$$

The precise syntax and semantics of legal assignment statements, including the legal form of the expression E, are determined during instantiation. Similarly, the valid syntax and semantics of the Boolean expressions that may appear in conditional and repetition statements are not defined in S*. They are determined during instantiation.

The machine-independent constructs in S* include the usual composite and control statements: sequential composition; the *if*, *while*, and *repeat* statements; the procedure *call*; and the *goto*. All procedures are declared without parameters. Of more interest are two constructs that allow the programmer to specify low-level *parallelism* within a microprogram. These can be explained as follows:

Let $S_1 \theta S_2$ signify either

$$S_1 \| S_2$$

or

$$S_1 ; S_2$$

where S_1, S_2 are statements; $S_1 \| S_2$ denotes the *parallel* composition of S_1, S_2; and $S_1 ; S_2$ denotes sequential composition. The execution of "$S_1 \| S_2$" causes these statements to be executed in parallel. It terminates when both S_1 and S_2 have terminated. The S* schema includes the constructs

cocycle $S_1\theta S_2$ **coend**
stcycle $S_1\theta S_2$ **stend**

such that in the *cocycle* statement S_1,S_2 are simple or composite statements and in the *stcycle* statement, S_1,S_2 are simple, composite or (embedded) *stcycle* or *cocycle* statements.[9]

The *cocycle* construct indicates that the composite event "$S_1\theta S_2$" begins and ends *in the same microcycle*. When "θ" is "||" then S_1 and S_2 *overlap* in their execution. When "θ" is ";" then S_1,S_2 execute *in sequence,* though still within the confines of a microcycle.

The *stcycle* statement signifies that the composite statement "$S_1\theta S_2$" begins executing in a new microcycle. Precisely when it will end is left unspecified but can, in principle, be known from the details of S_1 and S_2. Again, "θ" has the same significance as in the *cocycle* statement except that the termination is not confined to occur in a single microcycle.

Example 5.6

(a) /* Enable alu and cond.codes and do acc := acc + gpr[1] + 1 */
    cocycle
        alucode := 1; carryin := 1; acc := acc + gpr[1]
    coend
(b) /* read from memory and execute alu operation */
    stcycle
        ibr := mem[pc] || acc := acc + gpr[6]
    stend

In **(a)** the three statements are executed sequentially but within the same microcycle. The form of this *cocycle* implies the presence of a polyphase microcycle (see Volume 1, Chapter 5, Section 5.3.4); furthermore, the legality of this instruction depends on whether these particular assignments can be executed in distinct, relatively ordered phases of the microcycle as implied here. Thus, knowing the syntax and semantics of the schema S* allows a reader to *understand* the meaning of this statement; however, the writer of such a statement must know the timing attributes of its constituent assignment statements. It is in this sense that instantiated versions of S* are machine-specific.

In **(b)** the two statements begin together in a "new" microcycle, but the duration of the *stcycle* as a whole depends on the timing attributes of its components. The reason why the two statements were composed into a *stcycle* statement is that in this particular instantiated language the memory read statement "ibr := mem[pc]" may take several microcycles to complete. ∎

[9]A *simple* statement in an instantiated version of S* represents primitive microoperations in the host machine. A *composite* of simple statements $S_1, \ldots, S_n$, is the statement $S_1\theta S_2\theta \ldots \theta S_n$, possibly with the addition of parenthetic delimiters. The simple statements in S* include the assignment, the *if* statement, *call, return,* and the *goto.* For a complete definition of the syntax and semantics of S*, refer to Dasgupta (1984, Chapter 10 and Appendix B).

The first complete instantiation of S* was for the nanolevel architecture of the QM-1.[10] The resulting language was called S*(QM-1) (Klassen and Dasgupta, 1981; Dasgupta, 1984). There were several objectives in carrying out this instantiation:

1. To experiment with the viability of instantiating S* with respect to a rather complex micro-architecture such as the QM-1 provided.
2. To investigate the extent to which code generated from a HLML program could be compacted into highly horizontal code (Rideout, 1981; see also Section 5.4 in this chapter).
3. To provide a basis for constructing a proof theory for verifying horizontal microprograms (Dasgupta and Wagner, 1984; see also Section 5.5 in this chapter).
4. To see how a microprogramming language could be used in the systematic design of an architecture (Dasgupta and Olafsson, 1982; see also Section 5.5 in this chapter).

The AADL/S* System

A serious defect in the development of S*(QM-1) was that the instantiation process was ad hoc. A far more elegant approach to instantiation has been developed by Damm and coworkers in the AADL/S* system (Damm, 1984, 1985; Damm *et al.,* 1986).

The instantiation procedure is schematically shown in Figure 5.4. A host machine A is described formally in the *architecture description language* AADL.[11] An A-specific microprogramming language S*(A) is instantiated from

---

[10]The Nanodata QM-1 (Nanodata, 1979) is characterized by a *dual level* control store, each defining a distinct micro-architectural level. The lower and more complex of these is the "nanolevel" architecture. For more on this, see Volume 1, Chapter 5, Section 5.3.3.

[11]AADL is an acronym for *axiomatic architecture description language.* Within the framework of the hardware description space discussed in Chapter 3 (Section 3.2), it belongs to the class of functional languages and is, specifically, in the axiomatic style of functional languages (see Section 3.2.3). Thus, there are many points of similarity between AADL and the language S*M described in Chapter 4 (Section 4.3).

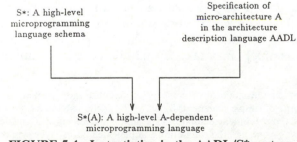

FIGURE 5.4   Instantiation in the AADL/S* system.

S* according to the AADL description of A. The process depicted in Figure 5.4 thus, in a sense, formalizes the notion of instantiation.

An AADL description has the general form shown in Figure 5.5. The clock description part specifies the clocking scheme controlling the host. This specification describes the various phases of the clock, their durations, and their positions relative to one another. The timing attributes of all microoperations are defined with respect to the clock specification.

The block diagram part specifies the storage elements and the data paths that are visible to the microprogrammer. The microinstruction format part describes the structure of the host microinstructions. The final component in an AADL description is a set of detailed functional specifications of the host machine's microoperations.

Figures 5.6 through 5.9 show examples of each of these components from an AADL specification of the Microdata 1600 micro-architecture (Doehmen, 1985).[12] While Figures 5.6 through 5.8 are reasonably self-explanatory, the micro-operation description in Figure 5.9 needs some clarification.

The *pattern* provides an appropriate *notation* for referring to the micro-operation within an S* (Microdata) program, for example,

primary-file[x] := primary-file[x] + directoperand

It also suggests the principal action performed by the operation.

Whereas the *sources* and *sinks* field denote the primary data objects used by the micro-operation, the *auxiliarysources* and *auxiliarysinks* fields list additional data objects, the values of which are required or set during the micro-operation's execution. The *conditions* field states the invariant conditions that must be true at the beginning of, and during, the execution of the operation.

The semantics of the microoperation are given by its *semantics* and *sideeffects* clauses. Each "side" effect is given in the form of a pre-/postcondition pair. As can be seen from Figure 5.9, the semantics of this particular microoperation have three distinct components.

---

[12]The Microdata 1600 (Microdata, 1970) is a vertically organized 8-bit user-microprogrammable emulation engine—a somewhat restricted "universal" host machine (see Volume 1, Chapter 5, Section 5.4.2). Its architecture and application in emulation has been described by Banerji and Raymond (1982, Chapter 9).

```
architecture Microdata 1600 :
    /* clock specification part */
    . . . . . . . . . . .
    /* block diagram part */
    . . . . . . . . . . .
    /* microinstruction format part */
    . . . . . . . . . . .
    /* microoperations definition part */
    . . . . . . . . . . .
endarchitecture
```

FIGURE 5.5 Structure of a micro-architecture description in AADL (based on Doehmen, 1985).

```
unittime 1 nanoseconds

clock microphases dur 200
    phase
        P1 dur 50,
        P2 dur 50,
        P3 dur 50,
        P4 dur 50
    endphase
    synchronization
        startof microphases = startof P1
        startof P2 = endof P1
        startof P3 = endof P2
        startof P4 = endof P3
        endof microphases = endof P4
    endsynchronization
```

FIGURE 5.6   AADL specification of the Microdata 1600 clocking scheme (based on Doehmen, 1985).

Figure 5.10 describes a S*(Microdata) procedure that is part of a Data General NOVA emulator written for the Microdata 1600 (Doehmen, 1985). The following comments will be helpful for understanding this program.

1. Each invocation of a Microdata 1600 microoperation can be specified in terms of an instance of its *pattern*, for example,

    IL := IL + **hex** B6

    or by augmenting the pattern instance with the micro-operation *name*, for example,

    <IL := IL + **hex** B6, add dir_op to file_register primary>

    Note that the pattern for this microoperation (Fig. 5.9) is:

    primary_file[x] := primary_file[x] + directoperand

2. The assignment

    U_register := LOR (. . .)

```
blockdiagram memory section:
    types
        data : sequence <7..0> bit
    variables
        M_register, N_register : register,
        input_bus : data,
        memory : array [0..65535] of data with A_register
    pseudovariables
        OD_register : data
    synonyms
        A_register = M_register : N_register
endblockdiagram    /* memory section */
```

FIGURE 5.7   A fragment of the block diagram part from the Microdata 1600 description (Doehmen, 1985).

```
microword controword :

    format address_instruction :
        op_code = <15..12>, address = <11..0>
    endformat
    ........
    format file_register_instruction :
        op_code = <15..12>,
        file_register_designator = <11..8>,
        literal = <7..0>
    endformat
    ........

endmicroword
```

FIGURE 5.8 Microinstruction formats (Doehmen, 1985).

```
function add_dir_op to file_register primary :
  pattern
      primary_file[x] := primary_file[x] + directoperand
  sinks primary_file[x]
  sources x : file_select, primary_file[x],
      directoperand : directop_bin or directop_hex
  auxiliarysinks modification_enable, modify_register
  auxiliarysources bank_select, modify_register
  sideeffects
    then
      modify :
        pre true
        post primary_file[x] = primary_file[x]'
           add (directoperand and modify_register'),
      enable modification :
        pre true
        post modification_enable = on,
      reset modify register :
        pre true
        post modify_register = ones
  conditions bank_select = primary
  semantics + : bit (8) × bit (8) → bit (8)
  timingvalidity P1..P4
  microfield file_register_instruction.opcode = hex 3,
      file_register_instruction.literal = directoperand,
      file_register_instruction.file_register_designator = X
endfunction
```

FIGURE 5.9 (Partial) description of a Microdata 1600 micro-operation (Doehmen, 1985).

```
procedure load_accumulator
  stcycle
    < T_register := memory[A_register], read memory > ;
    < memory[A_register] := T_register, refresh after read >
  stend;
  <IL := IL + hex B6, add dir_op to file register primary > ;
  U_register := LOR(IL, T_register, 0, select_zeroes, 0, 0);
  primary_file[F0 or U_register < 3..0 > ]
    := COP(primary_ file [F0 or U_register < 3..0 > ],
       0, 0, T_operand, 0, rewrite_file);
  N_register := LOR(OL, T_register, 0, select_zeroes, 0, 0);
  stcycle
    M_register := MOD(OU, no_operation, 0);
    T_register := memory[A_register];
    do
      memory[A_register] := T_register
      ||cocycle
        primary_file[F1 or U_register < 3..0 > ]
          := COP (primary_file[F1 or U_register < 3..0 > ],
                  0, 0, T_operand, 0, rewrite_file);
    coend
    od
  stend
endprocedure   /* load accumulator */
```

FIGURE 5.10   A sample S*(Microdata) procedure (Doehmen, 1985).

is an instance of the "logical or primary" microoperation that has the pattern (not shown here)

$$Y := LOR (\ . \ . \ . \ )$$

where the LOR operator is a rather complex function defined over arguments of the types specified in the pattern.

The AADL/S* system is significant in a number of different ways:

1. It provides a rigorous method for instantiating S* for any host architecture that can be described in AADL. One such instantiation—S* (Microdata)—has been completely carried out for the Microdata 1600.
2. It establishes a framework for the systematic design of computer architectures using stepwise refinement. The development of a Microdata 1600 emulator for the Data General NOVA was successfully realized using this method.
3. The system provides a basis for the axiomatic verification of firmware. This aspect will be further discussed in Section 5.5.
4. Finally, AADL not only allows for instantiating S*; it also paves the way for the construction of retargetable firmware development systems (see Section 5.6). Currently (1987), a team from the Technische Hochschule Aachen and the University of Kiel is implementing such a system.

5.3.3 "C" as a Microprogramming Language

Within the taxonomic framework described in Section 5.3.1, the class of HLMI languages represents the most ambitious approach to high-level microprogramming. In theory, a language in this category is one in which the constructs and features are independent of any particular micro-architecture. At the same time, the language and its associated compiler must have the power to generate satisficing microcode for a reasonably broad spectrum of micro-architectures.[13]

Of the many proposals for the attainment of the goals, some are based on new language designs (Dewitt, 1976; Lewis, Malik, and Ma, 1980; Davidson and Shriver, 1980). The more recent and, it seems, more profitable tendency has been to use variants and subsets of the programming language C (Kernighan and Ritchie, 1978) as a machine-independent microprogramming language. At least three such systems have been described (Gurd, 1983; Duda and Mueller, 1984; Hopkins, Horton, and Arnold, 1985).

The advantages of using an existing *programming language* for microprogramming are fairly obvious.

1. System designers are likely to be familiar with the language, thus making it not only easier for such persons to be brought into a firmware development project but also easier for them to understand, maintain, modify, or rewrite firmware that has already been written and documented in the language.
2. In any of the more well known and widely used programming languages there will be a considerable corpus of existing software that can, when needed, be compiled into microcode with little (re)microprogramming. This becomes a particularly useful fact when such software is to be *migrated* down into firmware.[14]

The particular advantages of C as microprogramming language (as opposed to other programming languages such as Pascal) are (Hopkins, Horton, and Arnold, 1985):

1. C has data types and operations that appear to be more directly mappable

---

[13]Ideally, one would like *optimal* code to be generated from such high-level microprograms. However, it has been shown by DeWitt (1976) that the problem of producing an optimal (i.e., minimal) sequence of microinstructions from a straight-like sequence of micro-operations is NP-hard, although under more restricted conditions the problem has been shown to be solvable in polynomial time by Vegdahl (1982a) (see also Section 5.4). Thus, in most practical cases the goal is to generate code that is *satisficing* (Simon, 1981)—that is, acceptably good—rather than optimal. One criterion of satisficability is that the executable microcode produced for some set of benchmarks is at least as efficient as functionally equivalent hand-produced microcode.

[14]In a multilayered, hierarchically structured system of the type depicted in Figure 5.1, *vertical migration* refers to the technique of reorganizing and redefining the system layers by moving functions implemented at a given level to some lower level. The objective is to improve the performance of the system. The most usual means of effecting vertical migration is to move software-implemented functions into microcode. The implementability of vertical migration in this case depends on the availability of writable control stores and the techniques of dynamic microprogramming (see Volume I, Chapter 5, Section 5.4.2). For more on vertical migration and its relationship to dynamic microprogramming, refer to Stankovic (1981) and Winner and Carter (1986).

into microcode than are constructs of other languages. C also has some features—for instance, the *register* class of stores—that are useful for the programmer to assist a C compiler in carrying out machine-independent optimizations.

2. Providing that the microprogramming version of C is compatible with standard C, microprograms can be tested and debugged on a standard UNIX environment (with all its attendent support tools) before compiling code for the actual host machine.

Given the many oddities of individual micro-architectures, and given the importance of microcode efficiency, the obvious question that comes to mind is whether *it is possible to specify a microprogram in a completely host machine independent way and still allow for the automatic generation of satisficing executable microcode?*

At this time, we do not have an answer to this question and in my opinion the answer is most likely to be negative. For example, an experimental retargetable microcode generation system has been described by Hopkins and coworkers.[15] The system uses a subset of C, named Micro-C, as the source microprogramming language. The ability of the Micro-C compilation system to generate satisficing code has yet to be reported. However, Hopkins and coworkers have noted the desirability of certain extensions to C that would both aid register allocation during compilation and also permit the microprogrammer to specify particular characteristics of the host machine itself.

5.4 MICROCODE OPTIMIZATION AND COMPACTION

As already noted, the practicality of HLMLs—regardless of whether they are partially or fully machine-independent—rests critically on the compiler's ability to carry out effective optimization of the microcode and produce code comparable in efficiency to that produced by the traditional (assembly language style) method. This observation has prompted a great deal of research during the 1970s and 1980s into the theory and practice of microcode compaction and optimization.

In microprogramming, the word *optimization* is used in essentially the same sense as in the context of conventional compilers (Aho and Ullman, 1977). Optimization refers to the menu of strategies used to improve the execution time of object code by *transforming* the code. *Compaction,* in contrast, does not attempt to transform code. Its objective is to take "vertical" microcode—a microprogram—and construct a sequence of micro-instructions (each of which

---

[15]In the context of microprogramming, "retargetability" is synonymous to "host machine independent." Thus, a retargetable microprogramming system is one that can be used to develop, debug, verify, and generate microcode (from a high-level language description of the microprogram) for a wide variety of host machines. For more on retargetability, see Section 5.6.

may consist of one or more of the original micro-operations) so as to minimize as far as possible the number of micro-instructions or the execution time. Compaction is, thus, an exercise in code *reorganization* and is associated with horizontally organized micro-architectures.

A *microprogramming system* is any integrated set of tools and techniques that can be used in the firmware design and implementation process. Figure 5.11 shows the principle components of such a system for generating, optimizing, compacting, and simulating microcode and the flow of the microprogram and other items of information through these components. Although the details and the composition of the individual components will differ, as also will the nature and extent to which the components interact with and depend on one another, most of the microprogramming systems that have been implemented (Ma and Lewis, 1980, 1981; Baba and Hagiwara, 1981; Sheraga and Gieser, 1983; Marwedel, 1984) or are under construction (Mueller and Varghese, 1985; Hopkins, Horton, and Arnold, 1985) exhibit this general structure.[16]

---

[16]See Section 5.6 for a discussion of such retargetable microprogramming systems.

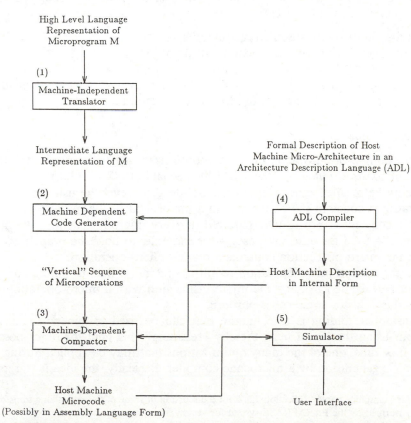

FIGURE 5.11 Structure of a retargetable microprogramming system.

For our purposes, we will assume that optimization techniques will be applied by components (1) and (2), whereas, of course, compaction is performed by component (3).

5.4.1 Optimization

As in the case of optimizing compilers for programming languages, optimization may be (host) machine-independent or machine-dependent. Strategies for *machine-independent* optimization are largely based on related techniques developed for software.[17] Many of these strategies and their relevance to the firmware domain were first discussed by Kleir and Ramamoorthy (1971). This was the earliest paper on microcode optimization; it provided the stimulus for the subsequent interest in optimization and compaction.

Of much greater interest are the kinds of *machine-dependent* optimizations that have been identified. In his work on STRUM—a high-level, machine-dependent, Pascal-like microprogramming language—Patterson (1976) listed a number of optimizations that, as far as can be determined, were performed by the STRUM compiler, which produced microcode for the Burroughs D Machine. These included

1. Removal of duplicate microinstructions.
2. Movement of literal assignments outside of loops.
3. Production of more efficient control structures.
4. Deletion of literal assignment microinstructions and placement of literal assignments in spare fields of other microinstructions.

Constant Unfolding

As an example of automatic microcode optimization I will describe the technique of *constant unfolding* developed by Vegdahl (1982a, 1982b).

It may be recalled that at the micro-architectural level the usual method of generating a constant is to encode it in a literal field in the micro-instruction. Since a constant is not usually required in every micro-instruction, the literal field is also used for other purposes—for example, to hold the branch address when the micro-instruction contains a branch micro-operation.

Clearly, then, a micro-operation requiring the literal field to hold a constant cannot be executed in the same micro-instruction with a micro-operation that needs this field for some other purpose.

Constant unfolding is a technique that can be used to generate constants without using the literal field, thereby "releasing" this field for other possible uses. It is, thus, one of the many optimizations that may be applied during and after code generation by a microcode compiler. Basically, the idea is to replace

---

[17]See, for example, Chapter 7, Section 7.5.2, for a discussion of some of the optimizing transformations performed by the PARAFRASE system for vector/array processors.

microprogrammer-defined constants (in the source microprogram) by expressions involving common *hardwired* constants available as part of the micro-architecture.[18]

To appreciate the nature of constant unfolding, one must understand the code generation procedure developed by Vegdahl. This is essentially a heuristic search procedure and can be characterized in terms of two functions SEARCH and TRANSFORM.

SEARCH takes some *goal* as input and returns a *sequence of microoperations* that realizes the goal. TRANSFORM takes a *goal* and a *current state* (of affairs) as input and returns a *sequence of microoperations* that resolves any differences between the goal and the current state. More precisely, these two functions can be defined as follows:

SEARCH ('goal'):

1. Select a *feasible* microoperation that is "semantically" close to 'goal.'
2. Apply TRANSFORM to 'goal' to resolve differences between 'goal' and 'feasible microoperation.'

TRANSFORM ('goal,' 'current state'):
If 'goal' = 'current state' **then** do nothing
else
either

1. Choose an axiom and apply it to 'goal' to produce 'new goal.'[19]
2. Call TRANSFORM ('new goal,' 'current state').

or

If 'goal' and 'current state' are both expressions with identical 'outermost' operators
then Call TRANSFORM on an operand-by-operand basis

or

If 'current state' is a storage resource
then
Apply **Fetch Decomposition:** Create the 'new goal' of transferring 'goal' value into 'current state' and invoke SEARCH ('new goal').

---

[18]Consider, for example, the von Neumann machine micro-architecture shown in Volume 1, Figure 5.1. This has a constant table (CT) that permanently holds constants that might be commonly used by the microprogrammer, including the 40-bit binary strings "00 . . . 0" and "10 . . . 0."

[19]Axioms, in Vegdahl's system, are a collection of rules of identity that may be used during code generation and optimization to effect transformations on the code. Examples of such axioms are

(i) The additive identity axiom: $X = 0 + X$
(ii) The And commutativity axiom: $X \wedge Y = Y \wedge X$

where X, Y, denote variables.

Example 5.7

Using these two functions, the goal of achieving 'W := X' might be resolved by the following search sequence.

```
SEARCH (W := X):
        Choose feasible operation 'W := Y + Z'
    TRANSFORM (X, Y+Z):
            Apply additive identity axiom 'X = O + X'
        TRANSFORM (O+X, Y+Z):
                Decompose operand-by-operand
            TRANSFORM (O,Y):
                    Apply Fetch Decomposition
                SEARCH (Y := O):
                        Choose feasible operation 'Y := O'
            TRANSFORM (X,Z):
                    Apply Fetch Decomposition
                SEARCH (X := Z):
                        Choose feasible operation 'Z := X'
```

Thus, the original goal of 'W := X' is transformed into the microoperation sequence

```
Y := O;
Z := X;
W := Y + Z
```

■

Returning to the constant unfolding problem, suppose that the host machine contains the hardwired constants 0, 1, 3, 7, 15. Consider the problem of generating microcode for the high-level microprogramming language statement

```
Reg := Reg + 8
```

where "Reg" is some host machine register. One possible code sequence is

1. Alu.left := Reg;
2. Alu.right := 8;
3. Alu.out := Alu.left + Alu.right;
4. Reg := Alu.out

Assuming an appropriate polyphase timing scheme in which the microoperations (1) and (2) can be activated in phase 1 of the microcycle, microoperations (3) and (4) in phases 2 and 3, respectively, the entire code sequence can be subsequently compacted into a single microinstruction with the literal field in the latter being used to encode and emit the constant "8." This will, however, preclude any other microoperation requiring this literal field (e.g., a branch that holds the branch-to-address, or a shift that encodes the shift amount in this same field) from being placed in the same microinstruction.

Alternatively, the search procedure can invoke the search sequence shown in

Figure 5.12 for unfolding the constant 8. The resulting microoperation sequence will be

5. Alu.right := %7; (hardwired constant)
6. Alu.out := *incr* Alu.right;
7. Alu.right := Alu.out:
8. Alu.left := Reg;
9. Alu.out := Alu.left + Alu.right;
10. Reg := Alu.out

Note that under the same timing assumptions, this code sequence can be compacted into two microinstructions. However, the literal field will not be required. Whether constant unfolding is useful in this particular case will, of course, depend on what uses the literal field can be put to during the execution of these microinstructions.

Several other examples of how constant unfolding can be used for code generation and optimization are given in Vegdahl (1982a, 1982b).

```
SEARCH (Reg := Reg + 8) :
  Choose feasible micro-operation 'Reg := Alu.out'
  TRANSFORM (Reg + 8, Alu.out) :
   Apply Fetch Decomposition
   SEARCH (Alu.out := Reg + 8)
    Choose feasible micro-operation 'Alu.out := Alu.left + Alu.right'
    TRANSFORM (Reg + 8, Alu.left + Alu.right) :
    Decompose on operand-by-operand basis
    TRANSFORM (Reg, Alu.left) :
     Apply Fetch Decomposition
     SEARCH (Alu.left := Reg) :
      Choose feasible micro-operation 'Alu.left := Reg'
     TRANSFORM (8, Alu.right) :
      Apply constant unfolding axiom
      TRANSFORM (1 + 7, Alu.right) :
      Apply Fetch Decomposition
      SEARCH (Alu.right := 1 + 7) :
       Choose feasible micro-operation 'Alu.right := Alu.out'
       TRANSFORM (1 + 7, Alu.out) :
       Apply Fetch Decomposition
        SEARCH (Alu.out := 1 + 7)
        Choose feasible micro-operation 'Alu.right := incr Alu.right'
         TRANSFORM (7, Alu.right) :
         Apply Fetch Decomposition
         SEARCH (Alu.right := 7) :
          Choose feasible micro-operation 'Alu.right := %7'
          TRANSFORM (7, %7) :
          Match
```

FIGURE 5.12 Search sequence for constant unfolding (based on Vegdahl, 1982a).

5.4.2 Compaction

Microcode compaction techniques fall into two classes:

1. *Local compaction,* which is concerned with compacting *straight-like micro-code segments* (SLMs) (Fig. 5.13). An SLM is an ordered set of microoperations with no entry points except at the beginning and no branches except possibly at the end. Following compiler terminology, SLMs may also be called basic blocks.
2. *Global compaction* in which the domain of compaction extends across several SLMs (Fig. 5.14).

We will discuss techniques from both these classes. In order to do so, however, some basic notation and definitions need to be introduced.[20]

Notation

For a microoperation Mi, the symbols SOURCE (Mi) and DEST (Mi) will denote, respectively, the sets of storage elements that serve as the *data source* and *result destination* of Mi. UNITS (Mi) will denote the set of functional units (ALUs, shifters, buses, etc.) required to execute the microoperation; the symbol PHASES (Mi) will denote the phase(s) of the microcycle during which Mi is active. Finally, FIELDS (Mi) will denote the field(s) of the microinstruction word required to encode the microoperation.

When the concern is only with source and destination sets, microoperations will be denoted by HLML-like statements—for example

---

[20]Since microcode compaction deals with the issue of detecting parallelism between microoperations and the placement of such microoperations in microinstructions, the issues are similar (though not identical) to such problems as hazard detection and the issue of instructions in pipelined uniprocessors. You may wish to compare the concepts presented here with those in Chapter 6 (Section 6.3.6).

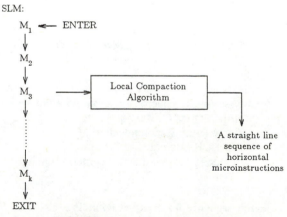

FIGURE 5.13 Local compaction.

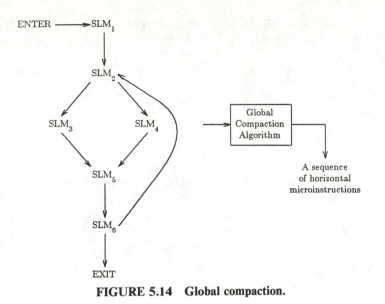

FIGURE 5.14 **Global compaction.**

```
Reg_out := Reg_in1 ∧ Reg_in2
if Reg_out ≠ 0 then goto start.
```

However, when necessary, microoperations will be symbolized by the complete *tuple* notation (Landskov *et al.,* 1980):

Mi = < OP, SOURCE, DEST, UNITS, PHASES, FIELDS >

where OP identifies the operations performed by Mi and the other components are as previously defined.

We may formulate the *local microcode compaction* problem in terms of the following concepts.

Definition 5.1

Two microoperations Mi, Mj are said to be (mutually) *data dependent* (denoted Mi **dd** Mj) if

1. DEST(Mi) ∩ SOURCE (Mj) ≠ ∅

or

2. DEST(Mj) ∩ SOURCE (Mi) ≠ ∅

or

3. DEST(Mi) ∩ DEST (Mj) ≠ ∅

where ∅ is the empty set.

Definition 5.2

Given two microoperations Mi, Mj within an SLM S, where Mi precedes Mj in S (denoted Mi < Mj), Mi *directly data precedes* Mj (denoted Mi **ddp** Mj) if Mi **dd**

Mj and there is no sequence of microoperations $M_1', M_2', \ldots, M_n'$ ($n \geq 1$) such that Mi **ddp** M_1', M_1' **ddp** M_2', $\ldots$, M_n' **ddp** Mj.

Definition 5.3

Mi *data precedes* Mj (Mi **dp** Mj) if Mi **ddp** Mj or there exists some Mk such that Mi **ddp** Mk and Mk **dp** Mj.

Definition 5.4

Two microoperations Mi, Mj within an SLM S, such that Mi < Mj in S, are said to be *data independent* (denoted Mi **di** Mj) if it is not the case that Mi **dp** Mj (i.e., ~ Mi **dp** Mj).

Based on these relationships, an SLM S may be represented as a directed acyclic graph in which the vertices represent the microoperations in S and there exists an edge from vertex i (representing microoperation Mi) to vertex j (representing microoperation Mj) if and only if Mi **ddp** Mj. Such graphs are called *data dependency graphs* (DDGs).

Example 5.8

Consider the following SLM S_1 for a machine with a monophase microcycle:

M₁: Alu_left := Reg1

M₂: Mbr := Mem[Mar]

M₃: Alu_right := Mbr

M₄: Alu_out := Alu_left + Alu_right

M₅: Reg1 := Alu_out

M₆: Reg2 := Alu_out

M₇: Reg3 := '10'

M₈: Reg1 := Reg 3

The DDG $G(S_1)$ for this is shown in Figure 5.15. We will also assume that the following *resource conflicts* exist:

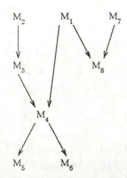

FIGURE 5.15   Data dependency graph $G(S_1)$ for SLM S_1.

FIELDS (M_2) ∩ FIELDS (M_7) ≠ ∅
FIELDS (M_3) ∩ FIELDS (M_7) ≠ ∅
UNITS (M_5) ∩ UNITS (M_6) ≠ ∅   ■

Definition 5.5

More generally, two microoperations Mi,Mj are said to have a *resource conflict* (denoted Mi **rc** Mj) if PHASES (Mi) ∩ PHASES (Mj) ≠ ∅ and either FIELDS (Mi) ∩ FIELDS (Mj) ≠ ∅ or UNITS (Mi) ∩ UNITS (Mj) ≠ ∅.

Local Compaction

The local microcode compaction problem can now be stated as follows:

Given

1. An SLM S = <M_1;M_2; . . . ;M_n>.
2. A partial order << on S based on the data precedence relation. That is, Mi << Mj if Mi **dp** Mj.
3. A set, RC, of microoperation pairs such that <Mi,Mj> ∈ RC if Mi **rc** Mj and Mi,Mj are in S.

Then

Minimize the total length of the microinstruction sequence S´ required to "hold" S such that

1. Every microoperation Mi in S is placed in exactly one microinstruction in S´.
2. If Mi << Mj in S, then when S´ is executed, Mi will execute before Mj.
3. If Mi **rc** Mj, for Mi,Mj in S, then when S´ is executed, the activation duration of Mi,Mj will never overlap.[21]

Several approaches to local compaction have been proposed. These are reviewed in Landskov *et al.* (1980), Davidson *et al.* (1981), and Vegdahl (1982a). Here I will briefly describe two of these approaches.

The First Come, First Served (FCFS) Algorithm:

This algorithm was originally proposed by Dasgupta and Tartar (1976). Given an SLM S = <M_1;M_2; . . . ;M_n> and an initially empty list of microinstruc-

---

[21]As we have had occasion to note, micro-architectures have a multitude of idiosyncrasies. Timing attributes, for example, vary widely, ranging from simple monophase to complex multicycle schemes; destinations of certain micro-operations may be transient variables. In this discussion we are, for the sake of exposition, assuming a relatively simple model of micro-architecture. The effect of such issues as polyphase and multicycle timing attributes and transient variables on microcode compaction are considered by Dasgupta and Tartar (1976); Landskov *et al.* (1980); Ma and Lewis (1980, 1981); and Mueller and Varghese (1985).

tions, for each successive microoperation Mi in S, the FCFS algorithm tries to place Mi in the earliest possible existing microinstruction subject to the data precedence relations and resource conflicts between the microoperations. If this is not possible—either because of a resource conflict between Mi and at least one microoperation in each of the existing microinstructions, or because data dependencies preclude inserting Mi in any of the existing microinstructions—a new microinstruction is created to hold Mi. If Mi is data independent of all the microoperations $M_1, \ldots, M_{i-1}$ already allocated to microinstructions, the new microinstruction is created at the beginning of the "current" microinstruction sequence; otherwise, it is created at the end.

Versions of the FCFS algorithm, also called the "Linear Algorithm" (Landskov *et al.*, 1980), have been used as the local compactor in at least two retargetable microprogram generation systems: the experimental Ma-Lewis system (Ma and Lewis, 1980, 1981) and the commercial JRS system (Sheraga and Gieser, 1983).

Example 5.9

Figure 5.16 shows the way that FCFS compacts the SLM S_1 of Example 5.8. Notice that M_2 can be inserted in I_1 since there are neither data dependencies nor resource conflicts between M_1 and M_2. M_3 cannot be placed in I_1, nor can it *precede* I_1 because of its data dependency on M_2. Hence I_2 is created. Similarly M_4 cannot be placed in either I_1 or I_2 nor can it precede I_2 because of its data dependency on M_3. Hence I_3 is created. A similar argument holds for the creation of I_4 for M_5. M_6 is data independent of M_5 but is data dependent on M_4. However because of the resource conflict between M_5, M_6, the earliest microinstruction for M_6 is I_5. In the case of M_7, the earliest instruction in which it can be placed is I_3 because of its resource conflicts with both M_2 and M_3. Finally, because of the data dependency between M_7 and M_8, the earliest microinstruction for M_8 is I_4.

It turns out that this sequence of five microinstructions is the optimal length for S_1. However, it is easy to construct examples for which FCFS produces suboptimal sequences of microinstructions. ∎

Microinstructions generated	SLM S_1: $<M_1$	M_2	M_3	M_4	M_5	M_6	M_7	$M_8>$
I_1	(M_1)	(M_1,M_2)	(M_1,M_2)	(M_1,M_2)	(M_1,M_2)	(M_1,M_2)	(M_1,M_2)	(M_1,M_2)
I_2	—	—	(M_3)	(M_3)	(M_3)	(M_3)	(M_3)	(M_3)
I_3	—	—	—	(M_4)	(M_4)	(M_4)	(M_4,M_7)	(M_4,M_7)
I_4	—	—	—	—	(M_5)	(M_5)	(M_5)	(M_5,M_8)
I_5	—	—	—	—	—	(M_6)	(M_6)	(M_6)

FIGURE 5.16 Compaction of S_1 by FCFS.

List Scheduling Algorithms: Generally speaking, *list scheduling* refers to a class of techniques for assigning tasks to processors in a multiprocessor system (Coffman and Denning, 1973, Chapter 3). Given a *task list* partially ordered according to the data precedence relation, a finite set of processors, and some externally imposed *priority scheme* on the set of tasks, whenever a processor P_i becomes free the *list scheduler* scans the task list and assigns to P_i the first task (as defined by the priority scheme) that is also unassigned and whose predecessor tasks have been completed.

In the case of microcode compaction, one such priority scheme proposed by Wood (1978, 1979) is based on assigning a *weight* W_i to a microoperation M_i in a DDG, where W_i is the number of (direct or indirect) descendents of M_i in the DDG.

The list scheduling compaction algorithm then proceeds as follows (Landskov *et al.,* 1980):

Given a *weighted* DDG G(S) for an SLM where weights are assigned to vertices according to the foregoing rule, and an initially empty list of microinstructions,

1. Determine the first *data available set* (Dset) of microoperations. A Dset is, simply, the set of all unplaced microoperations that are not data dependent on any unplaced microoperations.
2. Determine the microoperation in the Dset with the highest weight and assign it to the (initially empty) "current" microinstruction I_c.[22]
3. Identify the microoperation M_k with the next highest weight.[22] If M_k does not conflict with any microoperation already assigned to I_c, M_k is placed in I_c.
4. Repeat (3) until all the micro-operations in the Dset have been examined. The resulting "complete" micro-instruction I_c is added to the list of generated micro-instructions.
5. Repeat steps (1) through (4) until all the micro-operations in G(S) have assigned to micro-instructions.

Example 5.10

Consider once more the SLM S_1 of Example 5.8. Figure 5.17 shows the *weighted* DDG $G'(S_1)$ that reproduces Figure 5.15 with weights attached to the vertices. Figure 5.18 shows, for each iteration of steps (1) through (4), the Dset identified, the micro-instruction I_c produced from the Dset and the resulting, updated list of micro-instructions. As in the case of FCFS, an optimal sequence of micro-instructions is produced. ■

Davidson and coworkers (1981) conducted extensive studies on four different classes of compaction algorithms (reviewed in Landskov *et al.,* 1980), including

---

[22]When there is a tie between two or more micro-operations, that is, they have the same weight, select a micro-operation according to some priority scheme, for example, first come, first served.

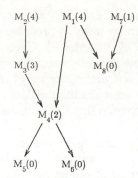

FIGURE 5.17 **Weighted DDG $G'(S_1)$ for SLM S_1.**

the two cited here. The two main performance measures used were (1) the number of micro-instructions generated for a set of benchmark SLMs that ranged in size from 32 to 375 micro-operations; and (2) the CPU time required on a Honeywell 68/80 system running under MULTICS, to produce compacted micro-instructions. Their main conclusion was that a modified version of the FCFS algorithm (called "FCFS with version shuffling") and the list scheduling algorithm performed most effectively on the benchmarks used.

Global Compaction

Extending the scope of compaction from SLMs to ordered sets of SLMs was the next obvious step in the development of compaction theory and technology. Because of the frequent occurrences of (possibly multiway) branches and loops in microprograms, the application of local microcode compaction alone may not suffice to produce satisficing microcode. It was expected that better compaction would be achieved if the analysis could be extended beyond SLMs. This expectation formed the rationale for the development of *global compaction* techniques.

D Set	Micro-instruction from D Set	List of Micro-instructions
(M_1,M_2,M_7)	$I_1 = (M_1,M_2)$	(I_1)
(M_3,M_7)	$I_2 = (M_3)$	$(I_1;I_2)$
(M_4,M_7)	$I_3 = (M_4,M_7)$	$(I_1;I_2;I_3)$
(M_5,M_6,M_8)	$I_4 = (M_5,M_8)$	$(I_1;I_2;I_3;I_4)$
(M_6)	$I_5 = (M_6)$	$(I_1;I_2;I_3;I_4;I_5)$

FIGURE 5.18 **Compaction of S_1 by list scheduling algorithm.**

Several global compaction algorithms have been proposed (Dasgupta, 1977; Tokoro, Tamura, and Takizuka, 1981; Wood, 1979; Isoda, Kobayashi, and Ishida, 1983). The most well known is the *trace scheduler* of Fisher (1981). Subsequent to its publication, trace scheduling has been further studied with respect to its performance (Grishman and Su, 1983; Su and Ding, 1985), application (Fisher, 1983), and improvements (Lah and Atkins, 1983; Linn, 1983; Su, Ding, and Jin, 1984). Here, I describe Fisher's original version of the algorithm.

In order to follow trace scheduling, some further definitions will be useful.

Definition 5.6

A *flowgraph* representation $G(M)$ of a microprogram M is a directed graph in which vertices denote SLMs and there exists an edge from vertex SLM_i to vertex SLM_j if on exit from SLM_i the next SLM that may be executed is SLM_j.

Definition 5.7

Given a flowgraph $G(M)$, a data object is *live* at the entrance to an SLM if its value may be read in that or some successor SLM without having been overwritten. A data object that is not live at some point is said to be *dead* at that point.

Definition 5.8

A microoperation is said to be *free at the top* of an SLM if no microoperation data precedes it. A microoperation is said to be *free at the bottom* if it does not data precede any other microoperation.

Based on these definitions, certain legal *rules of code motion* across SLMs can be established. Consider the flowgraph $G(M_2)$ of Figure 5.19 for some loop-free

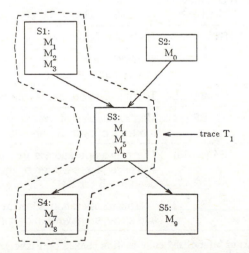

FIGURE 5.19 Flowgraph $G(M_2)$ for a microprogram M_2 with a trace outlined.

microprogram M_2. Then Figure 5.20 lists some legal rules of code motion that may be applied without violating the semantics of M_2.

Definition 5.9

Given a flowgraph G(M), a *trace* is a path through G(M) representing a sequence of microoperations, beginning at a source vertex and ending at a sink vertex,[23] that would be executed for some choice of values of the data objects.

Example 5.11

Consider the flowgraph $G(M_2)$ of Figure 5.19. There are four possible traces through this graph: $T_1 = <S_1; S_3; S_4>$, $T_2 = <S_1; S_3; S_5>$, $T_3 = <S_2; S_3; S_4>$, and $T_4 = <S_2; S_3; S_5>$. Each of these traces can be viewed as an extended SLM. ∎

Stated briefly, trace scheduling proceeds as follows:

1. Given a flowgraph G(M) of a microprogram M, assign to each vertex SLM a number indicating its frequency of execution. (This can be based on simulation, heuristic estimates, or actual runs of the vertical code.)
2. Select the *most probable* trace T through G(M) and compact this using list scheduling.
3. Using the menu of code motion rules, duplicate micro-operations of the trace into locations off the trace to preserve the semantics of the original microprogram M.

---

[23]In a directed graph, a source vertex is a vertex in the graph with no incoming edge; a sink vertex is a vertex in the graph with no outgoing edge.

Rule	Micro-operation can move From	To	Under the conditions that
1	S3	S1 and S2	The micro-operation is free at top of S3
2	S1 and S2	S3	Identical copies of the micro-operation are free at the bottoms of S1 and S2
3	S3	S4 and S5	The micro-operation is free at the bottom of S3
4	S4 and S5	S3	Identical copies of the micro-operation are free at the tops of both S4 and S5
5	S3	S4 (or S5)	The micro-operation is free at the bottom of S3 and all registers written by the micro-operation are dead in S5 (or S4)
6	S4 (or S5)	S3	The micro-operation is free at the top of S4 (or S5) and all registers written by it are dead in S5 (or S4)

FIGURE 5.20   Rules of inter-SLM code motion (based on Fisher, 1981. © 1981 IEEE; adapted with permission).

4. Repeat steps (2) and (3) for the remaining set of traces through G(M) until all traces have been compacted.

Example 5.12

Consider $G(M_2)$ (Figure 5.19) and suppose that the most-probable trace to execute is $T_1 = \langle S_1; S_3; S_4 \rangle$. The algorithm selects T_1 and produces, after compaction [step (2)] the following microinstruction sequence:

Original SLM	Micro-instruction		Microoperations			
	Number	Address	Field 1	Field 2	Jump 1	Jump 2
S_1	1	15	M_1	M_4	—	—
	2	16	M_2	M_3	17	—
S_3	3	17	M_5	—	18	"S5"
S_4	4	18	M_6	M_7	—	—
	5	19	M_8	—	—	—

The following inter-SLM movements have taken place here:

1. M_4 has been placed in micro-instruction 1 and has effectively been moved from S_3 up into S_1 (see T_1 in Fig. 5.21).
2. M_6 has been placed in micro-instruction 4 and has effectively been moved from S_3 down into S_4 (again, see the trace T_1 in Fig. 5.21).

Clearly, in order to preserve the original intended semantics of M_2 some additional duplications must be performed [by step (3) of the algorithm]. These adjustments will draw on the kinds of rules stated in Figure 5.20:

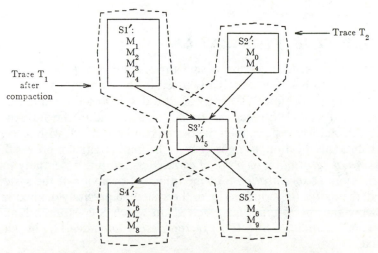

FIGURE 5.21   State of the flowgraph after compacting T_1.

1. M_4 will be copied into S_2.
2. M_6 will be copied into S_5.

The resulting state of the flowgraph is shown in Figure 5.21. The next most likely trace T_2 will now be selected, the procedure repeated, and so on. ■

Noted that because of (possibly extensive) copying of microoperations from the trace being compacted onto off-trace SLMs, the resulting sequence of micro-instructions may be larger than if the individual SLMs had been locally compacted. However, the average execution time of the resulting compacted micro-code is expected to be less.

Example 5.13

In the case of one microprogram cited by Fisher, Landskov, and Shriver (1981), the microprogram had a main trace of 12 micro-instructions when the SLMs in it were individually compacted, and a main trace of 7 micro-instructions when trace scheduling was used. However, the overall control store space requirements were 16 and 20 micro-instructions respectively. ■

To assess the efficacy of trace compaction, Grishman and Su (1983) studied the microcode produced for a horizontal host machine called PUMA. In their experiments, carefully handcrafted PUMA microcode served as the basis for comparison. The hand-coded segments were rewritten in sequential form and fed as input to the trace scheduler.

For the test segments, the trace scheduler's performance compared quite favorably with the hand-compacted code. For example, a floating-point divide routine required, on the average, 16.1 and 16.4 microcycles, respectively, when hand and trace compacted whereas the initialization part of a floating-point multiply routine required 14 microcycles in both cases.

5.5 FIRMWARE VERIFICATION

The place of verification in the design process for any kind of information processing system has been widely discussed in the computer science literature (see, for example, Volume 1, Chapter 3). If a design and the requirements that the design is intended to meet can be both stated within the framework of a formal mathematical system, then the design can be verified (with respect to the requirements specification) as rigorously as the mathematician proves theorems.

Such *formal verification* or *proof of correctness* requires essentially four types of information: A *specification* S of the intended behavior of the system being designed; the *design* (description) D, of the system; a precisely defined *semantics* SEM(SL) of the *specification language* SL in which S is expressed; and a precisely defined *semantics* SEM(DL) of the *design language* DL in which D is expressed.

A verification, then, is a logical argument or demonstration, using SEM(SL) and SEM(DL), that the system as described by D does indeed behave in the manner prescribed by S.

The overall logic of verification is recapitulated in the Appendix to this volume. Accordingly, the present discussion of formal *firmware verification* will assume that you are familiar with the material presented there.

Substantive research on firmware verification began in the early 1970s with the work by W. C. Carter and associates at the IBM T. J. Watson Research Center and has culminated in the contemporary (1986) work by W. Damm and coworkers in Aachen. Space does not allow us to survey or describe all this work in any reasonable fashion.[24] I will, instead, concentrate on a single line of development, namely, the evolution of the *axiomatic verification* of firmware — that is, verification based on the axiomatic semantics of the design (i.e., in this context, microprogramming) language.

Recall (from Section A.3 of the Appendix) that in the axiomatic approach the meanings of syntactic entities (of the design/description language) are specified in terms of formulas in some logical, deductive system. The basic formulas of interest are *correctness formulas* of the form $\{P\}S\{Q\}$ where P, Q are assertions called the pre- and postcondition, respectively, and S is some legal description of some design entity (e.g., an entire program or a microprogram).

The correctness of such formulas are proved using logical systems collectively termed Hoare logics. A Hoare logic essentially consists of *axioms* that characterize the semantics of the atomic constructs of the design (or programming or microprogramming) language and a collection of *proof rules* (or *rules of inference*) that define the semantics of the composite statements in the design language.

Recall also that such proof rules are usually expressed in the notation

$$\frac{F_1, F_2, \ldots, F_n}{F}$$

where the assertions or formulas $F_1, F_2, \ldots, F_n$ are the premises and the formula F is the conclusion.

Our discussion of firmware verification will, essentially, trace the progressive development of the nature of the axioms and proof rules for microprogramming languages. We will see how the proof theory became increasingly more applicable to the domain of "real" firmware. The development began with Patterson's (1976) work on STRUM, which, in turn, led to the work by Dasgupta and Wagner (1984) on S* (QM-1), and culminated in the Aachen/S* system of Damm and coworkers (1986).

5.5.1 STRUM

The first major investigation of the axiomatic verification of microprograms was carried out by Patterson (1976). His general approach is depicted in Figure 5.22.

---

[24]A very detailed survey of firmware verification is given in Dasgupta (1987).

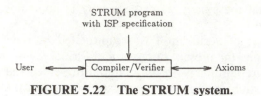

FIGURE 5.22 The STRUM system.

We have previously mentioned (see Section 5.3.1) that STRUM is a HLMD language. It is rooted in Pascal and oriented toward the Burroughs D Machine. In the STRUM system, a specification (in the architecture description language ISPS) of the target machine that the microprogram is intended to emulate is used as a basis for constructing assertions that are then inserted at key positions in the STRUM program. This is then passed to the verification system, which uses the axioms and proof rules for the language to prove that the microprogram does indeed satisfy the assertions.

The proof theory for STRUM is based on an axiomatic definition of the language much in the style of the Hoare-Wirth definition of Pascal (Hoare and Wirth, 1973). Since STRUM is somewhat machine-specific, many of the axioms reflect the idiosyncrasies of the D Machine.

Example 5.14

The **if** statements in STRUM have the same form as in Pascal and the same proof rules:

$$\frac{\{P\&B\}\ S\ \{Q\},\ P\&\neg B \supset Q}{\{P\}\ \textbf{if } B \textbf{ then } S\ \{Q\}}$$

$$\frac{\{P\&B\}\ S_1\ \{Q\},\ \{P\&\neg B\}\ S_2\ \{Q\}}{\{P\}\ \textbf{if } B \textbf{ then } S_1 \textbf{ else } S_2\ \{Q\}}$$

However, there are restrictions on the nature of the Boolean expression B. One class of admissible Boolean expressions is the class of machine-specific *test* expressions, which include the following:

lst(AE):   **if** AE < 15 > = 1 **then** TRUE **else** FALSE
mst(AE):   **if** AE < 0 > = 1 **then** TRUE **else** FALSE
ones(AE):   **if** AE = $FFFF_{16}$ **then** TRUE **else** FALSE

where AE denotes an arithmetic expression. An example of an **if** statement would be

   if ones (X + Y) **then** X := X-1   ■

Example 5.15

Consider the proof rules for the *parallel* statement. The general form for this statement in STRUM is

ASSGN [,ASSGN][,ASSGN], STMT

where ASSGN is an assignment statement, STMT is any other executable statement and "[. . .]" signifies an optional component. Informally, the assignment statements will execute in parallel followed by the execution of STMT. Thus the assignments must not *interfere* with one another.

Since the general form of the proof rule is somewhat complex, I will show a simplified version for the following special case of the parallel statement:

S: B1 := A1, B2 := A2, I := E, STMT

where B1,B2 are Boolean variables, A1, A2 are Boolean constants, I is an integer variable, and E is an integer-valued expression. The proof rule for this statement is (Patterson, 1977):

$$\frac{\{P\}\ STMT\ \{Q\}}{\{P[B1/A1][B2/A2][I/E]\}\ S\ \{Q\}}$$

where P[B1/A1][B2/A2][I/E] is the assertion P with all free occurrences of B1,B2,I replaced by A1,A2,E, respectively. ∎

The STRUM system has been used to emulate the architecture of the Hewlett Packard HP-2115 on the Burroughs D Machine. The emulator was verified and then translated and optimized to produce object microcode. In the course of verification, 10 errors were uncovered in the STRUM program, 11 errors in the specifications, and 10 errors in the assertions.

5.5.2 S*(QM-1)

Subsequent to the STRUM effort, Wagner and Dasgupta (Wagner, 1983; Dasgupta and Wagner, 1984) investigated the feasibility of verifying microprograms written in the language S*(QM-1). The main departure of this work from the STRUM project were the following:

1. There are significant differences in the languages. S*(QM-1) is an instantiation of S* (see Section 5.3.2) for the highly horizontal Nanodata QM-1 (Nanodata 1979; see also Volume 1, Chapter 5, Sections 5.3.1, 5.3.3); thus the language reflects specific characteristics of this particular host machine. As an example, the presence of *residual control* (see Section 5.2.4, Idiosyncratic Features of Host Machines) in the QM-1 posed rather unique problems in the axiomatization of S*(QM-1) and this necessitated the introduction of *structural* information (i.e., information concerning characteristics of the data-path structure) to be incorporated into the language. Similarly, the presence of *transient variables* (see Section 5.2.4, Idiosyncratic Features of Host Machines) necessitates restrictions on the appearance of transients in assignment statements in order to ensure proper proofs of correctness of S*(QM-1) programs.
2. The highly horizontal nature of the QM-1, together with the 10 buses around which its data-path structure is organized, posed problems of *side*

effects (see Section 5.2.4, Idiosyncratic Features of Host Machines) that had to be resolved in constructing the proof theory.

3. More generally, the aim was to construct a deductive system for *developing* correct microprograms, rather than automatic verification. The primary objective was to provide a basis for *reasoning formally* about firmware design so that the proof of correctness and firmware development could proceed hand in hand (Gries, 1981).

Because of the complexity of the QM-1, the proof rules and axioms for S*(QM-1) turned out to be complex. To illustrate the impact of residual control and side effects, we consider the axiom for the *simple* assignment statement:

X := Y

where X,Y are simple or substricted variables denoting QM-1 storage locations. A specific instance of this assignment is

local_store[15] := local_store[14].

In the QM-1, local store registers cannot be referenced directly as shown here. They can only be accessed by assigning constants to *residual control registers* that serve as array index variables with respect to the local store (array). Thus, the execution of the foregoing S*(QM-1) assignment results in side effects—the setting of appropriate residual control registers to 15 and 14, respectively.

Let P be an assertion. Then, as before, P[X/Y] denotes P with all free occurrences of X being replaced by Y. More generally,

P[X1/Y1][X2/Y2] . . . [Xn/Yn]

signifies *simultaneous substitution* of X1, X2, . . . , Xn by Y1, Y2, . . . , Yn, respectively.

Using this notation, the axiom of the simple assignment statement is defined as

{P[X/Y][SEL/V]} X := Y {P}

where SEL denotes locations side-effected as a result of the assignment statement and V denotes the set of corresponding values assigned to the variables in V. That is,

[SEL/V] ≡ [SEL1/V1][SEL2/V2] . . . [SELn/Vn].

The proof theory has been successfully applied to prove the correctness of a few nontrivial microroutines in S*(QM-1) (Wagner, 1983; Dasgupta and Wagner, 1984). Certain important lessons were also learned.

1. The proof rules were cumbersome. One of the reasons for this is the inherent complexity of the QM-1 architecture. Thus, if we really wish to design and implement demonstrably reliable firmware, the micro-architectures should be designed to support this goal.

2. Another cause for the complexity of proof rules was the fact that certain entities that are taken to be "primitives" are not primitives at all. For instance, the simple assignment statement in S*(QM-1) is not simply an

assignment to an output variable; it is, rather, an *atomic procedure* that causes several assignments to take place. Similarly, the evaluation of an S*(QM-1) expression does not return a single value; it involves the invocation of an atomic procedure that, in the course of returning a value, also modifies other locations.

5.5.3 The AADL/S* System

In describing this system in Section 5.3.2, I noted how the notion of instantiation was rigorously interpreted. The AADL/S* system has also greatly extended the results of the S*(QM-1) verification work in that

1. It uses a more accurate model of very fine-grained, low-level parallelism that reflects the timing characteristics of concurrently executable microoperations. As a result, the proof rules for such parallel statements as the *cocycle* are far more formal and general than those for S*(QM-1).
2. Using AADL, the semantics of microoperations are defined in terms of still more primitive entities, thereby making explicit the actual complexity of their behavior. Furthermore, the proof rules for statements in S*(A), where A is some micro-architecture described in AADL, are *derived formally* from the AADL specification.
3. The AADL/S* system is as much concerned with the exploitation of *hierarchical systematic design* as with verification issues.

Space will not permit me to describe with any degree of completeness the nature of the proof theory. I will, instead, describe the development of just one of its proof rules—namely, the proof rule for *low-level parallel statements* such as may appear within *cocycle* construct in S* (see Section 5.3.2). In particular, let the parallel statement be of the form

PAR: **do** $S_1 \parallel \ldots \parallel Sn$ **od**

where the Si's are microoperations or compositions of microoperations. Basically, we desire that the proof rule for PAR to be of the form:

$$\frac{\{P_1\}\ S_1\ \{Q_1\},\ \ldots\ \{P_n\}\ S_n\ \{Q_n\}}{\{P_1 \wedge \ldots \wedge P_n\}\ \text{PAR}\ \{Q_1 \wedge \ldots \wedge Q_n\}}$$

provided that certain additional conditions are met whenever Si,Sj, $(i \neq j)$ conflict in their use of microarchitectural resources.[25]

---

[25]Also see Section A.7 of the Appendix for a general discussion of proofs of parallel systems. This formulation of the proof rule for parallel *program* statements was first presented by Hoare (1972). An important subsequent refinement proposed by Owicki and Gries (1976) took the form

$$\frac{\{P_1\}S_1\ \{Q_1\},\ \ldots\ ,\{P_n\}S_n\{Q_n\}\text{are interferencefree}}{\{P_1 \wedge \ldots \wedge P_n\}\text{PAR}\{Q_1 4.\ \ldots\ \wedge Q_n\}}$$

This rule can be applied to the verification of asynchronous parallel subsystems in endo-architectures in which explicit clocking is either absent or is ignored. For an explanation and example of the application of the Owicki-Gries rule to architecture, see Dasgupta (1984, Chapter 8).

Several key ideas need to be formalized for an appropriate proof rule to be established.

Cooperation

To illustrate the notion of cooperation, consider the parallel statement:

```
PAR1: do
        do A1; A2 od
        || B1
        || do C1; C2; C3 od
      od
```

which exhibits the timing diagram shown in Figure 5.23. The proof rule must be able to express the fact that the properties assumed to be true prior to the execution of C3 are indeed established by those micro-operations in PAR1 that precede C3 (viz., A1, B1, and C2). Damm and coworkers refer to this as the *cooperation test;* its aim is to show that the pre-/postcondition pairs P_i/Q_i characterizing the behavior of a single microoperation S_i in PAR *cooperate* to establish the truth of the global formula $\{P_1 \wedge \ldots \wedge P_n\}$ PAR $\{Q_1 \wedge \ldots \wedge Q_n\}$.

This cooperation test is integrated into the proof rule in the form of a *verification condition* for those points in time at which cooperation occurs. For PAR1, the relevant verification condition would be

$$VC(\text{time} = 12): Q_{A1} \wedge Q_{B1} \wedge Q_{C2} \text{ implies } P_{C3}$$

In general, the verification condition for cooperation at time t will be denoted as VC(t).

Interference

Assuming the timing diagram of Figure 5.23, consider the statement

do A1: a := 4 || B1: b := 5 **od**

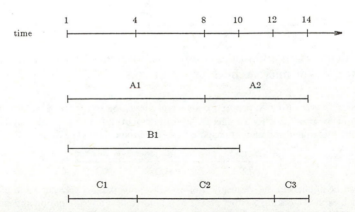

FIGURE 5.23   Timing diagram for PAR (based on Damm, 1984).

and suppose that the formulas for the individual microoperations are

{true} A1: a := 4 {true}

{a := 3} B1: b := 5 {b = a + 2}

Clearly, these formulas cooperate at time = 1 (see Fig. 5.23) in the sense of the verification condition VC(1): $P_{A1} \wedge P_{B1}$ implies the global precondition P: a = 3. However, the formula

{a = 3} **do** A1 || B1 **od** {b = a + 2}

certainly is not correct. Thus, we must ensure that a postcondition does not depend on the destination location of some concurrent microoperation.

Let S_i d|| S_j be true if S_i, S_j occur in parallel in the timing diagram of PAR such that S_j starts d time units after the start of S_i, and S_j starts before S_i terminates (Fig. 5.24a). Let S_i ||d S_j be true if S_i, S_j occur in parallel in the timing diagram of PAR such that S_j terminates d time units after the termination of S_i and S_j starts before S_i terminates (Fig. 5.24b).

When either of these conditions hold, S_i, S_j are said to constitute a *critical microoperation pair.*

The proofs of $\{P_i\}S_i\{Q_i\}$ (i = 1 . . . n) are *interference free* if and only if for all critical microoperation pairs (S_i, S_j):

1. If d = 0, then

    DESTINATIONS (S_i) ∩ FREE (Q_j) = ∅
    DESTINATIONS (S_j) ∩ FREE (Q_i) = ∅
2. If d > 0, then

    DESTINATIONS (S_i) ∩ FREE (Q_j) = ∅

    where ∅ is the empty set, DESTINATIONS (x) denotes the set of all locations that may be changed by x and FREE (y) denotes all free variables occurring in the assertion y.

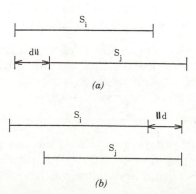

(a)

(b)

FIGURE 5.24 Critical micro-operation pair (Damm, 1984).

Static Disjointness

Interference is a property of *proofs of formulas* and not of the resources or of the critical micro-operations themselves. Thus a third condition must be met: There should not be any *resource conflicts* between pairs of critical micro-operations.

To ensure this requires the use of information available in the AADL definition of the host machine concerning the resource requirements of individual micro-operations.

For a micro-operation S_i, let

UNITS (S_i) denote the set of functional units used by S_i.

NEEDED (S_i, U) denote the duration for which S_i requires the Unit $U \in$ UNITS (S_i).

SOURCE (S_i) denote the source locations for S_i.

DESTINATIONS (S_i) denote the destination locations for S_i.

Then the parallel statement PAR is *statically disjoint* if and only if, whenever S_i, S_j are critical micro-operations in PAR and S_i d|| S_j (see Fig. 5.24*a*), then:

1. $\{L \in$ SOURCE $(S_i) \mid$ NEEDED $(S_i, L) > d\}$
   $\cap$ DESTINATIONS $(S_j) = \emptyset$
2. DESTINATIONS $(S_i) \cap$ SOURCE $(S_j) = \emptyset$
3. DESTINATIONS $(S_i) \cap$ DESTINATIONS $(S_j) = \emptyset$
4. $\{U \in$ UNITS $(S_i) \mid$ NEEDED $(S_i, U) > d\}$
   $\cap$ UNITS $(S_j) = \emptyset$
5. microinstruction_fields $(S_i) \cap$ microinstructions_field $(S_j) = \emptyset$

We can now formulate a proof rule for the PAR parallel statement that takes into account the timing relationships among its microoperations:

$$\frac{\{VC(t) \mid t \in ACT\}, \{\{P_i\}\ S_i\ \{Q_i\}, i=1, \ldots, n\}, VC(t_{end})}{\{P_1 \wedge \ldots \wedge P_n\}\ \textbf{do}\ PAR\ \textbf{od}\ \{Q_1 \wedge \ldots \wedge Q_n\}}$$

provided that

1. The proofs of $\{P_i\}\ S_i\ \{Q_i\}$ $(i = 1, \ldots, n)$ are interference free.
2. PAR is statically disjoint, where:
   (a) ACT $= \{t \mid$ there are some microoperations that are activated at time t$\}$.
   (b) $t_{end} =$ time when the last microoperation of PAR terminates.

Note the level of detail at which analysis of parallelism is done. Damm and coworkers have, in fact, carried the analysis still further and have derived conditions under which *dynamic data conflicts* may be detected. As an example, consider a declaration in S* of an array X

var X: **array** [. . .] **of** T

the elements of which are of type T (e.g., a 32-bit *sequence*), and suppose two micro-operations attempt to write to X[I], X[J] in parallel. Then a conflict will take place only if I = J. Damm and colleagues have formulated a proof rule taking into account the possibility of such *dynamic disjointness* that can be used to show that even though the microoperations are not *statically* disjoint, there will still be no conflicts *during* the execution of PAR. For further details, refer to Damm (1984,1985), Damm *et al.* (1986).

5.6 RETARGETABLE MICROCODE GENERATION SYSTEMS

The ultimate *practical* objective of firmware engineering is the development of retargetable microprogramming systems for the production and/or verification of microcode for arbitrary host machines.

Figure 5.11 shows the general structure of such a system for microcode generation. As I have recorded in Section 5.4, several such systems have been implemented in recent years. Of particular note are those by Ma and Lewis (1980,1981), Baba and Hagiwara (1981), Marwedel (1984), and the commercial system development by JRS Laboratories (Sheraga and Gieser, 1983).

Here, I will describe briefly one of the most recent and sophisticated of such systems, the Horizon retargetable compiler, implemented at Colorado State University by Mueller and coworkers (Allan, 1986; Mueller and Varghese, 1985; Mueller and Duda, 1986).

Figure 5.25 shows the detailed structure of the Horizon compiler. A number of features of this compiler that are of particular interest are discussed here.

5.6.1 Phase Coupling

In general, the most significant and problematic phases of the microcode generation process are to be found in the machine-dependent part of the microcode compiler; these are the following:

Register assignment, in which registers of the host machine are bound (or assigned) to symbolic registers or variables of the microprogram, the latter expressed in some symbolic intermediate language.

Code selection, which produces from an intermediate language specification of the microprogram, functionally equivalent, host machine-specific microcode.

Global optimization, which performs code motion and code transformations both within and beyond SLMs.

Local compaction, which generates host machine-specific (horizontal) micro-instructions from individual SLMs.

Because of the intrinsic computational complexity of the problem of producing optimal microcode (see footnote 13), the earlier systems, such as the Ma-Lewis and JRS systems considered each phase independently of the others. These are, then, instances of *phase-decoupled* methods. The advantage of relative simplicity is offset by the limits to which decisions made in an earlier phase

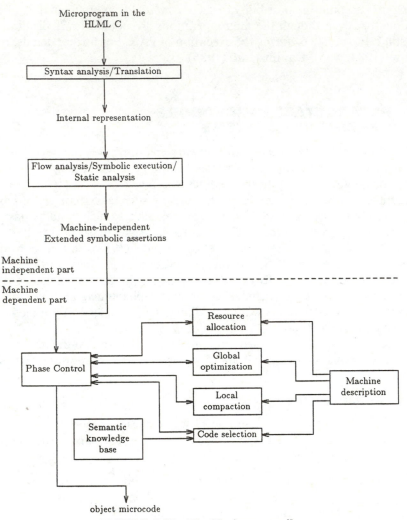

FIGURE 5.25 The Horizon compiler.

may impose on the efficacy of a later phase. For example, if register allocation is performed prior to code selection, and the latter prior to code compaction, then certain kinds of optimizations may simply not be possible.

In contrast, the Horizon compiler employs the method of *phase coupling,* where the various phases share information and cooperatively interact (in some fashion) to produce microcode. Although phase coupling will add to the complexity of the code generation process, its proponents (DeWitt, 1976; Vegdahl, 1982a, 1982b; Allan, 1986) believe that it has the potential for producing more optimized microcode.[26]

---

[26]Phase coupling is, of course, applicable to compilers in general, regardless of whether these are for generating executable software or firmware. The literature on phase coupling is reviewed by Allan (1986).

Example 5.16

Vegdahl (1982a) has described several methods for coupling phase:

1. One approach is to *iterate* through a set of phases, in which case, for example, information produced by a phase in one iteration may be useful to another phase in the next iteration, and so on.
2. Two phases may cooperate on a *master-slave* relationship, with the master invoking the slave as and when necessary.
3. The use of *AND/OR trees.* For instance, a code selection phase, rather than produce a single (vertical) sequence of microoperations, produces an AND/OR tree from which the compaction phase can select microoperations during compaction. An AND/OR tree is a tree in which each internal vertex is marked AND or OR and the leaf vertices are micro-operations. A solution to the tree (a) consisting of a single leaf is the microoperation designated by the leaf; (b) the root of which is an AND vertex is the solution to each of its subtrees; and (c) the root of which is an OR vertex is the solution to any one of its subtrees. Given the (partial) AND/OR tree shown in Figure 5.26, for example, possible sequences that may be generated are $<M_1; M_3; M_4>$, $<M_2; M_3; M_4>$, $<M_1; M_3; M_5>$ and $<M_2; M_3 M_5>$. ∎

5.6.2 Retargetable Code Selection

As Figure 5.25 indicates, retargetability is achieved by means of host-machine descriptions that serve as inputs to all the significant machine-dependent phases. A set of *machine tables* is defined for each host machine. The phases (which are themselves machine-independent) extract the machine-specific information from the tables.

The table-driven code selector produces microcode for one SLM at a time. The behavior or function of an SLM is defined by means of *symbolic assertions* (Mueller and Varghese, 1985; Mueller and Duda, 1986) defined as follows.

Given an SLM, its variables can be partitioned into two classes: *Use* variables, which are read before being written to within an SLM; and *Def* variables, which are live at the bottom of an SLM as a result of being written to within an SLM. We then have the following definitions.

Definition 5.10

Given an SLM S, a *symbolic assertion* is a mapping

$$I \rightarrow F$$

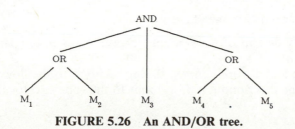

FIGURE 5.26   An AND/OR tree.

where I associates with each Use variable a symbolic constant that represents the value of that variable on entry to S, and F associates with each Def variable a symbolic representation of the expression assigned to that variable in terms of the symbolic constants associated with the Use variables.

Definition 5.11

Any mapping (or association) between a variable and a symbolic expression is called a *symbolic state mapping* (SSM). A tuple of SSMs for distinct variables is a *symbolic state vector* (SSV), with I being an *initial* SSV (ISSV) and F a *final* SSV (FSSV).

Example 5.17

Consider an SLM consisting of the following sequence of statements:

    J := A*B;
    J := J-I;
    C := H-J*I.

The corresponding symbolic assertion is

$$[A = a_1, B = b_1, H = h_1, I = i_1] \rightarrow$$
$$[J = a_1{}^*b_1 - i_1, C = h_1 - (a_1{}^*b_1{}^*i_1)]$$

where $a_1, b_1, \ldots$, are symbolic constants, the equalities "$A = a_1$," "$B = b_1$," ..., are SSMs, and I and F are instances of SSVs, specifically ISSVs and FSSVs, respectively. ∎

I and F are, respectively, restricted forms of pre- and postconditions as they appear in axiomatic proof techniques (see Section 5.5 and also the Appendix, Section A.3).

In general, the input to the code selector consists of a flowgraph of SLMs where each SLM is represented by means of an *extended* symbolic assertion, defined as follows.

Definition 5.12

An *extended symbolic assertion* (ESA) is a pair

    esa (I → F; C)

where I → F is a symbolic assertion and C is a control flow directive such as an unconditional branch ("**goto** L") or a conditional branch in the form

    cond_symbolic_expression **then** L₁ **else** L₂

Figure 5.27(*b*) shows an ESA flowgraph corresponding to the partial flowgraph of Figure 5.27(*a*).

From Figure 5.25 it will be noted that in addition to the flowgraph of ESAs and the machine description, a third input to the code selector is the *semantic*

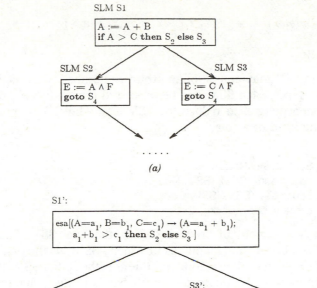

SLM S1

$$A := A + B$$
$$\text{if } A > C \text{ then } S_2 \text{ else } S_3$$

SLM S2

$$E := A \wedge F$$
$$\text{goto } S_4$$

SLM S3

$$E := C \wedge F$$
$$\text{goto } S_4$$

· · · · ·

(a)

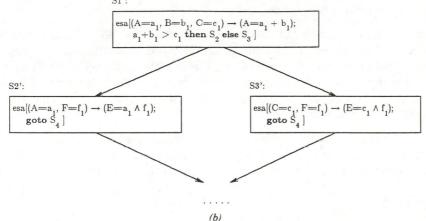

S1':

$$\text{esa}[(A{=}a_1,\ B{=}b_1,\ C{=}c_1) \rightarrow (A{=}a_1 + b_1);$$
$$a_1{+}b_1 > c_1 \text{ then } S_2 \text{ else } S_3\ ]$$

S2':

$$\text{esa}[(A{=}a_1,\ F{=}f_1) \rightarrow (E{=}a_1 \wedge f_1);$$
$$\text{goto } \check{S}_4\ ]$$

S3':

$$\text{esa}[(C{=}c_1,\ F{=}f_1) \rightarrow (E{=}c_1 \wedge f_1);$$
$$\text{goto } \check{S}_4\ ]$$

· · · · ·

(b)

FIGURE 5.27 *(a)* **Original flowgraph;** *(b)* **ESA flowgraph.**

knowledge base. This consists of procedures expressing facts and rules that may be applied during code selection. The following are some examples of the contents of the knowledge base (Mueller and Varghese, 1985).

Example 5.18

Given the SSM "X = a," the fact

    simple_assignment (X = a, X: = Y, <Y = a>)

expresses the SSM (the third argument) that results from the (backward) transformation of the SSM defined as the first argument by the microoperation specified as the second argument. ∎

Example 5.19

Given the SSM "$X = OP(a_1, a_2)$," the backward effect of the microoperation $X := OP(Y_1, Y_2)$ can be defined by the fact:

assignment
$$(X = OP(a_1,a_2), X: = OP(Y_1,Y_2), <Y_1 = a_1,Y_2 = a_2>)$$ ■

Example 5.20

In general, an SSV may consist of an arbitrary number of SSMs. Using facts of the foregoing types, each SSM can be processed (or "reduced") separately and the results then merged to reduce the SSV as a whole. This procedure is expressed in the form of a rule:

```
reduce_ssv (
      SSM.SSV, ISSV, Code) :−
            reduce_ssm (SSM, ISSV, Code₁),
            reduce_ssv (SSV, ISSV, Code₂),
            merge (Code₁, Code₂, Code).
```

Here, the first argument of "reduce_ssv" is the final SSV (FSSV), which is represented as a list of state mappings in which "SSM" is the first mapping and "SSV" denotes the rest. The second argument is the initial SSV (ISSV) whereas the third argument is the microcode produced from the reductions of the first argument. The meaning of the other procedures "reduce ssm" and "merge" should be intuitively apparent. ■

For detailed discussions of how the knowledge-based code selection mechanism is used, refer to Mueller (1984) and Mueller and Varghese (1985). We can only convey the flavor of their approach with a simple example.

Example 5.21

Given the symbolic assertion

SA_1 : <Reg1 = a, Reg2 = b> → <Reg1 = a+b>

representing the desired functional behavior of an SLM, and a machine description, the code selector constructs the microcode sequence *in reverse order of its execution.* Assuming that the host machine ALU performs the addition, the last microoperation might be selected as

M_4: Reg1 := Alu.out.

In that case, M_4 may be preceded by the micro-operation

M_3 : Alu.out := Alu.left + Alu.right

The original symbolic assertion SA_1 is thus transformed to

SA_2: <Reg1 = a, Reg2 = b> → <Alu.left = a, Alu.right = b>

which, when followed by the sequence $M_3;M_4$, satisfies SA_1.

To satisfy SA_2, the code selector can generate microcode that satisfies each of the individual symbolic assertions

SA_{21}: < Reg1 = a, Reg2 = b > → > Alu.left = a >

SA_{22}: < Reg1 = a, Reg2 = b > → < Alu.right = b >

Using the same backward reasoning and using appropriate facts and rules in the knowledge base, the selector generates the microoperations

M_2: Alu.left := Reg1

M_2: Alu.right := Reg2

to satisfy SA_{21} and SA_{22}, respectively. These, when merged with M_3 and M_4 produce the data dependency graph of Figure 5.28. ∎

5.7 SOME HISTORICAL REMARKS

The earliest reference to what is now called firmware engineering is Tucker's (1967) discussion of the microprogram control of the IBM System/360. In this paper, Tucker discusses not only the flowchart notation used for specifying 360 microcode but also the feasibility of using HLMLs. Even prior to this time, Falkoff, Iverson, and Sussenguth (1964) had used the APL notation developed by Iverson (1962) to formally describe the operational semantics of the 360 instruction set and the instruction interpretation cycle.

In 1970, the first book on microprogramming appeared (Husson, 1970). This contained a fairly extensive discussion of a Fortran-like HLML and its compiler. This discussion marked the beginning of firmware engineering as a topic of research and development in its own right, although the term "firmware engineering" appears to have been used much later (Davidson and Shriver, 1978).

PROBLEMS

5.1 "Microprograms . . . are, by their very nature, *machine specific*" (Section 5.2.1). Thirty years ago, when programming was almost entirely done in assembly languages, similar sentiments were expressed about programs. And, yet, programming has been liberated from the "tyranny

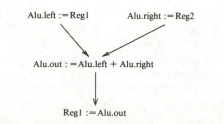

FIGURE 5.28   DDG for the microcode corresponding to SA_1.

of the machine" although microprogramming remains very much en-slaved to the machine.

   (a) Give an explanation as to why this has historically been the case, using as a basis for your argument the differences between program-ming and microprogramming.
   (b) To what extent will developments in firmware engineering change this state of affairs?

5.2 Draw timing diagrams to correspond to the following $S*$ statements.
   (a) **cocycle**
           alu.left := gpr[1] || alu.right := gpr[2]
       coend;
       cocycle
           aout := alu.left + alu.right
       coend
   (b) **cocycle**
           mar := ir.addr
       coend;
       stcycle
           mbr := mem[mar] || pc := pc + 1
       stend
   (c) **stcycle**
           mbr := mem[mar]
       ||
           pc := pc + 1;
           cocycle
             mar := pc
           coend
       stend

5.3 Write a report evaluating C as a high-level microprogramming language. Your evaluation should take into account the following perspectives.
   (a) The general ability to describe microprograms across a range of host machines. Issues to be considered here include the nature of micro-program-level data types and data objects, the specification of paral-lelism within microprograms, and the nature of control structures common to microprogramming.
   (b) The ability to capture the idiosyncrasies of a specific micromachine. Issues to be considered here include the semantics of machine-spe-cific micro-operations and the timing idiosyncrasies of particular micromachines.
   (c) The ease of compiling C microprograms into executable host-ma-chine-specific microcode.
   (d) The efficiency of the compiled microcode.
   (e) The verifiability of C microprograms.

[Note: Your approach to this exercise should be in the spirit of preparing an *a priori* assessment of C as a *potential* microprogramming language such that, given your report, one could make an informed decision as to whether or not to invest the time, resources, and money into a project for implementing a C-based microprogramming system.]

5.4   In Chapter 4, the architecture description language S*M was discussed. It will be recalled that S*M is specially suited for the description of clocked micro-architectures — the forte of the microprogrammer.

Write a report evaluating S*M as a *microprogramming language*. If your evaluation leads to the assessment that S*M is lacking in certain directions, make recommendations on how to extend or modify the language to rectify its shortcomings.

[*Note:* See the note for Problem 5.3.]

5.5   Consider the local compaction problem stated and discussed in Section 5.4.2. In the formal statement of this problem the sole recognition given to the complexities of micromachine timing is in the definition of the resource conflict relation (Definition 5.5), which allows for polyphase microcycles.

Consider, however, the situation that a particular micromachine may have one or more micro-operations (MOs) that span *several* microcycles. In the worst possible case such a "pathological" MO may begin execution somewhere within a microcycle (i.e., not necessarily at the start of a microcycle) and, after executing for several microcycles, may end somewhere within another microcycle.

Analyze the consequences of this situation and redefine the local microcode compaction problem to take this complication into account.

5.6   [Continuation of Problem 5.5.] Further timing complications might arise in the case of MOs whose execution duration may *vary* depending on some other condition being satisfied or not. For example, an MO whose "normal" execution duration is a simple 50-nsec-phase (say of a 200-nsec, 4-phase microcycle) may require two successive 50-nsec-phases when a particular flag or register in the micromachine happens to have a particular value at the time the MO begins execution.

Analyze the implications of the presence of such variable duration MOs and redefine the local compaction problem (from what it was in response to Problem 5.5) to take this complication into account.

5.7   The local compaction problem as stated in the text ignores the possibility of the presence of *transient stores* in a micromachine. A transient store, it will be recalled, is a store that retains its most recently written value for a particular duration only. Subsequently, the store may be reset to zero or some other arbitrary value by the hardware.

Thus, if an MO M_i writes to a transient store S_j, and a subsequent MO M_k is required to use that value, then M_k must execute within the duration for which S_j retains the value produced by M_i.

Analyze the problem of transient stores in the context of the local compaction problem and propose a general solution for this problem. In other words, redefine the local compaction problem so as to include the issue of transient variables.

5.8   The machine model underlying the local compaction problem (Section 5.4.2) assumes that each MO in the SLM is "bound" to a particular functional unit. That is, the UNITS$_i$ field of an MO M$_i$ refers to a specific set of functional units that will execute M$_i$.

However, it is quite feasible that the operation OP$_i$ performed by M$_i$ can be executed by two or more alternative functional units. For example, an INCR operation may, conceivably, be executed by a general purpose ALU or by a specialized increment unit.

In that case, the UNITS field of the MO (in an SLM) should not prematurely bind the MO to a particular set of functional units. Rather, all the available options should be kept open, leaving it to the compaction algorithm to analyze these alternatives and to *couple* the binding and compaction phases.

(a)   Redefine the local microcode compaction problem (as it is stated in Section 5.4.2) to take into account the fact that the UNITS field of an MO in the input SLM may specify two or more alternative sets of functional units that may perform that operation.

(b)   Modify or enhance the FCFS algorithm accordingly.

5.9   [Continuation of Problems 5.5 and 5.6.] Analyze the implications of multicycle MOs and variable timing MOs for the *global compaction model* discussed in Section 5.4.2. In particular, determine whether the rules of inter-SLM code motion (Figure 5.20) have to be changed to take these issues into account. If so, what would be the new set of rules?

5.10 [Continuation of Problem 5.7.] Analyze the implications of the presence of transient stores for the global compaction problem and determine whether or not (and if so, how) the rules of code motion (Fig. 5.20) have to be modified to take this complication into account.

5.11 The trace scheduling algorithm discussed in Section 5.4.2 makes no mention of the presence of *loops* in the microprogram. Analyze and discuss how global compaction (using trace scheduling or any other technique that you may like to use) can be done when the microprogram contains loops.

5.12 Suppose S* (X1) is an instantiation of S* for a (hypothetical) machine X1. It is required to develop a set of proof rules for the microprogramming language S* (X1) as the basis for (i) formally defining the semantics of the language, and (ii) developing proofs of correctness of S*(X1) microprograms.

The general syntax of *assignments* in S* (X1) is

V := E

where V is a simple or subscripted variable and E is an arithmetic, logical, or shift expression. There are, however, some complications:

(a)   When an expression, E, is evaluated, several other variables (i.e., other than V) may be set to values as "side effect." Instances of such side effects are condition code flags or carry out flip-flops. As a specific example, the execution of the S* (X1) assignment.

    sh_outbus := LLS (6) [sh_inbus]

causes the contents of "sh_inbus" to be left logical-shifted by six positions and the result placed in "sh_outbus." At the same time, the following side-effects take place: (i) the last bit shifted out is recorded in an overflow flag; (ii) the shift type ("left logical") is recorded in a micromachine register called "type-field"; and (iii) the shift amount ("6") is recorded in a micromachine register called "amt-field."

(b)   An operation may be specified in E *indirectly*. For instance, rather than describe the left logical shift as in (a), it may be described in S* (X1) in the form:

    sh_outbus := (type-field) (amt-field) [sh_inbus]

where the registers "type-field" and "amt-field" have been set to specific values by previous assignments. The result of executing this assignment is to place the shifted value into "sh_outbus" and to record the last shifted out value in an overflow flag.

    Construct a general axiom of assignment for the S* (X1) assignment statement V := E that allows for these two forms of the statement.

5.13 The general form of the *conditional* statement in S* (X1) (see Problem 5.12) is

    if TEST-COND then S fi

where S is any other legal statement in S* (X1). Here, TEST-COND is one of a set of Boolean conditions that are specific to X1. These Boolean conditions have the predefined names CARRY, SIGN, OVERFLOW, SHIFTHB, and SHIFTLB and denote particular condition codes that may be "set" by previous assignments. TEST-COND may also specify the *negation* of the foregoing Boolean conditions, for example, *not* CARRY.

    Evaluation of a particular TEST-COND causes, as a side-effect the resetting of that TEST-COND to zero after the evaluation has been performed.

    Construct a proof rule for the S* (X1) **if** statement.

5.14 [Continuation of Problem 5.13.] The general forms for the *iteration* statements in S* (X1) are

    repeat S until TEST-COND

    while TEST-COND do S od

where TEST-COND is defined as in Problem 5.13. Construct proof rules for these two S* (X1) iteration statements.

5.15 In Pascal-like programming languages, the statement

    repeat S until B

is equivalent to the sequential composition

    S ; while not B **do S od**

Using the proof rules developed in Problem 5.14, and a proof rule for sequential composition, determine whether or not this equivalence is true in S* (X1).

5.16 Because S* (X1) is a partially machine dependent microprogramming language it includes, as one of its repertoire of simple statements, the construct

goto L

where L is the label of some other statement. The **goto** corresponds directly to the unconditional branch MO in X1.

Construct an axiom or a proof rule for this statement.

5.17 [Uses the solutions to Problems 5.13, 5.14, and 5.16.] Using the proof rules for the **if, goto,** and **repeat** statements in S* (X1), show that the functional behavior of

repeat S **until** TEST-COND

is equivalent to the sequential composition

L : S ;
if not TEST-COND **then goto** L **fi**

5.18 [Continuation of Problem 5.12.] A particular characteristic of microprogramming is that one must not only know the functional properties of each MO, but also its *temporal* properties. Consider, once more, the assignment statement $V := E$ in S* (X1). In Problem 5.12 we ignored the temporal aspects of this assignment completely.

Let us suppose, however, that the micromachine X1 runs with a 2-phase microcycle, and that all the legal S* (X1) assignments fall into one of the following categories:

Type I: All the assignments of this type begin and end execution (including all side effects) in phase 1 of the microcycle.

Type II: All the assignments of this type begin and complete execution (including side effects) in phase 2 of the microcycle.

Type III: All the assignments of this type require *two complete microcycles* for their execution.

Type IV: All the assignments of this type are of the form $V := E$ where "V" is a transient variable. These assignments begin and complete execution in phase 1 of the microcycle. However, V retains its "new" value only for the duration of phase 2 at the end of which it assumes the value "zero."

For each of these assignment types, modify the axiom of assignment developed in Problem 5.12 so that the axiom (or axioms, if necessary) reflects both the temporal and the functional properties of the assignment types.

PART THREE

PARALLEL PROCESSING

CHAPTER 6

PIPELINING IN UNIPROCESSORS

6.1 INTRODUCTION

Within a computer system the phenomenon of *parallelism* comes in many forms and may appear at many different levels of abstraction.[1] The goal of parallelism in all cases is the same: to increase, through architectural means, the performance of a computer.

In uniprocessors, two such forms of parallelism can be seen in micro-architectures: first, in the case of horizontal machines, several micro-operations can be executed from the same micro-instruction. Second, in any micromachine, vertical or horizontal, one can overlap the execution of one microinstruction with the fetching of the next (see Volume 1, Chapter 5). This latter case is an instance of what has come to be known as *pipelining*.

Among the many different means by which parallelism may be achieved within a computer, pipelining is certainly one of the most distinctive, powerful, and ubiquitous. It is sufficiently *distinctive* that one can reasonably view pipelining as an architectural *style* — in the sense that once a design decision is made that pipelining is to be used, this decision will most likely inform and influence almost all other aspects of the machine's design.[2] It is *powerful* and *general* in that pipelining can be employed at different levels of abstraction within a computer and can be conjoined with many other architectural styles. Consequently, it is *ubiquitous,* appearing in virtually all classes of computers ranging from microprocessors (e.g., the Intel 8086) through superminis and mainframes (e.g., the VAX 8600 and certain IBM System/370 models) to supercomputers (e.g., the CRAY machines).

The focus of this chapter is, then, pipelining. More specifically, after introducing the basic vocabulary, concepts, and issues related to pipelining in general, I will examine its presence in single-processor systems in the form of *instruction*

---

[1]The *Erlangan classification system* discussed in Section 2.5 (Chapter 2) conveys some flavor of possible levels at which parallelism might appear in a computer system.

[2]See Chapter 2 (Section 2.7) for a discussion of "style" in computer architecture. A more elaborate analysis is contained in Dasgupta (1984, Chapter 12).

pipelines. As will be clarified later, such mechanisms contribute to the design of endo-architectures.

Other important forms of pipelining will be briefly mentioned in this chapter but are discussed further and in more detail in Chapter 7.

6.2 BASIC CONCEPTS AND TERMS

In its most general and abstract form, a *pipeline system* P is an ordered pair

$$<T,S>$$

where T is a set of computational processes or *tasks* and S is a set of processors termed *stages* such that

1. Each task $T_i \; \varepsilon \; T$ is composed of subtasks $t_{i1}, t_{i2}, \ldots, t_{in}$ that must be processed *sequentially* in time; that is, the output computed by t_{ij} is the input to t_{ij+1}. Symbolically, we denote such a subtask sequence as

$$T_i \equiv <t_{i1}; t_{i2}; \ldots ; t_{in}>$$

   and use the set-theoretic notation $t_{ij} \; \varepsilon \; T_i$ to refer to subtask t_{ij} in task T_i.[3]

2. For a given task T_i, each $t_{ij} \; \varepsilon \; T_i$ is processed by a stage $S_k \; \varepsilon \; S$ such that if the subtasks $t_{i1}, t_{i2}, \ldots, t_{in}$ of T_i are processed respectively by stages $S_1, S_2, \ldots, S_n \; \varepsilon \; S$, then the output resource of stage S_j must be the input resource of stage S_{j+1}.

3. At any given time, two or more tasks from the task set T may be in the pipeline. That is, if

$$T_i \equiv <t_{i1}; t_{i2}; \ldots ; t_{im}>$$
$$T_j \equiv <t_{j1}; t_{j2}; \ldots ; t_{jn}>$$
$$\cdots \cdots \cdots \cdots \cdots$$
$$T_k \equiv <t_{k1}; t_{k2}; \ldots ; t_{kp}>$$

   are tasks $(T_i, T_j, \ldots, T_k \; \varepsilon \; T)$ then at some particular time it may be the case that distinct stages of S are processing subtasks $t_{iqi} \; \varepsilon \; T_i$, $t_{jqj} \; \varepsilon \; T_j$, $\ldots$, $t_{kqk} \; \varepsilon \; T_k$.

For a given pipeline system P, the stages of S must satisfy an *ordering relation* such that for every task in T condition (2) holds. We can, thus, view S as an *ordered set* of n stages and, by convention, refer to S as forming an *n-stage pipeline* or more simply as a *pipeline* when the number of stages is not impor-

---

[3]It is quite possible for a *subsequence* of subtasks to appear repeatedly in T_i. That is, it is just as possible for T_i to be of the form, say,

$$T_i \equiv <t_{i1}; t_{i2}; t_{i3}; t_{i2}; t_{i3}; t_{i2}; t_{i3}; t_{i4}>$$

as it is to be of the simpler form, say,

$$T_i \equiv <t_{i1}; t_{i2}; t_{i3}>$$

tant. We will also on occasions find it more natural to refer to the subtasks as *phases*.

Informally stated, then, pipelining involves splitting a task into subtasks or phases in such a fashion that the latter can be sequentially performed by the successive processing elements or stages of a pipeline. Furthermore, the processing of several different tasks may be *overlapped* by the fact that different stages of the pipeline can be processing subtasks belonging to separate tasks.

Example 6.1

Figure 6.1 depicts an *instruction pipeline* system with five stages denoted as IFETCH, IDECODE, EADDR, OFETCH, and IEXEC. The tasks to be processed are instructions stored in main memory. Consider an instruction stream $I_1 I_2 \ldots$, that is to be processed by the pipeline. Viewed as a "task," each instruction I_j consists of the following subtasks.

1. Fetching the instruction from main store.
2. Decoding the instruction.
3. Computing the effective addresses of operands.
4. Fetching the operands from main or local stores.
5. Executing the instruction.

Since each of these subtasks are performed by a distinct stage of the pipeline, each instruction I_j will "flow" through all five stages.

In the ideal situation there may be up to five consecutive instructions I_j, I_{j+1}, I_{j+2}, I_{j+3}, I_{j+4} in the pipeline at any given time such that while IEXEC is processing subtask (5) of instruction I_j, OFETCH is processing subtask (4) of instruction I_{j+1}, . . . , and IFETCH is processing subtask (1) of I_{j+4}. ■

Example 6.2

A *floating-point ADD* computation is composed of several sequentially ordered subtasks. In particular, consider the addition of two floating-point numbers $N_1 = \langle E_1, M_1 \rangle$, $N_2 = \langle E_2, M_2 \rangle$, where E_i, M_i (i = 1,2) are the exponent and mantissa, respectively, for number N_i. Then, the addition of N_1 and N_2 involves, typically, the following subtasks.

1. Comparison of exponents E_1 and E_2.

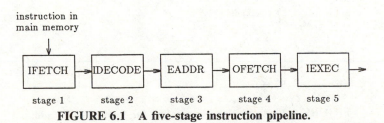

FIGURE 6.1 A five-stage instruction pipeline.

2. Alignment of the mantissas by shifting right the mantissa corresponding to the smallest exponent by an amount equal to the difference between E_1 and E_2.
3. Addition of the two mantissas.
4. Checking for the number of leading zeros in the result.
5. Normalizing the result by shifting left the result so as to eliminate the leading zeros and adjusting the corresponding exponent.

Figure 6.2 depicts a pipeline with stages specialized for the processing of these five sequential subtasks. This is an example of an *arithmetic pipeline*. ∎

The goal of implementing a pipeline is obvious: It is to increase the throughput of the system. Considering Example 6.1, assume, for the sake of simplicity, that each subtask of every instruction takes the same amount of time, N. Thus, each instruction in the instruction stream will require 5N time units to be processed regardless of whether the system is pipelined or otherwise. However, in a nonpipelined system instructions will be completely processed at the rate of one every 5N time units, whereas in a pipelined system, assuming the most optimistic conditions, instructions will be completely processed at the rate of one every N time units, a fivefold increase in throughput. Of course, as we will see later, there are many impediments to the attainment of such maximal performance.

Examples 6.1 and 6.2 also illustrate another feature of pipelined systems: A stage of a pipeline may itself constitute a pipeline in its own right. For example, the IEXEC stage of Figure 6.1 may be an arithmetic pipeline of the kind shown in Figure 6.2.

6.2.1 Categories of Pipeline Systems

A pipeline system $P = \langle T,S \rangle$ is said to be *unifunctional* if all the tasks in T that pass through the pipeline are functionally identical. That is, the pipeline S itself is capable of processing only one type of task. If the pipeline can process different task types—if T consists of tasks that are functionally distinct—the pipeline system is said to be *multifunctional*.

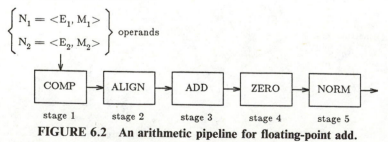

FIGURE 6.2 An arithmetic pipeline for floating-point add.

Example 6.3

The floating-point ADD system of Example 6.2 is an instance of a *unifunctional* pipeline system. The instruction pipeline described in Example 6.1 exemplifies a *multifunctional* system, since different types of instructions may be processed in different ways and may take different paths through the pipeline. ■

Multifunctional pipeline systems may be further classified into *statically configured* (or more simply, *static*) and *dynamically configured* (or *dynamic*) types, depending on how frequently the pipeline may switch from processing one type of task to another.

Since functionally distinct tasks may take different pathways through the pipeline, each such distinct path corresponding to a task may be called a *configuration* of the pipeline (Fig. 6.3), and the process of switching from one configuration to another, *reconfiguration* of the pipeline.

In a *static* system, the frequency of reconfiguration is relatively low, so that between changes the pipeline system behaves unifunctionally. In a *dynamic* system, the frequency of changing from one configuration to another is much higher.

Example 6.4

An important class of pipelined computers are *vector processors,* (see Chapter 7), in which a single type of operation may be applied to a stream of distinct operand sets. For example, given two n-element vectors

$$A = [a_1, a_2, \ldots, a_n]$$
$$B = [b_1, b_2, \ldots, b_n]$$

the computation of the vector sum

$$C = A + B$$

involves performing the following iterative statement:

for i := 1 **to** n
    do C[i] := A[i] + B[i] **od**

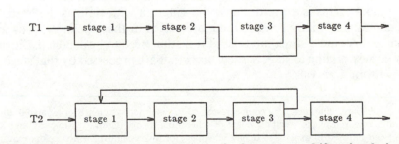

FIGURE 6.3 Two distinct configurations of a four-stage multifunctional pipeline.

That is, the same "+" operation is performed on different pairs of operands.

In a vector processor, a pipelined arithmetic/logical unit would be configured to overlap the execution of the add operation on successive pairs of operands:

(A[1],B[1]), (A[2],B[2]), . . . , (A[n],B[n])

The task stream entering the pipeline would consist of the same ADD instruction but operating on different pairs of operands. Thus, till all n pairs of vector elements have been processed, the pipeline will remain unifunctional, so to speak. At a different time, however, the same arithmetic pipeline may process a different instruction (e.g., a vector MULTIPLY), again, over many operand sets. Vector processors are, thus, examples par excellance of static multifunctional pipeline systems. Specific examples include (Kogge, 1981; Hwang, Su, and Ni, 1981; Hwang and Briggs, 1984): the IBM 2938 and 3838 Array Processors, the Texas Instruments ASC, the CDC STAR-100, the CRAY-1, and Floating Point Systems' AP-120B and FPS-164. ∎

Example 6.5

Instruction pipelines of the kind shown in Figure 6.1 are, typically, multifunctional dynamic systems. Consecutive instructions entering the pipeline are likely to differ from one to the next so that the pipeline configuration changes (or must have the capacity to change) very rapidly, on a task to task basis. As will be discussed later in this chapter, most high-performance uniprocessors incorporate such dynamic, multifunctional instruction pipelines. Important examples include IBM's System/360 Model 91, System/370 Model 165 and the 3033 (Kogge, 1981; Siewiorek, Bell, and Newell, 1982), the MU5 (Morris and Ibbett, 1979; Ibbett, 1982), the Amdahl 470/v6 (Ramamoorthy and Li, 1977), and, most recently, the VAX 8600 (Fossum, McElroy, and English, 1985, Troiani *et al.*, 1985). Instruction pipeline systems are also referred to as *lookahead processors* (Keller, 1975). ∎

6.2.2 Depiction of Pipeline Schedules: The Gantt Chart

Given an n-stage pipeline and an ordered set of tasks to be processed by the pipeline, a *schedule* is a description of the assignment of tasks to stages at each point of time. A convenient representation of pipeline schedules is the *Gantt chart* (Fig. 6.4). This is a two-dimensional diagram with time as the horizontal axis; it contains as many rows as there are stages in the pipeline and as many columns as there are distinct intervals of time that need to be depicted. Entries in the row corresponding to stage S_i show tasks that are processed by that stage over successive time intervals.[4]

---

[4]The use of the Gantt chart is not, of course, restricted to pipelined systems. It originated in the field of operations research in the specific context of scheduling theory (Conway, Maxwell, and Miller, 1967) and can be used in general to depict schedules for any system of n processors required to service an ordered set of tasks. Coffman and Denning (1973), for example, used Gantt charts extensively in their discussion of processor scheduling by operating systems.

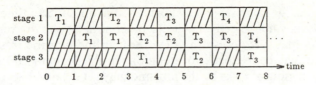

FIGURE 6.4 A Gantt chart for a three-stage pipeline processing a task stream T_1, T_2, ...

In the context of pipelines Gantt charts are also termed *space-time diagrams* (Chen, 1971; Ramamoorthy and Li, 1977) and *reservation tables* (Davidson, 1971; Kogge, 1981).

6.2.3 Performance Characteristics

Pipelining, like all other parallel processing techniques, is intended to enhance the performance of a computer system. To this end, one must consider a number of performance characteristics that are relevant to the design of pipelined systems. The most important of these are the following.

Throughout and Speedup

The *throughput* of a pipelined system is the number of tasks completely processed by the pipeline per unit time. Consider, for example, an n-stage pipeline where each stage requires the same unit of time to process any subtask and the tasks are delivered to the pipeline at the same unit intervals. The system will require n time units to "fill" the pipeline and process the first task; thereafter, it will process one task after every unit time interval. Therefore, the pipeline processes k tasks in time

$$T_p(k,n) = n + (k-1)$$

Hence, the system's throughput is

$$\frac{k}{n + (k-1)} \text{ tasks/time unit}$$

It is also natural to want to compare the throughput of a pipelined system with that of a nonpipelined system. In the latter case, k tasks will be processed in time

$$T_{np}(k,n) = nk$$

The *speedup* of the n-store pipelined system processing k tasks, relative to the nonpipelined system, is

$$SU = \frac{T_{np}(k,n)}{T_p(k,n)} = \frac{nk}{n + (k-1)}$$

With $k \gg n$, the speedup approaches n, the number of stages in the pipeline.

"Real" pipelined processors will rarely meet the ideal assumptions underlying this rather simple model. The stages of the pipeline may differ in their relative processing times; the same stage may take different amounts of time for different subtasks; tasks may not be delivered to the pipeline at regular or even predictable intervals; tasks may not necessarily flow through the pipeline in such a linear fashion: There may be feedbacks or iterations in the system (see Fig. 6.3); and, finally, the processing of tasks by the pipeline may get delayed because of certain dependencies between tasks or because of conflicts in their usage of stages.

These issues will be discussed later in this chapter. For the present, merely note that the throughput performance and speedups in realistic pipelined systems are very often assessed, especially at the design stage, using *simulation*.

Example 6.6

Weiss and Smith (1984) have investigated and compared the performance of a number of different instruction pipeline schemes using simulation. In their particular experiment, a collection of 14 benchmark programs developed at the Lawrence Livermore National Laboratory served as inputs to their simulated pipelined systems and the throughputs were measured empirically. ■

Initiation Rate and Latency

Throughput measures the rate at which tasks *leave* the pipeline. Kogge (1981) has defined an alternative measure called the *initiation rate,* which is the rate at which tasks may *enter* the pipeline. The inverse of initiation rate is the pipeline's *latency,* which is the average number of time units between two consecutive initiations.

Efficiency

Given an n-stage pipeline processing a stream of k tasks, it is also useful to be able to determine the extent to which the stages of the pipeline are kept busy, since this kind of information provides a basis for identifying bottlenecks in the pipeline. The *efficiency* (of utilization) of stage S_i is a measure of how often S_i is used to process tasks in a given task stream. It is defined as the ratio

$$\frac{\text{Number of time units for which } S_i \text{ is busy}}{\text{Total number of time units required to process k tasks}}$$

Similarly, the *efficiency of the pipeline* measures the extent to which all stages are busy in processing the task stream. Again, under the ideal assumptions that each stage requires unit time to process, that there are no delays within the pipeline, and that the initiation rate is one task per unit time, the efficiency of an n-stage pipeline processing a stream of k tasks is given by

$$\text{Eff}(n,k) = \frac{nk}{(n + (k - 1))n}$$

For $k \gg n$ and for very large k, we note that $\text{Eff}(n,k) \rightarrow 1$. In reality, of course, these assumptions will rarely be met.

6.2.4 Forwarding And hazards

Consider, once more, an n-stage pipeline; one may conceptually view the system as one in which an "unprocessed" set of tasks in some order enters the pipeline and the same set of tasks, but "processed," exits the pipeline, again in some order.

There are two possibilities regarding the ordering of the processed tasks. In the first, simpler case the tasks emerge from the pipeline in the same order that they are initiated (Fig. 6.5). The problem with this is that it does not take into account the facts that (1) different tasks may take different amounts of time to be processed by the pipeline; or (2) a task T_{i-1} may be held up at a particular stage in which case all tasks $T_i, T_{i+1}, \ldots$, following it will also be delayed.

Example 6.7

Consider the instruction pipeline of Example 6.1 (Fig. 6.1) and a task stream $I_1, I_2, I_3, \ldots$, being processed by this pipeline. A given instruction I_j in this stream may be a "long" instruction, for example, a storage-to-storage instruction requiring two main memory accesses as part of its operand fetch phase. An instruction following I_j could then be delayed from entering the OFETCH stage even though it was ready to do so. All other subsequent instruction would be correspondingly held up. ∎

Thus, the second and more efficient alternative is to relax the necessity of preserving the initiation order; if a task T_i is delayed at a given stage and it is possible for T_{i+1} to proceed to a stage further down the pipeline, then it is allowed to do so. This technique is referred to as *forwarding* (Tomasulo, 1967) and may lead to a situation where the order of the output task stream is some permutation of the initiation order (Fig. 6.6). Although this technique may increase the extent of overlap in the processing of instructions and consequently the pipeline throughput, quite a bit of additional machinery—both logical and physical—must be used to ensure not only that the throughput can be increased but also that forwarding preserves the *intended function* of the original task stream.

By recognizing the possibility of delays inside the pipeline, we have, in fact, injected the first dose of realism into our rather rarified model of pipelined systems. One of the first consequences is that the stages of the pipeline may operate *asynchronously* (relative to one another) rather than in fully synchronized, lock-step fashion.

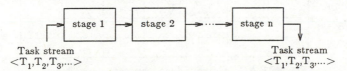

Task stream
$<T_1, T_2, T_3, \ldots>$

Task stream
$<T_1, T_2, T_3, \ldots>$

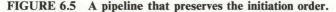

FIGURE 6.5 **A pipeline that preserves the initiation order.**

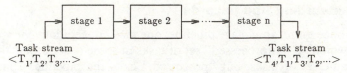

FIGURE 6.6   **A pipeline that alters the initiation order.**

Second, the pipelined system must ensure that for an ordered pair of tasks

$$<T_i, T_j>$$

where T_i precedes T_j in the task stream (denoted as $T_i < T_j$), if T_j (or one of its subtasks) is dependent on the result produced by T_i (or one of its subtasks), then T_j should be appropriately delayed until the result from T_i (or its relevant subtask) is available.

Example 6.8

Consider the instruction pipeline of Example 6.1 (Fig. 6.1) and suppose the instruction stream contains the subsequence:

I_j : R1 ← R1 + R2
I_{j+1} if R1 > 0 **then** goto I_k
I_{j+2} : R3 ← R4 + R2
· · · · · · · · ·

We see here two different types of dependencies:

1.   The branch condition in I_{j+1} cannot be tested until I_j has completed. More precisely, during the processing of I_{j+1}, the operand R1 cannot be accessed (by stage OFETCH) until the stage IEXEC has actually completed processing I_j and register R1 has been modified. A Gantt chart depicting the resulting delay is presented in Figure 6.7. This is an example of a *data dependency*—that is, a dependency induced by the fact that I_{j+1} requires, for its execution, data produced by I_j.
2.   The instruction I_{j+2} cannot be executed (by IEXEC) until the branch instruction I_{j+1} has been completely processed and it is "known" to the pipelined system whether or not a jump to I_k has taken place. In the former

IFETCH	I_j	I_{j+1}					
IDECODE		I_j	I_{j+1}				
EADDR			I_j	I_{j+1}	←delay→		
OFETCH				I_j		I_{j+1}	
IEXEC					I_j		I_{j+1}

time →

FIGURE 6.7   **Delay induced by data dependency.**

case, the instructions $I_{j+2}, I_{j+3}, \ldots$, already in the pipeline following I_{j+1} should not be allowed to complete their execution phases. This kind of dependency is termed *procedural* or *control dependency*.   ■

Dependencies between tasks form, in the terminology of pipelining, one class of *hazards* (Ramamoorthy and Li, 1977). In general, hazards are any conditions within the pipelined system that disrupt, delay, or prevent smooth flow of tasks through the pipeline. In addition to intertask dependencies, a hazard may also arise because, or when, two tasks in the task stream require the use of the same hardware resource at the same time. Such hazards are termed *collisions* in the pipelining literature (Kogge, 1981), although in the general context of parallel processing, they constitute what are called *resource conflicts.* The detection and resolution of hazards constitute a major aspect of the design and control of pipelined systems. I will deal with these aspects in the specific context of instruction pipelines later in this chapter.

6.2.5   Latches and Clocks

The primary role of a pipeline stage is to perform some subtask based on input presented to the stage and produce output that is passed on to the next stage for further processing. In the case of pipelines implemented in hardware, which is what we are interested in here, stages are essentially combinational circuits.[5] In general, stages may require different amounts of time to perform their work, in which case the output produced by stage i (say) may not be immediately accepted by stage i+1 if the latter is still processing a previous subtask. For this reason, high-speed registers termed *staging latches* (or simply *latches*) are introduced between the stages of a pipeline (Fig. 6.8).

The purpose of a latch is to hold the input to a stage (or, equivalently, the output of the previous stage) for a sufficient time until the stage is in a position to

[5]It is, of course, quite possible for pipelines to be implemented in *software*. For instance, many functions performed by a computer's operating system can be logically viewed, modeled, and designed as pipelined systems where each stage is realized as a software module and the stages collectively constitute a *concurrent program*. In the operating systems and concurrent programming literature, such pipelines are studied under the general rubric of "producer-consumer problems" (Brinch Hansen, 1973, 1977).

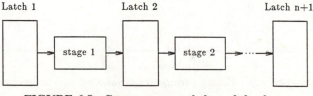

FIGURE 6.8   Stages connected through latches.

correctly accept the input for further processing. A latch, then, serves as a buffer between adjacent components of a pipeline. In the pipelining literature they are also referred to as *reservation stations*.

We assume that the pipelined systems of interest to us will be *clocked* systems. That is, the times at (and during) which significant events take place in the system will essentially be determined and regulated by a global clock. This is to be contrasted to a purely *asynchronous* pipelined system, where the times at which significant events take place — including the flow of information between stages — are not under the control of a central clock but are regulated by the stages communicating with one another through explicit synchronizing mechanisms.[6]

For the present, I will present a relatively straightforward model of timing. In later discussions, more complex timing situations will be considered.

In a clocked system, a clock pulse will be issued to the stages of the pipeline at regular intervals. When a clock pulse is received by stage i, it accepts the information held in its input latch i, performs its task, and outputs its result to the next latch, i + 1. This output must be received by latch i + 1 and be stabilized before the next clock pulse arrives at the pipeline.

We define for each stage i a *stage delay* sd_i as the time required for it to perform its subtask. Each latch will be associated with an identical *latch delay* ld, which is the time required for the latches to accept their respective inputs (Fig. 6.9). The *clock period* (cp), the interval between successive clock pulses arriving at the pipeline, is then determined as

$$cp = \underset{1 \le i \le n}{Max} (sd_i) + ld$$

The inverse 1/cp of the clock period is the *frequency* at which the pipeline operates.

---

[6]An example of an asynchronous pipeline is described precisely and in detail in Dasgupta (1984, Chapter 7).

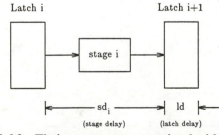

FIGURE 6.9 **Timing parameters associated with a pipeline.**

6.3 THE ORGANIZATION OF INSTRUCTION PIPELINES

We are now in a position to discuss in some detail the organization and principles of instruction pipelines. As we have already noted, such a pipeline is essentially an endo-architectural feature; indeed, the use of pipelining for the processing of an instruction stream has so many consequences that one may legitimately say that pipelined architectures constitute a distinctive endo-architectural style.

The assertion that instruction pipelining pertains to endo-architecture carries with it the implication that the pipeline need not be visible at the exo-architectural level. Thus, the programmer or the compiler writer may be quite ignorant of the fact that pipelining is being used. In the past this was largely true. For instance, in the case of the IBM System/360 and System/370 series, not all processors were pipelined, although they all shared a common exo-architecture. Thus one was expected to program these computers regardless of whether or not the instructions were processed through a pipeline.

However, if the existence of the pipeline *is* known to the programmer or the compiler writer, this knowledge may be very usefully employed in producing object code that can be efficiently processed by the pipeline. In other words, although awareness of the pipeline is not necessary for producing correct code, it may be important for the exploitation of the full power of the pipeline.[7] Rymarczyk (1982) has discussed how assembly language programmers and the compiler writer may take advantage of pipelining. And, in recent years, pipelined processors, such as the Stanford MIPS (Hennessy *et al.,* 1982; Gross and Hennessy, 1982), have emerged where it is essential for the compiler writer to be aware of the nature of the pipeline since otherwise, the resulting code would simply not be correct.

In this section (6.3), I will consider the organization of instruction pipelines. To make this discussion precise, I will first (in Section 6.3.1) suggest a model of the exo- and endo-architectures that is relevant for our purposes. In Section 6.3.2 I introduce the basic theory of hazards, which is at the heart of all pipelined systems. In the rest of Section 6.3, various design issues in pipelined systems are discussed.

6.3.1 The Architecture: Assumptions and a Model

We assume, to begin with, that the exo-architecture follows the register machine style (see Volume 1, Chapter 4) and exhibits the following characteristics.

1. Programmable storage consists of main memory and a local store of registers. Memory operands will be denoted as Mem[a], Mem[b], . . . , where a,

---

[7]These comments are made only in the context of instruction pipelines. The pipelining characteristics of a processor *must* be visible in the case of vector or array processors (see Chapter 7).

b, . . . , specify memory addresses using valid addressing modes. Register operands will similarly be signified as Reg[u], Reg[v], . . . , where u, v, . . . , specify register addresses using valid addressing modes.

2. Memory words and registers are all of width W; this is the word length of the machine.

3. Instructions will be symbolized by the forms:

    Dest := OP(source)
    Dest := OP(source$_1$, source$_2$)
    If BOOL (source) then goto L$_k$
    If BOOL (source$_1$, source$_2$) then goto L$_k$

where (a) "Dest" denotes a memory word or a local store register that serves as the destination of the value produced by the instruction; (b) "source," "source$_1$," "source$_2$" denote memory or register operands; (c) "OP" is the operation performed by the instruction; (d) BOOL is a Boolean value-returning expression with either one argument ("source") or two ("source$_1$," "source$_2$"); and (e) "L$_k$" is a label of some instruction.

Example 6.9

Concrete instances of such instructions are
(a) Reg[u] := LOAD (Mem[a])
(b) Reg[u] := ADD (Reg[u], Reg[v])
(c) Reg[v] := NOT (Reg[w])
(d) **if GREATER (Reg[u], Reg[w]) then goto** L$_1$ ■

4. All instructions are of length W, the machine's word length, and thus fit exactly into a memory word or a register. Furthermore, all opcode fields are of the same length.

5. All operands can be stored in a single memory word or a register either singly or in packed form.

6. Because of (4) and (5), an instruction or an operand can be fetched from main memory in one memory access.

7. Although we are not stipulating the precise addressing modes, we will assume that they fall into two broad classes: one based on using local store registers only and the other using main memory words (possibly in conjunction with registers). These will be termed *register-based* and *memory-based* modes, respectively. In the former case, the effective address is computed from register values only (as, for example, in the register and autoincrement modes in the PDP-11—see Volume 1, Chapter 4), whereas in memory-based modes memory words have to be accessed during the calculation of effective address (as in the register deferred or autoincrement deferred modes in the PDP-11).

For this particular machine model, instruction processing has four distinct phases: instruction *fetch,* instruction *decode, effective address computation,* and instruction *execution.* Since all instructions are of identical length and opcodes

TABLE 6.1 Instruction Processing Phases and Their Times

Phases of Instruction Processing	Time (microcycles)
Instruction fetch	5
Instruction decode	2
Effective address computation	
Register-based mode	2
Memory-based mode	5
Instruction execution (nonbranch)	
Load/store	5
Register-register functional	2
Register-storage functional	5
Instruction execution (branch)	
Unconditional branch	2
Conditional branch	
If branch taken	3
If branch not taken	2

are of the same size [assumption (4)], the times for instruction fetch and instruction decode will be constants. The address computation time will depend on the mode being register- or memory-based. The execution time will, of course, be instruction dependent.

Table 6.1 lists representative times required for these various phases measured in microcycles.

6.3.2 The Conditions for Hazard Formation

Recall from Section 6.2.4 that a hazard is any condition within the pipelined system that disrupts the smooth flow of the task stream through the pipeline. We also noted that there are two classes of hazards.

1. **Dependencies** between tasks. In the specific case of instruction pipelines, there may be either *data* or *control* dependencies.
2. **Collisions;** that is, two tasks require the use of the same hardware functional unit at the same time.

Let us consider somewhat more formally the general conditions under which hazards may arise between instructions in an instruction pipeline. For this purpose, we will denote a particular stream of instructions IS_k as

$$IS_k \equiv \langle I_{k1}; \ldots ; I_{k2}; \ldots ; I_{kj}; I_{k,j+1}; \ldots \rangle$$

where I_{k1} precedes I_{k2}, I_{k2} precedes I_{k3}, . . . , I_{kj} precedes $I_{k,j+1}$, . . . ; When I_{kj} precedes I_{kl} in the instruction stream we denote this as

$$I_{kj} < I_{kl}$$

Each instruction I_{kj} may be expressed in terms of its ordered subtasks as

$$I_{kj} \equiv <I_{kj}.\text{fetch}; I_{kj}.\text{decode}; I_{kj}.\text{addr}; I_{kj}.\text{exec}>$$

These instructions will be of the types described in the machine model of Section 6.3.1. Thus, for an instruction I_{kj} we will denote by

SOURCE(I_{kj})
DEST(I_{kj})

its *operand source set* and *result destination set,* respectively.

Example 6.10

Consider the following instructions.

I_{k1}: Reg[1] := LOAD (Mem [Reg[4]])
I_{k2}: Reg[2] := ADD (Reg[1], Reg[2])
I_{k3}: **if** GREATER (Reg[1], Reg[2]) **then goto** L₁

Their source and destination sets are:

SOURCE (I_{k1}) = {Mem; Reg[4]}, DEST(I_{k1}) = {Reg[1]}
SOURCE (I_{k2}) = {Reg[1], Reg[2]}, DEST(I_{k2}) = {Reg[2]}
SOURCE (I_{k3}) = {Reg[1], Reg[2]}, DEST(I_{k3}) = {   }   ∎

An instruction stream IS_k forms a *basic block* if (1) the only entry point in IS_k is by way of its first instruction and (2) the only exit point is the last instruction in the stream. In other words, a basic block is a straight-line sequence of instructions within which a branch may appear only as the last instruction in the stream.[8]

Data Dependency Hazards

Let $I_{kj} < I_{kl}$ in a basic block IS_k. Then the following kinds of *data dependency* hazards may arise:[9]

Read After Write (RAW):
    DEST (I_{kj}) ∩ SOURCE (I_{kl}) ≠ ∅
Write After Read (WAR):
    SOURCE (I_{kj}) ∩ DEST (I_{kl}) ≠ ∅
Write After Write (WAW):
    DEST (I_{kj}) ∩ DEST (I_{kl}) ≠ ∅

---

[8]The term *basic block* is borrowed from compiler theory (Aho and Ullman, 1977, Chapter 12). In the theory of microcode compaction, which is concerned with the automatic reorganization of vertical microcode into equivalent horizontal microcode and which has many points in common with the principles currently under discussion, basic blocks of microcode are also called "straight-line microprograms" (Landskov *et al.,* 1980; also see Chapter 5 of this volume.)

[9]I use the usual set theoretic notations here: If S_1, S_2 are sets, then $S_1 ∩ S_2$, $S_1 ∪ S_2$ denote their intersection and union, respectively, and ∅ denotes the empty set.

Informally, a RAW hazard occurs when the earlier instruction I_{kj} writes to a store that is to be read by the later instruction I_{kl}. A WAR hazard occurs when I_{kj} reads from a store that is being written into by I_{kl}. Finally, a WAW hazard occurs when both instructions wish to write to the same store.[10]

Example 6.11

Consider the following instruction stream IS_1:

$I_{11} \equiv$ Reg[1] := LOAD (Mem [Reg[4]]);

$I_{12} \equiv$ Reg[2] := ADD (Reg[1], Reg[2]);

$I_{13} \equiv$ Mem[Reg[u]] := STORE (Reg[2]);

$I_{14} \equiv$ Reg[2] := AND (Reg[6], Reg[3]);

$I_{15} \equiv$ Reg[6] := INCR (Reg[6]).

The instructions $<I_{11},I_{12}>$ pose a RAW hazard; $<I_{12},I_{14}>$ pose a WAW hazard, while the pair $<I_{14},I_{15}>$ constitute a WAR hazard. ∎

It is worth noting that although the RAW and WAR conditions appear symmetric, they differ in a rather fundamental way: a RAW hazard—such as between I_{11} and I_{12} in Example 6.11—arises because there may be a genuine *dependency between* the instructions: I_{12} requires the value in R[1] that was previously produced by I_{11}.

In contrast, a WAR hazard—as between I_{14} and I_{15} in Example 6.11—arises because the later instruction wishes to alter the value of a store at a time that the previous value is still required by the earlier instruction. Certainly, I_{14} does not *depend* on I_{15} nor I_{15} on I_{14}. To highlight this asymmetry, the condition leading to a WAR hazard was termed an *antidependency* by Banerjee and colleagues (1979).

Branch instructions do not produce results that are written into destination stores in the way other instructions do.[11] Thus a branch, when being processed as the last instruction in a basic block, cannot pose a WAW or a WAR hazard. It can certainly pose a RAW hazard relative to some earlier instruction in the instruction stream.

Example 6.12

Given the sequence of instructions IS_2:

$I_{21} \equiv$ Reg[2] := ADD (Reg[2], Reg[3]);

---

[10]Strictly speaking, these conditions identify the *potential* for hazards between I_{kj} and I_{kl}. If I_{kj} and I_{kl} are far enough apart, they will never be in the pipeline at the same time, in which case a hazard will never actually occur. Henceforth, we will assume, in order to make this discussion meaningful, that instruction pairs may, in fact, be in the pipeline at the same time so that potential hazards may actually occur.

[11]At least not when the instructions are viewed at the exo-architectural level. When we look at the implementation of a branch instruction at the endo- or micro-architectural level, then the picture changes: The result of executing a branch is to write a value (the "branch-to" address) into the program counter.

$I_{22} \equiv$ **if** ZERO (Reg[2]) **then goto** L_3

the pair $\langle I_{21}, I_{22} \rangle$ constitute a RAW hazard. ∎

Control Dependency Hazards

Data dependency hazards are problematic since they may prevent the simultaneous processing of two instructions in the pipeline and may, as a result, disrupt and reduce the throughput. These are not, however, the only sources of trouble in a pipeline. Looking beyond basic blocks, the presence of a branch in the instruction stream may lead to a *control dependency* hazard as follows: Let

$$IS_k \equiv \langle I_{k1}; I_{k2}; \ldots ; I_{kj}; I_{kj+1}; \ldots I_{kp} \rangle$$

be a stream of p instructions in which I_{kj} is a conditional or unconditional branch. For the sake of uniformity, all branches may be expressed in the form

if BOOL (. . .) **then goto** L_r

where L_r is the "branch-to" address and BOOL (. . .), the test condition, is always the predicate TRUE in the case of an unconditional branch.

A *control dependency* (CD) *hazard* is said to occur whenever a branch takes place and the instruction at the branch-to address is $I_{k,j+n}$ for some $n > 1$ or $I_{k,j-m}$ for some $m \geq 0$. The instructions $I_{k,j+1}, \ldots, I_{k,j+n-1}$ (in the first case) or the instructions $I_{k,j+1}, \ldots, I_{km'}$ (in the second case) are the *constituents* of the CD hazard with respect to the branch, I_{kj}.

In other words, a CD hazard results when the outcome of a branch is to transfer control (forward or backward) to an instruction such that some subsequence of instructions following the branch are skipped (Fig. 6.10). Instructions in this subsequence are the constituents of the CD hazard and must be prevented from being processed by the pipeline if the branch takes place.

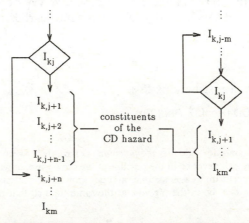

FIGURE 6.10   Control dependency (CD) hazards.

Example 6.13

Consider the following instruction stream IS_3:

$I_{31} \equiv$ Reg[2] := ADD (Reg[2], Reg[3]);

$I_{32} \equiv$ **if** ZERO (Reg[2]) **then goto** L_3;

$I_{33} \equiv$ Mem[500] := STORE (Reg[2]);

$I_{34} \equiv$ L3: Mem[600] := ADD(Mem[500], Reg[5])

The instruction I_{33} is the constituent of a CD hazard with respect to I_{32}. ∎

Collisions

Finally, instructions may be involved in a collision: that is, a pair of instructions may wish to use the same functional unit at the same time.

Let I_{kj}, I_{kl} be two instructions in the stream IS_k such that $I_{kj} < I_{kl}$. Let UNIT (I_{kj}), UNIT (I_{kl}) denote the sets of functional units needed to process I_{kj} and I_{kl}, respectively. Then a necessary condition for a collision hazard is

UNIT $(I_{kj}) \cap$ UNIT $(I_{kl}) \neq \emptyset$

6.3.3 Example of an Instruction Pipeline: The Principle Issues

We noted in Section 6.3.1 that for our particular machine model instruction processing has four phases: fetch, decode, effective address calculation, and execution. The pipeline will be partitioned along similar lines (Fig. 6.11), with the four stages designated as IFETCH, IDECODE, EADDR, and IEXEC, respectively. Since different instruction types have different processing needs, the pipeline must be multifunctional; and as consecutive instructions in the input stream may belong to the different instruction types, the pipeline must be dynamically reconfigurable.

The principle problems of interest in designing such a system are

1. What will be the timing characteristics of the pipeline?
2. At which stage (or stages) will data-dependency hazards be tested for, and what is to be done when such a hazard is detected?
3. At which point in the pipeline will control dependencies be tested for, and how will the system respond to them?
4. At which stage (or stages) will collisions be tested for, and what is to be done when collisions occur?
5. How will hazards be detected?
6. How will the pipeline as a whole be controlled?

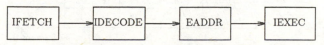

FIGURE 6.11 A four-stage pipeline.

We have purposely separated the questions concerning the three classes of hazards since they require, in some sense, distinct considerations; note also that (2) through (4) deal with policy questions whereas (5) and (6) are issues of implementation.

6.3.4 Timing Characteristics: Synchrony and Asynchrony

Based on Table 6.1, we can see that the delays to be associated with the four stages are

IFETCH:	5 microcycles
IDECODE:	2 microcycles
EADDR:	2 or 5 microcycles
IEXEC:	2, 3, or 5 microcycles

The simplest way of coping with these variations in stage delays is to take their maximum (viz., 5 microcycles) as the constant actual delay for all the stages and use this to determine the clock period and the pipeline frequency (as indicated in Section 6.2.5). Assuming that instructions can be fed into the pipeline at the required initiation rate, its maximum throughout will be one instruction every 5 microcycles (Fig. 6.12).

The main problem with this solution is obvious: There may be significant periods of time when the IDECODE, EADDR, and IEXEC stages are doing nothing, even assuming a hazard-free, idealized instruction stream. If we examine the use of the stages from one *microcycle* to the next, we may, in a rather pessimistic scenario obtain a Gantt chart of the type shown in Figure 6.13. Of course, the actual use of the stages will depend on the actual distribution of instruction types in the input stream.

Second, even if underuse of stages was acceptable, the smooth flow of instructions through the pipeline every 5 microcycles would be disrupted by the occurrence of hazards. Thus, a uniform timing structure for all stages of the pipeline will scarcely be possible.

As a first step toward improving this solution we note that the most serious impediment to reducing the average stage delay is the main memory access time. Memory is accessed during instruction fetch, effective address calculation, and instruction execution (in this last phase it is actually the fetching of operands

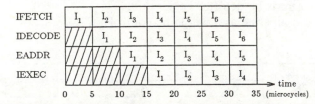

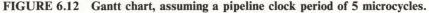

FIGURE 6.12 Gantt chart, assuming a pipeline clock period of 5 microcycles.

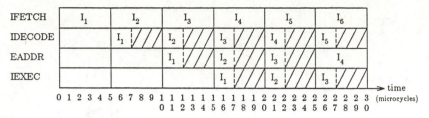

FIGURE 6.13 Gantt chart on a per-microcycle basis assuming stage delays of 5 microcycles.

that may demand memory access). However, the address calculation and instruction execution phases will not need to access main store all the time—thus, the delays of the corresponding pipeline stages may be as low as 2 microcycles. The instruction fetch time, on the other hand, will always require 5 microcycles.

We will, accordingly, attempt to revise our timing scheme as follows: *Assuming* that the IFETCH stage can be designed to deliver instructions to the IDECODE stage at the rate of one every 2 microcycles:

1. The stage delays in the "normal" case will be assumed to be 2 microcycles.
2. Whenever a particular stage requires more time (e.g., when a memory access is needed by EADDR or IEXEC), it is allowed to do so. The *idealized* flow through the pipeline (still disregarding, that is, the occurrence of dependency and collision hazards) will then only be affected by (what we hope are relatively rare) memory accesses.

The basic implication of this plan is that if the (constant) bottleneck (IFETCH) can somehow be reduced (how, we will see in Section 6.3.5), then providing that the other stages can perform at their highest speeds most of the time, a much higher average throughput may be attained.

Example 6.14

Consider the following instruction stream, IS_4:

$I_{41} \equiv$ Reg[1] := ADD(Reg[1], Reg[2]);

$I_{42} \equiv$ Reg[3] := LOAD(Mem [Reg4]);

$I_{43} \equiv$ Reg[5] := AND(Reg[1], Reg[3]);

$I_{44} \equiv$ Mem [Reg[4]] := STORE(Reg[5]);

$I_{45} \equiv$ **if** ZERO(Reg[5]) **then goto** L_k

If the earlier scheme of a constant delay/stage of 5 microcycles is adopted, these instructions will be processed in 40 microcycles (Fig. 6.12)—a throughput of 1 instruction in 8 microcycles. Using the revised timing scheme, and (1) noting that I_{42} and I_{44} need to access memory; and (2) assuming that the branch of I_{45} is taken, the timing requirements for IS_4 will be as shown in Figure 6.14. The total time to process the five instructions is 23 microcycles, a throughput of 1 instruction every 4.6 microcycles. ■

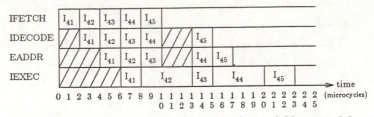

FIGURE 6.14 Gantt chart for IS₄ assuming variable stage delays.

Example 6.15

It is instructive to see how the pipeline performs with a more pathological instruction stream. Consider IS_5:

$I_{51} \equiv$ Reg[1] := LOAD(Mem [Mem[500]]);

$I_{52} \equiv$ Reg[2] := LOAD(Mem [Mem[501]]);

$I_{53} \equiv$ Reg[3] := ADD(Reg[1], Reg[2]);

$I_{54} \equiv$ Mem [Mem[500]] := STORE(Reg[3]).

Again, assuming the earlier scheme of a 5 microcycle/stage delay, IS_5 would be processed in 35 microcycles (Fig. 6.12), a throughput of 8.75 microcycles/instruction. Using the revised scheme, the Gantt chart of Figure 6.15 obtains, IS_5 is processed in 29 microcycles, a throughput of an instruction every 7.25 microcycles. Note that the fetching of I_{54} is shown to be delayed by 3 microcycles since it cannot, in any case, be passed to EADDR till I_{52} has completed execution. ■

From the perspective of pipeline logic it should be obvious that the control of the new scheme will be considerably more complex. In the earlier version the pipeline stages are completely synchronized with the clock cycle time: Each successive clock signal advances the instruction one further stage along the pipeline.

In the current version we have to introduce a measure of *asynchrony* into the pipeline. The problem can be described by referring to Figure 6.16.

Assume, in the most general case, that both stages i and i + 1 have variable delays. Advancing a task from stage i to latch i, and a task already in latch i to stage i + 1 cannot simply be effected at regular clocked intervals.

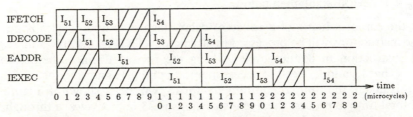

FIGURE 6.15 Gantt chart is IS₅ assuming variable stage delays.

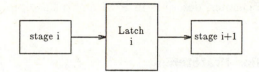

FIGURE 6.16   Typical fragment of a pipeline.

For example, assuming that the two stages begin their activations together, stage i may require 5 microcycles to deposit its task T_j in latch i whereas stage i + 1 may have completed processing its task T_{j-1} (previously in latch i) in 2 microcycles. Stage i + 1 must then wait till it "knows" that the next task T_j has been placed in latch i.

Latch i, then, constitutes a kind of hazard; we may call it a *synchronization hazard,* and it poses the classical problems of interprocess communication and mutual exclusion that are encountered whenever concurrent processing involves shared variables (Brinch Hansen, 1973; Hoare, 1985, Chapter 7; Filman and Friedman, 1984, Chapter 3).

The pipeline control must, therefore, guarantee that when stage i deposits its task into latch i the latter is *empty;* otherwise, stage i must *wait* till the latch is empty. When it can do so, stage i deposits its task into latch i and must indicate that the latch is now *full.* A *flag* bit associated with latch i can be used to detect and set the state of the latch (Fig. 6.17).

Similarly, when stage i + 1 requires a task from latch i, the latter must have such a task — as indicated by the flag bit's state; otherwise the stage must wait till the latch has been filled. When it is able to do so, stage i + 1 accepts the task in latch i and sets the flag bit to "empty."

Note that a completely asynchronous system is not required. The overall system may still be clocked in the sense that the significant events (viz., processing by a stage, testing the latch's state, depositing the task in the latch, setting the latch's state) are enabled by clock signals.

Describing concurrent systems of any kind in natural language can only convey the *flavor* of the concurrency involved. For a more precise, more rigorous understanding, it becomes necessary to introduce formal descriptions. Thus, for those readers familiar with S*M (see Chapter 4, Section 4.3), Appendix 6.A,

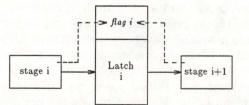

FIGURE 6.17   Flag associated with a latch and accessible to adjacent stages.

at the end of this chapter, describes in S*M a two-stage pipeline with variable stage delays.

6.3.5 Instruction Prefetching

I noted in the preceding section that the relatively low bandwidth of memory can seriously reduce the potential throughput of an instruction pipeline. I then made the assumption that memory bandwidth can, in some manner, be increased so that IFETCH would deliver instructions to IDECODE at the rate of an instruction every 2 microcycles.

A technique called *instruction prefetching,* first used in the IBM 7094 machines (Kogge, 1981), will achieve this goal. As the term suggests, instructions are fetched ahead, and in anticipation, of the time they will actually be required by the rest of the pipeline. More precisely, given an instruction stream IS_k, whenever an instruction I_{ki} is required to be fetched from main memory, a *sequence* of N instructions,

$$\langle I_{ki}, I_{k,i+1}, \ldots , I_{k,i+N-1} \rangle$$

is read from consecutive memory words and stored in an instruction buffer. The instructions $I_{k,i+1}, \ldots , I_{k,i+N-1}$ can subsequently be supplied to IDECODE at a rate dictated by logic speeds rather than memory access times.

Obviously, for this scheme to work demands that the time to fetch N instructions (a *prefetch* of $N-1$ instructions) will be of the same order as that to fetch one instruction. If N is rather small, say 2 or 3, if instruction sizes are small, and if the word length is large, then instructions may be packed two or three to a word so that each memory word access effectively fetches 2 or 3 instructions.

A more general implementation method is to use a $N - way\ interleaved$ *memory* scheme. The basic idea here is to organize a set of N *memory modules* such that N sequential addresses, say a, a + 1, . . . , a + N − 1 are distributed uniformly across all the modules: address a falls in module 0, a + 1 in module 1, a + 2 in module 2, . . . , a + N − 1 in module N − 1. Thus, if an instruction at address a is requested, then not only that instruction but also those at a + 1, a + 2, . . . , a + N − 1 will be accessed in parallel, read into N distinct memory buffer registers, and then stored in an instruction buffer (Fig. 6.18). As an example, suppose that the *degree of interleaving* is $N = 2^n$ and that the capacity of each memory module is $M = 2^m$, for some pair of integers n,m. Then an (m + n)-bit address will be delivered to the memory system, the high-order m bits will be used to access a word in each module, while the low-order n bits will determine which of the accessed words is to be placed first in the instruction buffer. Once the first instruction has been forwarded to IDECODE, the remaining instructions will be advanced one step along the buffer, so that the time lag between successive instructions delivered to IDECODE will essentially be the time for the instructions to be shifted down the buffer (Fig. 6.19).

The success of memory interleaving relies on the notion that instructions at successive memory locations will be executed sequentially in time—a reason-

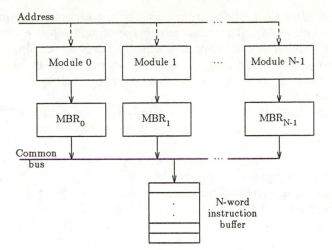

FIGURE 6.18   N-way interleaved memory for prefetching instructions.

able assumption when processing basic blocks. Naturally, the presence of branches will upset this apple cart and will demand special solutions (see Section 6.3.7).

The interleaved memory scheme just outlined is a fully sychronous scheme in that all N memory modules are read in lock-step fashion. Alternatively, one may uncouple the accesses to the N modules; an address request presented to the *controller* of an interleaved memory system is forwarded to the relevant module M_i if M_i is not busy, and a read is initiated. The controller then accepts the next address request and initiates a read to a memory module M_j if that is not busy, and so on. If any particular module is busy, then the request must be delayed.

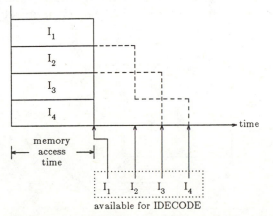

FIGURE 6.19   Availability of instructions for I-decode using a four-way interleaved memory scheme.

Thus requests for instructions are serviced by the memory system in a pipe-lined fashion (Fig. 6.20). The main advantage of this scheme over the fully synchronized version is that while it is equally adept at fetching instructions located in consecutive addresses, it can also service a set of *nonconsecutive* address requests—as long as these addresses remain distributed across the N memory modules.

Memory interleaving is important not only because it supports instruction prefetching in uniprocessors—the reason for its original development—but also because it enables concurrent access to memory modules in certain classes of multiprocessors. It is, in fact, a general principle of memory organization used to increase memory/ processor bandwidth.

For this reason, determining the effectiveness of interleaved memory systems is of great interest and has been analytically studied by several investigators (Hellerman, 1967; Burnett and Coffman, 1970, 1973, 1975; Knuth and Rao, 1975). The results of some of these studies have been summarized in Volume 1, Chapter 8 (Section 8.3).

6.3.6 Resolution of Data Dependencies and Collisions

In Section 6.3.2 I described the conditions for hazard formation. The principle relevant issues when designing a pipeline is to determine at which point or points in the pipeline hazard detection is to be done, what the hazard detection algo-rithm is to be, and what action to take when a hazard is detected. These issues are discussed here in the context of data dependency and collision hazards; the question of control dependencies is deferred to Section 6.3.7.

When to Detect

With regard to the point of detection, there are really only two possibilities. One is to conduct all detection at a fixed point in the pipeline, usually at the instruction decode stage. One may call this the *static* approach. The other is to

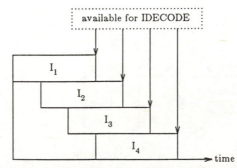

FIGURE 6.20 A four-way interleaved memory system with staggered instruction fetches.

permit the instruction to proceed down the pipeline as far as it can go and to perform hazard detection at each stage. In this case, hazards are identified *dynamically*.

The main disadvantage of static detection is that not all dependencies or collisions can be resolved a priori and thus a rather conservative policy may have to be pursued: *potential* hazards have to be treated as *actual* hazards. In the dynamic approach, hazards are uncovered as and when they occur "on the fly," hence only actual rather than potential hazards are resolved.[12]

Example 6.16

Consider the two-instruction stream IS_6:

$I_{61} \equiv$ Mem [Reg[3]] := STORE(Reg[1]);

$I_{62} \equiv$ Reg[2] := LOAD(Mem [Mem[500]])

and suppose that I_{62} has been fetched and is in the IDECODE stage. I_{61} is in the EADDR stage.

If static hazard detection is performed, then we see that according to the conditions set forth in Section 6.3.2 a potential for a RAW hazard exists: at this point, the actual memory word to be written by I_{61} will not be known, although the memory word (holding the indirect address) to be read by I_{62} is known. A conflict between the source set of I_{62} and the destination set of I_{61} is thus perceived resulting in a RAW hazard.

In contrast, if dynamic detection is performed I_{62} will be allowed to proceed to EADDR. At this stage it may be determined that I_{61} wishes to write to an address that is distinct from location 500. If interleaved memory is also used to hold data (operands and indirect addresses), then the two memory words may well be in distinct memory modules, in which case there will be no hazard between I_{62} in EADDR and I_{61} in IEXEC. ■

The disadvantage of dynamic detection will be evident: It demands far more complex logic at each stage of the pipeline with all the attendant problems of design, implementation, and debugging.

Finally, it is important to note that the choice between the two approaches is as valid an issue for detecting collisions as it is for data dependencies. Essentially the same considerations apply.

How to Detect

The algorithm to detect data dependency and collision hazards will be independent of the static or dynamic nature of hazard detection. Here I will describe a

---

[12]In this respect, the contrast between static and dynamic hazard detection is very similar (for obvious reasons) to that between the detection of parallelism between instructions as performed by the compiler (static parallelism detection) and as performed by the hardware (dynamic parallelism detection).

method devised originally by Tomasulo (1967; see also Keller, 1975 and Baer, 1980).

We associate with each distinct store S_i a *usage counter* C_i, which may take values in the range $\{1,0,-1,-2, \ldots ,-n_i\}$ where n_i is the maximum number of concurrently executable instructions that may have S_i as a *source*. If the value of C_i is 1 at any given time, this indicates that some instruction with store S_i as a destination is being processed by the pipeline. If the value of C_i is $-m$ for some integer $m \le n_i$, then there are m instructions in the pipeline with S_i as a source. If it is the case that store S_i is both a source and a destination of an instruction then, by convention, the value of C_i is 1. Finally, when the value of C_i is 0 this indicates that S_i is being used neither as a source nor as a destination in any instruction.

In the context of our machine model, stores include local store registers and the main memory. If the latter is interleaved, then each distinct memory module constitutes a distinct store with its own usage counter. Recall also that a store will be a source of an instruction if its value is needed not only as an operand but also to compute the effective address of an operand.

Corresponding to each distinct functional unit FU_n there will also be a binary-valued *busy flag* B_n. At any given time, $B_n = 1$ if a pipeline stage is using FU_n; otherwise, $B_n = 0$.

Let us assume that the presence or absence of a (data dependency or collision) hazard is tested for in the IDECODE stage. If no hazard is detected, IDECODE completes its task in the normal 2 microcycles and issues the instruction to EADDR. If, however, a hazard *is* detected, IDECODE will hold the instruction in a latch until the hazard condition disappears. It is further assumed that IDECODE will consume its normal 2 microcycles *after* the hazard condition disappears before issuing the instruction to EADDR.

Consider an instruction I_k with SOURCE(I_k), DEST(I_k) as its operand source and result destination sets, respectively, and UNIT(I_k) as its set of functional units. Tomasulo's procedure involves essentially three independent processes:

1. IDECODE will issue I_k when the following conditions are met:

$$C_i = 0 \text{ for all } S_i \ \varepsilon \ \text{DEST}(I_k)$$
$$C_j \le 0 \text{ for all } S_j \ \varepsilon \ \text{SOURCE}(I_k) \qquad (6.1)$$
$$B_n = 0 \text{ for all } FU_n \ \varepsilon \ \text{UNIT}(I_k)$$

Informally, these conditions stipulate that (a) none of the destination stores of the instructions are being used either as a source or as a destination by any other preceding instruction in the pipeline; (b) each of the source stores of the instruction is only being used (if at all) as a source for other preceding instructions in the pipeline; and (c) each of the functional units required to process the instruction (either during the EADDR or IEXEC stages) is free.

2. Having issued the instruction I_k to the next stage, IDECODE will alter the usage counters and busy flags so that[13]

---

[13] We are using the S*M-like notation **new** x = y to denote that the process performs the appropriate actions (in any order it chooses) such that on its termination the "new" value of x equals the "old" value of y.

> **new** $C_i = 1$ for all $S_i \ \varepsilon \ \text{DEST}(I_k)$
> **new** $C_j = C_j - 1$ for all $S_j \ \varepsilon \ \text{SOURCE}(I_k)$
> **new** $B_n = 1$ for all $FU_n \ \varepsilon \ \text{UNIT}(I_k)$

3. When the instruction has been completely processed the usage counters and busy flags will be updated such that

> **new** $C_i = 0$ for all $S_i \ \varepsilon \ \text{DEST}(I_k)$
> **new** $C_j = C_j + 1$ for all $S_j \ \varepsilon \ \text{SOURCE}(I_k)$
> **new** $B_n = 0$ for all $FU_n \ \varepsilon \ \text{UNIT}(I_k)$

Resolution of Hazards

As previously stated, when a hazard is detected between an instruction I_k and some earlier instruction, the issue of I_k to the next stage is delayed until the hazard condition disappears. This means that I_k will remain in one of the buffers (or the latch) associated with IDECODE and the latter will continually test the values of the usage counters and busy flags until conditions (6.1) are satisfied.

If it is decided that instructions will be decoded and passed onto EADDR strictly in the order in which they appear in the instruction stream, deferring I_k's issue implies that the instructions $I_{k+1}, I_{k+2}, \ldots ,$ following it will also be halted in their tracks, even though one or more of these instructions might not have any data dependencies or collisions with its predecessors. These succeeding instructions are prevented from being issued only because I_k is being delayed.

One way in which it may be possible to partly resolve this problem is by introducing *virtual functional units* (Keller, 1975).

Thus far, we have associated with an instruction I_k *real* functional units $FU_n \ \varepsilon$ $\text{UNITS}(I_k)$. We now associate with each such FU_n, a set of *virtual* functional units $\{VFU_{n1}, VFU_{n2}, \ldots , VFU_{nq}\}$ where the size, q, of the set can be made as large as one wishes. The basic idea of virtual functional units is that an instruction I_k being examined in the IDECODE stage should not be prevented from being *issued* to EADDR because of the unavailability of a functional unit. Instead, as long as there are no data-dependency hazards, I_k will be dispatched to the next stage by assuming the availability of a virtual functional unit capable of processing the instruction. Thus, the only condition that may prevent I_k from being sent to the next stage is a data-dependency hazard.[14]

Virtual functional units will not allow an instruction I_k to be necessarily *completed* earlier; that will still depend on the availability of a real functional unit to which the instruction can be assigned. It will, however, allow other succeeding instructions I_{k+j} ($j \geq 1$) to be issued providing that data-dependency hazards are not detected.

---

[14]These remarks hold regardless of whether hazard detection is done statically or dynamically or the number of pipeline stages. In general, each stage of a pipeline may have associated with it a set of *real* functional units that are needed for that stage's operation. Each real functional unit will, in turn, be associated with a set of virtual functional units. Stage i will then be able to pass an instruction I_k to stage i + 1 as long as there are no data dependencies detected by stage i between I_k and some earlier instruction in the pipeline. Of course, the more dynamic the hazard detection scheme and the larger the number of pipeline stages, the more complex will be the resulting pipeline logic.

Example 6.17

Consider the instruction stream IS_7:

$I_{71} \equiv \text{Reg}[2] := \text{LOAD (Mem [Reg[6]])};$
$I_{72} \equiv \text{Reg}[4] := \text{ADD (Reg[2], Reg[4])};$
$I_{73} \equiv \text{Reg}[3] := \text{AND (Reg[3], Reg[1])};$
$I_{74} \equiv \text{Mem [Reg[6]]} := \text{STORE (Reg[2])};$

Figure 6.21 shows the Gantt chart for processing this stream assuming that Tomasulo's hazard detection and resolution procedure is used and that there are no virtual functional units and only one real arithmetic/logical unit. Hazard detection is performed during IDECODE.

Figure 6.22 shows the revised Gantt chart when the availability of virtual arithmetic/logical units are assumed. The main difference is that since there are no collisions between I_{72} and I_{73} the latter can be decoded as soon as IDECODE is available and can be issued to the next stage. Overall, a saving of four microcycles result. ∎

A set of q virtual functional units corresponding to a real functional unit FU_n can be most simply realized by attaching a queue of q latches with FU_n. Assigning an instruction I_k to a virtual functional unit then amounts to placing I_k at the tail of the queue. Scheduling an instruction on the real functional unit is achieved by servicing the contents of the queue on a first in/first out basis. The instruction pipeline will be of the form shown in Figure 6.23.

Forwarding

We saw in Example 6.17 that virtual functional units can reduce the delaying of instructions from being issued by IDECODE due to collision hazards. Indeed, at the time hazard detection is performed the test for

$$B_n = 0$$

can be avoided altogether.

Delaying instruction issue due to RAW type data-dependency hazards can be further reduced by a technique called *forwarding*—also introduced first by

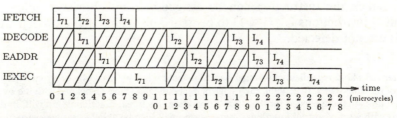

FIGURE 6.21 Gantt chart for IS_7 with no virtual functional units.

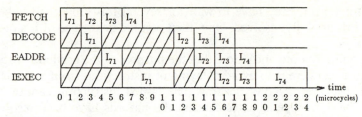

FIGURE 6.22 Gantt chart for IS$_7$ with a virtual arithmetic/logic unit.

Tomasulo (1967). The discussion that follows is based on Keller (1975), suitably modified for our particular machine and pipeline models.

In this technique, each distinct store S$_i$ may have attached to it, a *tag* T$_i$. The latter, when present, is an indicator of a functional unit FU$_n$ that is being, or will be, used by some instruction in the pipeline to produce a value to be written into S$_i$. A tag T$_i$ is attached to the store S$_i$ whenever S$_i$ is a destination of an instruction and the instruction has been issued by IDECODE.

Suppose IDECODE is in the process of determining whether or not instruction I$_k$ can be issued to the next pipeline stage. If for some S$_i$ ε SOURCE (I$_k$) there is a tag T$_i$ attached to S$_i$, then a potential RAW hazard is posed. The store S$_i$ has yet to receive the value that is required by I$_k$. Let FU$_n$ be the functional unit that is to produce this value; the tag T$_i$ will then indicate "FU$_n$."

Under these conditions, I$_k$ is *conditionally* issued to the next stage (EADDR) along with the tag T$_i$.[15]

When FU$_n$ completes the operation that produces a value to be written to S$_i$, the pipeline control checks all the stores and the latches to see if any of these possesses a tag indicating FU$_n$. Since such a match will be found for store S$_i$, the latter is set to the new value and its tag removed. When such a match is found with a latch holding an instruction, then this indicates the conditionally issued instruction I$_k$. In this case the output value is *forwarded to the conditionally issued* instruction I$_k$ or (equivalently) the tag associated with I$_k$ may be reset, indicating elimination of the hazard. Note that, depending on the particular type

---

[15]If S$_q$ ε DEST(I$_k$) and some functional unit FU$_p$ is involved in producing this value to be written into S$_q$, then a tag T$_q$ indicating FU$_p$ must, of course, be also attached to S$_q$ as soon as I$_k$ is conditionally issued.

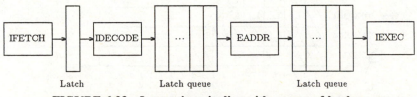

FIGURE 6.23 Instruction pipeline with queues of latches.

of the instruction, I_k may have to wait for several forwarded values before its RAW hazards are fully resolved. Only then can the next stage of I_k's processing actually begin.

It is important to note once more that the purpose of the particular forwarding scheme described here is to avoid delaying of instructions from being issued by IDECODE because of RAW hazards. The issued instruction cannot be completed till the data dependencies causing the hazards have been resolved. We may also point out here that the concepts of conditional issue and forwarding as described in 1967 by Tomasulo anticipates some of the principles of *data flow computation* suggested some years later by J. B. Dennis and others (see Chapter 9).

Example 6.18

Consider once more, the instruction stream IS_7 of the previous example (6.17). When both virtual functional units and forwarding are employed, the instructions can be scheduled according to Figure 6.24. Note, first, that I_{72} is data-dependent on I_{71} with Reg[2] constituting the RAW hazard. I_{72} is, thus, decoded and conditionally issued by IDECODE before I_{71} has terminated. EADDR can, therefore, begin processing I_{72} as soon as I_{71} has been completely processed (by the end of the eleventh microcycle). I_{72} is, thus, completely processed by the end of the fifteenth microcycle. The overall time to process IS_7 is reduced from 24 microcycles (Fig. 6.22) to 22 microcycles. ■

6.3.7 Resolution of Control Dependencies

Recall from Section 6.3.2 that a control dependency (CD) hazard results when the outcome of a branch instruction's execution is to transfer control to an instruction that is "out of sequence" with the branch; subsequently, a subsequence of instructions—the constituents of the hazard—will not be executed (Fig. 6.10).

CD hazards will arise whenever there is an abrupt and explicit transfer of control within an instruction stream, due not only to conditional or unconditional branches but also to procedure calls and returns. (For convenience, I will collectively refer to these as "branch instructions.") From the perspective of instruction pipelines, the problem it raises is that of what action to take to

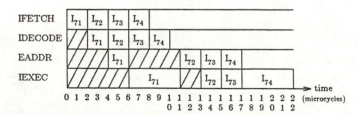

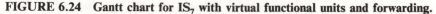

FIGURE 6.24 Gantt chart for IS_7 with virtual functional units and forwarding.

minimize the disruption of the pipeline—minimize, that is, its latency and throughput—while preserving the intended semantics of the instruction stream.

The seriousness of the effect of CD hazards will depend, at least partly, on the number of hazard constituents, that is, the number of instructions following the branch instruction that will have entered the pipeline when it is determined that the branch is to take place, thus making it necessary to prevent their further processing. Consider as an extreme example an instruction pipeline consisting of 10 stages (Fig. 6.25). In the absence of any special precautions, when the branch is executed in stage 9, eight other instructions will be in the earlier stages of the pipeline, and if the branch transfers control elsewhere, all these constituents of the hazard must be "flushed out"—that is, prevented from proceeding further down the pipeline.

In contrast, in a four-stage pipeline, as in our machine model, the number of hazard constituents will be at most three. The larger this parameter, the greater will be the disruption of the pipeline after the branch is executed: The number of microcycles expended uselessly in the partial processing of the hazard constituents will be larger and more cycles will be consumed to refill the pipeline with the "new" sequence. Thus, the greater the potential performance drop due to a CD hazard, the more will be the desire on the part of the designer to minimize the actual performance drop.

Let us now consider how one may cope with control dependencies in our particular machine model. Recall from Section 6.3.1 that branch instructions in this model are of the form

if BOOL (source) **then goto** L_k

if BOOL (source$_1$, source$_2$) **then goto** L_k

An unconditional branch is simply an instance of the first form where "BOOL (source)" is the non-ary predicate TRUE. I will, for convenience, refer to the instruction at label L_k as the branch *target* instruction; the address corresponding to L_k is termed the *branch-to* address while that corresponding to the branch instruction itself is called the *branch-from* address. The instruction streams beginning at these two addresses will, correspondingly, be termed the *branch-to* and *branch-from* instruction streams.

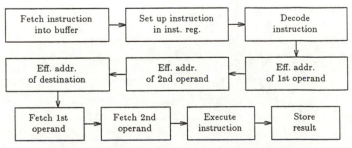

FIGURE 6.25   A ten-stage instruction pipeline.

Flushing and Refilling the Pipeline

Conceptually, the simplest solution is to stop processing the hazard constituents that are already in the pipeline—to flush them out as it were—and refill the pipeline with a new stream beginning with the branch target instruction. As with all other instructions, a branch will actually be executed by the IEXEC stage of the pipeline. Thus, there may be several hazard constituents—instructions that sequentially follow the branch—in the earlier pipeline stages, all of which must be ignored by the pipeline if and when the branch is executed.

Example 6.19

Consider the instruction stream IS_9:

$I_{91} \equiv L_1$: **if** ZERO (Reg[1]) **then goto** L_2;

$I_{92} \equiv$ Reg[2] := INCR (Reg[2]);

$I_{93} \equiv$ Mem [Reg[3]] := STORE (Reg[4]);

$I_{94} \equiv$ **if** TRUE **then goto** L_1;

$I_{95} \equiv$ . . .

where we assume that at the instruction sequence beginning at the branch-to address L_2 is $I_{100};I_{101}; \ldots$

Taking into account the data dependencies between the instructions, and assuming that virtual functional units and forwarding are used, the Gantt chart for IS_9 will be as shown in Figure 6.26 if the branch in I_{91} is not taken and as shown in Figure 6.27 if it is.[16]

As Figure 6.27 indicates, when I_{91} has completed execution, the process of fetching the next instruction in sequence, I_{95}, will have started. Thus, the branch target instruction, I_{100}, will be fetched from the beginning of the tenth microcycle. However, it is important to "stop" the pipeline as soon as I_{91} has terminated and, in particular, to prevent I_{92} from entering IEXEC.

One way in which this can be achieved is not to stop the pipeline's *physical* operation but to introduce "dummy" or NOOP ("no operation") instructions

---

[16]In interpreting these charts, you must take into account the timing of the various phases of instruction processing as listed in Table 6.1.

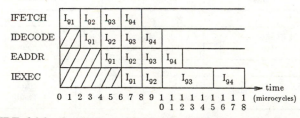

FIGURE 6.26   Gantt chart for IS_9 when branch is IS_{91} is not taken.

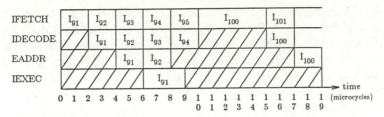

FIGURE 6.27 Gantt chart for IS_9 when branch in IS_{91} is taken.

into the relevant pipeline buffers and allow the pipeline to proceed in its normal manner. The NOOP's will, of course, be processed without causing any change in the states of the stores. The resulting Gantt chart is depicted in Figure 6.28.

◼

Prefetching the Branch-To Stream

From Example 6.19 and Figure 6.28 we see that because the branch instruction I_{91} does not complete execution till the end of the ninth microcycle, fetching the target instruction, I_{100}, can begin no earlier than the tenth microcycle and several cycles are consumed before the pipeline is refilled with the branch-to stream. Furthermore, the initiation of the latter requires a full 5 microcycles to fetch I_{100}.

On the other hand, the nature of an instruction can be determined during its decoding. If the instruction is an unconditional branch, a procedure call, or a return, then the inevitability of a change in the flow of control will be known at the IDECODE stage. Thus, *prefetching of the branch-to instruction stream* can begin as soon as the branch instruction is decoded by IDECODE and the effective branch-to address has been computed.

Example 6.20

Consider, once more, the instruction stream IS_9. Assume now that the branch in I_{91} did not take place; thus IS_9 will be processed by the pipeline according to the Gantt chart shown in Figure 6.26.

I_{94}, however, is an unconditional branch. Without prefetching, the branch-to instruction stream (which happens to be IS_9 once more) will not be initiated into the pipeline until the end of the eighteenth microcycle. Furthermore, the first

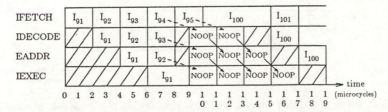

FIGURE 6.28 Gantt chart for IS_9 when branch in IS_{91} is taken and NOOPs inserted.

instruction in this stream, I_{91}, will require 5 microcycles to fetch. That I_{94} is an unconditional branch will, however, be known at the time I_{94} is decoded. If the effective address corresponding to the label L_1 is also known at this time (by what mechanism, we will ignore for the moment), prefetching the branch-to stream starting with I_{91} can begin immediately. Furthermore, the branch instruction I_{94} need not be processed by IEXEC anymore. The resulting Gantt chart is shown in Figure 6.29.

If the effective address corresponding to the label L_1 cannot be determined before EADDR has processed I_{94}, then prefetching the branch-to stream with I_{91} cannot begin till the end of the twelfth microcycle. ∎

The Use of a Cache

The effectiveness of prefetching the branch target instruction and its successors will really depend on initiating this prefetch as early as possible. In Example 6.20, for instance, we assumed that the effective address of the target instruction, I_{91}, is known when the unconditional branch, I_{94}, is in IDECODE.

One means of achieving this is as follows: The pipeline control manages a *table* of words, each of which consists of the ordered pair:

[branch-from address, branch-to address]

Let us call this the *branch address table* (BAT). When IDECODE detects an unconditional branch (or a procedure call or a return) at (branch-from) address BFA, it searches the BAT using BFA as the key. If a match is found, the search returns the corresponding branch-to address, BTA, which is the effective address of the branch target instruction; prefetching of the branch-to instruction stream can thus begin.

If a match is not found, then prefetching must at least be deferred till the effective address BTA has been computed by EADDR. In this case, a word in the BAT will be loaded with the ordered pair

[BFA, BTA]

either in an unoccupied location or, if the BAT is full, replacing some previous entry. The BAT, thus, functions as a *cache* store that keeps track of the most

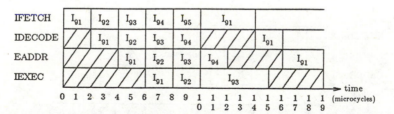
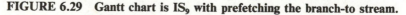

FIGURE 6.29 Gantt chart is IS_9 with prefetching the branch-to stream.

likely to occur, or most recently encountered, branches in the instruction stream.[17]

The interesting point about this approach is that it can be used to prefetch a branch-to instruction stream even in the case of conditional branches when the direction of the flow of control will not be known till the branch is actually executed. In this more general situation, entries in the BAT will not only correspond to unconditional branches but also to previously encountered conditional branches. For an instance of the latter, an entry of the form

[branch-from address, branch-to address]

represents a conditional branch where the "branch-to" address represents the beginning of the *most probable* instruction stream to be processed when the conditional branch is executed. Thus, this address may be that of the instruction immediately following the branch (e.g., in IS_9, if we consider the conditional branch I_{91}, this would be the address of I_{92}) or of the branch target instruction (e.g., the address corresponding to L_2), whichever is viewed as most probable.

Conditional and unconditional branches can, thus, be treated uniformly in this way. The significant difference is that if the conditional branch does not actually execute so as to follow the most probable (or, in a sense, predicted) path, then there will be a performance drop since the pipeline has to be flushed and refilled as indicated previously (see Example 6.20).

An elaboration of this scheme was used in the MU5 system (Morris and Ibbett, 1979). Simulation experiments indicated that some 75% of branch executions could be successfully processed using a BAT with only eight entries; increasing the number of words in the table did not lead to any significant improvement in the performance.

Delayed Branches

The methods for detecting and resolving CD hazards just discussed rely on hardware implementations. A very different solution is the use of what is termed, quite misleadingly, the *delayed branch* scheme.

This method has already been described in Volume 1, Chapter 5, in the context of micro-architectures. Indeed, delayed branching has been used in the past to construct microprograms for machines in which *micro-instructions* were fetched and executed in a pipelined mode. Its principles have become more widely disseminated in more recent years, largely because of its use in *reduced instruction set computers* (RISCs) such as the Berkeley RISC-I and RISC-II (Patterson and Sequin, 1982; Katevenis, 1985) and the Stanford MIPS (Hennessy *et al.,* 1982) (see Volume 1, Chapter 7). We will re-examine the delayed branch method by way of an example.

---

[17]The organization and functioning of cache memories and their other applications are discussed in some detail in Volume 1, Chapter 8.

Example 6.21

Consider the following instruction stream IS_{10}, as may be generated by a conventional compiler:

$I_{10,1} \equiv$ Reg[1] := INCR (Reg[1]);

$I_{10,2} \equiv$ Reg[3] := ADD (Reg[3], Reg[2]);

$I_{10,3} \equiv$ Mem [Reg[0]] := STORE (Reg[1]);

$I_{10,4} \equiv$ **if** TRUE **then goto** L_3;

where the instruction at L_3 is assumed to be $I_{10,11}$. Given this sequence, notice that the branch instruction $I_{10,4}$ is not dependent in any way on the preceding instructions $I_{10,1}$, $I_{10,2}$, or $I_{10,3}$.

Now, if this output of the compiler is passed through another program that *reorganizes* IS_{10} so as to produce the stream IS_{10}':

$I'_{10,1} \equiv$ **if** TRUE **then goto** L_3;

$I'_{10,2} \equiv$ Reg[1] := INCR (Reg[1]);

$I'_{10,3} \equiv$ Reg[3] := ADD (Reg[3], Reg[2]);

$I'_{10,4} \equiv$ Mem [Reg[0]] := STORE (Reg[1]);

then a pipeline can process IS_{10}' according to the Gantt chart of Figure 6.30. Here it is assumed that forwarding is in effect. It is also assumed that the address corresponding to L_3 is calculated in EADDR so that fetching $I'_{10,11}$ can begin even before $I'_{10,1}$ has actually completed execution. Notice that *no* special precaution is taken by the pipeline control in the event that the branch is taken. Since, according to IS_{10}, the instructions $I_{10,1}-I_{10,3}$ were intended to be executed before the branch, by reorganizing IS_{10} into IS_{10}', these same instructions can legitimately be processed by the pipeline regardless of the branch at $I_{10,4}$ ($I'_{10,1}$). ∎

Thus, in the delayed branch approach, the burden of resolving the CD hazards is transferred from the pipeline control hardware to a postcompilation "code reorganizer." This latter program will analyze the generated code and reorganize the instructions, if possible, so that branch instructions are followed by instructions that (1) are independent of the branch as far as RAW or WAR hazards are

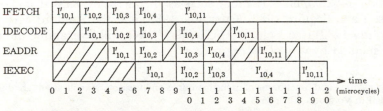

FIGURE 6.30 Gantt chart is IS_{10}, if branch is taken.

concerned; and (2) would execute regardless of whether or not the branch takes place.

If the code reorganizer is unable to append the appropriate number of instructions to the branch, then it will insert the necessary number of NOOP instructions.

As already noted, the delayed branch method was adopted in the design and implementation of some recent RISC machines where reducing the complexity and amount of control logic hardware was a major objective. In the case of the Berkeley RISC machines, the compiler itself inserted NOOPs after branch instructions whereas a postcompiler reorganizer would, when possible, replace the NOOPs with instructions moved from elsewhere in the instruction sequence (Katevenis, 1985). Based on measurements of code generated from C programs, the reorganizer was found to be able to remove some 90% of the NOOPs following unconditional branches (including calls and returns) and between 40 and 60% of the NOOPs following conditional branches.

6.4 BIBLIOGRAPHIC AND OTHER REMARKS

The single most authoritative discussion of pipelining in all its aspects is, no doubt, Kogge (1981), which as far as we know is the only book-length treatise on this topic. Hwang and Briggs (1984) also has useful chapters on pipelining in the general context of parallel processing. Ramamoorthy and Li (1977) is an earlier survey; Keller (1975) provides a very elegant discussion of some of its logical problems.

Arguably, the "classic" exemplar of a pipelined uniprocessor is the IBM System 360/Model 91 — a remarkable instance of a computer famed for its architectural ideas rather than its commercial success. The January 1967 issue of the *IBM Journal of Research and Development* was dedicated to this system and includes the well-known paper by Anderson, Sparacio, and Tomasulo (1967). The 360/91 pipeline consisted of an *I-unit* and two *E-units*. The I-unit was responsible for instruction fetching, partial decoding, and effective address calculation and was, itself, internally pipelined. The E-units were responsible, respectively, for fixed and floating-point operations and were also internally pipelined. Many of the theoretical ideas discussed in this chapter were first conceived and implemented on the 360/91.

Kogge (1981) provides a brief but useful discussion of the System 360/Model 91. He also describes some other well-known processors employing instruction pipelining, including the CRAY-1 and the Intel 8086.

An experimental computer attractive for a variety of reasons is the MU5, conceived, designed, and implemented at the University of Manchester roughly during the period 1968–1974. Morris and Ibbett (1979) provide a detailed discussion of this computer along with a bibliography of research papers on this system.

The MU5 has two pipeline systems. The *primary* pipeline takes packets of instructions and outputs individual instructions consisting of the operation and its operands. Not all types of operands, however, can be accessed by the primary pipeline. The *secondary* pipeline, which takes its input from the primary system, is responsible for accessing and processing operands that are parts of complex data structures (such as arrays). Instructions emerging from the secondary pipeline are ready for execution and are passed to the main arithmetic (A-) unit.

A relatively recent example of a pipelined uniprocessor is the VAX 8600 system (Fossum, McElroy, and English, 1985; Troiani *et al.,* 1985) a high-performance addition to the VAX family. Logically speaking, its pipeline consists of seven stages, these being, respectively, responsible for instruction address calculation, instruction fetch, decode, operand address computation, operand fetch, instruction execution, and result store. The 1985 issue of the *Digital Technical Journal* is devoted to various aspects of this system.

Appendix 6.A

Consider a two-stage instruction pipeline separated by a latch (Fig. 6.16). Assume that stage 1 has two possible delays depending on the kind of subtasks it performs and that stage 2 also has two delays associated with it, the durations of which are not necessarily the same as those of stage 1 delays. The delays associated with these stages account solely for the times taken for them to process their subtasks. Thus, there is also a delay associated with the latch — this being the lag between the time at which data arrive at the input to the latch and the time at which the data are available at the latch's output.

Figure 6.A.1 is a specification, in S*M, of one possible synchronization scheme involving stage 1, latch, and stage 2. The durations of the clocks clk11, clk12 define the possible delays through stage 1; similarly the durations of clocks clk21, clk22 define the two possible delays through stage 2.

In arriving at this specification, the issues of stage 1 performing its computational subtask and the deposition of the processed task in the latch have been uncoupled. Similarly, the issues of stage 2 accepting the contents of the latch and processing this task have been uncoupled. Thus, the detailed structure of the pipeline is as shown in Figure 6.A.2. Stage 1 has an output buffer and a synchronization flag associated with it. Similarly, there are an input buffer and a synchronization flag associated with stage 2. The latch is composed of a buffer that holds the partially processed task produced by stage 1 (to be further processed by stage 2) and a synchronization flag.

PROBLEMS

6.1 Consider the hypothetical register machine described in Section 6.3.1 for which the delays associated with its four pipeline stages are as stated at the beginning of Section 6.3.4. Thus, the time a given instruction spends in each stage will depend both on the stage and on the nature of the instruction itself.

Consider now, the following instruction stream:

I_{11}: Reg[1] := LOAD (Mem[Reg[4]]);
I_{12}: Reg[2] := LOAD (Mem[500]);
I_{13}: Reg[4] := ADD (Reg[1], Reg[4]);
I_{14}: **if** GREATER (Reg[4], Reg[2])
         then goto I_{16};
I_{15}: Reg[4] := ADD (Reg[1], Reg[2]);
I_{16}: Mem[500] := STORE (Reg[4])

(a) Identify all the hazards in this instruction stream.
(b) Construct a Gantt chart and compute the throughput assuming the branch is taken in I_{14}.
(c) Construct a Gantt chart and compute the throughput assuming the branch is not taken in I_{14}.

```
module stage1
    inoutport flag1
    outport outbuffer1

    guard {cond_11, clk_11}, {cond_12, clk_12}

    effects
        if flag1 = empty
            then
                /* ...some computation... */
                & new outbuffer1 = /* ...processed task... */
                & new flag1 = full
        end if
end module

module deposit_in_latch
    inport outbuffer1
    inoutport latch_flag; flag1
    outport latch_buffer

    guard {true, latch_clk1}

    effects
        if flag1 = full
            then
                if latch_flag = empty
                    then
                        new latch_flag = full
                        & new flag1 = empty
                        & new latch_buffer = outbuffer1
                end if
        end if
end module
```

FIGURE 6.A.1 S*M description of pipeline. (Part 1 of 2)

```
module accept_from_latch
    inport latch_buffer
    inoutport latch_flag; flag2
    outport inbuffer2

    guard {true, latch_clk2}

    effects
        if flag2 = empty
            then
                if latch_flag = full
                    then
                        new latch_flag = empty
                        & new flag2 = full
                        & new inbuffer2 = latch_buffer
                    end if
            end if
end module

module stage2
    inport inbuffer2
    inoutport flag2

    guard {cond_{21}, clk_{21}} {cond_{22}, clk_{22}}

    effects
        if flag2 = full
            then
                /* ...some computation involving inbuffer2... */
                & new flag2 = empty
        endif
end module
```

FIGURE 6.A.1   S*M description of pipeline. (Part 2 of 2)

6.2   [Continuation of Problem 6.1.] Assume the same stage delays except that now assume that IFETCH will deliver instructions to the IDECODE stage at the rate of one every 2 microcycles.

(a)   Construct a Gantt chart and determine the throughput for the instruction stream shown in Problem 6.1 assuming that the branch is taken.

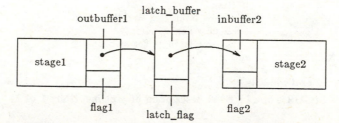

FIGURE 6.A.2   Detailed structure of the two-stage pipeline.

    (b) Construct a Gantt chart and determine the throughput for the instruction stream assuming the branch is not taken.

6.3 [Continuation of Problems 6.1 and 6.2.]

    (a) Compute the efficiency of each stage of the pipeline for the instruction stream shown in Problem 6.1 under the delay assumptions stated

        (i) In Problem 6.1.

        (ii) In Problem 6.2.

    (b) Compute the efficiency of the pipeline as a whole for this instruction stream under the delay assumptions stated

        (i) In Problem 6.1.

        (ii) In Problem 6.2.

  assuming in each case that the branch is taken.

6.4 [A design project.] In Section 6.3.1 a hypothetical pipelined register machine architecture was outlined. Assume that this machine contains 16 programmable registers and a single ALU. As the initial phase in the development of a detailed formal design, you are required to conduct a *preliminary* design of the pipeline. The main components of this preliminary design will be the following.

    (a) Identification of the key performance and functional goals or requirements for the pipeline as a whole.

    (b) Decisions regarding the number of stages in the pipeline (Note that in the text, a four-stage pipeline was assumed. There is nothing sacrosanct about this number.)

    (c) Decisions concerning the stage (or stages) in the pipeline at which data and control dependency hazards will be tested for, and the means to resolve such hazards.

    (d) Decisions as to when collisions are to be detected and how to deal with collisions when they are found to occur.

    (e) Decisions concerning the extent to which latches (or buffers) will be inserted between stages.

    (f) Decisions concerning the overall mode of pipeline control, that is, whether it would be fully synchronous or partly or wholly asynchronous.

  The outcome of the preliminary design will be a report that discusses and rationalizes each of these "top level" policy decisions and provides an informal or semiformal "profile" of the pipeline structure and behavior.

[*Note*: In the course of preliminary design, certain additional assumptions may be required to be made about the architecture. Whatever assumptions are made should be explicitly stated and justified.]

[Note also that design being invariably of an evolutionary nature (see Volume 1, Chapter 3) decisions may be revised at later stages. Thus, your goal should be to make policy decisions that are as independent of one another as possible so that later revision of one has minimal impact on the others—admittedly easier said than done!]

6.5   [Continuation of Problem 6.4.] In this phase, you are required to develop a detailed design of the entire pipeline system (at the endo-architectural level, of course). What is of interest in this exercise is the structure, control, and mode of operation of the *pipeline*. In other words, your detailed design may abstract from the gory details of instruction fetching, decoding, address calculation, and so forth, and characterize these individual phases only to the extent that they are relevant to the flow and control of instructions through the pipeline.

The result of this phase will be a comprehensively documented specification of the pipeline system expressed in an architecture description language (ADL) or (less preferably) in a programming language such that the operation of the pipeline may be simulated by executing your description.

6.6   [Continuation of Problem 6.5.] Clearly, a crucial issue in the design of such a parallel processing system is the certification of its *correctness*. You are, thus, required to describe the procedures you have used—these may be experimental, mathematical, or a combination thereof—to demonstrate the correctness of the pipeline design.

6.7   [Continuation of Problem 6.5.] Evaluate your pipeline design. For this purpose, construct a set of *benchmark instruction streams* and simulate the execution of these benchmarks on your pipeline system. The result of your evaluation studies will be
    (a)   A critical report on the performance of the pipeline vis-à-vis the requirements established during preliminary design.
    (b)   An analysis of the design flaws and bottlenecks (if any) that were identified.
    (c)   Suggestions for possible design changes that could reasonably be explored to further improve the design.

6.8   [A design project.] In a microprogrammed processor, the instruction interpretation cycle (ICycle) is implemented using a judicious combination of hardware and firmware, with the latter being mostly responsible for controlling, sequencing, and manipulating the hardware resources (see Volume 1, Chapter 5).

Consider the problem of developing a microprogrammed implementation of a four-stage pipelined ICycle of the type discussed in Section 6.3.1.

Assuming, to begin with, that all stages will take the same amount of time (viz., the time required by the slowest stage), design the architecture of a microprogrammed control unit (MCU) for controlling the four-stage pipelined ICycle. The main components of your design will be
    (a)   The structural organization of the MCU.
    (b)   Its timing characteristics.
    (c)   The nature of the microinstruction fetch/decode/execute cycle.
    (d)   The next microinstruction address generation logic.
    (e)   The microinstruction formats.

(f) Details of the microprogram given only to the extent needed to show how it helps to control the pipeline.

6.9 Solve the design Problem 6.8, but this time under the assumption that each stage of the ICycle pipeline will require the times shown in Table 6.1.

6.10 The execution of a *floating-point ADD* instruction involves several sequentially ordered tasks. In particular, consider the addition of two floating-point numbers.

$$N_1 = <E_1, M_1>$$
$$N_2 = <E_2, M_2>$$

where E_i, M_i ($i = 1, 2$) are the exponent and mantissa respectively for number N_i. (See, for example, Volume 1, Chapter 4, Section 4.6.2, for more information on floating-point number representation). The addition of N_1 and N_2 involves, typically, the following subtasks:

(a) Comparison of E_1, E_2.

(b) Alignment of the mantissas by shifting right the mantissa corresponding to the smallest exponent by an amount equal to the difference between E_1 and E_2.

(c) Addition of the two mantissas.

(d) Checking for the number of leading zeros in the result.

(e) Normalizing the result by shifting left the result so as to eliminate the leading zeros and adjusting the corresponding exponent.

You are required to conduct a *preliminary design* of a *pipelined* floating-point add unit such that the execution of successive ADD instructions can be overlapped in time. The main components of your design will be

(i) Identification of the pipeline stages and an informal or semiformal specification of the functional characteristics of each stage and of the overall performance goals for the pipeline.

(ii) Estimated times for each stage.

(iii) Decisions concerning the extent of interstage buffering.

(iv) Decisions concerning the stage (or stages) of hazard detection and the method of resolving such hazards.

(v) Decisions concerning the overall mode of pipeline control—for example, synchronous, asynchronous, or a combination thereof.

The outcome of the preliminary design will be a report discussing and justifying each of these design (policy) decisions and concluding with an outline of the pipeline system.

[*Note*: You might find it prudent to develop, as part of this phase, a set of benchmarks that may be useful both in guiding the preliminary design itself and in evaluating the design in a later phase.]

6.11 [Continuation of Problem 6.10.] Using an appropriate ADL or (less preferably) a programming language, develop a detailed design of the floating-point ADD unit such that the operation of this unit can be simulated by executing your description. Your detailed design report should also document the procedure (or procedures) you have used to verify the design.

6.12 [Continuation of Problem 6.11.] In this final phase, you are required to evaluate your floating-point pipelined add unit (with respect to the requirements established as part of the preliminary design). As usual, this will involve "executing" your design using the benchmarks as experimental inputs.

Your evaluation report should include

(a) A critical assessment of the pipeline performance relative to performance goals initially established.

(b) Identification of the design flaws and bottlenecks (if any) in your design.

(c) Suggestions for improving the design so as to minimize such flaws or bottlenecks.

CHAPTER 7

VECTOR PROCESSORS

7.1 INTRODUCTION

Consider the problem of computing the *inner product*

$$C = \sum_{i=1}^{n} a_i \, b_i$$

of two vectors

$$A: [a_1 \; a_2 \; \ldots \; a_n]$$
$$B: [b_1 \; b_2 \; \ldots \; b_n]$$

In an ordinary uniprocessor this computation would have to be performed in a sequential fashion, for instance, by means of a machine-code equivalent of the program fragment:

```
C := 0;
for i := 1 to n
    C := C + a[i] * b[i]
```

It is easy to see, though, that the inner-product computation exhibits *natural parallelism* in the sense that the products a[i] * b[i] can be calculated independently and in parallel before they are summed. Furthermore, the summation of the n products can itself be organized so as to take advantage of *its* intrinsic parallelism. For instance, by first adding product pairs

```
a[1] * b[1] + a[2] * b[2]
a[3] * b[3] + a[4] * b[4]
    . . . . . . . . . . . .
```

in parallel, then adding pairs of the results in parallel, and so on. The inner product of two vectors is a ubiquitous operation in that it or its variations appear in many important kinds of scientific computations, for example, convolution and matrix multiplication.[1] In this chapter I will discuss architectural styles that have been explicitly developed to exploit the natural parallelism in such types of problems. The objective of these styles as of all systems for parallel processing is, of course, to enhance the performance of the computer.

The fundamental characteristic of the inner product and other similar computations is that some sort of an identical operation (e.g., a multiplication) is required to be performed repeatedly on independent sets of operands (e.g., pairs of vector elements a[i], b[i] for i = 1, . . . n). The following possibilities have emerged for exploiting this characteristic:)

1. If the repetitive operation can be decomposed into a linearly organized set of tasks or phases, then *pipelining* may be used to overlap the processing of the independent sets of operands (Fig. 7.1). The pipeline consisting of, say, m stages would be fed at the input side with operand sets after fixed intervals of time and, at any given point of time, the different stages would be executing different phases of the operation on different sets of operands.[2] Computers based on this principle are referred to as *pipelined vector processors* (or *pipelined array processors*). The most notable examples of these are (Kogge, 1981; Hwang, Su, and Ni, 1981; Hwang and Briggs, 1984; Riganati and Schneck, 1984): the Texas Instruments ASC, the CDC STAR-100 and the CYBER-205, the IBM 2938 and 3838, the CRAY-1 and CRAY X-MP, Fujitsu's VP-200, the Hitachi S810/20, and Floating Point Systems' AP-120B and FPS-164. For convenience, I will refer to these simply as "vector" processors.

---

[1]The *convolution* problem is defined as follows: Given a sequence of weights $\{w_1, w_2, \ldots, w_k\}$ and a sequence of input values $\{x_1, x_2, \ldots, x_n\}$, to compute an output sequence $\{y_1, y_2, \ldots, y_{n+1-k}\}$ defined by

$$y_1 = w_1 x_i + w_2 x_{i+1} + \ldots + w_k x_{i+k-1}$$

Let $A = [a_{ij}]$ be an n $\times$ m matrix and $B = [b_{jk}]$ an m $\times$ r matrix. Then their *product* is the n $\times$ r matrix $C = [c_{ik}]$ where

$$C_{ik} = \sum_{j=1}^{m} a_{ij} b_{jk}, \quad 1 \leq i \leq n, \quad 1 \leq k \leq r$$

[2]I assume that you are familiar with the principles of pipelining as enunciated, for instance, in Chapter 6, Section 6.2.

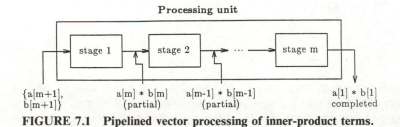

FIGURE 7.1 **Pipelined vector processing of inner-product terms.**

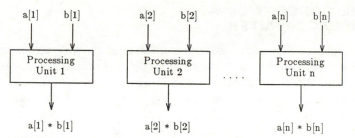

FIGURE 7.2 Parallel array processing of inner-product terms.

2. If the repetitive operation as a whole can be performed by independent processing units, then each of the latter can operate on an independent set of operands *concurrently* (Fig. 7.2). Computers based on this principle are usually referred to as *parallel array processors* or, within the framework of Flynn's taxonomy (see Chapter 2), as *SIMD machines.* Important examples of this style are the ILLIAC IV (Barnes *et al.,* 1968; Hord, 1982; Bouknight *et al.,* 1972); the ICL Distributed Array Processor (DAP) (Reddaway, 1973); the Burroughs Scientific Processor (BSP) (Kuck and Stokes, 1982); the Goodyear Massively Parallel Processor (MPP) (Batcher, 1980); and Staran (Batcher, 1974). I will use the term "array processor" to refer to these machines.

3. In recent years, for problems such as convolutions and matrix computations, a class of algorithms has been defined, originally by H. T. Kung and associates (Kung and Leiserson, 1979; Kung, 1979; Foster and Kung, 1980; Kung, 1982) that exhibit the following characteristics (Foster and Kung, 1980):

   (a) The algorithm can be implemented using a few different types of very simple operations.

   (b) The flow of data and control within the algorithm is highly regular.

   (c) The algorithm relies heavily on pipelining and parallel processing.

Because of the regularity of the data and control flow, such algorithms were termed *systolic algorithms* by Kung and coworkers and were found to be ideal for direct implementation using VLSI technology. Such special-purpose processors are known as *systolic processors,* and they combine some of the characteristics of both pipelined vector and SIMD processors (Fig. 7.3).

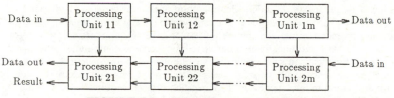

FIGURE 7.3 A systolic array processor.

7.2 THE CONCEPT OF A SUPERCOMPUTER

It is to be expected that at any given time, "state of the art" vector and SIMD processors will far outperform "state of the art" uniprocessors. Thus, in a trivial sense, any parallel processor that operates at the limits of performance at a point of historical time may be viewed as a *supercomputer*. Furthermore, as the performance of parallel computers improves over time, processors that once were regarded as supercomputers may rapidly lose this exalted status.

At this time of writing (1987) the general opinion appears to be that a supercomputer is a computer that has a *sustained* performance rate (i.e., the rate at which computations are performed throughout a working day) of at least 100 mflops and a *maximum* rate of 1000 mflops (or 1 gflops) or more (Lincoln, 1986; Riganati and Schneck, 1984; Hwang and Briggs, 1984).[3] This can be contrasted to the situation in the mid- to late 1970s, when sustained rates of about 20 mflops were expected of supercomputers (Lincoln, 1986; Baer, 1980). These figures also convey some idea of the remarkable rate of progress in the development of these very high performance computers. Table 7.1, based on Riganati and Schneck (1984), summarizes the important characteristics of some contemporary supercomputers along with two that were in the design stage circa 1984.

In passing, it is also worth noting that the demand for performance in the typical range of supercomputing applications is far in excess of actual capabilities. Lincoln (1986), for example, has presented projections up to the year 2000. The projected user demand for 1990 and 2000 are approximately 100 gflops and 1000 gflops, respectively, whereas the projected maximum performance (based on the present rate of increase) for these same years are 10 gflops and 100 gflops, respectively. There is, then, an order of magnitude shortfall in performance.

7.3 A COMPARISON OF VECTOR AND ARRAY PROCESSORS

The notions of vector and array processors were briefly introduced at the beginning of this chapter. These two classes of processors share several characteristics:

1. The principle that only one instruction stream, monitored by a single control unit and a single program counter, is processed by the system (see also Flynn's classification scheme discussed in Chapter 2).

---

[3] 1 mflops (i.e., 1 megaflops) $= 10^6$ million floating-point operations per second; gflop is an abbreviation for "gigaflops." The processing power of computers in general is measured in terms of millions of instructions per second (mips) (see Volume 1, Chapter 2, Table 2.4). Since vector, array, and other parallel processors have traditionally been developed for scientific computation, the type of operation that is most significant in such applications is the floating-point operation. For the emerging class of high-performance computers for "knowledge" processing—for example, the inference engines that are central to the Japanese Fifth Generation Project (Moto-oka, 1982)—the significant type of operation is logical inferences per second (LIPS).

TABLE 7.1 Characteristics of Some Supercomputers

	First Installation	Performance		Max Main Memory Size (mbytes)	Technology	
		Max (mflops)	Cycle-time (nsec)		Logic (gate delay)	Main Memory
Fujitsu VP-200	1983	500	15 (vector) 7.5 (scalar)	256	ECL (350 psec)[a]	64K MOS static (55 nsec)
Hitachi S-810/20	1983	630	15	256	ECL (350 psec)	16K MOS static (40 nsec)
Cray-1M	1983	250	12.5	32	ECL (0.7 nsec)	16K MOS (70 nsec)
Cray-X-MP	1983	630	9.5	32	ECL (0.5-1 nsec)	4K ECL (25 nsec)
Cyber 205	1982	400	20	64	ECL (700 psec)	MOS (45 nsec)
Cray-2	1984	1000	4	1024	ECL	MOS
ETA-GF10	1986	10,000	NA[b]	256	CMOS (0.5-1 nsec)	MOS

[a]psec = picosecond = 10^{-3} ns.
[b]Not available.
Source: Riganati and Schneck (1984). © 1984, IEEE; reprinted with permission.

2. They are both designed to execute a common class of computational problems, namely, those involving arrays of data. There is, thus, a commonality of language and compilation issues, as will be discussed in Section 7.5.
3. The grain of parallelism is the instruction; that is, parallelism is of the *interinstruction* type.
4. Finally, they are both member groups of the supercomputer class.

Yet the fact remains that vector and array processors belong to indisputably distinct architectural styles. This distinction can be explained in terms of two functional aspects of parallel processing: the means for achieving concurrency between the instructions; and the means by which data are shared and communicated between instructions.

In the vector processor, *parallelism* is achieved by

1a. A multiplicity of concurrently executable, possibly distinct, and specialized functional units that collectively constitute the overall arithmetic/logical unit in the processor.
1b. Pipelining the individual functional units.

Data sharing and *communication* between instructions have the characteristics that

1c. They are achieved through shared memory and shared registers.
1d. The functional units do not communicate with one another.
1e. There exists only a single stream of data traffic at the processor-memory interface (Fig. 7.4).

In the case of the array processor, *parallelism* is achieved through the following mechanisms:

2a. A multiplicity of (usually identical) general-purpose processing elements (PEs), each of which constitutes a distinct arithmetic/logical unit in its own right.
2b. At the processor–memory interface there exists several concurrent streams of data traffic (Fig. 7.5).

The characteristics of interinstruction *data communication* include

2c. The fact that this can be achieved either through shared memory or through direct transmission between the PEs; and, consequently,
2d. The PEs can communicate with one another directly, without having shared memory mediate.

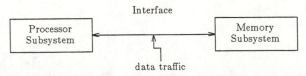

FIGURE 7.4 **The processor–memory interface in vector processors.**

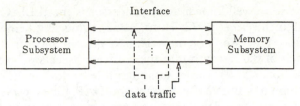

FIGURE 7.5 The processor–memory interface in array processors.

Because of (2b), (2c), and (2d), there is, at the endo-architectural level, a profound distinction between array and vector processors: the necessity for the former to contain *interconnection networks* (INs)—also called *alignment networks*—that facilitate multiple processor-memory data streams or inter-PE communication.

A very general picture of an array processor's endo-architectural structure thus emerges, as shown in Figure 7.6. The memory-processor IN allows multiple streams of data to flow concurrently between the m memory modules and n PEs while the inter-PE IN allows PEs to communicate with one another directly. The design of INs is, thus, a fundamental aspect of array processor architectures.

Interconnection networks also play a basic role in the design of multiprocessor systems; hence, their discussion is deferred to Chapter 8.

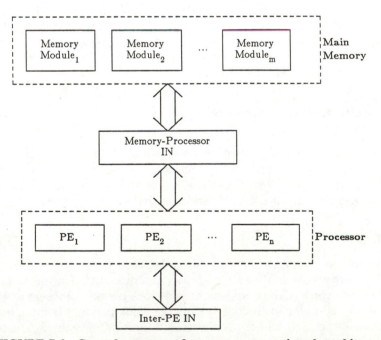

FIGURE 7.6 General structure of an array processor's endo-architecture.

Certainly the most well-known array processor is the ILLIAC IV (Barnes *et al.,* 1968; Bouknight *et al.,* 1972; Hord, 1982), which by being the first fully operational array processor not only defined this architectural style but also motivated much of the research into the software aspects of vector/array processing (see Section 7.5). However, although a few additional array processors have since been built — BSP, MPP, Staran, and DAP, for example — most of the recent work in supercomputer design and research has been in the domain of vector processors and certain types of multiprocessors. Precisely why this is so needs to be investigated. In the remainder of this chapter, I will, therefore, focus our attention on vector processors.

7.4 VECTOR PROCESSORS

As indicated by the list in Table 7.1, many vector processors have been designed, implemented, and marketed since the early 1970s. Of these, perhaps the most well known is the CRAY-1, developed by Cray Research and first introduced in 1976 (Russell, 1978).

This machine was considered to be the fastest supercomputer in the late 1970s. The CRAY-1 and its recent multiprocessing *alter ego,* the CRAY-X-MP, introduced in 1983, also appear to be the vector processors that have been most widely studied both in the field (Baskett and Keller, 1977; Jordan, 1982; Kershew, 1982; Lubeck, Moore, and Mendez, 1985; Mendez, 1984; Riganati and Schneck, 1984) and through simulation (Srini and Asenjo, 1983; Weiss and Smith, 1984; Kunkel and Smith, 1986). Thus, the Cray machines provide a rich source of information and insight on the principles, applications, and performance of vector processors. For this reason, I will use the CRAY-1 as the primary vehicle for our discussion on vector processors.

7.4.1 Architecture of the CRAY-1

The principle structural components of the CRAY-1 endo-architecture are shown in Figure 7.7. As with all vector processors, the CRAY-1 contains *vector processing* and *scalar processing* subsystems since, typically, any application run on such machines will consist of a mix of scalar and vector computations. The processor cycle time or, in CRAY-1 terminology, the *clock period* is 12.5 nsec.

Main Memory

The main memory is organized into 16 banks, each consisting of 64K, 64-bit words. This organization allows for 16-way interleaving.[4] The memory cycle time is 50 nsec, which is, thus, equivalent to 4 clock periods. Since up to 4 words can be transferred to the instruction buffers per clock period, the main memory has a bandwidth of 320 million words/second (or 1280 megabytes/second).

---

[4]See Chapter 6, Section 6.3.5, for a discussion of interleaving.

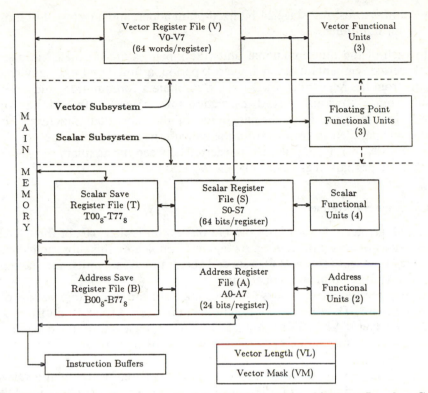

FIGURE 7.7   Structural components of the CRAY-1 endo-architecture (based on Cray, 1984).

The Scalar Subsystem

The scalar processing subsystem consists of instruction buffers and the associated instruction issue logic, two files of scalar registers (S and T) and an associated set of dedicated *scalar functional units,* and two files of address registers (A and B) along with an associated set of dedicated *address functional units.* In addition, a set of *floating-point functional units* are shared by both the scalar and the vector subsystems.

There are 8 64-bit-wide *scalar* registers (the S file) and 64 auxiliary *scalar save* registers (the T file). Similarly, 8 24-bit *address* registers (the A file) are supported by 64 *address save* registers (the B file). As Figure 7.7 suggests, the functional units in the scalar subsystem interact directly only with the S and A registers.

The three sets of functional units consists of a total of nine fully pipelined components as follows:

1. The floating-point units: A 6-stage 64-bit adder; a 7-stage 64-bit multiplier; and a 14-stage reciprocal approximation unit.
2. The scalar units: A 3-stage 64-bit fixed-point adder; a 1-stage 64-bit shifter; a 1-stage 64-bit logical unit; and 2/3-stage 64-bit leading zero count unit.

3. Address units: A 2-stage 24-bit fixed-point adder; and a 6-stage 24-bit fixed-point multiplier.

In each of the nine functional units the pipelines are organized into single clock period segments. During any clock period, a functional unit may receive inputs from the relevant registers (A or S), initiate a computation, and deliver a result from a previously issued instruction into a register. In addition to the parallelism resulting from the pipelining of the individual functional units, additional parallelism obtains from the concurrent activation of the functional units. Finally, words may also be transferred between the auxiliary register (B or T) and the primary registers in one clock period.

The Vector Subsystem

Of much greater interest to our present discussion is that part of the CRAY-1 responsible for vector processing. As Figure 7.7 indicates, this subsystem consists of a file of 8 *vector registers* (V), a set of 3 vector functional units, and the shared set of 3 floating-point functional units.

Each of the vector registers is 64 words long and can, thus, store vectors of up to 64 elements. The three vector functional units are a 3-stage 64-bit fixed-point adder, a 4-stage 64-bit shifter, and a 2-stage 64-bit logical unit. Each vector and floating point unit can accept inputs from, and deliver results to, the V or S registers.

Let us consider the behavioral aspect of the endo-architecture that is relevant to vector processing (Jordan, 1982). As in the case of scalars, the functional units cannot operate directly on memory operands; the former can only access vector data located in the V registers. To transfer data between memory and a V register, instructions are executed to load a vector length (≤ 64) into the *vector length* (VL) register (see Fig. 7.7), the starting address of the vector into one of the A registers, and the indexing value into another A register. On executing a memory read/store, instruction words of the referenced vector are transferred between memory and one of the V registers. The transfer continues up to and including the number of elements specified in the VL register.

Instruction Formats

All CRAY-1 instructions are composed of either one or two 16-bit "parcels" (Fig. 7.8). The precise formats are as follows:

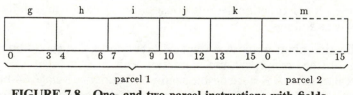

FIGURE 7.8 **One- and two-parcel instructions with fields.**

1. For binary *arithmetic and logical* instructions, the fields are interpreted as shown in Figure 7.9(*a*). The fields j and k may also combine to designate a B or a T register.

2. The unary *shift and mask* instructions have the format shown in Figure 7.9(*b*).

3. Memory *read and store* instructions are two-parcels long and have the format shown in Figure 7.9(*c*). The 22-bit address field (jkm) specifies, in the case of scalars, the address of a single 64-bit main memory word and, in the case of vectors, the starting address in memory where the vector is to be read from or written to. The h field is used to specify an index register.

   The 22-bit jkm field can also be used to hold *immediate operands* for the "immediate operand" instructions.

4. Finally, the low-order 24 bits of a two-parcel instruction can be used to specify the target address of a *branch instruction*. Of the 24 bits, the high-order 22 bits specify a memory address and the low-order 2 bits identify which of four 16-bit parcels within the addressed word to branch to.

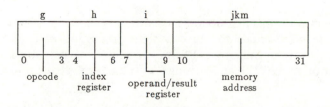

(a)

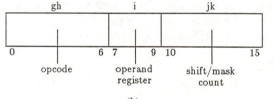

(b)

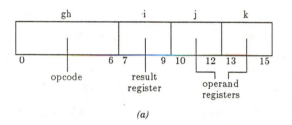

(c)

FIGURE 7.9 Instruction formats.

7.4.2 Parallelism and Vector Chaining in the CRAY-1

The conditions under which parallel processing may prevail in a vector processor such as the CRAY-1 are basically the same as those we have already discussed in earlier chapters on pipelining (Chapter 6, Section 6.3.2) and firmware engineering (Chapter 5, Section 5.4.2). Consider a pair of instructions I_j, I_k in the instruction stream with I_j immediately preceding I_k. Then I_k can be issued one clock period after I_j has been issued provided that

1. There are no data dependencies between I_j and I_k.[5]
2. There are no conflicts in their functional units requirements.

Example 7.1

Consider the following sequence, IS_1, of vector instructions in which the V_i's denote vector registers and the S_j's denote scalar registers:

I_{11}: V3 := V1 * V2

I_{12}: V4 := V3 + V6

I_{13}: V0 := V0 + V7

I_{14}: S2 := V1 * S3

After I_{11} has been issued, I_{12} will be prevented from being issued until I_{11} is completed because of the RAW hazard involving V3. On issue of I_{12}, I_{13} will be held back till I_{12} has completed and has released the floating-point adder. Finally, since there are no dependencies or conflicts between I_{14} and its predecessors, I_{14} can begin execution one clock period after the issue of I_{13}. ∎

Notice that parallelism may be manifested at two distinct levels: between functional units (or, equivalently, between instructions) and between stages of a functional unit (or, equivalently, within phases of an instruction). The former results from the concurrent activation of two or more functional units (as when I_{13} and I_{14} in Example 7.1 are executing in parallel on the adder and multiplier, respectively); the latter results from the pipelined operation of the individual functional units.

Example 7.2

Consider the execution of the multiplication instruction

I_{21} : V3 := V1 * V2

A timing diagram for this instruction's execution is shown in Figure 7.10. Each horizontal line corresponds to the complete processing of a pair of vector elements and involves reading ("r") from the vector registers to the multiplier, the computation itself ("*"), and writing ("w") the results back into the destina-

---

[5]That is, in the terminology of pipelining, there are no RAW, WAR, or WAW dependency hazards between I_j and I_k. See Chapter 6, Section 6.3.2.

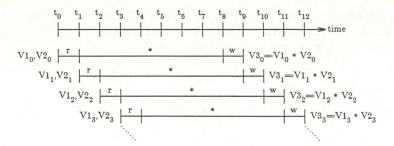

FIGURE 7.10 **Timing diagram for the pipelined execution of vector instructions for V3 := V1 * V2.**

tion vector register. Successive pairs of vector elements from V1 and V2 can be read into the multiplier at one clock period intervals starting at time t_0; the 7-stage multiplier produces its first output at time t_8 and successive outputs at one clock period intervals. An additional clock period is required to write the product of the multiplier into an element of the vector register; thus, each successive element of V3 is written into successive clock periods. The notation $V1_i$, $V2_i$, $V3_i$ denotes, the i-th element (i = 1, 2, 3, . . .) of vector registers V1, V2, and V3, respectively. ∎

In the CRAY-1, the general data-dependency conditions can be relaxed somewhat by virtue of a hardware mechanism called vector *chaining* that enhances the possibility of interinstruction parallelism.

This mechanism may be explained using the following example. Consider the instruction sequence IS_3:

I_{31} : V2 := V1 * S2
I_{32} : V3 := V2 + V0

In I_{31}, the elements of the vector are each multiplied by the scalar quantity in S2 while I_{32} is a vector add instruction. We will assume that I_{31} involves the floating-point multiplier and I_{32}, the floating-point adder, and that the vectors are all of length 64.

Because of the RAW data dependency associated with V2, it would appear that I_{32} cannot be issued before the termination of I_{31}. Assuming that the processing of I_{31} begins at time t_0, the first result of I_{31} (viz., $V2_0$) will be available at time t_9, the second result at time t_{10}, . . . , the 64th result (viz., $V2_{63}$) at time t_{72}.

Instruction I_{32} will then be issued beginning at time t_{72}; its first output ($V3_0$) will be available at time t_{80}, the second output at time t_{81}, . . . , the 64th output at time t_{143}. Thus, the time to process the sequence IS_3 is 143 clock periods.

In the process called *chaining*, whenever there is a RAW dependency between a pair of vector instructions and no other data dependency or functional unit conflict prevails, the successor instruction is issued *as soon as the first output of the predecessor instruction is produced*. In CRAY-1 terminology, the time at which this happens is called the *chain slot time* (Johnson, 1978); this comes up only once for each instruction. Thus, a successor instruction can be issued at the chain slot time for the predecessor instruction.

Example 7.3

Consider once more the instruction sequence IS_3:

I_{31} : V2 := V1 * S2
I_{32} : V3 := V2 + V0

Apart from the RAW data dependency involving V2, there are no other dependency or conflict conditions. Without chaining we saw that a total of 143 clock periods would be required to process IS_3.

Figure 7.11 shows the timing diagram when chaining is enforced. Each horizontal line indicates the production of one element of the vector V3. The chain slot time for I_{31} is t_9 and that for I_{32} is t_{17}. Thus, the first element $V2_0$ of V_2 is available at t_9 and immediately becomes an operand for I_{32}, which is then issued. The first output of I_{32}, $V3_0$, is produced at time t_{17}. It can easily be seen that the total time to process IS_3 is 80 clock periods. ∎

7.4.3 Performance Aspects of the CRAY

As we have previously noted, at the time of its introduction the CRAY-1 was considered the supercomputer *par excellence* with a maximum throughput of 250 mflops. However, such peak performance is obtainable only under the most ideal of conditions. Of much more realistic interest is how the CRAY performs over specific benchmarks and how it compares with other high-performance computers.

A number of such studies have been conducted both on the CRAY-1 and its successor, the CRAY X-MP. This section summarizes the main data resulting from these studies. But prior to that, it is worthwhile to review the architectural and technological sources of CRAY-1's high performance. These may be enumerated as follows.

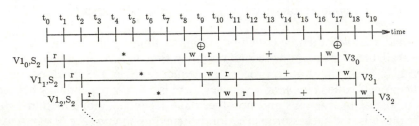

FIGURE 7.11 Timing diagram for IS_3 using chaining (⊕ indicates chain slot times).

1. Because of the pipelined functional units, several *identical operations* (corresponding to a single vector instruction) may be executed in parallel on distinct elements of array data.
2. Because of the multiplicity of functional units, several *distinct operations* (corresponding to distinct instructions in the instruction stream) may be executed in parallel on distinct sets of operands.
3. The use of ECL technology throughout the CRAY-1 processor.[6]
4. The ability of the functional units to accept operands and transmit partial results from one segment to another every 12.5 nsec. Furthermore, transfers between registers (e.g., between S and T registers or A and B registers) can be effected in 12.5 nsec.
5. The large number of programmable registers, particularly, the presence of the vector registers, makes it possible to execute many register-register per memory references. In fact, the CRAY-1 is fundamentally a register machine in that only LOAD/STORE type instructions can access main memory whereas all computational instructions take operands from and deliver results to registers.[7]
6. A block of B or T registers can be stored in or loaded from main memory at the rate of 1 clock period (12.5 nsec) per word by executing a single "block load" or "block store" instruction. Thus, these instructions can transmit data between main memory and the large register files at the rate of 5 gigabits per second. In contrast "direct load" from memory to an A or S register or "direct store" from an A or S register to memory requires 10 cycles.

   Baskett and Keller (1977) have suggested that this rate of block transfer involving the large B and T register files can be effectively exploited by using the B and T files as programmable caches to hold local variables and parameters of subroutines during their execution. The objective is to avoid the possibility of wasting 10 clock periods for data to arrive at an A or S register from memory. Data can, instead, be read from B(T) to A(S) in a single clock period.

   When a procedure P_1 is being executed, all its address, index, and pointer data are held in a block of B registers while all its 64-bit scalars are held in a block of T registers. When P_1 calls another procedure P_2, the contents of the relevant B and T registers are block-stored into main memory prior to

---

[6]Only four distinct chip types were used in implementing the CRAY-1 (Russell, 1978): 16×4 bit register chips with 6-nsec cycle time, 1024×1 bit memory chips with 50-nsec cycle time, and two types of logic chips with less than 1-nsec propagation time. Baskett and Keller (1977) in their evaluation of the CRAY-1 have pointed out that the small number of distinct components contributed not only to economy through volume purchase of parts but also to the reliability of the machine by simplifying circuit design and mass-production testing of components.

[7]This characteristic is, of course, one of the key features of the reduced instruction set computer (RISC) philosophy (see Volume 1, Chapter 7). Indeed Patterson (1985) has acknowledged this particular debt on the part of RISC architects to Seymour Cray, the principal architect of the CRAY-1 and its predecessors, the CDC 6600 and the CDC 7600.

transferring control to P_2. When control is to be returned to P_1, these saved words will be block-loaded back into the B and T registers.

The performance of the CRAY-1 has been assessed in two ways. On the one hand, its *scalar* performance has been compared with that of the CDC 7600, which was an SISD machine with multiple pipelined functional units but no vector-processing capability. This comparison is of some interest as both machines were largely designed by Seymour Cray.

On the other hand, the *overall* performance of the CRAY has been compared with other contemporary vector processors. We will consider both types of comparison.

Scalar Performance

The scalar performance of the CRAY-1 and its comparison to that of the CDC 7600 was investigated by Baskett and Keller (1977). A selection of 23 FORTRAN kernels—none involving vector operations—were implemented in the assembly languages of the CRAY and the 7600. The kernels were selected from five production programs that represented the most likely workload on the CRAY-1 at the particular installation of interest to the investigators.

The experiment did not yield a statistically significant "scalar" speed ratio between the two machines. They did, however, show that the scalar speed of the CRAY-1 relative to the speed of the CDC 7600 was greater than a factor of two with 90% confidence for the particular benchmarks considered. The actual speed ratios for the 23 kernels ranged from 2.03 to 4.12.

Overall Performance

I have already noted that the peak performance rate of a vector/array processor can only be obtained under the most ideal circumstances. For this reason, comparisons of high-performance computers based on peak rates, as is often done, has been severely criticized (Hack, 1986). Of much greater validity are sustained performance rates. However, as Hack (1986) has pointed out, the sustained performance of a computer is somewhat difficult to determine since it will depend on a number of factors, notably:

1. The level of vectorization—that is, the fraction of the total computation to be performed by a program that can be accomplished by means of vector operations.
2. The average vector length.
3. The ability to chain vectors.
4. The ability to overlap vector, scalar, and memory operations.
5. The extent of memory contention.

The overall performance behavior of a machine with two different modes and speeds of operation—serial and parallel, scalar and vector—has been quantified in the form of a "law" attributed to G. M. Amdahl. For a vector processor, *Amdahl's law* is given as (Lubeck, Moore, and Mendez, 1985):

$$S = \frac{1}{(1 - f) + f/k}$$

where:

f is the fraction of vectorized code.

k is the speed of the vector unit relative to the scalar unit and is a function of vector length and type of operation.

S is the net speedup.

This law can be derived as follows. For a given program P:

Let Ts be the time to execute P entirely in scalar mode. Then Ts/k is the time to execute P entirely in vector mode. Since f is the fraction of P's code that can be executed on the vector unit, the actual execution time for P in a mixed scalar/vector mode is

$$Tsv = (1 - f)Ts + \frac{f \cdot Ts}{k}$$

Thus, speedup is

$$S = \frac{Ts}{Tsv} = \frac{1}{(1 - f) + f/k}$$

A typical plot of S against f according to this relationship is shown in Figure 7.12, assuming k = 20. It can be seen that a significant increase in speedup is only attained when f > 0.8. In other words, unless a program is very heavily

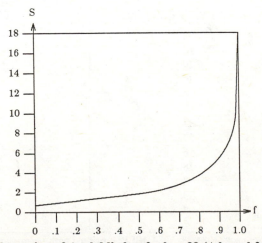

FIGURE 7.12 Illustration of Amdahl's law for k = 20 (Adapted from Lubeck, Moore, and Mendez, 1985 © 1985 IEEE; adapted with permission).

vectorized, the slower (scalar) mode of operation will dominate the overall performance.

Measurements of sustained or actual performances of vector and other high-performance processors must, therefore, rely on the identification of benchmarks that reflect accurately the types of workloads that these computers will typically carry. Possibly because the most significant users of supercomputing power have been the U.S. National Laboratories, the most widely known benchmarks have emerged from these centers. One such well-established set of benchmarks is the collection of 14 FORTRAN kernels known as the Livermore Loops, developed at the Lawrence Livermore National Laboratory. These kernels are quite small, ranging from 2 to about 20 lines of FORTRAN code. Descriptions of these loops are given in Riganati and Schneck (1984).

Another collection of 10 benchmarks have been developed at the Los Alamos National Laboratory (Lubeck, Moore, and Mendez, 1985). Most of these workloads are typical of the Los Alamos environment and are much larger than the Livermore Loops, ranging from 400 to 3000 lines of FORTRAN statements.

Table 7.2 lists the observed performances of the CRAY-1 and the CRAY X-MP on the Livermore Loops. The CRAY X-MP is an improved and later version of the CRAY-1, the most significant difference probably being a clock period of 9.5 nsec (in contrast to 12.5 nsec). Furthermore, 2- or 4-processor configurations (denoted, respectively, as X-MP/2 and X-MP/4) can operate as multiprocessors. As Table 7.1 shows, the peak performance of the X-MP/2 has been measured at 630 mflops. The figures shown in Table 7.2, however, are

TABLE 7.2   Performance of the CRAY-1 and a Uniprocessor CRAY X-MP on the Livermore Loops

Loop Number	Performance (mflops)	
	CRAY-1 (CFT Compiler)	CRAY X-MP (Uniprocessor) (CFT 113+)
1	68	155
2	16	138
3	29	136
4	21	48
5	4	11
6	3	9
7	87	165
8	52	91
9	56	123
10	28	64
11	3	8
12	23	76
13	4	5
14	7	7

Source: Riganati and Schneck (1984). © 1984, IEEE; reprinted with permission.

based on a uniprocessor version. The codes for the two machines were obtained from CRAY FORTRAN (CFT) compilers.

The performance of the CRAY X-MP/2 on the Los Alamos benchmarks has also been investigated (Lubeck, Moore, and Mendez, 1985). Table 7.3 shows the results of one of these experiments indicating the performance of some basic vector loops at various vector lengths. The loops also differ in the modes of memory accesses: for example, contiguous vector element access; access of vector elements separated by a constant amount[8]; and arbitrary accesses. With the exception of the last two entries, all the operations in the table are heavily vectorized.

The data from which these rates were extracted were also used to determine the *startup time* for the loops and the *rate of loop execution.* The total execution time, T, for a vector loop was found to satisfy the linear function

$$T = T_s + nT_e$$

where T_s is the vector startup and loop overhead time, n is the vector length, and T_e is the rate of execution per vector element.

Table 7.4 shows values of T_s (in nanoseconds) and T_e (in number of 9.5 nsec clock periods) for the vector loops. Note that the last two examples, not being vectorized, are vastly slower than the others.

7.5 SOFTWARE ASPECTS OF VECTOR AND ARRAY PROCESSORS

Amdahl's law tells us that the effectiveness of a vector processor will depend heavily on the extent to which programs are vectorized. Indeed, this law is

---

[8]This kind of an accessing mode is also called a constant *stride.*

TABLE 7.3   Rates in mflops for Vector Loops as a Function of Vector Lengths

	Vector Length				
	10	50	100	200	1000
Vector Loops			Rates (mflops)		
1. A(I) = B(I) + S	14.4	57.6	63.9	69.5	76.6
2. A(I) = B(I) + S(I = 1,N,23)	9.6	39.3	52.0	61.4	77.7
3. A(I) = B(I) + S(I = 1,N,8)	9.6	39.3	52.1	61.5	77.7
4. A(I) = B(I)*C(I)	14.0	53.5	58.6	61.6	68.7
5. A(I) = B(I)*C(I) + D(I)*E(I)	33.5	97.7	102.5	108.6	115.2
6. S = S + A(I)*B(I)	5.2	21.7	36.9	58.6	117.4
7. A(I) = B(J(I)) + S	2.3	2.5	2.5	2.5	2.5
8. A(J(I)) = B(I)*C(I)	3.1	3.5	3.5	3.5	3.5

Source: Lubeck, Moore, and Mendez (1985). © 1985, IEEE; reprinted with permission.

TABLE 7.4 **Startup and Execution Times for Vector Loops**

Vector Loops	Ts (nseconds)	Te (clock periods)
1. A(I) = B(I) + S	444	1
2. A(I) = B(I) + S(I = 1,N,23)	798	1
3. A(I) = B(I) + S(I = 1,N,8)	792	1
4. A(I) = B(I)*C(I)	468	1
5. A(I) = B(I)*C(I) + D(I)*E(I)	558	2
6. S = S + A(I)*A(I)	3723	2
7. A(I) = B(J(I)) + S	1142	27
8. A(J(I)) = A(I) + B(I)	1191	23

Source: Lubeck, Moore, and Mendez (1985). © 1985, IEEE; reprinted with permission.

applicable not only to the vector processors we have been considering so far but also to array processors.

It follows that architectural and hardware technology constitute just one side of the coin of vector and array processing. On the other side are the issues of algorithm design, program design, and compiling that must be necessarily considered to exploit the parallelism embedded in these computers. Thus, what might broadly be termed the *software issues* of vector and array processors— and these issues are essentially similar for both these classes—have been investigated hand in hand with architectural issues; and often by the same group of investigators. This holistic approach to computer systems design and research is, thus, a rare example of how the stereotypical schism between "hardware" and "software" may be bridged in order to solve effectively a particular design problem.

The most extensive investigation of the software aspects of vector/array processing has been conducted over a period of almost two decades by D. J. Kuck and colleagues at the University of Illinois (Kuck, 1968; Kuck, 1976; Kuck, 1977; Sameh, 1977; Kuck, 1978; Kuck *et al.*, 1980). These studies were first motivated by the design of the ILLIAC IV SIMD computer but have continued far beyond the ILLIAC IV project. Many of the results of these investigations have been embodied in the PARAFRASE vectorizing compiler (Kuck *et al.*, 1980). Our discussion of software aspects will rely heavily on the Illinois work.

7.5.1 Array Data Organization in Multiple Memory Modules

One crucial factor for the efficacious execution of programs by a parallel processor is the *latency* of the main memory system—that is, the elapse of time between a request by a processor to memory and the delivery of the requested item by the memory (see also Volume I, Chapter 8, Section 8.2, and Chapter 8, Section 8.5 of this volume). Architectural solutions to this problem include the use of *interleaved memory modules,* which are used both in uniprocessors (see Chapter 6, Section 6.3.5) and in vector processors (see Section 7.4.1), and independent *parallel memory modules* as used, for example, in array processors

Main Memory

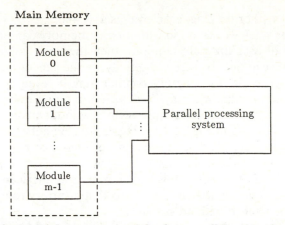

FIGURE 7.13   Multiple memory modules in a parallel processing computer.

and multiprocessors (see Chapter 8, Section 8.2).[9] Collectively, these will be referred to as *multiple memory modules.* A very general picture of such memory organizations and their relationship to a parallel processor is given in Figure 7.13.

Because the primary data structure in vector and SIMD computers is the array, the organization of arrays in multiple memory modules is of considerable importance since the potential parallelism of memory access can be significantly lost because of inappropriate data organization. This problem has been investigated by Budnick and Kuck (1971) (see also Kuck, 1977).

The problem is illustrated by Figure 7.14. Here, a 4×4 matrix has been stored in a 4-module memory with each column vector in a module. If a row vector

[9]Another solution to the latency problem not germane to the present discussion is the use of caches (see Volume 1, Chapter 8, Section 8.5).

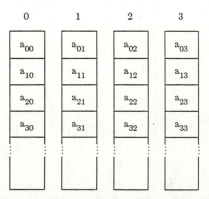

FIGURE 7.14   A 4×4 matrix stored in a 4-module memory.

(e.g., $[a_{10} \ a_{11} \ a_{12} \ a_{13}]$) or the diagonal elements a_{ii} ($i = 0, \ldots, 3$) are required to be accessed in parallel, we can do so without any memory contention. However, if the elements of a column are required, then there are contentions and the column elements can only be accessed serially. In the general multidimensional array case, the potential for memory conflict may be even more exacerbated since many different subarrays may be required to be accessed.

One way to access row and column vectors without memory conflict is to *skew* the data, as shown in Figure 7.15. Here, the elements of a column vector are in distinct memory modules as are the elements of a row vector. Note, however, that now the diagonals can no longer be accessed in parallel. In fact, Budnick and Kuck (1971) have shown that an mxm matrix can never be stored in m memory modules (where m is even) so that arbitrary rows, columns, and diagonals can be fetched without conflicts.

Consider the general problem of storing a k-dimensional matrix in an m-module memory so as to avoid conflict in accessing a particular partition of n elements (such as a row or a column). Let d_i be the *skewing distance* in the i-th dimension. That is, each element in the i-th dimension is stored d_i (mod m) modules away from its predecessor element.

Example 7.4

Figure 7.15 denotes a (1,1) skewed storage with $k = 2$, $m = 4$, and $d_1 = d_2 = 1$ where d_1 refers to the column dimension ($i = 1$) and d_2 refers to the row dimension. ∎

For a two-dimensional array in general with a (d_1, d_2)-skewing scheme, the columns will be said to be d_1-ordered, the rows d_2-ordered, and the main diagonal $(d_1 + d_2)$-ordered.

Let a *d-ordered n vector* (mod m) denote a vector of n elements, the i-th element of which is stored in memory module $(d_i + c)$ (mod m), where c is an arbitrary constant. Then a sufficient condition for a conflict-free access to such a vector is

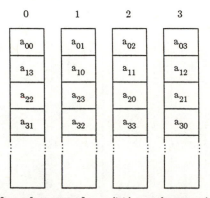

FIGURE 7.15 Skewed storage for a 4×4 matrix on a 4-module memory.

$$m \geq n * gcd(d,m)$$

where gcd (d,m) is the greatest common divisor of d and m. For a proof of this, you may consult Budnick and Kuck (1971) or Kuck (1977).

Example 7.5

Consider storing a 4×4 matrix in a sufficient number, m, of memory modules such that any row, column, or the main diagonal can be accessed without conflict. Figure 7.16 shows a (2,1)-skewed organization with $d_1 = 2$, $d_2 = 1$, $m = 5$.

1. Any d_1-ordered 4-element column can be accessed without conflict since m $> n * gcd(d_1,m)$.
2. Any d_2-ordered 4-element row can be accessed without conflict since m $> n * gcd(d_2,m)$.
3. The $(d_1 + d_2)$-ordered main diagonal can be accessed without conflict since m $> n * gcd(d_1 + d_2, m)$. ■

It is important to note that, in order to exploit skewing schemes effectively, it must be possible to index into each of the memory modules in an independent manner so that a different (relative) location in each module can be accessed. In the specific case of the CRAY-1 this is not possible since a LOAD instruction will use a single A register as an index register.

7.5.2 Vectorization Strategies

The responsibility of exposing the parallelism in an algorithm to be executed by a vector or an array processor can be assigned either to the programmer (who will specify explicitly what is to be done in parallel using a suitable vector programming language) or to the compiler, which will analyze the program (originally expressed, perhaps, in an ordinary sequential programming language)

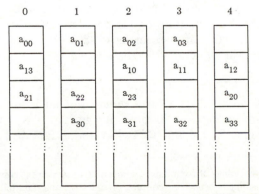

FIGURE 7.16   Skewed storage with n = 4, m = 5, $d_1 = 2$, $d_2 = 1$.

and apply appropriate strategies to transform the program into a form suitable for execution.

The debate over where this responsibility should lie is, of course, not unique to the vector/array processing domain. It surfaces whenever the issue of parallelism and parallel processing arises as, for example, in the context of horizontal microprogramming (see Chapter 5, Sections 5.3 and 5.4) or the programming of multiprocessors (see Chapter 8, Section 8.7) and data flow computers (see Chapter 9, Section 9.2.2). In fact, they need not and should not be considered to be alternative choices but rather as complementary and mutually enhancing approaches to the problem of parallel processing.

Aspects of the design of vector programming languages will be considered in Section 7.5.3. In this section I describe techniques that may be adopted by an optimizing compiler in order to expose the parallelism in a program and thereby enhance its speed of execution on a vector/array processor. Such techniques are termed *vectorization strategies.* As stated earlier, this discussion of vectorization will rely heavily on the work by Kuck and colleagues on the PARAFRASE vectorizer (Kuck *et al.*, 1980, Kuck *et al.*, 1981).

PARAFRASE is really a compiler *preprocessor* that performs a series of *source to source* transformations on Fortran programs. It is also *retargetable* in that its transformations include both target machine independent strategies (called by Kuck *et al.*, *front-end* strategies), *intermediate* strategies for particular classes of parallel processors such as vector processors, and *back-end* strategies for even more specific types of target machines such as register-based vector processors as the CRAY-1.[10] The output of the vectorizer is, thus, Fortran code that is functionally equivalent to the original input to the vectorizer. This code can then be compiled into target-machine object code by a nonoptimizing Fortran compiler.

Dependence Graphs

The basis for the catalog of transformation strategies used in PARAFRASE is the *data dependence graph* (DDG), which was introduced in Chapter 5 (Section 5.4.2). Here we recall the basic definitions couched in a form more suitable to the present context. The notations and definitions given here are mostly based on Kuck (1978) and Kuck and associates (1980).

A program *loop* will be denoted in the abstract as

$$L = (I_1, I_2, \ldots, I_d)(S_1, S_2, \ldots, S_p)$$

where I_j is a *loop index*, S_k is a *body statement* that is an assignment, and d signifies the maximum *depth* of loop nesting in L.

Given a statement S_i, let SOURCE (S_i) and DEST (S_i) denote its *source*

---

[10]Recall that in the terminology of compiling, the machine for which the compiler generates code is termed the *target* machine—hence the concept of a retargetable compiler or (as in this case) vectorizer.

variable set and *destination variable set,* respectively.[11] We will also use the notation

$$S_k(i_1, i_2, \ldots, i_d)$$

to refer to a statement S_k during a particular iteration step in which the values of $I_1, I_2, \ldots, I_d$ are $i_1, i_2, \ldots, i_d$, respectively.

Furthermore, if $S_i(k_1, k_2, \ldots, k_d)$ is executed before $S_j(l_1, l_2, \ldots, l_d)$, this will be denoted as

$$S_i(k_1, \ldots, k_d) < S_j(l_1, \ldots, l_d)$$

where the symbol "$<$" denotes the *execution order* or *precedence* relation. When the values of the loop index variables are irrelevant or there is no scope for ambiguity, the precedence relation will be signified simply as

$$S_i < S_j$$

Example 7.6

Consider the Fortran-like loop

```
DO S₂ I = 1,10
    DO S₂ J = 1,10
        S₁ : A(I,J) := A(I,J) + B(I,J)
        S₂ : D(I,J) := A(I,J) * E
```

Then this can be abstractly represented as

$$L = (I, J)(S_1, S_2)$$

Furthermore, we have SOURCE $(S_1(1,3)) = \{A(1,3), B(1,3)\}$, DEST $(S_1(1,3)) = \{A(1,3)\}$; SOURCE $(S_2(1,2)) = \{A(1,2), E\}$, DEST $(S_2(1,2)) = \{D(1,2)\}$. Finally, the following are some of the precedence relationships.

$$S_1(1,1) < S_2(1,1)$$
$$S_2(1,1) < S_1(1,2)$$
$$S_2(1,2) < S_1(1,3)$$
$$S_1(1,3) < S_2(1,3).$$

■

Definition 7.1

Let S_i, S_j be a pair of assignments appearing within a basic block of assignment statements such that $S_i < S_j$.[12] Then, denoting by $\emptyset$ the empty set:

---

[11]In the literature on parallel processing these are also referred to as the *input* and *output* variable sets, respectively.

[12]A *basic block* (also called a "straight-line code segment") is an ordered set of statements or instructions in a program with no entry points except at the beginning and no branches except possibly at the end.

1. S_j is *data dependent* on S_i, denoted S_i dd S_j if DEST $(S_i) \cap$ SOURCE $(S_j) \neq \emptyset$.
2. S_j is *data antidependent* on S_i, denoted S_i da S_j if SOURCE $(S_i) \cap$ DEST (S_j) $\neq \emptyset$.
3. S_j is *output dependent* on S_i, denoted S_i od S_j if DEST $(S_i) \cap$ DEST $(S_j) \neq$ $\emptyset$.[13]

Definition 7.2

If any of the foregoing *general data dependence* relations hold between S_i and S_j, then we denote this as S_i GDD S_j. Furthermore, S_j is said to be *indirectly data dependent* on S_i, denoted S_i IDD S_j, if there exists statements $S_p, S_q, \ldots, S_r$ such that

$$S_i \text{ GDD } S_p, \ S_p \text{ GDD } S_q, \ \ldots, \ S_r \text{ GDD } S_j$$

Definition 7.3

Given a loop $L = (I_1, \ldots, I_d) (S_1, \ldots, S_p)$, then for a pair of statements S_i, S_j in the loop body:

1. S_i dd S_j if DEST $(S_i (k_1, \ldots, k_d)) \cap$ SOURCE $(S_j (l_1, \ldots, l_d)) \neq \emptyset$ and S_i $(k_1, \ldots, k_d) < S_j (l_1, \ldots, l_d)$.
2. S_i da S_j if SOURCE $(S_i (k_1, \ldots, k_d)) \cap$ DEST $(S_j (l_1, \ldots, l_d)) \neq \emptyset$ and S_i $(k_1, \ldots, k_d) < S_j (l_1, \ldots, l_d)$.
3. S_i od S_j if DEST $(S_i (k_1, \ldots, k_d)) \cap$ DEST $(S_j (l_1, \ldots, l_d)) \neq \emptyset$ and S_i $(k_1, \ldots, k_d) < S_j (l_1, \ldots, l_d)$.

Definition 7.4

Let B be a basic block or a loop body of S statements. Then, a *data dependence graph* (DDG) corresponding to B is a directed graph $G = (V,E)$ where each vertex $V_i \ \varepsilon \ V$ corresponds to a statement S_i in B and there is an edge $l_k \ \varepsilon \ E$ from V_i to V_j if S_i GDD S_j. In particular, the edge is *labeled* "d," "a," or "o" if S_i dd S_j, S_i da S_j or S_i od S_j, respectively.

Example 7.7

For the following sequence of assignment statements:

$S_1 : A := A + 1;$

$S_2 : B := A*C;$

$S_3 : B := E - C;$

$S_4 : E := A + G.$

the DDG is as shown in Figure 7.17. ■

---

[13] These three data dependence relations correspond to RAW, WAR, and WAW hazards as discussed in Chapter 6 on pipelining (see Section 6.3.2).

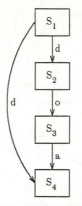

FIGURE 7.17   DDG for Example 7.7.

Example 7.8

For the loop of Example 7.6, the DDG is as shown in Figure 7.18. Note that this is not an acyclic graph as is Figure 7.17 since there is a *dependency cycle* between S_1 and S_2. ∎

PARAFRASE uses the information in a DDG to extract both *local* dataflow information (involving only pairs of statements) and more *global* information involving an entire program segment such as a procedure. For this latter purpose, a DDG is further analyzed into a Π-*partition* defined as follows.

Definition 7.5

Given a DDG G for a loop L, a Π-*partition* is a maximal partitioning of the statements $\{S_1, \ldots, S_p\}$ of L such that S_i, S_j are in the same subset, called a Π-*block*, if and only if S_i GDD S_j and S_j GDD S_i.

Definition 7.6

Given a Π-partition $\{\Pi_1, \ldots, \Pi_m\}$ where the Π_i's are the Π-blocks, the partial ordering relations "pidd," "pida," and "piod" can be defined such that for $i \neq j$:

1. Π_i pidd Π_j iff there exists $S_k \varepsilon \Pi_i$, $S_l \varepsilon \Pi_j$ such that S_k dd S_l.

FIGURE 7.18   DDG for Example 7.8.

2. Π_i pida Π_j iff there exists $S_k \, \varepsilon \, \Pi_i$, $S_l \, \varepsilon \, \Pi_j$ such that S_k da S_l.
3. Π_i piod Π_j iff there exists $S_k \, \varepsilon \, \Pi_i$, $S_l \, \varepsilon \, \Pi_j$ such that S_k od Π_l.

Definition 7.7

A Π-*block graph* (also called a "partial ordering graph by Kuck *et al.*, 1980) is a directed graph in which the vertices corresponds to Π-blocks of a Π-partition and there is an edge (labeled "d," "a," or "o") from the vertex corresponding to Π_i to the vertex corresponding to Π_j if the corresponding partial-ordering relation "pidd," "pida," or "piod" holds between Π_i and Π_j.

Example 7.9

For the DDG of Figure 7.19 (*a*) the corresponding Π-block graph is shown in Figure 7.19(*b*). For simplicity, the edge labels have been omitted. ∎

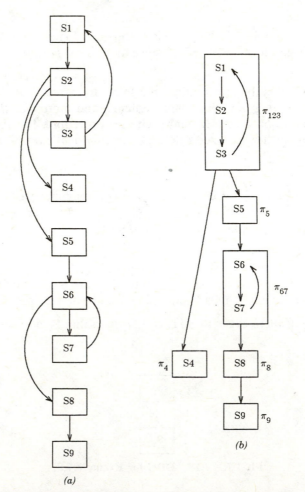

FIGURE 7.19   A DDG *(a)* and its π-block graph *(b)*.

Note that by definition, if a Π-block contains more than one statement, there will be a cyclic dependency between the statements and the corresponding subgraph of the DDG will be strongly connected. Such a Π-block is called a *recurrence* Π-block. Note also that because each cyclic dependence in the DDG will be contained *within* a vertex of the Π-block graph, the latter itself is acyclic.

A recurrence Π-block denotes a set of statements (within a loop) that cannot be executed in parallel. Many of the transformations carried out by PARA-FRASE seek to change recurrences so that the statements can be parallelized.

Examples of Vectorizing Transformations

PARAFRASE, like other optimizing compilers, contains a catalog of optimizing strategies. In this section I give examples of some of the transformations that are relevant to pipelined vector processors such as the CRAY-1.

Example 7.10: Induction Variable Substitution

A scalar variable, I, to which the only assignments within a loop are of the form

```
I := I ± constant
```

is called an *induction variable*.[14] Induction variable substitution replaces the right-hand expression of such an assignment by a linear function of the index variable. Such a transformation is useful in that it eliminates the recurrence from the assignment.

For instance, in the following code segment A is an induction variable:

```
A := −1
DO I = 1,21,2
    A := A + 2
    . . .
```

This can be transformed to:

```
A := −1
DO I = 1,21,2
  A := I
  . . .
```

Example 7.11: Scalar Renaming

Consider a variable A that is assigned a value, then read, is reassigned a value that is then again read. For instance,

---

[14]In the compiler literature these are also called *basic* induction variables. Aho and Ullman (1977, Chapter 5, Section 5.5) define an induction variable more generally as a variable appearing within a loop that is either a basic induction variable I, or a variable J for which there is a basic induction variable I such that each time J is assigned in the loop, J's value is the same linear function of the value of I. As, for example, when J appears in the assignment statement J := 4*I. Example 7.10 is only concerned with basic induction variables.

```
DO I = 1,10
      S1 : A := Z*W
      S2 : X[1] := U*A

      . . . . .
      S3 : A := V/E
      S4 : Y[I] := U*A
      . . . . .
```

Clearly there is a data dependence between S2 and S3 that can be eliminated by renaming the second instance by A1:

```
DO I = 1,10
      S1 : A := Z*W
      S2 : X[1] := U*A

      . . . . .
      S3 : A1 := V/E
      S4 : Y[I] := U*A1
      . . . . .
```
∎

Example 7.12: Scalar Forward Substitution

Consider the following code:

```
R := 11 − K
J := 10 − K
DO I = 1,20
      S1 : A(I,J) := A(I,R)*D
      . . .
```

Without knowing the values of J and R, it would not be clear to a compiler whether or not S1 is a recurrence. However, by substituting for J and R so as to obtain

```
R := 11 − k
J := 10 − k
DO I = 1,20
      S1 : A(I,10 − k) := A(I,11 − k)*D
```

this problem can be resolved. In general, a scalar that is assigned and then used as an array index variable is a candidate for forward substitution. Its main purpose is to enhance the data dependence testability of a program. ∎

Example 7.13: Dead Code Elimination

Any statement that assigns a value to a variable that either is never used again or is reassigned before being used is an instance of *dead code*. Dead code usually arises as a result of other transformations. For example, the outcome of the scalar forward substitution performed in Example 7.12 is the dead code fragment that assigns values to R and J. This fragment can be eliminated. ∎

Example 7.14: Scalar Expansion

Consider the loop fragment

```
DO I = 1,10
    S1 : A := B*I
    S2 : Y(I) := A*Z(I)
```

On each iteration of the loop the scalar A is assigned a value in S1 that is then used in S2. There is, as a result, a data antidependence between S2(i) and S1(i + 1) for $1 \le i \le 9$. This can be avoided by automatically *expanding* the scalar A into an *array* with one element for each iteration of the loop—thus:

```
DO I = 1,10
    S1 : AA(I) := B*I
    S2 = Y(I) := AA(I) + Z(I)
```
∎

Example 7.15 Loop Distribution

If a multiple statement loop body is such that its constituents can be partitioned into two or more mutually *data-independent* groups (i.e., there are no general data dependence relations between statements belonging to different groups), then the loop may be transformed into a number of smaller loops. Consider, for instance, the following:

```
DO I = 1,10
    S1 : A(I) := B(I) + C(I)
    S2 : D(I) := R(I)/A(I)
    S3 : XX(I) := YY(I)*T
```

There is a data dependence between S1 and S2, but S3 is independent of both S1 and S2. The loop may then be distributed so as to obtain

```
DO I = 1,10
    S1 : A(I) := B(I) + C(I)
    S2 : D(I) := R(I)/A(I)
DO I = 1,10
    S3 : XX(I) := YY(I) + T
```

The advantages of loop distribution are twofold. First, a loop distributed around a single statement creates a single vector operation, as in the case of S3. Second, loop distribution may increase the *locality* characteristic of a program. This happens because when an array is referenced in a distributed loop, all its elements will have been referenced before control transfers to other arrays referenced in the succeeding loops. ∎

Example 7.16: Loop Fusion

The converse of loop distributions is *loop fusion* (also called *loop jamming*). If a pair of loops are executed the same number of times with the same indices, then they can be combined into a single loop. In register-based vector machines this transformation is useful for reducing the processor-memory traffic. Consider, for instance, the following code fragment.

```
DO I = 1,10
    S1 : A(I) := B(I) + C(I)
DO I = 1,10
    S2 : D(I) := R(I)*A(I)
```

When compiled, each of these two loops would generate a vector instruction for the arithmetic operations. However, the vector elements computed by S1 would be stored back into memory (in the array A) and then again read back into a vector register when S2 is executed. This can be avoided by fusing the two loops as follows.

```
DO I = 1,10
    S1 : A(I) := B(I) + C(I)
    S2 : D(I) := R(I)*A(I)
```

Note, however, that if fusion results in the number of variables referenced inside the loop body exceeding the number of available processor registers, then additional memory references to store and load temporaries may be necessary. ∎

7.5.3 Languages for Vector and Array Processors

As noted in the previous section, the parallelism within a computation can be detected by a compiler or can be explicitly exposed in the source program. This latter capability demands the development of languages for programming vector/array processors—or more simply, *vector programming languages.*[15]

In fact, the development of such languages has, perhaps, not received the amount of attention that it should have. The general tendency has been to use slightly extended versions of sequential programming languages—especially, Fortran—and rely on vectorizing compilers to produce appropriate code for the target machine. Thus, for example, the use of CFT (Cray Fortran) in programming the CRAY-1 (Russell, 1978) and the development of IVTRAN, a version of Fortran, for the ILLIAC IV (Millstein, 1973). In the case of the ILLIAC IV, however, two different vector programming languages were developed: CFD (Stevens, 1975; Hord, 1982), a Fortran-like language; and Glypnir (Lawrie, *et al.,* 1975; Hord, 1982), based on Algol.

The desirability of high-level vector programming languages can hardly be held in doubt. Vector and array processors are special purpose systems designed to perform computations demanding very high rates of throughput. Their effectiveness in meeting such demands rests critically on how well their specific architectural features are taken advantage of. In other words, it may be a

---

[15]These constitute a subclass of the class of *parallel programming languages,* which also include (horizontal) *microprogramming languages* (see Chapter 5, Section 5.3) and languages for programming *multiprocessors* (see Chapter 8, Sections 8.4.3 and 8.7).

disadvantage for the endo-architecture of a vector/array processor to be hidden from the programmer—even to the high-level language programmer. Rather, one may reasonably expect that if the programming language allows the programmer to represent explicitly the inherent parallelism in the algorithm—in a manner that can be easily exploited by the target machine—this would greatly enhance the ease of compilation.

Although a detailed consideration of vector programming languages is beyond the scope of this book it is of interest to point out their important and distinctive features. For this purpose, I will describe some aspects of a vector programming language called Actus, designed by Perrott (1979). Actus is based on, but extends, the Pascal notation (Jensen and Wirth, 1975).

The Array Data Type

As can be expected, the *array* data type is of central interest in the design of any vector programming language. Consider Figure 7.20, which shows an Actus program for multiplying an mxn matrix "mata" by an n-element vector "vectb."

In Actus, a *scalar array* is represented in the same way as in Pascal. Thus, for example, we have from Figure 7.20:

var vectb : **array**[1 . .n] **of** real

The elements of this array can be referenced only one at a time. To specify *parallel* reference along any dimension of an array, the symbol ". ." is replaced by ":". For example, in Figure 7.20, the declaration

var mata : **array**[1:m,1..n] **of** real

states that the elements of mata along any one of the n columns can be accessed up to m at a time. Thus, in the second iteration of the **for** statement the elements

mata[1,2], mata[2,2], . . . ,mata[200,2]

are referenced in parallel. Although multidimensional arrays are permitted in Actus, the *extent of parallelism* can only be specified along one dimension.

```
const m=200; n=100;
var
    mata : array[1:m,1..n] of real;
    vectb : array[1..n] of real;
    vectu : array[1:m] of real;
    i : integer;

begin
    vectu[1:m] := 0.0;
    for i := 1 to n do
        vectu[1:m] := vectu[1:m] + mata[1:m,i] * vectb[i]
end
```

FIGURE 7.20 An Actus program to multiply a matrix by a vector (Perrott, 1979).

Although not shown in Figure 7.20, an ordered set of integers can be declared in the form of *parallel constants.* For example,

const n = 1:(3)22

defines a parallel constant n, consisting of the sequence of integers 1,4,7, . . . , 22; the quantity in parenthesis specifies the increment between two successive values. When the increment is one, it may simply be omitted as, for example, in

const d = 1:100

Subarrays other than rows or columns may be accessed by means of *array indices,* which are parallel integer vectors, the values of which serve to access a parallel array variable. For example, given the foregoing constant declaration and the declaration:

var main_diag : **array**[1:50] **of** integer;
    matc : **array**[1:50,1..50] **of** integer;

the assignment

main_diag[1:50] := d

writes the values 1, . . . ,50 into main_diag's elements 1, . . . ,50, and the expression

matc[1:50, main_diag[1:50]]

accesses the elements of matc's diagonal in parallel.

Another indexing mechanism in Actus is the *index set,* which is an ordered set of integer values, each of which identifies particular elements of an array to be accessed in parallel. For example, given the declarations

var aa : **array**[1:100, 1..100] **of** real;
index interior = 2:99

the expression aa[interior,3] references the elements aa[2,3], aa[3,3], . . ,aa[99,3]. The more general forms of the index set are exemplified by the declarations:

index top_bottom = 1:2, 99:100;
    odd = 1:(2)99;

These may be used to reference only specific elements of an array. The "," in "top-bottom" signifies a break in the range of the index set whereas "odd" has the same format as parallel constants.

Actus contains two powerful alignment operators for moving data between or within parallel variables. These are the **shift** and the **rotate** operators and their forms and meanings are illustrated by the following example.

Given the declarations

var bb : **array**[1:100] *of* integer;
index firsthalf = 1:50

the expression

bb[firsthalf] + bb[firsthalf **shift** 1]

causes elements 1 through 50 of bb to be added to elements 2 through 51 of bb, respectively, whereas the expression

bb[firsthalf] + bb[firsthalf **rotate**-1]

causes bb[1] to be added to bb[50] and bb[2], . . . ,bb[50] to be added to bb[1], . . . ,bb[49], respectively. Thus, **shift** and **rotate** shift data linearly and circularly, respectively, to the left or to the right (indicated by a positive or a negative shift amount, respectively).

Statements

As Figure 7.20 suggests, the statements in Actus are very similar to the related constructs in Pascal, except that the former may execute on parallel sets of data.

Each Actus statement may have associated with it a single *extent of parallelism*. Obviously, the assignment is the smallest statement for which the extent of parallelism can be specified. As an example, given the declaration

var aa,bb : **array**[1:m, 1. .n] **of** integer;

the assignment

aa[1:m,1] := bb[1:m,1]

assigns all elements of bb's column 1 to aa's column 1 in parallel. Similarly, the **if, while, for,** and **case** constructs may also be associated with extents of parallelism, as shown in the following examples.

Example 7.17

1. **if** a[1:50] > b[1:50] **then** a[#] := b[#]
2. **if any** (a[1:50] > b[1:50]) **then** a[1:50] := a[1:50]-1
3. **if all** (a[10:20] > b[20:30]) **then** a[10:20] := b[20:30]

In (1) the ">" relation between the a[i]'s and the b[i]'s (i = 1, . . ,50) are evaluated in parallel. For those that are true, the assignments involving the corresponding array indices are executed. Thus, the "#" symbol designates the extent of parallelism.

In (2), if any one of the parallel relational expressions are true, then the specified parallel assignment statement is executed. Finally, in (3) the assignment will be executed only if all the ">" relations are true. ∎

Example 7.18

1. **while** a[1:10] < b[1:10] **do** a[#] := a[#] + 1
2. **while any** (a[1:10] < b[1:10]) **do** a[1:10] := b[1:10]
3. **while all** (a[1:25] > b[1:25]) **do** a[1:25] := a[1:25]−1

These may be interpreted in a similar fashion. The statements terminate when [in the case of (1)] *none* of the "<" relations are true; [in the case of (2)] *none* of the "<" relations are true, and [in the case of (3)], *any one* of the ">" relations is false. ■

Given a sequence of assignments with the same (unvarying) extent of parallelism, one may avoid having to repeat the extent explicitly by using the *within* statement. For instance, the statement

```
within 1:50 do
    begin
        a[#] := b[#] + C[#];
        b[#] := b[# shift 1]
    end
```

specifies that the extent of parallelism are elements 1 through 50 and the "#" symbol represents this extent implicitly within the assignments.

7.6 BIBLIOGRAPHIC REMARKS

At the time of this writing, Hwang and Briggs (1984) is the most comprehensive treatise on parallel processing computers and Kogge (1981) provides detailed discussions on all aspects of pipelined architectures, including those of vector processors. Hwang (1984) is a useful anthology of some of the important papers on supercomputing and Metropolis *et al.* (1986) present papers from a recent conference on the scientific, technological, and economic aspects of supercomputers.

The ILLIAC IV has a long and rich history. In addition to the papers cited in the text, Hord (1982) recounts the development, architecture, programming, and applications of this processor in detail.

Russell (1978) is an overview of the CRAY-1. The principles underlying vector processing and chaining in this system are expounded by Johnson (1978). For a detailed technical review of CRAY systems, refer to Cray (1984).

PROBLEMS

7.1 The CRAY-1 achieves its computing power through a combination of technological and architectural means. Analyze the CRAY architecture and identify and explain briefly the principal architectural mechanisms that contribute to its computing power.

7.2 Referring to the taxonomic systems discussed in Chapter 2, describe the place of the CRAY-1:
  (a) In the Erlangen Classification Scheme.
  (b) Within the framework of the Flynn/Hwang-Briggs classification scheme.

7.3   Consider the instruction sequence

$I_1 : V_6 := V_1 + V_2$
$I_2 : V_3 := V_6 * S_1$
$I_3 : V_5 := V_3 + V_1$

where the V_i's are all 64-element vectors and S_1 is a scalar. Assume that the executions of I_1 and I_3 involve a six-stage pipelined floating-point adder whereas the execution of I_2 involves a seven-stage pipelined floating-point multiplier. In executing each vector instruction, one clock period is expended in reading from the source vector to the relevant functional unit and one clock period is required to write back from the functional unit to the destination register. Each stage of the adder and the multiplier consumes one clock period.

(a) Draw a timing diagram showing the execution of this instruction sequence assuming that vector chaining is used.

(b) Indicate the chain slot times on the timing diagram.

(c) What is the speedup attained by this instruction sequence over the situation when chaining is *not* used?

7.4   Amdahl's law indicates that unless a program is heavily vectorized, the speedup will not be significant. Clearly, programs that are executed on vector processors such as the CRAY-1 must, for the sake of efficiency, contain a high proportion of functions or operations that are fundamentally vector-oriented.

   Consider, in particular, the following functions commonly encountered in scientific computations.

(a) Dot product of two vectors.

(b) Matrix transpose.

(c) Matrix multiply.

(d) Matrix inverse.

(e) Convolution.

Using an appropriate vector programming notation (such as Actus, described in Section 7.5.3) construct "vectorized" procedures for each of these functions. Assuming a processor capable of performing primitive vector add, subtract, multiply, and reciprocal operations (instructions), estimate for each procedure the fraction of the executable code that would be vectorized.

7.5   Given an n-th degree polynomial

$$P(x) = p_n x^n + p_{n-1} x^{n-1} + \ldots + p_1 x + p_0$$

where $p_n, p_{n-1}, \ldots, p_0$ are integer coefficients, suppose we wish to evaluate it for $x = v$ Using an appropriate vector programming notation (such as Actus) construct a vectorized algorithm to compute $P(x)$ at $x = v$. Under the same assumptions as stated in Problem 7.4, estimate the fraction of executable code that would be vectorized.

7.6 [A project.] Investigate and analyze thoroughly the vectorization possibilities of the discrete Fourier transform.

7.7 Vector processors are conventionally viewed as machines that are designed for numerical computations. Consider, however, the problem of *sorting* very large arrays of numbers—a classic instance of a nonnumerical computation. Investigate and analyze thoroughly whether and how vector processors can be effectively exploited for large-scale sorting.

7.8 Explain with examples how each of the following vectorizing transformations can be taken advantage of during program execution on a vector processor.
 (a) Induction variable substitution.
 (b) Scalar renaming.
 (c) Scalar forward substitution.
 (d) Scalar expansion.
 (e) Loop distribution.
 (f) Loop fusion.

7.9 [Based on an example due to D. J. Kuck.] Consider the following FORTRAN-like segment:

```
DO I = 1, 50
    MM(I) := NN(I) * PP(I)
    DO J = 1, 50
        QQ(J) := MM(I-1) − SS(J-1)
        SS(J) := QQ(J-1) * X
    DO K = 1, 50
        RR(K) := TT(I-1) + Y
        TT(I) := MM(I) **2
```

 (a) Draw the data dependence graph for this program.
 (b) Draw the corresponding Π-block graph.
 (c) Apply as many vectorizing transformations as you can on this program and show the program resulting from each such transformation.
 (d) Show the final data dependence graph and explain its advantage(s) over the original graph from the viewpoint of its execution on a vector processor.

7.10 Consider the following program loops and show how you can transform each of these so as to speed up the execution of the corresponding object codes on the CRAY-1.
 (a)
```
DO I = 1, 64
    DO J = 1, 16
        A(I,J) := B(I,J) * C
```
 (b)
```
DO I = 1, 64
    A(I) := A(I) * C
    B(I) := B(I) + A(I-1)
```

CHAPTER 8

MULTIPROCESSORS

8.1 THE IDEA OF MULTIPROCESSING

A computer system in its day-to-day operation is fed with a stream of independent "jobs." Each job, in turn, is a collection of communicating, interacting processes.

The concept of a *process* is fundamental to this chapter, so it is worth beginning this discussion by characterizing it in some precise terms. The word "process" is used somewhat casually in the literatures of architecture, operating systems, and performance modeling and yet, as has been noted in the past (Horning and Randell, 1973; Wilkes, 1975), it is an elusive concept that is hard to define formally in any satisfactory way.[1]

Following a line of thinking from Wilkes (1975), we will view the process concept in the following way. Given a particular function to be computed—a job to be done—a process is a (possibly interruptible) thread of control through one or more logically distinct code segments (or procedures) that, when allowed to proceed, enables the function to be computed.

A process, then, exhibits several interesting characteristics:

1. A collection of code segments residing in memory does not by itself constitute a process. It is, rather, a collection of code segments that forms a unit of computation by virtue of a thread of control through the segments (Fig. 8.1). A process is, thus, a dynamic entity.

2. A process may involve a code segment or procedure that may also be the constituent of some other process (Fig. 8.1).

3. A process can, for one or more reasons, be interrupted. This suggests that it can be in one of several *process states*. The most obvious of these is the *running* state during which the computation that the process defines is actually taking place. When interrupted, the process enters the *wait* state indicating its (temporary) suspension. A process can also be in the *ready* state indicating its willingness to resume execution.

In general, then, at any given time it is convenient to view the work load of a

---

[1]See, however, Horning and Randell (1973) for one formal interpretation of the process concept.

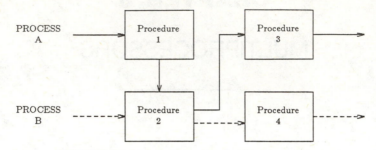

FIGURE 8.1 Two processes sharing a procedure.

computer system as consisting of a population of processes some of which belong to one job, others to some other job, and so on. Furthermore, the processes belonging to a particular job may be such that some of them can (logically, at least) run in parallel whereas some can only be executed in a well-defined sequential manner (Fig. 8.2). In the event that processes can execute in parallel, they may be completely independent of one another, they may need to access common code or data, or they may be required to pass messages between one another.

The task of a *processor* in the computer system is to execute processes in some orderly fashion. There is, therefore, a clear distinction to be made between process and processor. In the terminology of operating systems, when a process is in the running state — that is, it is actually progressing through a computation — it is said to *own* the processor that is executing it. Alternatively, that process may be said to have been *assigned* to the processor.

It is clear that in the case of a *uniprocessor* computer system we have the following problems:

1. Given a population of processes, the processor will have to be time-shared among the processes. This means that even when a single job consists of

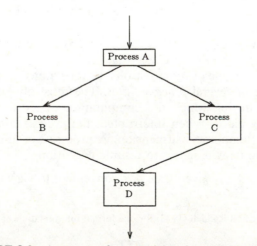

FIGURE 8.2 A system of sequential and parallel processes.

several concurrently executable processes these processes can only be executed in a serial fashion. Likewise, processes belonging to different jobs will also be executed serially in a time multiplexed manner even though the jobs are independent of one another.

2. If the processor *fails* for some reason, the system as a whole will fail till the cause of the failure has been identified and corrected.

The basic purpose of *multiprocessing* is to circumvent these problems. More specifically, multiprocessing is the *cooperative and integrative use of programming, architectural, and technological means to establish multiple processor-based computer systems capable of executing two or more processes in parallel.* The goals of multiprocessing are, then, threefold:

1. To reduce the execution time of a single program (job) by decomposing it into processes, assigning processes to distinct processors, and executing processes concurrently whenever possible.
2. To increase the overall throughput of a system's work load by allowing several jobs to be processed simultaneously by the system.
3. To establish, through redundancy, a level of fault tolerance for the system such that the failure of a processor will still allow the system to function correctly, though perhaps at reduced performance.

The relative importance of these three goals depends on one's viewpoint. There is general agreement that fault tolerance is an important and pleasant *consequence* of multiprocessing, but it is not the fundamental objective. To the more pure-minded, the *essential* purpose of multiprocessing is the parallel processing of individual programs for the purpose of speeding up their executions (Baer, 1973; Arvind and Ianucci, 1983). The more pragmatically inclined continue to view the potential for parallel processing of individual programs somewhat skeptically. Instead, it is the ability to concurrently process several jobs (using shared resources)—and thereby increase overall system throughput—that makes the idea of multiprocessing attractive (Satyanarayanan, 1980).

In my opinion, it seems that the designer of multiprocessing systems can hardly afford to ignore *any* of these objectives. Nevertheless, I would tend to view such a system as particularly disappointing if its capability to effect the parallel processing of individual programs was found to be poor. Accordingly, the primary measure of performance for multiprocessing systems must surely be the *speedup* in the execution of individual programs relative to their executions on single processor systems.

8.2 FUNDAMENTAL CHARACTERISTICS OF A MULTIPROCESSOR

Because of the objectives just discussed, a *multiprocessor* is necessarily distinct from vector processors or other forms of supercomputers. Rather, the multiprocessor concept is a generalization of the general purpose uniprocessor concept, and the entire discussion in this chapter presumes this to be axiomatic. A multiprocessor is, accordingly, an integrated computer system with the following characteristics.

1. It involves two or more processors all of roughly the same computational power and each capable of executing processes autonomously. This implies that there is no central control unit; each processor contains its own control unit and, thus, effectively, control logic is distributed throughout the system.
2. The processors share a (logically) single, systemwide, memory address space.
3. The hardware system as a whole is managed by a single operating system.

Figure 8.3 depicts, in very abstract terms, the principal structural characteristics of a multiprocessor's endo-architecture. The components of interest are a set of $m \geq 1$ memory modules, a set of $n > 1$ processors, and one or more interconnection networks (INs) that allow processors to access the address space and to communicate with one another.[2]

I stated previously that the multiprocessor concept is a generalization of the uniprocessor concept. This generalization is achieved, however, at a stiff price. A multiprocessor is not simply a set of identical or similar uniprocessors. Following the basic adage of systems theory, the whole is not simply the sum of its parts; rather, it is the interaction and integration of such parts that is the essence of the whole.

Thus, the design of *any* multiprocessor architecture involves the resolution of a common set of fundamental problems, some of which are new to the multi-

---

[2]Figure 8.3 may be compared with Figure 7.6, which shows the structure of an array processor's endo-architecture. The principal distinction is that in Figure 7.6 the individual processing elements (PEs) are not capable of autonomously executing processes; rather, they are under the command of a single, "master" control unit, which, though not shown in Figure 7.6, is contained in the box labeled "processor," and which is solely responsible for fetching and interpreting instructions. There is, thus, a single "processor" in array processors in contrast to the situation depicted in Figure 8.3, which shows several autonomously controlled processors.

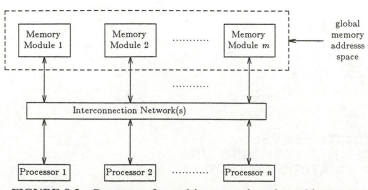

FIGURE 8.3 **Structure of a multiprocessor's endo-architecture.**

processing context whereas others are inherited from the uniprocessor domain but in an exaggerated form. The most important of these problems are

1. The "grains" of parallelism to be supported by the multiprocessor.
2. Synchronization mechanisms for access to shared memory and interprocess communication.
3. Memory latency and its resolution.
4. The interconnection network problem.
5. Processor scheduling strategies.
6. Concurrent programming languages and techniques.

Although these are *all* important problems in the design, implementation, and use of multiprocessor systems, some—in particular (1) through (4)—are more specifically architectural issues than are others. We will, thus, focus on these issues in Sections 8.3 through 8.6. The literature on scheduling and language issues will be discussed in the Bibliographic Remarks at the end of the chapter.

8.3 GRAINS OF PARALLELISM

I have already noted that a multiprocessor must have the capability of executing two or more processes autonomously and in parallel. It would appear, then, that the basic unit or *grain* of parallelism in a multiprocessor is the process; thus, the grain of parallelism is relatively *coarse,* as it would be determined by the average length (in number of instructions) of a process. Whether this statement is completely true or not for a given multiprocessor will actually depend not only on the global structure and capability of the multiprocessor but also on the endo-architecture of the individual processors.

Granularity of parallelism has become a contentious issue in recent discussions of multiprocessor design (Gajski *et al.,* 1982; Gajski and Peir, 1985; Gurd and Kirkham, 1986); this may be explained as follows.

Given the objective of minimizing the execution time of a particular program (or job), one would ideally like to maximize the extent of parallel processing of the program's components—that is, make the grain of parallelism as *fine* as possible. In the case of single instruction-stream systems, such as pipelined uniprocessors (Chapter 6) or vector processors (Chapter 7), the parallelism grain is the instruction in that two instructions belonging to the same stream can be simultaneously executed by the processor. Indeed, these architectural styles are determined by the a priori fine-grained parallelism in pipelined and vector modes of computation.

Consider, however, the case of the multiprocessor, which, we have earlier stated (axiomatically), is a generalization of the uniprocessor concept (Fig. 8.3); in particular, consider the problem of executing a single program component on such systems. A program can be conveniently represented by a data dependence graph (DDG), previously discussed in Chapter 5 (Section 5.4.2) and 7 (Section 7.5.2). One such DDG is depicted in Figure 8.4. Here, the vertices represent

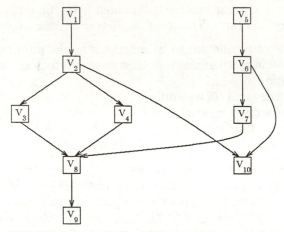

FIGURE 8.4   A DDG with instructions as vertices.

individual instructions, and an edge from some vertex V_i to some other vertex V_j indicates that V_j is data dependent on V_i.

If we wish to exploit the parallelism in this program to its utmost, the grain of parallelism would be the *instruction*. In that case, instructions would be assigned for execution to processors subject to the constraints imposed by the data dependence and resource requirements of the individual instructions.

The price to be paid for this fine-grained parallelism is twofold. First, there is the overhead of *scheduling* vertices of the DDG (in this particular case, individual instructions) to processors. Second, there is the cost of *synchronizing* each edge of the DDG, that is, ensuring that an instruction is not scheduled for processing if the processing of an instruction on which it is data dependent has not been completed.

When the grain size is increased, the scheduling and synchronization cost decreases since the number of vertices and edges in the DDG is less. In Figure 8.5, for example, the vertices of Figure 8.4 have been partitioned into four groups, each group constituting a vertex of a more abstract DDG. Each vertex $V_{ij \ldots k}$ in this DDG can be scheduled for execution on a single processor but, clearly, with an attendant loss of parallelism. For example, the parallelism between V_3 and V_4 or between V_7 and V_{10} can no longer be exploited.

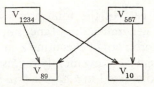

FIGURE 8.5   A DDG with instruction groups as vertices.

The situation can be summarized as follows: The overall speedup in processing a job or program depends both on the degree of parallelism and on the synchronization-scheduling overhead. If the latter can be reasonably reduced, then fine-grain parallelism is a laudable objective. Otherwise, the designer must accept a certain loss in parallelism in order to reduce the costs and complexities of scheduling and synchronization.

It is worth noting that the very fine-grain parallelism present in vector processors such as the CRAY-1 is achieved through special (vector) instructions that operate simultaneously on multiple operand sets contained in highly regular data structures, namely, arrays (see Chapter 7, especially, Section 7.4.2). Since in many computations array elements can be accessed or modified independently, the problem of synchronization does not arise. Furthermore, the vector instruction as a whole is scheduled on the relevant functional unit and not the individual identical instances of the instruction. Fine-grain parallelism in pipelined (scalar or vector) processors where data are not necessarily structured does, on the other hand, involve substantial synchronization overheads, as discussed in Chapter 6 (Section 6.3.6).

I stated earlier that granularity in the context of multiprocessors has become a contentious issue in the more recent past. This is probably because many of the earlier multiprocessors and even some of the very recent ones were not designed *ab initio* as multiprocessors but were extensions or modifications of *previously existing* uniprocessors. The grain of (simulated) parallelism in the uniprocessor — the unit assigned to a processor — was the process, and this concept carried over to the multiprocessor.

Example 8.1 (Satyanarayanan, 1980)

1. The IBM System 370/168 multiprocessor configuration consists of two identical 370/168 CPUs.
2. A Univac 1100 Model 80 multiprocessor configuration can be structured from two or more 1100/80 central processors.
3. The C.mmp multiprocessor developed at Carnegie-Mellon University consists of 16 (slightly modified) PDP-11 minicomputers. ■

Example 8.2

The recent CRAY X-MP and CRAY-2 multiprocessors developed by Cray Research (Cray, 1984; 1986) are two or four processor configurations based on the CRAY-1 vector processor. ■

The advocacy of fine-grain parallelism as a basis for very high speed general purpose multiprocessor design is largely a result of the emergence of the *data flow* styles of computation and architecture as first proposed by Dennis (1974) and since developed extensively by several investigators. I will discuss data flow architectures in Chapter 9 and will examine how the issues of synchronization and scheduling are dealt with in these machines.

8.4 PROCESS SYNCHRONIZATION MECHANISMS

In a general parallel processing environment, two or more concurrently executing processes may need to communicate with each other. For example, process P2 cannot enter a particular code segment until process P1 allows it to do so; or at some point in its execution, P2 needs data that are produced by P1. Thus, a multiprocessor architecture must contain some capabilities to facilitate *interprocess communication.*

A fundamental axiom governing the problem of interprocess communication in multiprocessors is that *no assumptions can be made about the relative speeds of processes.*[3] This means that in order for P1 and P2 to communicate or exchange data at well-defined points, they must be properly *synchronized* so that communication can take place. Furthermore, such synchronizations must be built into the processes themselves — that is, must be programmed — rather than be imposed by the processors (say, through some clocking mechanism). Thus, the problem of interprocess communication translates into the problem of *process synchronization.*

Traditionally, process synchronization mechanisms have been based on the use of *shared variables.*[4] As we will see, this approach continues to dominate in the domain of shared memory multiprocessors. An alternative approach is the use of *message passing;* this has attracted considerable interest in recent times with the development of such languages as CSP (Hoare, 1985) and Occam (INMOS, 1984) where processes communicate by passing or exchanging messages. At the architectural level, message-passing synchronization mechanisms prevail when multiprocessors are composed from multiple, intercommunicating microprocessors.

Both types of mechanisms will be discussed in the next section.

8.4.1 Kinds of Synchronization

Figure 8.6 depicts two processors, i and j, executing processes P1 and P2, respectively. Consider, first, the following interpretation of this diagram. P1 and

---

[3]Contrast this to the situation in pipelined uniprocessors (Chapter 6) or vector processors (Chapter 7) where very strong assumptions are usually made about the time required to perform the phases of an instruction by the pipeline stages.

[4]The process synchronization problem has a (relatively) long and rich history that significantly predates the recent large-scale developments in multiprocessors. Synchronization was first studied in the mid-1960s in the context of operating systems responsible for controlling multiprogrammed (uniprocessor) systems. In such environments, although processes were not executed concurrently by independent processors, it was found to be convenient to organize a program as a collection of communicating, cooperating processes rather than as a single sequential program. A simple example is that of a copying program, consisting of an input process reading from a file of records into a buffer and an output process writing from the buffer into an output file. The two processes constitute a pair of communicating, concurrently executing processes. The developments in process synchronization have been discussed very elegantly by Brinch Hansen (1973; Chapter 3), Andrews and Schneider (1983), and Hoare (1985; Chapter 7).

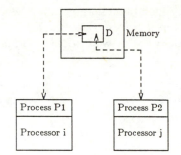

FIGURE 8.6   Processes sharing a data structure D.

P2 are two independent processes, executing in parallel. At some points in their execution, P1 and P2 are both required to modify a common data structure D, held in main memory. For the sake of exactness, we will assume that the code segments executed by P1 and P2 for modifying D are, respectively:

```
P1 : . . . . .
    LOAD D, Reg 1  ⎫
    ADD Reg 1, #1  ⎬  CS₁
    STORE Reg 1, D ⎭
    . . . . .
P2 : . . . . .
    LOAD D, Reg 2  ⎫
    ADD Reg 2, #2  ⎬  CS₂
    STORE Reg 2, D ⎭
    . . . . .
```

Since P1 and P2 are concurrent processes and since we make no assumptions regarding their relative speeds, it is possible that the instructions from these code sequences may *interleave* in time, leading possibly to unpredictable results: Assuming that the initial value of D was 0, the value of D after P1 and P2 have both executed can be 1, 2, or 3, depending on the relative times at which the instructions are actually executed. To avoid this situation of *functional indeterminacy* (Brinch Hansen, 1973)—that is, to guarantee that the value of D is always 3 whenever P1 and P2 have executed on the processors—what is required is to treat each of these code segments as *indivisible* units that access and modify D in a *mutually exclusive* manner. Such code segments were termed *critical regions* by Dijkstra (1968), but are now more commonly termed *critical sections*.

The twin requirements of indivisibility and mutual exclusion for a critical section can be implemented, conceptually, by a *locking* mechanism of the following nature. Let us associate with the shared data structure D a "key" k and two operations LOCK (k) and UNLOCK (k) that set k to 1 ("closes the lock") and 0 ("opens the lock"), respectively. A process can only execute LOCK (k) when it is in the unlocked state, that is, when the value of k is 0. The result of executing LOCK is to set k to 1 and thereby exclude all other processes from executing LOCK (k). Any such process must, then, wait. The result of executing an UNLOCK (k) operation is to reset k to 0.

Assuming that k is initially 0, the two critical sections in P1 and P2 can now be implemented as

```
P1 : . . . . .
     LOCK (k)
     critical section CS₁
     UNLOCK (k)
     . . . . .
P2 : . . . . .
     LOCK (k)
     critical section CS₂
     UNLOCK (k)
     . . . . .
```

The important point to note in this example is that P1 and P2 have to be synchronized so as to execute CS_1 and CS_2 in a mutually exclusive manner. Mutual exclusion, then, is one kind of synchronization that a multiprocessor architecture must support.

Consider, next, the following interpretation of Figure 8.6. This time, processes P1 and P2 are two cooperative, communicating, iterative processes in that P1 produces a stream of results and deposits them sequentially in D, which are taken in the same sequence and consumed by P2.

For simplicity, we assume that D can hold a single value only; thus, it must be ensured that (1) when P1 produces a value V_i and places it in D, it waits till P2 has consumed V_i before depositing the next value V_{i+1} in D; and (2) after P2 consumes value V_i from D, it waits till P1 has produced the next value V_{i+1} before reading from D again.

Thus, P1 and P2 must be mutually synchronized in the following sense: P1 must be delayed (from writing into D) till some particular *condition* is set by P2; and P2 must be delayed (from reading from D) till some particular condition is set by P1. Andrews and Schneider (1983) termed this type of synchronization, *condition synchronization.*

The interesting point to note at this stage is that condition synchronization can be achieved using the same conceptual locking mechanism that can be used to enforce mutual exclusion. We associate two keys, k_1 and k_2, with D. P1 unlocks k_2 to signal to P2 that it has deposited a new value in D whereas P2 unlocks k_1 to inform P1 that it has consumed the value last placed in D. Assuming that k_1 and k_2 are initially set to 0 and 1, respectively, the relevant code segments in P1 and P2 are

```
P1 : . . . . .
     LOCK (k₁)
     produce value and deposit in D
     UNLOCK (k₂)
     . . . . .
P2 : . . . . .
```

LOCK (k$_2$)
consume value in D
UNLOCK (k$_1$)

. . . . .

In the next section I describe how these locking mechanisms can be realized by means of synchronizing primitives that use shared variables.

8.4.2 Synchronization Based on Shared Variables

From the foregoing discussion, it will be evident that the LOCK operation involves two actions: *testing* the state of the key k, and *setting* it to 1 if its value is 0. UNLOCK, however, only involves the single action of setting the key to 1.

Clearly, any implementation of LOCK/UNLOCK must resolve two issues. First, the operations must be sufficiently *primitive* as to be themselves indivisible. Otherwise, each of the (two or more) concurrent processes may test k's value and find it to be 0 before any of the others set it to 1; in which case they will all enter their respective critical sections.

Second, a process that is locked out must, logically, wait till the key has been unlocked. It must somehow know when to reattempt the execution of LOCK.

A number of mechanisms have been developed that propose different ways of resolving these issues. Some of these are next described.

The TEST-AND-SET Primitive

The earliest solution to the problem appears to be the TEST-AND-SET instruction, which was first implemented as part of the IBM System/360 instruction set (Blaauw and Brooks, 1964) and later in the System/370 (IBM, 1981). The general form of the instruction is

C := TEST-AND-SET (k)

where k is a memory-based variable and C is a processor-based (or "local") variable. Its effect is to copy the value of k into C and set k to 1 as a single, indivisible, operation.[5]

The LOCK operation can now be implemented as

LOCK(k) : **repeat** C := TEST-AND-SET(k) **until** C=0

whereas, of course, the UNLOCK is simply realized, indivisibly, as

UNLOCK(k) : k := 0

---

[5]The precise form of this instruction on the System 360/370 is

TS Addr

where "Addr" is a memory byte address. In executing the instruction, the left-most bit of the addressed byte is used to set the condition code (0 if the left-most bit was 0, otherwise 1) and the addressed byte is set to all ones.

Variations of the TEST-AND-SET instruction are provided in many contemporary processors. Its presence in the form of the *interlocked* instruction on the NS32032 microprocessor is the basis for the synchronization mechanism provided on the recent Encore Multimax multiprocessor system (Encore, 1986; see also Section 8.6.4 of this chapter).

It will be evident that there are basically two drawbacks to the TEST-AND-SET instruction as a means for implementing the LOCK operation.

First, referring to Figure 8.6, a process P1 (say) attempting a LOCK operation and waiting to acquire control of a shared variable will be continuously executing the TEST-AND-SET. Consequently, processor i, executing P1, will be in a state commonly known as *busy-wait* or *spin-lock,* since it does nothing but wait for the LOCK to complete successfully. In the event that P1 is locked out because P2 is executing a prolonged code segment before it unlocks the key relevant to P1, valuable *processor cycles* are wasted on processor i.

Second, each busy-waiting processor attempting a LOCK operation requires memory access in order to TEST-AND-SET the value of the key and, thus, consumes *memory cycles* that might otherwise have been more productively used. In a general multiprocessor, many processors may be waiting on, and testing, a single key, in which case available memory cycles for other operations may be seriously degraded.

FETCH-AND-ADD Type Primitives

The aim of synchronization operations is to *serialize* two or more parallel code segments involving a shared data structure D. However, as I have just noted, serialization may seriously delay a process waiting for a particular key to be unlocked so that it may enter the relevant code segment. Note also that when two or more machine instructions (such as LOADs and STOREs) are attempted on a single memory word, the indivisibility of these instructions must be preserved so as to guarantee serialization. The memory controller will interleave the LOADs and STOREs.

The designers of the New York University (NYU) Ultracomputer multiprocessor (Gottlieb *et al.,* 1983) have recently proposed a new primitive called the FETCH-AND-ADD, which, when appropriately implemented, may be used to accomplish some degree of simultaneity of access to a shared variable while preserving the serialization requirement.

The form of this operation is

FETCH-AND-ADD (V,e)

where V is a variable, and e an integer expression. The execution of this operation causes the value of V to be returned and the value of V to be replaced by V + e as a single, indivisible operation. The FETCH-AND-ADD also satisfies the serialization property in the following sense: If several FETCH-AND-ADDs attempt to access V simultaneously, the effect of these operations is equivalent to the serial execution of these operations (in some unspecified order). Thus, for example, assuming the original value of V is Vo, the simultaneous execution of

```
R1 := FETCH-AND-ADD (V,ei)
R2 := FETCH-AND-ADD (V,ej)
```

will result in V's value set to Vo + ei + ej (as a *single* operation) while either

```
R1 = Vo, R2 = Vo + ei
```

or

```
R2 = Vo, R1 = Vo + ej
```

Gottlieb and colleagues have shown how the FETCH-AND-ADD can be used to implement several highly parallel algorithms (Gottlieb *et al.,* 1983; Gottlieb, Lubachevsky, and Rudolph, 1983). Our interest here is its use in the implementation of synchronization primitives.

For this purpose, consider the following generalization of the FETCH-AND-ADD:

```
FETCH-AND-OP (V,e)
```

where V is a variable and e is an expression that is type-compatible with V. This operation returns the value of V and at the same time replaces it with the value OP(V,e). Now, the

```
C := TEST-AND-SET (k)
```

primitive can be realized by the instruction

```
C := FETCH-AND-OR (k, TRUE)
```

where k is a Boolean variable.

Let us now consider what advantage the FETCH-AND-OR has over the original TEST-AND-SET. Consider two concurrent processes P1 and P2 that enforce mutual exclusion on a variable by means of critical sections. Using TEST-AND-SET, we have

Version 1   (initially, k = 0)

```
P1 : . . . . .
     repeat C₁ := TEST-AND-SET (k) until C₁ = 0 ("LOCK")
            critical section₁
     k := 0 ("UNLOCK")
     . . . . .
P2 : . . . . .
     repeat C₂ := TEST-AND-SET (k) until C₂ = 0 ("LOCK")
            critical section₂
     k := 0 ("UNLOCK")
     . . . . .
```

Using FETCH-AND-OR, we have

Version 2 (initially, k = FALSE)

```
P1 : . . . . .
     repeat C₁ := FETCH-AND-OR (k,TRUE) until C₁ = FALSE
            critical section₁
     k := FALSE
     . . . . .
P2 : . . . . .
     repeat C₂ := FETCH-AND-OR (k,TRUE) until C₂ = FALSE
            critical section₂
     k := FALSE
     . . . . .
```

In version 2, if simultaneous executions of the two FETCH-AND-ORs are attempted, the serialization property will guarantee that either

$$C_1 = \text{FALSE}, \ C_2 = \text{TRUE}$$

in which case P1 will enter its critical section, or

$$C_1 = \text{TRUE}, \ C_2 = \text{FALSE}$$

in which case P2 will enter its critical section. In either case, k = TRUE. Furthermore—and this is the important thing—the two updates of k will be *combined* into a single memory access. In contrast, the modification of k by the two TEST-AND-SET operations in version 1 will, necessarily, be done serially.

The efficiency of FETCH-AND-ADD type operations, thus, relies on combining the two or more simultaneous operations (ADD, OR, etc.) on the shared variable. It is of interest, then, to understand the mechanism proposed by Gottlieb and coworkers (1983) for this purpose.

Suppose the interconnection network between the processors and the memory modules (see Fig. 8.3) is a network of 2-input, 2-output (i.e., 2×2) *switches* and that each switch can accept two FETCH-AND-OP requests on its input lines and transmit a FETCH-AND-OP onto one of its two output lines (Fig. 8.7). If two requests, FETCH-AND-OP (V,ei) and FETCH-AND-OP (V,ej) from processes P1 and P2, referencing the same variable V, reach a switch at (roughly) the same time, the switch computes the value OP(ei,ej), transmits out the combined request FETCH-AND-OP (V,OP(ei,ej)), and stores one of the values (say ei) in a register contained within the switch. When the value of V, say Vo, is returned to the switch in response to the operation FETCH-AND-OP (V,OP(ei,ej)), the switch transmits Vo to P1 and computes and transmits the value OP(Vo,ei) to P2.

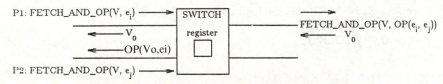

FIGURE 8.7   Implementation of FETCH-AND-OP.

Semaphores

As we noted earlier, a serious drawback of implementing the LOCK operation with a TEST-AND-SET primitive is that it places the processor executing the LOCK in a busy-wait state. In recognition of this problem, Dijkstra (1968) proposed two new indivisible operations denoted as P and V, defined on a special variable that he named *semaphore*.[6]

A semaphore is a nonnegative integer-valued variable. Given a semaphore S, the operations P(S) and V(S) are defined as follows.

```
P(S) : if S > 0
         then S := S − 1
         else Block the process executing P(S) and place it in a "wait queue" asso-
              ciated with S;
              Allocate processor to some other process from the "ready queue"
V(S) : S := S + 1;
         if there are any processes in the "wait queue" associated with S
         then select such a process from the "wait queue" and place it in the "ready
              queue"
```

In other words, P(S) will block the calling process unless S has a positive value. However, the blocked process itself will not tie up the processor, which will be released to execute some other "ready" process. V(S) will cause a process that had been previously blocked on this semaphore to be placed in the ready state so that it can be eventually allocated to an available processor. Thus, the busy-wait condition is avoided.

Using a semaphore, the mutual-exclusion problem can be solved as follows. Assume that a semaphore S is initialized to 1. Then

```
P1 : . . . . .              P2 : . . . . .
      P(S)                        P(S)
        critical section CS₁        critical section CS₂
      V(S)                        V(S)
    . . . . .                    . . . . .
```

Similarly, the condition synchronization problem described previously can be solved using two semaphores S_1 and S_2. Assume that S_1 is initialized to 1 and S_2 to 0. Then

```
P1 : . . . . .              P2 : . . . . .
      P(S₁)                       P(S₂)
        Produce value and           Consume value in D
        deposit in D
      V(S2)                       V(S1)
    . . . . .                    . . . . .
```

[6]Andrews and Schneider (1983) record that P stands for the Dutch word *passern* ("to pass") and V stands for the Dutch word *vrygeven* ("to release").

A semaphore itself is a shared variable, and the P and V operations on S must satisfy the mutual exclusion property. Thus, P and V must be programmed as critical sections—using the TEST-AND-SET primitive, for example. Since these will be very small critical sections, the busy-wait time that will be incurred by a waiting P or V operation will be relatively short.

For further discussions of semaphores, their uses and limitations from the programming viewpoint, and the means of their implementation, refer to Brinch Hansen (1973), who used the terms *wait* and *signal* for P and V, respectively, and Habermann (1976).

8.4.3 Synchronization Based on Message Passing

Conservative thinkers on multiprocessors and their use in parallel processing have mainly envisioned systems consisting of a relatively small number of processors—up to about 16—linked by means of an interconnection network to a global shared memory, also composed of a relatively small number of memory modules. In the last decade or so, however, progress in VLSI technology, availability of low-cost off-the-shelf microprocessors, and the possibility of customized components (see Volume 1, Chapter 2, Section 2.5) have produced a technological climate in which multiprocessors composed of several hundreds or even thousands of processors are being contemplated.

The basic structure of multiprocessors in this line of thinking differs significantly from that depicted in Figure 8.3. Rather, what is being envisioned are structures in which each processor is attached to its own (small) local memory, thus forming a processor/memory (PM) complex; and the PMs are connected directly to one another according to some appropriate geometry. As a small example of such a structure, Figure 8.8 shows a collection of 8 PMs connected in the form of a *Boolean 3-cube,* an instance of the more general *hypercube* structure (Seitz, 1985).

In such multiprocessor organizations, processes can truly be distributed among the PMs. Each process has direct access to its local memory and, thus, pays a price (in latency) when having to access data in some other PM.

It is, then, natural that in such multiprocessing systems synchronization

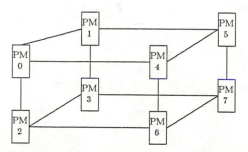

FIGURE 8.8 Eight-processor/memory multiprocessor organized as a Boolean 3-cube.

between processes running on the distinct PMs should be based on the principle of *passing messages* instead of shared variables. Indeed, message passing becomes the basis of interprocess communication as well as of process synchronization.

Primitive operations for effecting message passing are usually of the SEND/RECEIVE type. A process sends a message by executing an operation of the form

SEND expression TO destination process

which causes the message—the value of the expression—to be transmitted to the destination process. A message is received by a process when it executes

RECEIVE variable FROM source process

which causes a message from the source process to be received into the variable.

When a sending process PSend and a receiving process PReceive name each other as destination and source processes, respectively, a *channel of communication* is (logically) established. Message-passing schemes in which processes must explicitly name destination/source processes are the simplest and most restricted means of establishing communication channels. This protocol is termed *direct naming* (Andrews and Schneider, 1983). Other more flexible and more complex mechanisms have also been established, but I will not discuss them here. You may consult Andrews and Schneider (1983) for further details.

In message-passing schemes based on direct naming, the means for *synchronization* between sending and receiving processes may be effected in a number of ways. In (fully) *synchronous* message passing, there are no *buffers* associated with the communication channel. Thus, the execution of a SEND by a sending process PSend is always delayed until a RECEIVE is executed by the corresponding receiving process—that is, until the destination process named by PSend executes a RECEIVE naming PSend as the source process. Conversely, the execution of a RECEIVE is delayed until a corresponding SEND is executed.

In contrast, messages may also be *buffered* between the time that they are sent and the time that they are received. Assuming that the buffer is bounded—has finite capacity—a SEND operation will only get delayed when the buffer is full and a RECEIVE operation will only get delayed if the buffer is empty. Thus, in general, the sending process can potentially get as much ahead of the receiving process as the buffer capacity allows. Such message passing schemes are termed *asynchronous.*

The Occam/Transputer Model of Message Passing

As a specific illustration of a message-passing scheme available in a contemporary commercial system, we will discuss the features available in the Occam[7] programming language (INMOS, 1984). On one hand, Occam was designed to

---

[7]Occam is a trademark of the INMOS Group of Companies.

facilitate concurrent programming in which several processes execute independently and interactively. However, Occam is also the programming (or assembly) language for the *transputer* that was developed by INMOS as a "programmable VLSI component" (Whitby-Strevens, 1985). Occam has been designed to program a single transputer but was more specifically intended to program multiple-transputer multiprocessors where two transputers can be directly connected to each other through communication links. Transputers communicate with one another by sending messages along the links.

Occam, in fact, defines the model of concurrency, communication, and synchronization underlying the envisioned architecture of multiple-transputer systems. Indeed, one can describe such a system as a collection of Occam processes that executes concurrently and asynchronously and passes messages through named channels according to the message-passing protocol defined in the language.

As a specific example, consider the producer-consumer problem described in Section 8.4.1 in which process P1 produces a stream of values that are consumed by process P2 in the same order in which they are produced. Our earlier description had been based on the shared-variable model: The produced values were deposited by P1 in a shared data structure D that also served as P2's source of values. Correct access to D required the use of condition synchronization.

Using Occam, this same problem can be solved as follows (Fig. 8.9). The solution consists of two (in this example, unnamed) nonterminating Occam *processes* running in parallel, and communicating through a *channel* X (Fig. 8.10). The composition of the overall parallel process is indicated by the textual form

```
par
    [component
    [component
```

where the components are indented with respect to the keyword *par*. Each of the two components of the parallel process is an iterative *sequential* process, indicated by the textual form

```
chan X :
    par
        while true
            var a :
            seq
                compute value and place in a
                X ! a
        while true
            var b :
            seq
                X ? b
                consume value in b
```

FIGURE 8.9 Occam solution to a simple producer-consumer problem.

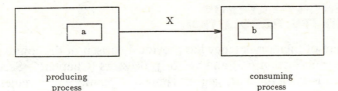

producing
process

consuming
process

FIGURE 8.10   Structure of Occam processes and their communicating channel.

while.   .   .   .
   seq
      [component
      [component

where, again, indentation is used to identify the components of the sequential process.

Of specific interest to us are the means by which the two sequential processes communicate and synchronize with one another. This is effected by the producing process executing an *output* statement

X!a

which sends the value of the local variable a onto the channel X; and the consuming process executing an *input* statement

X?b

which causes the value on channel X to be read into the local variable b.

Input and output statements are two of the three primitive statements in Occam. The third primitive statement is the assignment.[8]

The two sequential processes, then, *communicate* by means of input and output statements involving a common named channel X. *Synchronization* is achieved by the fact that an input statement involving X will not complete until an output statement involving the same channel X is executed. The converse also holds. The processes will wait on their input/output statements for one another, thereby effecting synchronization and, consequently, communication. Once this is done, the two processes will resume their parallel execution till they need to communicate again.

---

[8]It is important to note here that the conceptual and theoretical foundations for Occam were laid by Hoare's (1978) work on *communicating sequential processes* (CSP), which has since been further developed by Hoare (1985). An important distinction between (the original) CSP and Occam is that in the former channels are not named. Thus, two processes P1 and P2 communicate by executing output and input statements, respectively, of the form

P2 ! a
P1 ? b

That is, an output statement names the destination *process* and an input statement names the source *process*. In Hoare's later discussion of CSP (Hoare 1985), channels are introduced. For further comparison of CSP and Occam, see Hoare (1985, Chapter 7).

8.5 MEMORY LATENCY AND ITS RESOLUTION

The problem of memory latency has previously arisen in the context of pipelining (Chapter 6, Section 6.3) and vector processors (Chapter 7, Section 7.4). It was also discussed in the more general context of memory hierarchies in Volume 1, Chapter 8.

Latency, you will recall, is the time that elapses between a request by a processor to memory and the receipt by the processor of the associated data item. Memory latency, clearly, is a serious issue and a potential bottleneck that must be grappled with in the design of any high-performance system.

In the case of a shared memory multiprocessor system of the type depicted in Figure 8.3, the latency problem is greatly heightened by (1) the presence of many processors that may need to access the same memory module, thus leading to the possibility of *memory contention*; (2) the presence of the interconnection network, which introduces an inherent delay between a processor issuing a memory request and receiving a response; and (3) the potential for conflict in any particular component of the interconnection network itself. The larger the *size* of the multiprocessor—the larger the number of processors—the greater will be the average latency.

Interconnection networks are discussed in Section 8.6. Our concern in this section is to assume that memory latency can hardly be avoided in multiprocessors and to consider ways for *tolerating* (or hiding) its effect.

8.5.1 Process Switching

One possible method of hiding the effect of latency is to perform a process or "context" switch whenever a process Pi makes a memory request: Pi is suspended and the processor executing Pi is assigned to some other waiting-to-run process Pj.

This technique was developed originally for time-multiplexing a processor in multiprogrammed/time-shared systems (see, for example, Brinch Hansen, 1973; Habermann, 1976). The problem with this approach in a multiprocessor is that the process state (contained in the processor's registers) for the suspended process Pi will itself have to be saved and the process state for Pj will have to be loaded into these processor registers in order to effect a context switch.

If the process state is saved in memory, then this in itself will involve memory access and thus aggrevate still further the latency problem. One can avoid this by providing multiple sets of processor registers to hold multiple process states, at the cost of increasing processor complexity. Furthermore, as pointed out by Arvind and Ianucci (1983) and Gajski and Peir (1985), there must be at all times a sufficient number of concurrent processes available to take advantage of this scheme: Whenever a process makes a memory request, there should be a nonempty set of processes waiting to be executed.

Example 8.3

A variation of process switching was used in the Denelcor HEP multiprocessor for minimizing latency effects (Jordan, 1985). ■

8.5.2 The Use of LOAD/STORE Architectures

The CRAY-1 (Chapter 7, Section 7.4) attempts to minimize the effect of memory latency by using "LOAD/STORE" instruction sets: The only instructions that reference memory are the LOAD and STORE type instructions; all other instructions refer to data in (programmable) processor registers. (This characteristic was also implemented in the RISC machines—see Volume 1, Chapter 7.)

Such LOAD/STORE architectures must necessarily have a large number of processor registers, as in the case of the CRAY-1 (see Fig. 7.7). Furthermore, such LOAD/STORE instruction sets are frequently designed in conjunction with pipelined processing so that memory access (for both instructions and operands) form part of the pipeline; thus, while memory access is in progress, the pipeline is busy with the processing of other instructions.

Example 8.4

Recall the CRAY-1 architecture from Chapter 7, Section 7.4. Single instructions load entire sets of vector elements into vector (V) registers; all other vector arithmetic instructions process these elements in pipelined mode. Other special instructions can block transfer from the auxiliary B (or T) registers into memory or vice versa. ■

A large set of programmable registers (or a local store) in LOAD/STORE architectures suggests the notion of a cache memory, except that the registers are programmable.[9] The problem in using this method in the context of multiprocessors is the following: Each processor will have its own local store. Furthermore, two or more local stores may, at some point, be loaded with data from identical main memory words. However, if a processor updates one of these common data items in its own local store, then the same data item must also be updated in all the other relevant local stores as well as in main memory. This, in fact, is the *coherence problem* manifested in the presence of multiple caches in multiprocessors. It is discussed in the next section.

8.5.3 The Cache Coherence Problem

Probably the most widely established method of tolerating memory latency in uniprocessors is the use of a *cache* (discussed in Volume 1, Chapter 8). This same idea is applicable in the multiprocessor domain: Each processor can have associated with it its own private cache, as shown in Figure 8.11.

---

[9]You may recall that a cache memory is usually an endo-architectural feature and, thus, is not normally visible to the programmer (see Volume 1, Chapter 8).

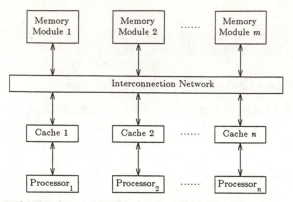

FIGURE 8.11 **Multiprocessor with private caches.**

Unfortunately, the presence of multiple caches introduces the *cache coherence problem,* which is defined as follows (Censier and Feautrier, 1978). A memory system is *coherent* if the value returned on a LOAD instruction is always identical to the value written to the same address by the latest STORE instruction.

In the case of uniprocessors, whenever a word in the cache is modified, then the *write-through* policy ensures that the corresponding word in main memory is also updated (see Volume 1, Chapter 8). In multiprocessors where each processor has its private cache, this policy cannot be easily enforced for, as we saw in the previous section, the same data item may be present in several of the private cache memories. If a processor modifies this data item in its own cache, then to maintain coherence the same modification must be effected on that data item in all the other caches (as well as in memory).

The cache coherence problem has attracted a great deal of attention, and methods for circumventing this problem have been proposed (Censier and Feautrier, 1978; Dubois and Briggs, 1982; Yeh, Patel, and Davidson, 1983; Hwang and Briggs, 1984, Chapter 7).

One solution that is being used in both the Cedar (Kuck *et al.,* 1986) and the Ultracomputer (Gottlieb *et al.,* 1983; Gottlieb, 1986) projects is to partially avoid the coherence problem altogether by allowing only *read only* information (e.g., code segments) or read-write data that is local to a process to be moved into private caches. Other read-write data access will incur longer latencies.

An alternative scheme is the *shared* cache organization (Dubois and Briggs, 1982) in which, rather than associating caches with processors, a cache is associated with one or more memory modules such that all processors can reference the cache. Figure 8.12 shows the structure of a shared cache-based multiprocessor where a cache is associated with each set or cluster of memory modules. Thus, when a processor updates cache i, coherence is maintained by a write-through to the relevant memory in module i. No other copies of the same data reside in any of the other caches.

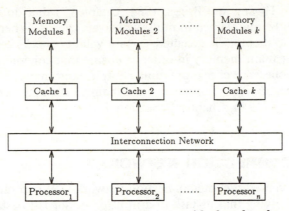

FIGURE 8.12   Multiprocessor with shared caches.

The main problem with this approach is that an access to a cache must still traverse the interconnection network. Thus, the latency effects due to network delays will remain.

The advantages of the private and shared cache schemes can be combined as shown in Figure 8.13. Shared read/write data are placed in the shared caches while read-only or local read/write information is placed in the private caches. A variation of this scheme is being used in the Cedar system (Kuck *et al.,* 1986).

The foregoing schemes avoid the cache coherence problem by not allowing multiple copies of a data item to exist. In contrast, schemes called *dynamic coherence checks* have been proposed (Censier and Feautrier, 1978; Papamarcos

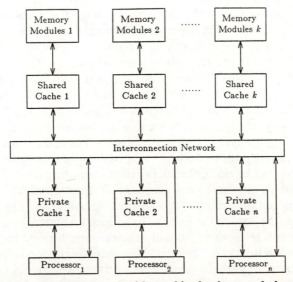

FIGURE 8.13   Multiprocessor with combined private and shared caches.

and Patel, 1984; Hwang and Briggs, 1984, Chapter 7) that do allow multiple copies of data to be maintained in multiple private caches. Whenever a read or write operation to memory is executed, certain validity checks are performed in the cache and/or main memory in order to ensure that coherence is preserved. Such dynamic coherence checks are quite complex and may themselves lead to performance degradations. For more on dynamic coherence checks, refer to Hwang and Briggs (1984, Chapter 7, Section 7.3).

8.6 INTERCONNECTION NETWORKS

So far, we have viewed the interconnection network (IN) in a rather functional way, merely specifying that its task in a multiprocessor is to establish connections between processors and memory either directly (Fig. 8.3) or by involving caches as intermediaries (Figs. 8.11 and 8.12). We have not yet considered the internal architecture of INs.

Our discussion of the latency problem also indicated that one of the contributions to the latency phenomenon is the ubiquituous presence of the IN. Thus, much research and thinking has gone into the design, analysis, and implementation of INs, as a result of which an almost bewildering array of IN architectures have been developed over the past two decades.

8.6.1 Terminology

In very general terms, given a set of devices that need to communicate with one another, an IN is a network of *switching elements* that facilitates paths of communication between pairs of such devices. In the case of shared memory multiprocessors of the kind we have been discussing, the paths of interest are of the *processor-memory* type. In the case of message-passing multiprocessors (see Section 8.4.3) or array processors (see Chapter 7, Section 7.1), the paths of interest are primarily of the *processor-processor* type.

The two principal factors that determine the overall architecture of INs are the *switching method* used to establish a path through the IN and the *network topology* that characterizes the interconnection pattern or structure of the IN.

The two main switching methods are circuit switching and packet switching. In *circuit switching,* a physical path is established between the source device and the destination device prior to the beginning of data transmission. Once a path is established, there will be no further delay in transmitting data. The only subsequent delay will be due to signal propagation time along the selected path. Circuit switching is, thus, suitable for transmitting bulk data or long messages. In *packet switching,* the data in the form of fixed length segments called *packets* are routed through the IN without actually establishing a prior physical path between source and destination. Each packet is individually forwarded through the IN along the best path available at its time of transmission. Packet switching is, then, advantageous for transmitting short data messages, since in the interest of maintaining simple switching elements, the buffers used to store packets at the switching elements should not be large.

Network topologies can be categorized as static or dynamic (Feng, 1981). In a *static* topology, links between the devices of interest are fixed whereas in a *dynamic* topology, links can be reconfigured by setting the network's switching elements.

Example 8.5

Figure 8.14 shows an example of a static topology:—the nearest neighbor connection as was used in the ILLIAC IV (Barnes *et al.,* 1968; Hord, 1982). Another example is shown in Figure 8.8: the 3-cube, a special case of the Boolean hypercube as used in the Cosmic Cube multiprocessor (Seitz, 1985). In both cases, the nodes in the network are processors. ■

Example 8.6

Figures 8.15 and 8.16 shows two examples of dynamic topologies: a crossbar switch that was used in the C.mmp system (Wulf and Bell, 1972; Satyanarayanan, 1980) and a banyan network (Goke and Lipovsky, 1973). In both cases, the nodes in the network are switches. ■

Dynamic topologies, in turn, consist of three network subclasses:

1. **Single-stage** networks, which consist of just one stage of switching elements. In such a network data may have to be recirculated through the single stage several times in order to reach a given destination from a given source.
2. **Multistage** networks, which consist of two or more stages of switching elements. In such networks it is usually possible to establish a transmission path between arbitrary pairs of devices.
3. **Crossbar** switches, in which every source device can be connected to every destination device without blocking.

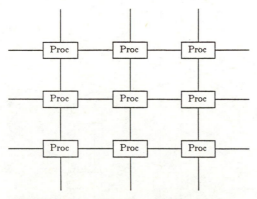

FIGURE 8.14   Nearest neighbor topology.

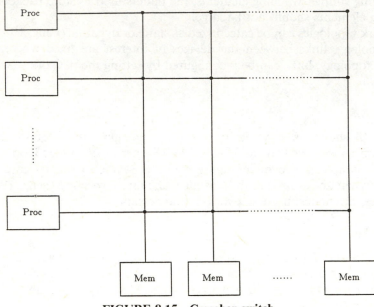

FIGURE 8.15   Crossbar switch.

Example 8.7

An example from the single-stage class is the *perfect shuffle* (or *shuffle exchange*) network (Stone, 1971) in which a processor i is connected to a processor j such that j's address is obtained from i's address by a circular left shift of one position of the binary representation of i. Figure 8.17 shows an 8 × 8 perfect shuffle network in which the same processors are shown on both sides of the one stage of switches for clarity. ∎

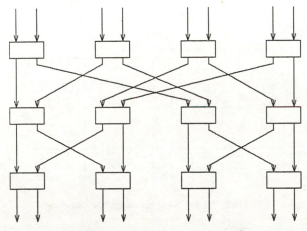

FIGURE 8.16   A banyan network.

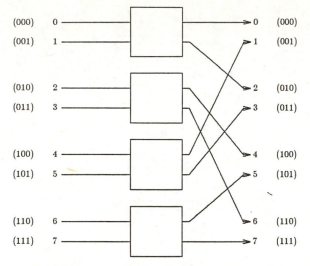

FIGURE 8.17   An 8×8 perfect shuffle network.

Example 8.8

The banyan network shown in Figure 8.16 exemplifies the class of multistage networks. ■

A network is said to be *blocking* if simultaneous connections between two or more pairs of devices may cause contention in the use of switching elements. It is said to be *nonblocking* if it can effect all possible pairwise device connections without conflicts. A network is said to be *rearrangeable nonblocking* if it can achieve all possible connections between source and destination devices by "rearranging" existing connections.

Finally, we note that single or multistage INs can be constructed from a single type of *switching element*. Possibly the most established switching element is the 2-input, 2-output (2 × 2) switch shown in Figure 8.18(*a*). The functional behavior of the switch is determined by the setting of the control input C according to the specifications:

if C = 0 **then** /* direct connect */
 new $O_1 = I_1$ &
 new $O_2 = I_2$
 else /* cross connect */
 new $O_1 = I_2$ &
 new $O_2 = I_1$

Direct and cross connections are shown in Figures 8.18 (*b* and *c*, respectively). Note that this particular switch is a *nonblocking* type: It can handle parallelism to the extent of direct connection of inputs to outputs or cross connection of inputs to outputs.

Another, more flexible, type of 2 × 2 switch is shown in Figure 8.19(*a*). The switch behavior is now controlled by two independent control lines. This is a

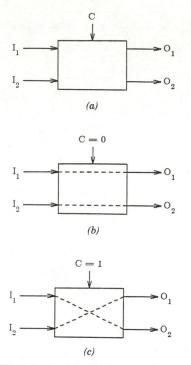

FIGURE 8.18 **Nonblocking 2×2 switch.**

blocking switch, since both inputs may contend for O_2 (Fig. 8.19b) or for O_1 (Fig. 8.19c).

As previously noted, a large number of INs have been designed and studied in the past two decades and the literature on the topic is vast.[10] Many of these were developed for array computers, some for specialized processors, and others for multiprocessors. Some of the INs that were originally designed for array processors are now being applied to the multiprocessor domain. In the following sections I will describe a small number of INs that have been selected either because they have been used most commonly in past multiprocessors or because they are viewed to be the most appropriate for a number of multiprocessor systems currently under development. Examples of multiprocessors employing these INs are also given.

8.6.2 The Crossbar Switch and C.mmp

The crossbar switch (Fig. 8.15) is the most direct and most expensive method of establishing paths between processors and memory modules. Given a set of m

---

[10]Significant surveys include Benes (1965); Enslow (1977); Siegel (1979); Masson, Gingher, and Nakamura (1979); Feng (1981), Siegel (1984), and Bhuyan (1987). Selected research papers relevant to specific INs include Goke and Lipovski (1973), Barnes *et al.* (1968), Wulf and Bell (1972), Lang, Valero, and Alegre (1982), Bhuyan and Agrawal (1983), Stone (1971), Lawrie (1975), Patel (1981), Seitz (1985), and Batcher (1977).

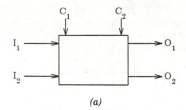

(a)

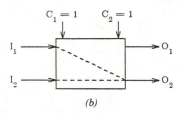

(b)

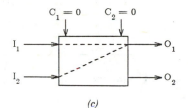

(c)

FIGURE 8.19   Blocking 2×2 switch.

processors and n memory modules, the crossbar requires m × n switching elements or *crosspoints;* thus, when m ~ n, the number of crosspoints is $O(n^2)$.[11] Thus, in the case of very large multiprocessors the cost of the switch can become a dominating factor.

Example 8.9

Certainly the most well-known example of the use of the crossbar is the C.mmp system (Wulf and Bell, 1972, Satyanarayanan, 1980). The maximum configuration consists of 16 shared memory modules providing a total of 32 Mbytes of global memory, connected to 16 processor modules (Fig. 8.20).[12] The processors are all slightly modified versions of the PDP-11 (5 PDP-11 Model 20s and 11 PDP-11 Model 40s) and all have identical access to any part of shared memory.

Taking into account the switch delay time, and assuming no contention at the destination memory module, the time to access memory is 1 μsec. Although private cache memories on a per processor basis had been envisioned to reduce latency, they were never implemented. In the absence of caches, it was found experimentally that approximately three processors could simultaneously refer-

[11]The notation $O(f(n))$, where $f(n)$ denotes a function of n, means "order of $f(n)$)."

[12]According to Jones and Schwarz (1980), the actual configuration, about 1980, consisted of 11 processors and 2.5 Mbytes of shared memory.

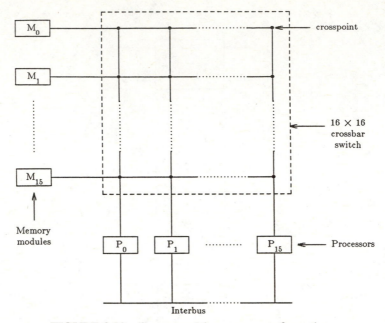

FIGURE 8.20 C.mmp multiprocessor configuration.

ence the same memory module without serious performance degradation (Jones and Schwarz, 1980).

Figure 8.21 shows the structure of the individual processor's endo-architecture. Each processor contains 8 kbytes of local store that, along with I/O devices communicate with the PDP-11 by means of the Unibus. The local bus is used by C.mmp's operating system kernel—called Hydra—for holding frequently executed system routines and locally used data structures.

Synchronization and interprocess communication in the C.mmp/Hydra system is effected by a combination of message passing, semaphores, and busy-waiting locks. The processor modules communicate with each other through the *Interbus* and interface with the crossbar switch through a mapping device, DMap, the function of which is to map each address appearing in the Unibus onto local memory, global memory, or local I/O devices. ∎

The performance of crossbar switches has been studied analytically quite extensively (Bhandarkar, 1975; Baskett and Smith, 1976; Rau, 1979), and the principal results are summarized by Lang, Valero, and Alegre (1982). These studies were based on the assumptions that

1. Processors are synchronized.
2. Memory requests have a uniform distribution.
3. Memory cycle time is constant.
4. Processing time has a binomial distribution.

Given these assumptions, and further assuming that a processor issues a new request as soon as the previous one has been serviced, the effective bandwidths of a crossbar switch for 2, 4, 8, 16 processors are as follows (Lang, Valero, and Alegre, 1982).

Number of Processors	Bandwidth
2	1.50
4	2.62
8	4.95
16	9.59

Consequently, the actual bandwidth of the crossbar switch is not nearly as good as one would hope. This, coupled with the quadratic cost of the crossbar, and its poor fault-tolerance—failure of a crosspoint would seriously disable the switch—make the crossbar relatively unattractive for large multiprocessor structures.

8.6.3 Multiport Memories

In the crossbar switch, the switching function and its control are distributed across the m.n crosspoints. It is also possible to concentrate the switching function at each of the n memory modules, resulting in a *multiport memory system.*

The general structure of such a system is shown in Figure 8.22. Each memory module has m ports, one port per processor. The switching element associated with a memory module also contains *arbitration logic:* Given the arrival at its ports of memory requests issued by two or more processors, the arbitration logic selects the processor with the highest priority.

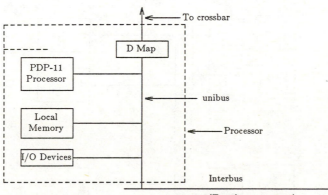

FIGURE 8.21   Structure of a C.mmp processor.

As in the case of the crossbar switch, the potential parallelism of memory access is Min(m,n). The amount of switching hardware is also of the same magnitude except that it is localized in the n memory modules. However, the number of processors in a system with multiport memories will obviously be bounded by the number of ports in the memory modules. The modularity of such multiprocessor structures is, thus, poor.[13] This is to be contrasted to the crossbar, where the modularity of the multiprocessor is a function of the crossbar array, which can be more easily expanded.

Example 8.10

One of the most recent examples of multiported memory-based multiprocessors is the CRAY-2 (Cray, 1986), which, at the endo-architectural level, exhibits the general structure shown in Figure 8.23. Four *background processors,* each having computational power that exceeds that of the CRAY-1 (see Chapter 7, Section 7.4), and a *foreground* processor share a global memory of 256 Mwords, 64 bit/word capacity. The foreground processor provides overall system supervision and, in particular, is responsible for information flow between memory and I/O controllers.

Process-memory interconnection and communication is provided through the four memory ports. Memory itself consists of four quadrants with 32 banks/quadrant. Each quadrant has a data path to each of the four memory ports. Thus, each memory port is associated with all four quadrants and contains four quadrant *buffers,* each of which can hold two memory references for the relevant quadrant. A memory *backup* is said to occur when a quadrant buffer is full and another reference to that quadrant occurs. Appropriate action is taken in such circumstances, namely, temporary termination of instruction issue and suspen-

---

[13]By *modularity* of a structure, I mean the property that the size of the structure can be incrementally increased without substantial redesign of the structure.

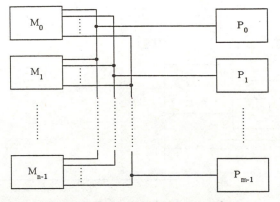

FIGURE 8.22   Multiport memories.

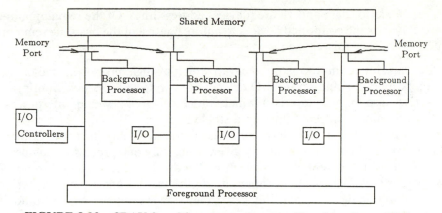

FIGURE 8.23   CRAY-2 multiprocessor structure (based on Cray, 1986).

sion of vector transfers for the particular background processor requesting memory access.   ∎

8.6.4   Single-Bus Communication

The interconnection structure that is most directly inherited from the uniprocessor domain is the time-shared *bus*. This is also one of the least costly and most modular means for effecting processor-to-processor and processor-to-memory communication, both for uni- and multiprocessors.

Generally speaking, a bus is a communication path between two devices. More specifically, a bus is a single shared collection of wires (along with its associated control logic) used for transmitting all necessary signals between a collection of processors, memories, and I/O devices.

Example 8.11

One of the most well-known and widely used buses is the PDP-11 *Unibus,* developed by Digital Equipment Corporation (Digital, 1978) as the basis for PDP-11 systems (Figure 8.24). The Unibus consists of a set of 56 signal lines of

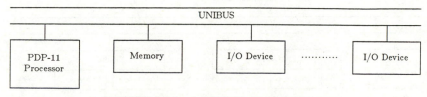

FIGURE 8.24   A PDP-11/Unibus system.

which 16 are for data and 18 are (device) address lines. Of the remaining lines, 14 are used by the connected devices to aquire control of the bus. The remaining lines serve other miscellaneous roles.[14]   ■

Generalizing a uniprocessor system in which a single processor, one or more memory modules, and several I/O devices are connected to a bus, multiprocessors may also be developed in which processor-memory and interprocessor communication is effected through a single bus.

From the perspective of our present discussion, probably the most significant characteristic of a bus is that at any given time, only one processor may use the bus—that is, the potential parallelism or bandwidth is 1. A second important characteristic is that in such configurations the bus becomes the single critical interconnection device. Thus, if it were to fail, the system as a whole would fail. On the other hand, buses exhibit good modularity characteristics, although with excessive overloading of the bus (with additional processors) there may be serious performance degradation of the system.

Example 8.12

A recently developed bus-based multiprocessor is Encore Computer Corporation's Multimax system (Encore, 1986; Bell, 1985). Multimax is a microprocessor-based multiprocessor system [an instance of a class that Bell (1985) terms "multis"] in which up to 20 central processors can address 32 Mbytes of memory using a very high speed bus called the Nanobus. The Nanobus can transmit 100 Mbytes/sec.

Figure 8.25 shows a typical Multimax configuration. Each of the processors is a National Semiconductor 32-bit NS32032. Pairs of processors are physically packaged together and share a cache memory. The presence of the caches reduces considerably the potential performance fall due to bus contention. According to Bell (1985), some 95% of a processor's memory request are serviced by the processor's (shared) cache.   ■

---

[14]Unibus is a registered trademark of Digital Equipment Corporation. For a formal description of the Unibus in a hardware description language, refer to Parker and Wallace (1981).

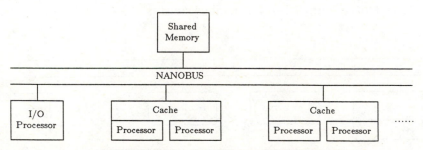

FIGURE 8.25   A Multimax configuration.

8.6.5 Multiple-Bus Communication

As noted previously, the very low bandwidth of a bus interconnection scheme and the obvious possibility of overloading place serious limits on the size of a single bus-based multiprocessor. One way of overcoming this problem is to increase the number of buses.

The general structure of such a *multiple-bus* organization is shown in Figure 8.26. The m processors (possibly with private caches) and n memory modules are each connected to all b buses so that each processor can reference any memory module through any of the buses. In this situation, the number of connections is proportional to $b(n + m)$ or, for $n \sim m$, is $O(bn)$. It can also be observed that this organization has better fault tolerance since the failure of a bus will not disable the functional capacity of the interconnection structure (Das and Bhuyan, 1985). However, the arbitration logic required to assign buses to servicing memory requests can be quite elaborate, as discussed by Mudge, Hayes, and Winsor (1987).

The performance of a b-bus, m-processor, n-memory system was first studied using simulation by Lang, Valero, and Alegre (1982). The question of interest is, how the bandwidth of the interconnection scheme behaves as a function of b and n (assuming $n = m$).

For the purpose of their simulation model, Lang and associates made the following assumptions.

1. Processor requests on the bus are synchronized.
2. Processor requests are independent and are uniformly distributed random variables.
3. The memory cycle times are identical and constant for all memory modules.
4. Processors issue request immediately after the previous request has been served.
5. Propagation delays and arbitration times are included in the memory cycle times.

Simulations for 4, 8, 12, 16 processors and up to 16 buses were carried out and the main results obtained were

1. The bandwidth of the system changed very little after b reached $n/2$.

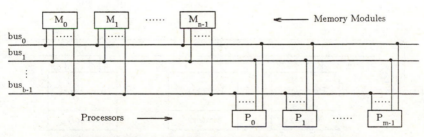

FIGURE 8.26 A multiple-bus multiprocessor structure.

2. A multiple-bus organization consisting of $b \sim n/2 + 1$ buses yields a band-width that is more than 90% of the bandwidth obtained for the crossbar switch.

These results were also derived analytically in a later study by Mudge and coworkers (1984).

The bandwidth profile just stated, coupled with its attractive fault-tolerant characteristic, seems to suggest that multiple buses might serve as a better alternative to the crossbar switch. However, general multiple-bus schemes where all processors and memory modules are simultaneously connected to several buses have yet to appear, either in the laboratory or in the market. I next give two examples of multiple buses that differ somewhat from the structure just discussed.

Example 8.13

The Tandem-16 NonStop system[15] (Katzman, 1977) consists of up to 16 proces-sors where each processor (containing its own dedicated memory of up to 512 Kbytes capacity) is connected to a two-bus system called the Dynabus (Fig. 8.27). The two buses are named, respectively, X- and Y-buses. These buses are, however, mutually independent, being controlled by two independent bus controllers. ∎

Example 8.14

Undoubtedly, one of the most interesting variations on the multiple-bus theme can be seen in the Cm* system, which, like the C.mmp, was developed (though later) at Carnegie-Mellon University (Fuller *et al.,* 1978; Swan *et al.,* 1977a, 1977b; Satyanarayanan, 1980). More accurately stated, though, the Cm* design defines a new class of interconnection structures, being composed of a *hierarchical organization of buses and switches.*

The Cm* hierarchy consists of components at three levels: the computer module, the cluster, and the system.

The basic computational unit is the *computer module* (Cm) consisting of an LSI-11 processor, up to 128 Kbytes of memory and I/O devices, all attached to

[15]NonStop is a trademark of Tandem Computers.

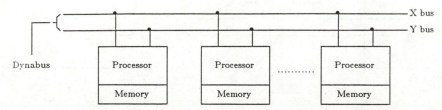

FIGURE 8.27   The Tandem-16 interprocessor bus structure.

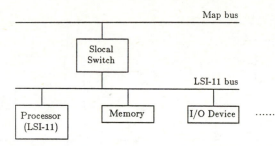

FIGURE 8.28 A computer module (Cm) in Cm*.

an LSI-11 bus (Fig. 8.28).[16] Also attached to the LSI-11 is a *local switch* named *Slocal,* which provides the basis for a Cm to communicate with other Cm's belonging to the same cluster. Slocal is, thus, a switch for *intracluster* interaction.

At the next level of the hierarchy is the *cluster* (Fig. 8.29) that is a set of up to 14 Cm's attached to a bus called the *Map bus.* Also attached to the Map bus is a microprogrammed processor, the *KMap,* which serves as a powerful switching device allowing Cm's in one cluster to communicate with Cm's belonging to a different cluster. KMap is, then, a switch for *intercluster* interaction.

At the highest level of the hierarchy is the complete Cm* *system.* This consists of clusters connected to one another through *intercluster buses* (Fig. 8.30). System fault tolerance is partly provided by each cluster being connected to two intercluster buses so that a single bus failure does not disable the cluster.

One can see that Cm* systems of different sizes can be built by varying the size of a cluster (up to a limit of 14 Cm's) and the number of clusters. The implementation at Carnegie-Mellon University (circa 1979) was a 5-cluster, 50 Cm

[16]The LSI-11, developed by Digital Equipment Corporation, is a complete PDP-11 (including 4K words of 16-bit memory) on a single board. It is, thus, a microcomputer that is fully compatible with the PDP-11 family of minicomputers (Sebern, 1978), and it is implemented using a combination of LSI NMOS technology and MSI/SSI TTL circuits. The LSI-11 bus is similar to the PDP-11 Unibus except that it is "narrower" (in terms of lines). For instance, instead of the 16 data and 18 address lines present in the Unibus, there are 16 data lines in the LSI-11 bus that are time-multiplexed (shared) between data and addresses.

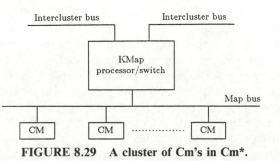

FIGURE 8.29 A cluster of Cm's in Cm*.

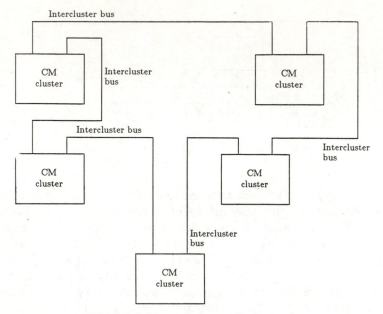

FIGURE 8.30   A 5-cluster Cm* system.

system (Jones and Schwarz, 1980; Satyanarayanan, 1980). One may also note that although physically each Cm has its own memory, the memory address space is accessible to all Cm's. The Cm* is thus, a shared memory multiprocessor.

From the perspective of our current discussion of interconnection structures, several aspects of the Cm* architecture are of interest.

1. Consider, first, the connectivity cost. As pointed out by Satyanarayanan (1980), Cm* is economical in its interconnection scheme (even after providing for the possibility of an intercluster bus failure). Adding a Cm to a cluster requires one connection—that of the Cm to the Map bus. Even when the addition of a Cm requires the creation of a new cluster, this entails three connections: two for the intercluster buses and one for attaching the Cm to the new cluster. Basically, then, the number of interconnections in a system with n Cm's is O(n).

2. Consider, next, how a 16-bit (virtual address) memory reference is serviced in Cm*. Such a reference originates in a particular Cm. First, Slocal determines whether or not the reference is local to the Cm. It does so using an address translation mechanism similar to that used in virtual memory systems (see Volume 1, Chapter 8). If the reference is local, Slocal generates an 18-bit physical address for that Cm's memory, otherwise a "trap" is generated indicating a nonlocal reference.

    In the latter case, Slocal transmits the originating Cm identifier and the virtual address to KMap, which determines whether or not the reference is located in another Cm within the same cluster. If so, KMap produces a message consisting of the real 18-bit address and an identifier of the destination Cm, which is then passed to the Slocal of the destination Cm.

If KMap had found that the reference lies outside the cluster, it constructs a message consisting (among other things) of its own identifier, a virtual address, and the identifier of the destination Cm. The KMap then acquires control of one of its two intercluster buses and sends the message to the KMap of the destination cluster (either directly or through intermediate KMaps and intercluster buses). The destination KMap then translates the virtual address to a physical address and transmits the reference to the relevant Slocal in its own cluster.[17]

Clearly, the time to reference memory will depend on whether the reference is to the local Cm, to a Cm within the same cluster, or to a Cm in some other cluster. The approximate times for these references are 3, 9, and 26 μsec, respectively (Jones and Schwarz, 1980). Thus, the performance of the system will depend critically on the mapping of applications onto the hierarchical structure of Cm* so as to maximize intra-Cm memory reference and minimize intercluster references.

3. Finally, from the foregoing description it will be evident that the Cm* interconnection structure is *packet switched*. ■

8.6.6 The Omega Network

Among the many multistage INs that have been designed, one that has been shown to be economical in terms of the number of switches is the *omega network* developed by Lawrie (1975).

For $n = 2^k$, where k is an integer, an $n \times n$ omega network consists of $k = \log_2 n$ identical stages such that each stage (1) is a perfect shuffle interconnection (see Fig. 8.17 and Example 8.7) and (2) is followed by a stage of n/2 switching elements. Such a network thus requires $O(n \log_2 n)$ switches.

Example 8.15

Figure 8.31 shows an 8×8 omega network consists of three stages, each containing four 2×2 switches. The path connecting input device 4 to output device 7 is traced through the network. ■

Each of the 2×2 switching elements can be set to one of four switching states: *direct connection* of the upper and lower inputs to the upper and lower outputs, respectively (Fig. 8.32a); *cross connection* of the upper and lower inputs to the lower and upper outputs, respectively (Fig. 8.32b); *upper broadcast* of the upper input to both upper and lower outputs (Fig. 8.32c); and *lower broadcast* of the lower input to both upper and lower outputs (Fig. 8.32d).

Data can be transmitted through the network from a particular input to a particular output by setting the switches to specific states. In general, consider

---

[17]This description of memory referencing is necessarily sketchy. For more detailed discussions, refer to Swan *et al.* (1977a, 1977b) or Satyanarayanan (1980).

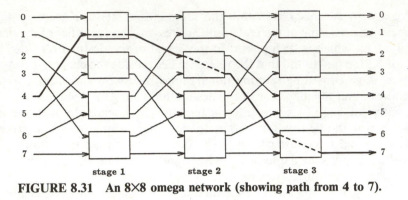

FIGURE 8.31 An 8×8 omega network (showing path from 4 to 7).

sending data from input device number I to output device number O, and let the binary representation of I and O be

$$I = i_1 i_2 \ldots i_k$$
$$O = o_1 o_2 \ldots o_k$$

Initially, device I is connected to a switch in stage 1 of the network. Then, the following algorithm allows the relevant switches in stage 1, stage 2, . . . , stage k to be set successively so that transmission can be effected from I to O.

For j = 1 .. k **do**
    If o_j = o **then** set the switch in stage j connected to I to upper output
            else set the switch in stage j connected to I to lower output
endfor

The boldface path from I = 4 to O = 7 in Figure 8.31 shows the setting of the switches required to perform the mapping.

In the omega network, there is, in fact, exactly one path between any input and any output. Thus, for a given mapping from one set of inputs to one set of outputs, the algorithm will always produce a unique set of paths to achieve the mapping. It may turn out, however, that a particular pair of such unique paths

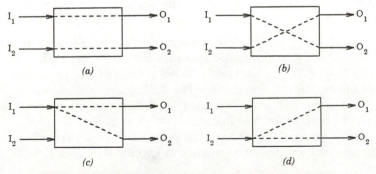

FIGURE 8.32 Permissible states of the 2×2 switches.

may *conflict* with one another because they require two different states of the same switch or require use of the same wire-connecting two stages. You may verify, for example, that a mapping of inputs (0,4) to outputs (4,7) will produce such a conflict.

More formally stated, the omega network cannot produce all possible mappings from input to output. Lawrie (1975) presents and proves several theorems that establish certain classes of mappings that can be realized by the omega network.

The design and properties of multistage networks have been studied extensively. As we saw earlier, the most attractive feature of the omega network is that it requires $O(n \log n)$ switches compared to $O(n^2)$ switches for the crossbar or multiport memories. However, perhaps because the design and implementation of multistage INs is complex, their use in multiprocessor systems remain rather sparse. Very recently a number of experimental systems have been designed and are under development that do propose to use multistage networks. These include the Cedar system (Kuck *et al.*, 1986), the Ultracomputer (Gottlieb *et al.*, 1983), and the IBM RP3 (Pfister *et al.*, 1985).

Example 8.16

The Ultracomputer is being designed as a shared-memory multiprocessor consisting of several thousands of processors connected through a packet switching IN to a global memory consisting of an identical number of memory modules.[18] The IN will be an enhanced omega network. One of the important enhancements is that there will be buffers associated with each switch in order to facilitate concurrent processing of requests for the same port.[19] ∎

8.7 BIBLIOGRAPHIC REMARKS

Probably the most encyclopaedic discussion of almost all aspects of parallel processing, including multiprocessing, in the current literature is Hwang and Briggs (1984). On a more modest scale, Satyanarayanan (1980) is also a useful survey of some of the earlier multiprocessors.

For lack of space, a number of specific machine designs and multiprocessing issues were omitted. For example, most of the discussion of multiprocessor architectures were concerned with shared memory based systems. For a description of message-passing systems, in particular, the Cosmic Cube, refer to Seitz (1985). A system that in recent times is exciting a great deal of attention is the

---

[18]The actual number of processors planned is not explicitly stated in either Gottlieb *et al.* (1983) or Gottlieb (1986). However, in giving estimates of chip count, Gottlieb *et al.* (1983) assumes a 4096 processor machine. The overall structure of the Ultracomputer is identical to the structure shown in Figure 8.3.

[19]The reason for buffered switches in the application and implementation of the FETCH-AND-ADD primitive is discussed in some detail in Section 8.4.2.

Connection Machine, a 64-K processing element system also based on message-passing principles (Hillis, 1985). Finally, Kowalik (1985) is a detailed exposition of the Denelcor HEP computer.

The topic of scheduling in a sense predates current developments in multiprocessors: Work in this area began with the advent of multiprogrammed uniprocessors. Scheduling principles are discussed in Brinch Hansen (1973) while much of the formal theories of scheduling, both deterministic and probabilistic, is elaborated by Coffman and Denning (1973). Deterministic scheduling strategies are also discussed by Gonzalez (1977). Hwang and Briggs (1984) contains a recent summary of the issues.

The most important programming issue in multiprocessing is probably the synchronization problem as discussed in Section 8.4. However concurrent programming languages were, and continue to be, a fertile area of research and discussion. See Andrews and Schneider (1983) and Hoare (1985, Chapter 7) for fine discussions of the evolution of concurrent programming concepts. Perhaps the languages Ada (U.S. Department of Defense, 1981) and Occam (INMOS, 1984) are most representative of current ideas on concurrent programming languages based, respectively, on the shared variable and message-passing paradigms.

PROBLEMS

8.1 A fundamental idea in multiprocessing is the notion of the *process* as the meaningful unit of computation rather than the instruction. A multiprocessor is, thus, a *process processor* rather than an *instruction processor.*
  (a) Construct a model of a multiprocessing computer system on the basis of this viewpoint. That is, formulate an abstract characterization of a multiprocessor viewing it as a "process processing" system.
  (b) Describe how the following issues and problems can be formulated within the framework of, or can be mapped onto, this model.

  (i) Granularity of parallelism
  (ii) Synchronization
  (iii) Memory latency
  (iv) Interprocess communication
  (v) Processor scheduling

8.2 Consider the problem of designing a general purpose multiprocessor system "from scratch." Identify the functional and performance requirements (or characteristics) that each *constituent processor* of the system would be expected to satisfy.

8.3 Consider the problem of designing a high-performance, "scientifically oriented" multiprocessor system. Describe a scheme (at the endo-architectural level) or, preferably, two or more alternative schemes, for integrating the need to support vector computation with the need to support general purpose multiprocessing.

8.4 **(a)** What are the basic disadvantages of the TEST-AND-SET instruction?

(b) How are these problems circumvented through the use of P and V operations?

(c) P and V operations can themselves be implemented using the TEST-AND-SET instruction. In that case, won't the disadvantages cited in response to (a) apply here? If not, why not?

8.5 The generalization of the FETCH-AND-ADD is the FETCH-AND-OP (v,e) operation, where v is a variable and e is an expression that is type-compatible with v. This operation returns the value of v and, at the same time, replaces it with the value OP (v,e).

What motivated the invention of this operation, and what are its advantages (if any) over other, older synchronization primitives?

8.6 Consider the general producer-consumer problem consisting of two concurrent, cooperating processes P and C. P produces a stream of results and deposits them sequentially in an (initially empty) circular buffer B of b > 1 elements whereas C consumes the elements in exactly the same order that they were deposited. Clearly, P must always write a result to an empty (or emptied) buffer element whereas C must never read a filled buffer element twice in succession.

(a) Write a solution to this problems (or more specifically, to the problem of synchronizing the actions of P and C with respect to the buffer, B), using the TEST-AND-SET instruction.

(b) Write a solution to this (synchronization) problem using semaphores.

(c) Can the FETCH-AND-OP primitive be used to solve this problem? If so, then present a solution using this primitive. Otherwise, explain why not.

(d) Construct a solution using message-passing synchronization primitives (e.g., using Occam).

(e) Compare the advantages and disadvantages of these various solutions.

8.7 [A design project.] You have been commissioned to write a fast simulator for simulating arbitrary *uniprocessor instruction pipelines*. Thus, the simulator is specialized toward a particular architectural style. Yet it is general purpose in that it should be possible to simulate different instruction pipelines.

The simulator will be executed on a shared-memory multiprocessor (call this Mp.Xbar) consisting of 16 processors communicating with 16 memory modules through a 16×16 crossbar switch. (There are no caches associated with Mp.Xbar.)

Based on this information concerning the underlying multiprocessor, develop a *preliminary design* of the pipeline simulator. The output of this design activity will be the following:

(a) A functional specification of each component (process) of the simulator (where a process is to be executed on a single processor).

(b) A description of the nature of the interprocess synchronizations and communications that will be necessary for coordination of the simulator processes.

(c) A detailed discussion of the trade-offs that were considered and analyzed in the course of developing this design.

[*Note:* An appropriate high level design notation should be used for the specification of parts (a) and (b).]

8.8 [Continuation of Problem 8.7.] You are now informed that the pipeline simulator will be executed on a successor model to Mp.Xbar (call this Mp.Xbar.Cache) in which each processor will have a dedicated cache. Analyze and discuss the consequences of this fact and, if necessary, modify the previous design so as to make the simulator appropriate for execution on Mp.Xbar.Cache.

8.9 [Related to Problems 8.7 and 8.8.] Suppose you have a computing environment of the type shown in Figure 8.26. Specifically, it consists of a set of 16 processors, each with its own cache, and a set of 16 memory modules communicating through a set of four high-speed buses. Call this system Mp.Mbus.Cache.

Develop a preliminary design of the pipeline simulator (as described in Problem 8.7) under the assumption that the simulator will be executed on Mp.Mbus.Cache. The components of your design will be as described in (a), (b), and (c) of Problem 8.7.

8.10 Based on your responses to Problems 8.7 through 8.9, write a report assessing the extent to which the underlying multiprocessor structure may influence multiple process program design.

8.11 [This and the following problems further explore the implications of the underlying multiprocessor structure on high-level-language multiprocess programming.] Using an appropriate high-level language (such as Ada or Modula-2), consider the development of a parallel program for *sorting* large integer arrays (consisting of up to 1024 elements) on shared memory multiprocessors.

(a) Construct your program assuming that its compiled form will be executed on the Mp.Xbar.Cache system described in Problem 8.8.

(b) Construct your program assuming that its compiled form will be executed on the Mp.Mbus.Cache system described in Problems 8.9.

(c) Discuss the extent to which the two program designs were influenced by the underlying multiprocessor structure.

(d) Which of the two programs do you consider to be the more efficient? Justify your answer.

8.12 Using an appropriate high-level programming notation, consider the development of a parallel program for *matrix multiplication,* where the matrices may consist of up to 512 rows and 512 columns.

(a) Construct your program assuming that after compilation, it will be executed on the Mp.Xbar.Cache system (described in Problem 8.8).

(b) Construct your program assuming that its compiled form will be executed on the Mp.Mbus.Cache system (described in Problem 8.9).

(c) Analyze and discuss the extent to which the program designs were influenced by the particular computing environment in which it would be executed.

(d) Estimate the efficiencies of the two programs.

CHAPTER 9

THE DATA FLOW STYLE

9.1 FINE-GRAIN PARALLELISM REVISITED

In Chapter 8 (Section 8.3) I discussed the "grains of parallelism" issue in the context of multiprocessors. Let us reconsider this issue. Figure 9.1 shows a hypothetical data dependency graph (DDG) for some program fragment where each vertex of the DDG denotes an instruction and the edges denote data dependencies between instructions.[1] Such a DDG renders explicit all the "natural" interinstruction parallelism.

I also pointed out in Chapter 8 (section 8.3) that supporting such fine-grain parallelism in a multiprocessor of the kind discussed there would be inefficient: first because of the scheduling overhead of assigning individual statements to distinct processors; and second because of the synchronization cost that would be incurred for preserving the ordering of, and dependency between, instructions in the DDG. Yet, clearly, it is highly *desirable* to exploit all the parallelism one can, especially in the case of very high performance systems.

Scheduling and synchronization costs of such fine-grain parallelism in von Newmann style multiprocessors (i.e., multiprocessors that are generalizations of von Neumann style uniprocessors) comes about because of the nature of the von Neumann computation model and, in particular, because (1) in order to execute an instruction it must be fetched from memory and allocated to a processor; and (2) execution of the instruction necessitates not only evaluation of an expression but also the concomitant "side effect" of updating a variable. Thus a new instruction I_k in memory can only begin execution after the completion of some prior instruction I_j (on which I_k is data dependent). In a parallel processing environment, then I_k must *wait* till it receives a *signal* that I_j has completed execution and some variable has been updated.

Referring to Figure 9.1 assume, however, that instead of assigning values of expressions to variables the result of an expression evaluation is passed directly to the operations that use this value. Instead of the DDG of Figure 9.1 we now have the graph of Figure 9.2 in which values produced at a vertex are transmitted

---

[1] See Chapter 7, Section 7.5.2, and Chapter 8, Section 8.3, for other references to DDGs.

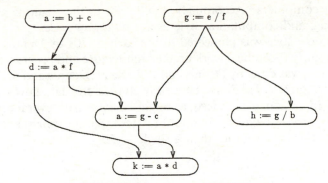

FIGURE 9.1   An acyclic DDG.

along the relevant edges to the vertices that require these values as inputs. Data may be viewed as "flowing" from one vertex to another and, for this reason, such graphs are termed *data flow graphs* (DFGs).

Let us now imagine a multiprocessing computer system in which instructions and data do not have to be fetched from memory into a processor for execution. Instead, an instruction is executed whenever all its input operands are available just as shown in the DFG of Figure 9.2. In other words, the execution of an instruction is *data driven;* synchronization between instructions is achieved implicitly by the flow of data between instructions rather than by an explicit synchronization mechanism; and, furthermore, there is no need to assign the result of an expression evaluation to a variable in memory. Such an ideal computer system would support fine-grain parallelism without the attendant overhead of synchronization or the redundancy of side effects.

One class of computers that was conceived to support these ideals is the class

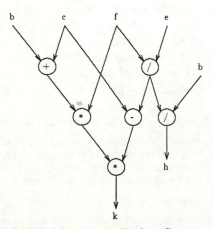

FIGURE 9.2   An acyclic data flow graph.

of *data flow* computers.[2] Accordingly, I will refer to the resulting architectural, programming, and computation style as the *data flow style.*

The data flow style was pioneered in the early 1970s by Dennis (1974), and much of the early theoretical work on the architecture and programming of data flow computers was done by Dennis and coworkers (Dennis and Misunas, 1974, 1975; Rumbaugh (1977).[3] Since these early studies, the data flow style has been investigated in great depth. Indeed, as might be expected, several divergences of the original concepts have occurred to the extent that one might even talk of the *class of data flow styles* rather than a single style.

9.2 DATA FLOW GRAPHS

Because it constitutes, in some sense, a distinct departure from the von Neumann style, the data flow style has produced new concepts and a new vocabulary. In this section I present the fundamental concepts, terms, and definitions, related to data flow graphs.

9.2.1 Notation, Terms, and Semantics

A *data flow graph* (DFG) is a directed graph in which the vertices (or nodes) denote entities called *actors* and *links* and the edges (or arcs) represent *paths* that carry either data values or control values (Boolean signals) between nodes. The presence or absence of a value on an arc is indicated by the presence or absence of *tokens.*

In the *static* model of data flow computation, an actor can execute or *fire* when there is a token on each of its input arcs and its output arcs are all empty. Thus, at any time there can be at most one token on any arc. In the *dynamic* model of data flow, an actor can fire when there is a token on each of its input arcs. The absence of tokens on the output arcs is not a necessary condition. Thus, at any time, there can be several tokens on an arc. In both models the result of an actor's firing is that the actor "consumes" its input tokens and produces a new token on each of its output arcs.[4] The type and value of the output token is determined by the nature of the operations performed by the actor (as will be explained). Because of the nature of this firing semantics, values need not be written into variables—hence, the absence of side effects.[5]

---

[2]Also termed *data-driven* computers by Treleavan, Brownbridge, and Hopkins (1982).

[3]The formal basis for, and the ancestor of, the data flow model of computation is the *theory of Petri nets* developed originally by Petri (1962) and the work by Adams (1968) and Rodriguez (1969). Another important theoretical antecedent was the work by Karp and Miller (1966). For a discussion and comparison of data flow and Petri nets, see Filman and Friedman (1984).

[4]The implications of static and dynamic models are discussed later.

[5]This ideal situation is somewhat rudely disturbed when data structures participate in computations. This is discussed later.

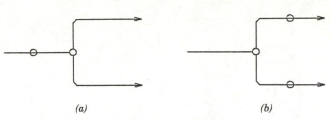

(a)   *(b)*

FIGURE 9.3   A link.

A *link* is a node in a DFG with one input arc and two or more output arcs. The function of a link is simply to copy a token on its input arc to all its output arcs. Graphically, a link is depicted as shown in Figure 9.3.

A data flow program, then, constitutes a machine language program for a data flow computer. The features of such a graphical language and the nature of data flow programs can be illustrated by examining the language proposed originally by Dennis (1974).

Figure 9.4 shows the primitive actors out of which a DFG can be constructed. An *operator* (Fig. 9.4*a*) performs some basic arithmetic or logical function f and fires by consuming its input tokens $i_1, \ldots, i_n$ and producing an output token $f(i_1, \ldots, i_n)$. In the case f is a Boolean function, it accepts as input (Boolean) control tokens and produces a control token as output.

A *decider* (Fig. 9.4*b*) represents some n-ary predicate p: It fires by consuming its inputs $i_1, \ldots, i_n$ as arguments and producing a Boolean token as determined by the predicate $p(i_1, \ldots, i_n)$.

A *constant* actor (Fig. 9.4*c*) produces a constant value as its output. It fires whenever its output arc is empty.[6]

A *gate* actor accepts two input tokens—one data, the other control. In the case of the *T gate* (Fig. 9.4*d*), if the control token input has the value *true,* then the gate allows the input data token to pass through; otherwise, the data token is consumed without an output being processed. In the case of the *F gate* (Fig. 9.4*e*), if the control token input has the value *false,* the gate allows the data token to pass through; otherwise, the input is consumed and no output is produced.

Finally, the *merge* actor (Fig. 9.4*f*) accepts two input data tokens on its "T" and "F" sides, respectively, and a control token. If the latter value is *true,* the T input is transmitted as output, otherwise the F input is transmitted. In either case, the input token that is not selected remains unaffected. Furthermore, there need not be a token on the unselected arc.

In a modified version of this language, the separate T and F gates can be replaced by a *switch* actor, as shown in Figure 9.5 (Arvind and Gostelow, 1982). This accepts two tokens—one data, the other control—and has two output

---

[6]A constant actor is meaningful only in the static model since the production of a constant token is triggered by the consumption of the previously produced token. Constant actors are not available in the dynamic data flow model. Instead, a constant is permanently associated with the actor using that constant (see Example 9.1).

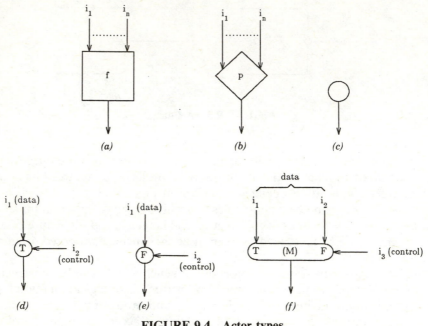

(a) (b) (c)

(d) (e) (f)

FIGURE 9.4 Actor types.

arcs—one designated T, the other F. If the control token value is *true,* the input data token is transmitted to the T arc; if the control token value is *false,* the data token is transmitted to the F side. In the examples that follow, I will illustrate the use of both switches and gates.

Example 9.1

Figure 9.6 shows the DFG corresponding to the conditional expression

    result = **if** x≤y **then** a*b **else** a*3   ∎

Example 9.2

Consider the computation of n! A "parallel" version of this computation, appropriate for a (von Neumann style) multiprocessor is as follows:

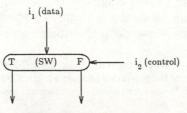

FIGURE 9.5 A switch.

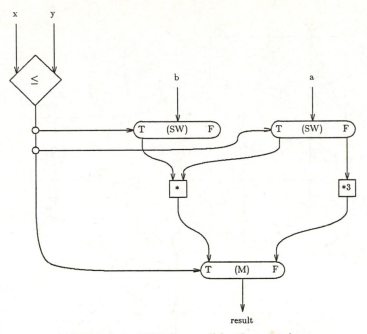

FIGURE 9.6 DFG for conditional expression.

```
function FACT(n) returns max;
    begin
        max: = n; min: = 1; k: = n − 1; l: = 2;
        while k > l do
            begin
                cobegin
                        max: = max*k
                ||    min: = min*l
                coend;
                cobegin
                        k: = k − 1
                ||    l := l + 1
                coend
            end
        max: = max*min
    end
```

FACT computes max = n! and returns max, where n is assumed even and greater than two. The notation **"cobegin S₁∥S₂ coend"** means that S_1 and S_2 are executed in parallel.

Figure 9.7 is a DFG for this function. Some of the arcs carrying control tokens are set to the initial value FALSE as shown. There are several cyclic subgraphs (or more simply, loops) in this DFG:

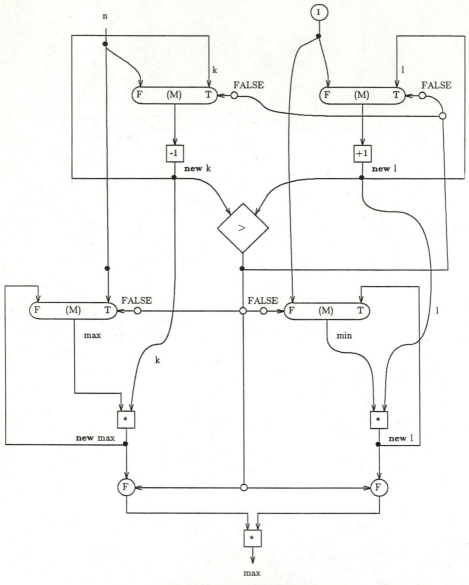

FIGURE 9.7 DFG for n!

1. The loop on the upper left controls the value of k: After initially computing k = n − 1, the loop decrements k in each iteration.
2. The loop on the lower left computes max*k in each iteration.
3. The loop on the upper right controls the value of l: After initially computing l = 2 (using a constant "1"), the loop increments l in each iteration.
4. The loop on the lower right computes min*l in each iteration.

The two multiplication loops terminate when the ">" decider returns a *false* value. The final "max*min" operation is thus invoked producing the desired result. Note that when ">" returns *false,* this will suspend the upper left loop until or unless a new token for n appears on the input line.   ■

9.2.2   Data Flow Languages

Clearly, writing programs directly in the language of DFGs (or reading such programs) can be an impossibly complex affair. Quite naturally, the need for high-level *data flow languages* (DFLs) was felt and has led to the design and implementation of several DFLs. The best known of these are Val (McGraw, 1982; Ackerman, 1982), Id (Arvind, Gostelow, and Plouffe, 1978; Arvind and Gostelow, 1982), and SISAL (McGraw *et al.*, 1983, Gurd and Bohm, 1986).

I will not enter here into a detailed discussion of DFLs but simply present the key notions underlying such languages. For a comprehensive exposition of the topic, refer to Ackerman (1982); compilation aspects of DFLs are discussed in Gurd and Bohm (1986).

The two fundamental requirements to be met by a DFL are

1.   The language must allow the programmer to specify side-effect-free computation. Thus, the notion of the assignment statement as it exists in imperative (or von Neumann style) programming languages should be absent. As we have seen, computational actions should return values that are then consumed as arguments by other computational actions.

2.   It should be easy for the DFL compiler to detect data dependencies between the operations of a data flow program and thereby facilitate the generation of DFGs.

In imperative languages the constructs used for returning values are expressions and function invocations. Ignoring syntactic issues, such value returning constructs may be represented as

OP(arg$_1$,arg$_2$, . . . ,arg$_n$)

That is, an operation (or function) OP is *applied* to a set of arguments arg$_1$, . . . ,arg$_n$ in order to produce a value. OP does not modify any of its arguments. Languages in which computation proceeds in this fashion are called *applicative* languages. A DFL, in order to be side-effect-free, must be an applicative language.

In imperative languages, the assignment statement executes by updating the left-hand variable as a side-effect. However, consider the following statement

d: = a*e

An alternative way of interpreting this statement is to view it as simply associating a new *name* with the right-hand expression. Thus, this statement is nothing but a *definition* of d, equivalent to the statement "let d = a*e."

A language that interprets assignment statements in this way is called a *definitional* language (Ackerman, 1982). The most obvious and useful property of definitional interpretation is that it allows us to view an assignment as an algebraic equation. Thus "d: = a*e" implies "d = a*e." Note that the *same name* cannot be defined more than once. There are two reasons for this. First, the equational property could be violated. Consider, for example, the statement

j: = j + 1

which would definitionally be interpreted as "j = j + 1" which, of course, is algebraically meaningless. Second, renaming reintroduces all the shortcomings of the imperative assignment statement. Consider, for example, the following sequence

a: = b + c

. . .

a: = e*f

From the viewpoint of detecting parallelism, an artificial dependency has been created between the two statements. Furthermore, program verification is rendered more difficult. If renaming was not allowed, the equation "a = b + c" resulting from the first definition would hold throughput the rest of the program and it would be known exactly where this equality was created. However, if the second definition of a is permitted, the assertion "a = e*f" would result and the original equality would not necessarily hold. This would obviously obscure program clarity and, consequently, complicate program verification.

Thus, a definitional language must necessarily satisfy the *single assignment rule* (Tesler and Enea, 1968): a name can appear only once on the left side of an assignment.

It may be noted that the single assignment rule poses a problem when a variable is to be modified iteratively within a loop (as in the FACT function of Example 9.2). Specifically, consider the need for the equivalent of an imperative statement such as

j: = j + 1

to be iteratively executed. Different data flow languages resolve this problem in different ways, but basically they all use constructs to resolve the fact that the left side j is a *new instance* of j that is distinct from the "old" j on the right side. Thus, for example, in Id (Arvind and Gostelow, 1982), this statement would be expressed as[7]

new j ← j + 1

9.2.3 Static and Dynamic Data Flow Models

In Section 9.2.1 I made a distinction between static and dynamic data flow models. In the *static* model only one token can occupy an arc at any time. The

---

[7]An example of an architecture description language that is definitional but not applicative is S*M, which is discussed in Chapter 4 (Section 4.3). It uses a similar notation to enforce the single-assignment rule.

implication of this for both data flow programming and machine architecture is illustrated in Figure 9.8. Part *(a)* shows fragment of a DFG corresponding to the computation $(x*y)-(y + z)$. Actors (1) and (2) can fire only when the input arcs of actor (3) are token-free; that is, when this actor has consumed any tokens that may have been previously placed on these arcs. It is, therefore, necessary for actor (3) to *signal* back to actors (1) and (2), *acknowledging* that tokens on its input arcs have been consumed.

The general instruction format for these actors will, then, be as indicated in Figure 9.8*(b)*. Each instruction has places for accepting its operands, a place that holds the pointers (addresses) of successor instructions, and also places to accept acknowledge signals from its successor instructions.

In an implementation of the static model, an instruction's operand places and acknowledge signal places must all be filled for the instruction to fire. A static model, then, necessitates the use of some form of synchronization between instructions.

The original data flow scheme proposed by Dennis (1974) was based on the static model, and much of the subsequent work done by Dennis and colleagues has been concerned with the development of *static data flow machines.*

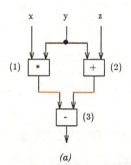

(a)

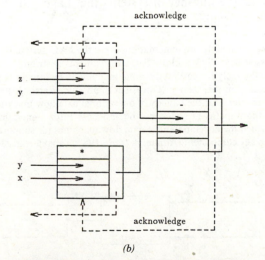

(b)

FIGURE 9.8 **The static data flow model.**

Apart from the necessity of using acknowledge signals, there are other problems associated with the static model. For one thing, it does not allow general recursion. Furthermore, it limits the actual amount of parallelism during the execution of a DFG. Consider, for example, a subgraph S of a DFG that serves as a procedure that can be invoked from several other places in the DFG. Suppose further that at two successive time points S has been invoked from different places. However, the earlier invocation cannot proceed because not all the input tokens have arrived at a particular node—the actor cannot fire. In contrast, the later invocation could proceed if so permitted because the corresponding tokens are available. In the static model the second invocation would not be permitted.

The *dynamic* data flow model, also known as the *tagged token* model, was developed in response to this problem. In this scheme, several tokens may be present simultaneously on an arc corresponding to different *instantiations* of that part of the DFG. The tokens on an arc are distinguished from one another by distinct *tags* that form part of the token.

Figure 9.9 illustrates this situation. Clearly, provisions must be made for tokens on distinct arcs to an actor to be *matched* (as belonging to the same instantiation) and only when matching tagged tokens on all the input arcs are detected will the actor consume them and fire. Thus, as we will see, a key component of *tagged-token data flow machines* is the use of a *matching* unit.

The concept of the dynamic model also originated in the seminal paper by Dennis (1974). However, the initial development of dynamic data flow schemes is largely the result of a number of independent and almost simultaneous efforts by Arvind and colleagues (Arvind, Gostelow, and Plouffe, 1978), Davis (1978), and Gurd and associates (Gurd, Watson, and Glauert, 1978).

9.3 DATA FLOW ARCHITECTURES

Although a great deal of theoretical work has been produced on the principles of data flow computers, the number of systems that have actually become operational remains rather small.[8]

[8]Among static machines, two early implementations were the LAU system developed in Toulouse, France, by Syre and associates (1977) and the Texas Instruments Distributed Data Processor (DDP) (Johnson *et al.,* 1980). Probably the earliest dynamic machine to be implemented is the Manchester prototype further discussed in this section (Gurd, Kirkham, and Watson, 1985).

One may surmise, however, that the paucity of operational data flow machines may change soon, largely as a result of the impetus provided by the Japanese Fifth Generation Computer Project (Moto-oka, 1982) in which the development of data flow machines for supporting knowledge-based systems appears to be a key component (Amamiya *et al.,* 1982; Tanaka *et al.,* 1982; Amamiya *et al.,* 1986).

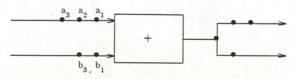

FIGURE 9.9   The dynamic data flow model.

To illustrate in some detail the design, organization, and performance of data flow computers, I will describe the Manchester Dataflow Machine (MDM), which is based on the tagged-token model. A prototype version of the MDM has been operational since October 1981, and its design and performance have been widely documented in a series of publications (Watson and Gurd, 1982; Gurd, Kirkham, and Watson, 1985; Gurd and Kirkham, 1986; Barahona and Gurd, 1986; Sargeant and Kirkham, 1986; Gurd and Bohm, 1986; Kawakami and Gurd, 1986). I will also consider some extensions to the Manchester machine.

9.3.1 The Manchester Dataflow Machine

The overall structure of the MDM prototype is shown in Figure 9.10. It consists of a *single ring* of five modules, each of which operates independently and, collectively, forms a pipeline. The switch allows MDM to be connected to a host machine that is responsible for all input/output functions.

Tokens are organized in the form of 96-bit packets; each token packet consists of a 37-bit data field, a 36-bit tag, a 22-bit destination address, and a 1-bit marker. Tokens generated by the processing unit pass through the switch and (if they are not final values to be output to the Host) arrive at the Token Queue from which they are sent to the Matching Unit. The main function of the Token Queue is to maintain an even flow of tokens along the ring.

A token arriving at the Matching Unit and intended for a single operand instruction is passed onto the Instruction Store. A token that is part of an operand pair will be matched with the tokens already in the Matching Unit and, if a match is found, is dispatched with its partner to the Instruction Store. The selected instruction along with its operands are, then, forwarded to the Processing Unit for execution.

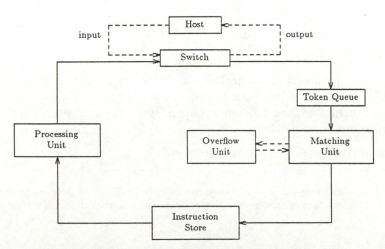

FIGURE 9.10 The MDM single-ring structure.

The Matching Unit

The main component of the Matching Unit is a pseudo-associative *match store* capable of holding 1M unmatched tokens. The store is physically organized in the form of 16 parallel memory banks each of 64K token capacity. It will be recalled that the 96-bit token consists of a 36-bit tag and a 22-bit destination address. The latter is actually composed of three fields:

> < instruction address (18 bits),
>   left/right input (1 bit),
>   matching function (3 bits) >

The *matching function* allows for eight different modes of matching to be performed, of which the two most important for our purposes are BYPASS and EXTRACT-WAIT (Watson and Gurd, 1982).[9] These are next explained.

A 96-bit token arriving at the Matching Unit is matched (according to the matching function) against the stored tokens on a key consisting of the 36-bit tag field and the 18-bit instruction address field. If the matching function is BYPASS, the token does not need a partner (i.e., the destination is a single operand instruction) and is subsequently passed onto the Instruction Store. If the matching function is EXTRACT-WAIT, the token is matched in the following manner: Using a hardware hash operation on the 54-bit key, a 16-bit hash address is generated, which is used to address in parallel, the 16 memory banks. Each memory bank is accessed and the contents checked against the 54-bit key. If a match occurs, the stored and the new tokens are formed into a 133-bit packet composed of

> < data (37 bits), data (37 bits), tag (36 bits),
>   destination (22 bits), marker (1 bit) >

and transmitted to the Instruction Store. If no match is found, the new token is written into the first available address generated by the hash function. However, if the matching store is full, the token is held in the store inside the *Overflow Unit.*

The Instruction Store

The main components of the Instruction Store are a random access memory capable of holding 64K instructions and an address translation mechanism. The 22-bit instruction address arriving as part of the token-pair packet is actually a segment/offset virtual address:

---

[9]The remaining matching-functions are variations of EXTRACT-WAIT designed to increase the efficiency of the matching operation under specific circumstances. For details, see Watson and Gurd (1982).

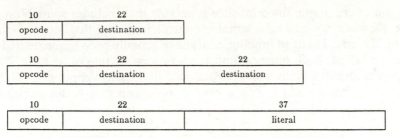

FIGURE 9.11 Instruction formats in the MDM.

and the address translation hardware generates from this virtual address a 16-bit physical address of the destination instruction.

The formats of instructions for the MDM are shown in Figure 9.11. The selected instruction and the input token-pair are combined into an *execution packet* consisting of the following fields:

> < data (37 bits), data (37 bits), opcode (10 bits),
> tag (36 bits), destination (22 bits),
> destination (optional) (22 bits), marker (1 bit) >

and is forwarded to the Processing Unit.

The Processing Unit

The internal structure of the Processing Unit (ignoring some additional buffers not shown) is as indicated in Figure 9.12. It contains, in addition to the input and output buffers, a special purpose *preprocessor* that executes a small number of special instructions and up to 20 identical *function units*. Each of the function

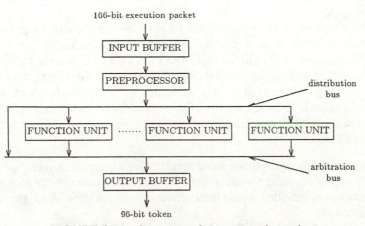

FIGURE 9.12 Structure of the processing unit.

units is a microprogrammed bit-slice processor that includes some 50 registers and a 4K word, 48-bits/word writable control store and that has a microcycle time of 229 nsec. Up to 14 function units have actually been implemented in the prototype MDM. Each function unit has a processing rate of up to 0.27 MIPS, and the ensemble has shown an aggregate maximum throughput of 2 MIPS. The output of the processing unit is a new 96-bit token that is dispatched to the Switch.

9.3.2 Performance Evaluation of the MDM

Most of the research effort in data-flow computing to date has been expended in the discovery of design principles. Far less attention has been paid to the analysis and evaluation of the designs or of their implementations. One of the most valuable aspects of the Manchester project has been the emergence of some welcome data — preliminary though they are — on the performance of such systems (Gurd and Watson, 1983).

I have already noted that the maximum throughput of the MDM is estimated to be 2 MIPS. Clearly, given a particular design and a particular implementation of that design, and given some estimated bound on the performance of that implementation, the principal performance questions of interest are of the following nature.

1. How close is the sustained throughput of the MDM to the maximum throughput?
2. How does the throughput vary with the number of function units?
3. How does the speedup vary with the number of function units?
4. How well are the function units used?

In designing experiments to respond to these questions, a software simulator of the MDM was used in conjunction with actual measurements on the hardware prototype.

The simulator was used to execute a total of 14 benchmark programs. These were written either in high-level data flow languages (specifically, two single-assignment languages called SISAL and MAD were used) that were then compiled or in an assembly language called MACRO (Gurd, Kirkham, and Watson, 1985). The programs ranged over a spectrum of problem domains, including numerical analysis, fast Fourier transforms, and circuit and logic simulations.

The simulator itself was based on some simplifying assumptions, the most important of which were

1. All instructions require the same amount of execution time.
2. The time to forward the output of an executed instruction to a successor instruction is included in the instruction execution time. And, perhaps most significantly:
3. An unlimited number of function units are available at every simulated time step.

Several measures were recorded during simulation. The most useful of these were

S_1 = The total number of instructions executed.
= The number of simulated time steps required if only one function unit was available.

Sinf = The number of simulated time steps required assuming that an unlimited number of function units are always available.

Pby = The proportion of executed instructions that bypassed the Matching Unit (i.e., the proportion of single-operand instructions).

For a given program, the ratio

$$\text{Par} = \frac{\text{S1}}{\text{Sinf}}$$

is an approximate measure of the average amount of parallelism available in the program. The parameter Pby was found to be in the range 0.56–0.70 for all the benchmarks.

As regards the prototype, the only measurement that could be made on it was the time interval between the start of a program and the arrival at the host of the first result. This is denoted by the measure

T(n) = Execution time for first output token as a function of n, the number of active function units.

Using T(n) and the measure S1 obtained from simulation, the following measures of system performance can be determined:

P(n) = T(1)/T(n)
= The *effective* number of function units when n function units are active.
= The *actual parallelism* or *speedup* obtained as a function of n.

$E(n)$ = $\dfrac{P(n)}{n} \times 100$
= Percentage utilization of n active function units.

$M(n)$ = $\left(\dfrac{S1}{T(n)}\right)$
= The *actual* rate of instruction execution (in MIPS) as a function of n.

$M'(n) = \dfrac{S1}{T(1)} n$
= The *potential* rate of instruction execution (in MIPS) as a function of n.

The specific values of these measures obviously vary from benchmark to benchmark and space does not allow me to elaborate on the quantities for the different benchmarks. Details of these are provided by Gurd and Watson (1983). We may, however, summarize the general nature of the results as follows.

Figure 9.13 shows the general shape of the performance graph for the benchmarks as a function of n. Actually, two performance measures are shown: the speedup P(n) against n; and the actual throughput M(n) against the potential throughput M′(n). The band is bounded with lines corresponding to 50% and 100% utilization (of function units). Finally, the curves within the band are for different values of Par, such that

$$Par_1 > Par_2 > Par_3 > \ldots$$

The important interpretations of these curves are

1. For low values of n, speedup is almost linear in n (and En ≈ 100%); this is followed by gradual deterioration until a program-constrained limit is reached.
2. Par, the average amount of parallelism is a consistent indicator of execution performance, regardless of all other factors. The higher the value of Par, the closer the performance curve is to the 100% utilization line.
3. Although not indicated explicitly by Figure 9.13, specific instances of this graph for the different benchmarks indicate that *a program is suitable for data flow execution if Par > 40* (Gurd and Watson, 1983).

9.3.3   Extensions to the Manchester Model

The implementations of the MDM and the experiments (just cited) on its performance have prompted further investigations of the effect of modifying its architecture on performance. Patnaik, Govindarajan, and Ramadoss (1986) have recently reported the results of simulation experiments on the performance of an extended version of the MDM that they called EXMAN. One significant extension was founded on the observation that the Matching Unit in the MDM

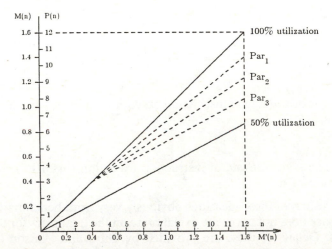

FIGURE 9.13   General nature of performance graph: (1) M(n) versus M′(n); (2) P(n) versus n (based on Gurd and Watson, 1983).

is likely to be a critical bottleneck. Thus, *multiple* Matching Units were considered as an extension to the original design.

Three benchmarks were executed on the simulator: a matrix multiplication algorithm and two graphics algorithms. For all these benchmarks, Patnaik and associates showed that

1. The speedup is very effectively improved by increasing the number of Matching Units from 1 to 2, but very little improvement ensued with further increases in the number of Matching Units. The investigators conjectured that this is due to the fact that with two Matching Units the rate of token-pair packet production is the same as the rate at which these packets were processed by the other units.
2. The reduction in the execution time due to multiple Matching Units is more effective when the number of function units is large (say 6 to 8) than when it is small (say 4). This was attributed to the fact that when the number of function units are low they become the critical factor influencing performance rather than the number of Matching Units.

Very recently, Ghoshal and Bhuyan (1987) have formulated an *analytical queueing network* model of the MDM and have studied the effect of varying the parameters of this model on performance. The Matching Unit, the Instruction Store and the Processing Unit are each viewed as a service center with a queue associated with it. Since the Processing Unit has several function units, it is modeled as a multiple server queue. The token queue being itself a FIFO buffer is combined with the Matching Unit queue. The overall structure of the network is shown in Figure 9.14.[10]

[10]The reader unfamiliar with the basic principles of Queueing Theory may wish to consult Trivedi (1982).

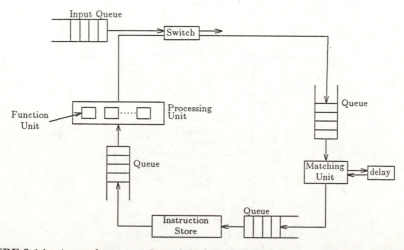

FIGURE 9.14 A queuing network model of the MDM (based on Ghoshal and Bhuyan, 1987).

Results obtained from this model also indicate that the Matching Unit becomes the limiting component. This is in essential agreement with the observation made by Patnaik, Govindarajan, and Ramadoss (1986). However, the queueing network model further indicates that increasing the number of Matching Units from 1 to 2 causes a congestion at the Instruction Store as the number of function units in the Processing Unit is increased.

Various other configurations of the MDM components were considered. Of these, the most attractive turned out to be a *dual ring* configuration, consisting of two independent paths through the switch, each involving a Matching Unit, a Processing Unit, and an Instruction Store. (This is, in fact, an instance of the multiring configuration to be discussed.) Ghoshal and Bhuyan (1987) point out that taking into account both performance and reliability, the dual-ring configuration proved to be the best of those studied.

I conclude this section by briefly mentioning the *multiring* data-flow machine currently being studied at the University of Manchester (Barahona and Gurd, 1986). Figure 9.15 shows the structure of this multiring MDM. Basically, each of the Matching Unit/Instruction Store/Processing Unit ensemble in the MDM becomes a single *processing component* in the multiring system. The number of processing components envisioned are of the order of 100. Preliminary results obtained by simulating a 64-ring system indicates that such a multiring MDM can operate with more than 90% efficiency, that is, it gives speedup greater than 64×0.9 compared to a single ring MDM. These speedup results have also been supported by a 16-ring hardware simulator (Gurd and Kirkham, 1986).

9.3.4 Handling Data Structures

At the level of data flow graphs we have seen that tokens (containing values) are transmitted from one node of the DFG to another. There are no variables or storage elements in which data are held. Since we have not placed any restrictions on the type of data that may be held in a token, it is theoretically possible to

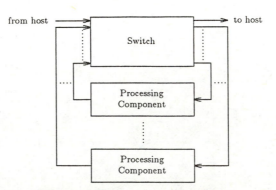

FIGURE 9.15   Multiring MDM.

include *data structures* (such as arrays) among the possible token types. Thus treated, data structures, like other, more elementary data values, would serve as input tokens to appropriate nodes of the DFG: The enabling of these node operations would produce *new* data structures on the output arcs. The original input data structure would be consumed in the usual way.

Instances of value-returning operators that can be applied to data structures have been described by Arvind and Culler (1986). These include CONS, which when applied to two lists, produces as output a token that is the ordered pair of these inputs. Conversely, the operators FIRST and REST applied to an ordered pair of values returns, respectively, the first and the second components. Similarly, for array structures the APPEND operator may be defined, which takes as arguments an array A, an index I, and a value V and produces a new array A' identical to A except that A'[I] = V.

In all these cases, to preserve the applicative property of the operators, extensive *copying* of input to output must be done.

Clearly, at the level of the data flow machine architecture, data structures cannot be passed around in this manner. They will be required, instead, to be held in a store and it would be the *pointers* to the stored structures that would be passed around as tokens.

The problems of dealing with data structures in data flow machines have been one of the sources of criticism concerning the data flow style, since it appears to detract from the formal elegance of this whole paradigm. Naturally, much attention has been paid by the proponents of data flow to the solution of this problem.

Probably the most influential proposal in this regard is the concept of *I-structures,* proposed by Arvind (Arvind and Thomas, 1981; Arvind and Ianucci, 1986). An I-structure is basically an arraylike storage structure (Fig. 9.16). Each word in the array is sufficiently large to hold a value and a *word status value* (to be explained). Each word can be written to at most once. However, a word can be read as many times as desired.

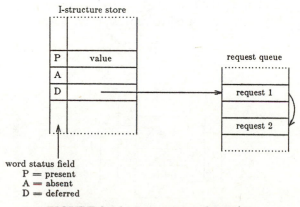

FIGURE 9.16   I-structure schematic.

The semantics of the read and write operations are

1. When a *read* is attempted on an I-structure word and the status field = P for that word, then the read can proceed in the usual manner since the status indicates the *presence* of data in the word.
2. When a *read* is requested and the status field = A, then the read must be *deferred* since the referenced word does not contain a value—data is *absent*. In that case, the status field is changed to D and the read request is held in a *request queue*. A pointer is set from the referenced word to the location in the request queue where the deferred request is stored.
3. When a *read* is requested on a word in I-structure that has status field = D, then the new request is appended, via links, to its predecessors in the request queue (see Fig. 9.16).
4. When a *write* operation is attempted on an I-structure word that has status field = A, the value is written in and the status field is changed to P, indicating that data is now present.
5. When a *write* operation is attempted on a word with status field = P, this indicates an error condition: The most recently written value must be consumed before a new value is written in.
6. Finally, when a *write* is requested on a word with status field = D, then, in addition to performing the actions stated in (4), the deferred requests on the request queue are allowed to proceed.

In the case of the Manchester machine, a number of alternative methods for storing and manipulating data structures were investigated (Sargeant and Kirkham, 1986). The scheme finally chosen for the hardware prototype involves a unit called the *structure store,* which is connected through the switch to the rest of the machine (Fig. 9.17).

The operating principles of the Structure Store is based closely on the principles of the I-structure already described. The internal organization of the Structure Store is shown in Figure 9.18. The *Data Memory* (DM) is a conventional random access memory that corresponds to Arvind's I-structure store (Fig. 9.16). The *Deferred Queue* (DQ) similarly corresponds to the request queue. A few bits in each DM word are used to represent the status field. Inputs to the

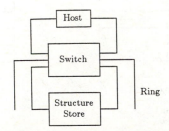

FIGURE 9.17 **The structure store in the MDM.**

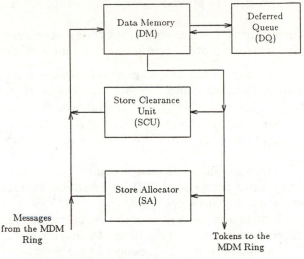

FIGURE 9.18 **Organization of the structure store.**

Structure Store arrive in the form of *messages* (carrying read, write, and other types of requests) and the outputs are tokens.

In addition to the DM and DQ, the Structure Store contains a *Store Clearance Unit* (SCU) and a *Store Allocator* (SA). As the names suggest, these are responsible, respectively, for clearing the status fields of DM words and allocating part of DM for a new data structure.

The principal types of messages that may be serviced by the Structure Store are

1. WRITE (address, data type, value): This causes the value to be written into the specified address (subject, of course, to the read/write semantic constraints described previously for I-structures).
2. READ/DEFER (address, destination, tag): This reads the value in the addressed word (subject to the read/write semantic constraints of I-structures) and returns it to the specified destination. Thus, this operation will either return a "normal" 96-bit token to the MDM ring or defer the message in the DQ.
3. POINTER REQUEST (size, destination, tag): Unlike the foregoing messages, this message is processed by the SA. The "size" argument specifies the minimum amount of storage that must be allocated. A token consisting of the pointer (which is composed, in turn, of the starting address and the size of the allocated space), the destination, and the tag is returned by the Structure Store.
4. START CLEAR (address, size): This message is intended for the SCU and directs it to clear the data structure of the specified size and at the specified address (specifically, to set the status fields of the addressed words to A).

Other types of messages are provided for garbage collection (i.e., for reclaiming storage).

At the exo-architectural level, several instructions have been provided for manipulating the Structure Store. These include, amongst others,

1. STORE: Functionally defined, this takes a *token stream* as input and returns a pointer to a data structure holding the token stream. Internally, the execution of this instruction causes several Structure Store messages to be processed, resulting in space to be allocated in DM, the token stream to be written to it (using a sequence of WRITE messages), and the pointer to be returned.
2. SELECT: This uses a pointer to a data structure, D, and an index value I as operands and returns the value of D[I]. Its execution obviously generates a READ message for the Structure Store.
3. FETCH: This instruction uses a pointer to a data structure, D, as an operand and returns the elements of D in the form of a token stream. Its execution, thus, involves a stream of READ messages to the Structure Store.

9.4 BIBLIOGRAPHIC REMARKS

For a comprehensive collection of papers on various data flow projects, refer to the special issue of *Computer* on data flow, edited by Agerwala and Arvind (1982). Of some interest in this collection is the paper by Gajski *et al.* (1982), which offers criticisms of the whole paradigm and suggests alternative approaches to the parallel–processing problem.

The paper by Gajski and colleagues may be contrasted with Arvind and Ianucci's (1983) critique of von Neumann style multiprocessing. In Arvind and Ianucci (1986), these authors elaborate and refine some of their earlier arguments.

A particularly thoughtful "state of the art" review and assessment of data flow computing, based on their experiences with MDM, is provided by Gurd and Kirkham (1986).

Data flow computing is but one of the alternatives to von Neumann style computing that has emerged in the last decade and a half. Another paradigm that has recently attracted a great deal of attention, stimulated largely by an influential paper by Backus (1978), is *reduction-based* computation. Treleavan, Brownbridge, and Hopkins (1982) discusses and compares these two paradigms and describes both data flow and reduction machine architectures.

PROBLEMS

9.1 Much has been said in the architectural literature about the so-called "semantic gap" in von Neumann machines (see Chapter 1). Practically no attention has been paid to the presence of a similar phenomenon in data flow systems—that is, the presence of a "semantic gap" between the data flow *model of computation* on the one hand and the actual data flow machine *architectures* on the other.

If you agree with this statement, analyze the nature of this semantic gap in the context of the data flow style. If you deny the existence of such a gap, present an argument in support of your view.

9.2   Recall that at the heart of the von Neumann machine style are the facts that (i) in order to execute an instruction it must be *fetched* from memory; (ii) execution of an instruction may necessitate the side effect of *updating* variables in memory; and (iii) a new instruction in memory must wait till it receives an *explicit signal* (either through the updating of a program counter or a synchronizing condition being satisfied) before it can begin execution.

Thus, there are two important *costs* inherent to the von Neumann style: the memory *latency* cost [because of (i) and (ii)]; and the cost of *synchronization* [because of (iii)]. Proponents of data flow computers claim that the data flow style eliminates or, at any rate greatly reduces, these costs.

Deeper reflections on the actual designs of current data flow machines indicate, however, that these intrinsic problems of the von Neumann style have *not* been eliminated. They appear in data flow machines in a different guise!

Using the Manchester Dataflow Machine as a working example, discuss the form or nature of the latency and synchronization costs as they appear in data flow machines.

9.3   Using Dennis's graphic data flow language (see Section 9.2), construct data flow graphs (DFGs) corresponding to the following von Neumann style programming statements.

(a)   x := (a + b) * (b − d)

(b)   **if** (a ∧ b) v (c ∧ d)
    then
        x := y * z
    else
        x := w − v

(c)   **for** i := 1 **step** 1 **until** η
      x := x + a[i]

(d)   z := 0;
    repeat
      z := z + x;
      y := y − 1
    until y = 0

9.4   Construct a data flow graph to compute the function

$$f(n) = n \text{ for } n = 1,2$$
$$= f(n − 1) + f(n − 2) \text{ for } n > 2$$

Annotate and clearly explain your program.

9.5 [Continuation of Problems 9.4]

    (a) Describe completely (but concisely) how the foregoing Fibonnaci program would be executed on a single-ring Manchester machine.

    (b) How would a multiring MDM effect the execution of this program?

9.6 Using the graphical data flow language, construct a data flow program to transform arbitrary infix arithmetic expressions (which may be wholly parenthesized or may contain parenthesized subexpressions) into parenthesis-free postfix (i.e., reverse Polish) forms. Annotate and clearly explain your program.

9.7 [Continuation of Problem 9.6]

    (a) Describe concisely, how the infix-to-postfix transformation program would be executed on a single-ring Manchester machine.

    (b) Discuss the effects of a multiring MDM on the execution of this program.

9.8 Let A be a $m \times n$ matrix and B be a $n \times p$ matrix where $2 \leq m, n, p \leq 10$.

    (a) Develop a data flow graph program for computing $C = A * B$.

    (b) Analyze this matrix multiplication program and compute or estimate "Par," the average amount of parallelism in the program.

9.9 [A design project inspired by some ideas due to Yale N. Patt.] As noted in Section 9.3.4, the formal elegance of the data flow paradigm is subdued somewhat by the intrusion of data structures, since these cannot be passed around as tokens in the way that scalars can.

Consider, however, the *micro-architecture* of uniprocessors. At this abstraction level, the fundamental data entities that are passed around are *bit sequences* (see, for example, Volume 1, Chapter 5 or Chapter 5 of this volume). Furthermore, in any given micromachine, the sizes of these bit sequences are limited to only a few values and the maximum size is bounded by the width of the data path. For instance, in a 64-bit micromachine, the maximum (and usual) size of the bit sequence "token" will be 64-bits; other tokens will mostly be restricted to 8-, 16-, or 32-bit sizes.

It follows, then, that much of the elegance of the data flow style may be actually retained if one considers the design of *data flow micro-architectures* (even though the exo-architecture is of the von Neumann style).

Assuming that it will support a fairly conventional (possibly reduced instruction set) register-style exo-architecture, develop the *preliminary design* of a *data flow micromachine.* The principal components of this design will be

    (a) A specification of the exo-architecture to be supported by your micromachine.

    (b) A specification of the functional components of the micromachine and the data path connecting these components.

    (c) An informal specification of the flow and control of information through the micromachine.

    (d) A detailed discussion of the trade-offs that were considered and analyzed in the course of this design activity.

9.10 [Continuation of design project 9.9.] In this second phase, develop the detailed design of the micromachine and, in particular, implement a microprogram that realizes the exo-architecture specified in Problem 9.9.

Based on this experience, what are your conclusions concerning the efficacy of data flow as a micro-architectural style?

9.11 [Continuation of Problem 9.10. For those familiar with architecture description languages.] The language S*M discussed in Chapter 4: (i) was designed specifically for the micro-architectural level; and (ii) is an axiomatic, nonprocedural language. Using the micromachine designed in Projects 9.9 and 9.10 as a working reference, discuss the suitability (or otherwise) of S*M as an ADL for the description of data-flow micro-architectures.

9.12 [Also for those familiar with architecture description languages.] Using the "hardware description space" of Chapter 3 as a classificatory framework, write a *requirements specification document* for an architecture description language (ADL) that would be suitable as a description tool for data flow machine design.

9.13 [Continuation of Problem 9.12.] Using your requirements specifications as a reference, discuss the strengths and limitations of VHDL as an ADL for data flow machine design.

APPENDIX

APPENDIX

THE LOGIC OF FORMAL VERIFICATION

In this Appendix I will introduce, very briefly, the logical foundations of formal verification as it may apply to the design of information processing systems. Much of this topic was constructed in the context of program development, but, in recent years, it has evolved in directions appropriate for the verification of firmware, architecture, and circuit designs. Thus, the exposition here will be very general and is intended to provide the foundations for understanding the discussion of firmware verification in Chapter 5, Section 5.5.

Given the design of an information processing system, its verification or proof of correctness requires, essentially, four pieces of information:

1. A *specification* S of the intended behavior of the system.
2. A *design* (or description) D of the system itself.
3. A precisely defined *semantics* SEM (SL) of the *specification* language SL in which S is expressed.
4. A precisely defined *semantics* SEM (DL) of the *design* language DL in which D is expressed.

A verification, then, is a logical argument or demonstration, using SEM (SL) and SEM (DL), that the system as described by D does indeed behave in the manner prescribed by S.

As will be seen herein, there are a number of approaches to design verification, the differences between them depending partly on the differences in the nature of the 4-tuple

< S, D, SEM (SL), SEM (DL) >

and partly on the methods of proofs. In particular, it has become customary to classify these approaches according to the nature of the semantic definitions of the design languages: The semantics of a language may be *operational, denotational,* or *axiomatic* (or propositional) (Donahue, 1976; Apt, 1981; de Bakker, 1980; Stoy, 1977; Gordon, 1979; Berg *et al.,* 1982). Accordingly, verification approaches are broadly classified as belonging to one of these classes.

A.1 OPERATIONAL SEMANTICS

Intuitively, the operational semantics of a language characterizes the meaning of the language in terms of how the language constructs would be executed by an abstract machine.

Wegner (1972a, 1972b) has made the distinction between compiler-oriented and interpreter-oriented operational semantics. A *compiler-oriented* language definition associates with each production rule

X : := Y

in the grammar for the language (where X is a nonterminal symbol and Y a symbol string) a *compile-time* semantic function $F_x(Y)$ that specifies the generation of target language code together with some updating of compile time state variables. At the same time, Y is replaced in the input string representing the program by the symbol X. Thus, in compiler-oriented definitions, "meaning" is specified in terms of a set of *translations* performed on the syntactic entities of the language.

Example A.1

In an obvious sense, a compiler generating code for some "standard" machine defines a compiler-oriented operational semantics for the language. Consider, for example, the ADL S*M (Chapter 4, Section 4.3). "Programs" in S*M are translated by the S*M compiler into machine code for an abstract S*M machine called SMC, which is then interpreted for execution on SMC by a simulator. Thus, a possible compile-oriented semantics for S*M could be defined in terms of the SMC code generated for each construct in S*M. ■

An *interpreter-oriented* language definition associates with each construct in the language a state transformation from the "current" state of an abstract interpretive machine to a "new" state. The *state vector* of the abstract machine includes an *instruction pointer* component that is updated during each state transformation to point to a new instruction. Thus, in an interpreter-oriented definition, the occurrence of a given syntactic entity—an assignment statement, for example—causes the execution of a sequence of state-transforming operations of the abstract interpretive machine.

If a compiler-oriented definition characterizes the meaning of a construct by specifying the *code generated for* some abstract machine, an interpreter-oriented definition characterizes meaning by specifying how the construct would be *interpretively* (i.e., directly) *executed by* some abstract machine.

Example A.2

In a microprogrammed computer, each instruction at the exo-architectural level is interpreted by a sequence of microinstructions executed on the host machine. Thus, in a sense, the microprogram running on the host machine provides an interpreter-oriented definition of the semantics of the exo-architectural level instruction-set. Of course, such a definition is only valid for this particular instruction set interpreted by this particular microprogrammable host machine. However, we can easily conceive a very general, very abstract microprogrammable host machine—a *universal host machine* (or UHM)—and define the semantics of *any* exo-architecture in an interpreter-oriented way in terms of the microcode for this UHM.

Similarly, the semantics of a programming, hardware description, or microprogramming language can be specified in terms of the microcode executed by the UHM and the associated state transformations of the UHM's storage elements (its state vector) for each construct in the language.

Probably the best known example of interpreter-oriented operational semantics is the use of the Vienna Definition Language (VDL) for specifying the semantics of PL/1 (Lucas and Walk, 1969). VDL is, perhaps now of more historical importance; however, the interested reader may consult Wegner (1972a) for an exposition on this formalism. ■

A.2 DENOTATIONAL SEMANTICS

The most obvious feature of operational semantics (at least of the interpreter-oriented model) is that the actions performed by the abstract interpretive machine in interpreting language statements result in *state sequences*. This may seem to be a case of overspecification. For example, to understand the "meaning" of the expression "a + b + c" it is enough for us to infer the value of this expression in terms of the semantics of the operator "+" and the states (values) of the variables. The order in which we choose to evaluate the expression or the intermediate values of subexpressions are not important. In general, the only states that matter are the initial and the final states; how we *arrive* at a final state is irrelevant for the meaning of a syntactic entity. State sequences or intermediate values do appear in the operational meaning of a construct because, in a sense, an operational definition of a language is specified in terms of its implementation on a *particular* machine, albeit an abstract one.

In *denotational semantics* (Stoy, 1977; Gordon, 1979; de Bakker, 1980) the underlying interpretive mechanism is abstracted away. In this approach, purely mathematical meanings (in terms of mathematical objects such as sets and functions) are assigned to syntactic entities in such a way that the meanings or *values* of relatively more complex entities may be determined in terms of the meanings or values of its components.

Example A.3

The idea of denotational semantics may be illustrated with a simple example taken from (de Bakker, 1980).

A *state* is defined as a function from the set of integer variables to the set of integers. Thus, if S is a state and a,b are integer variables, it may be that $S(a) = 3$, $S(a) = 4$. Let V be the function that maps integer expressions to their *values*. The latter will, of course, be from the set of integers but will also depend on an additional argument, the state in which V is being applied. Thus V is a function that maps integer expressions to the *set of functions from states to integers*. Using the notation "V(e)(S)" to signify "the application of the function V to expression e in state S," we may define the function V as follows.

$$V(a)(S) \quad = \quad S(a)$$
$$V(e_1 + e_2)(S) = V(e_1)(S) + V(e_2)(S)$$
$$V(e_1 * e_2)(S) = V(e_1)(S) * V(e_2)(S)$$

Thus, if S is such that $S(a) = 3$, $S(b) = 4$, we may obtain

$$V(a)(S) = S(a) = 3$$
$$V(a+b)(S) = V(a)(S) + V(b)(S) = S(a) + S(b) = 3 + 4 = 7$$

Now, let M be the function that maps *statements* to their values that are functions from states to states. Thus

$$S' = M(T)(S)$$

denotes that the effect of statement T is to transform the initial state S to the final state S'. S and S' will determine the values of the variables before and after executing T, respectively. A typical example in the definition of M is, for the assignment statement $y := e$:

$$M(y := e)(S) = S\{V(e)(S)/y\}$$

where $S\{V(e)(S)/y\}$ denotes a state S' identical to S except that its value at y is set to $V(e)(S)$, that is, to the value of e in S. Applying this definition to the statement "$y := a + b$" we obtain

$$M(y := a + b)(S) = S\{7/y\}.$$

That is, the effect of executing this statement in state S is another state that differs from S only in that the value of the variable y is 7.
Additional examples of the definition of M are

$$M(T_1; T_2)(S) = M(T_2)(M(T_1)(S))$$
$$M(\textbf{if}\,b\;\textbf{then}\;T_1\;\textbf{else}\;T_2\;\textbf{fi})(S) =$$
$$\textbf{if}\;B\,(b)(S)\;\textbf{then}\;M(T_1)(S)\;\textbf{else}\;M(T_2)(S)\;\textbf{fi}$$

That is, the meaning of the sequential composition of statements T_1 and T_2 is given by the composition of the functions $M(T_2)$ and $M(T_1)$. The semantics of the **if. .then** statement should be clear once it is understood that B is a function that maps Boolean expressions to functions from states to the Boolean values.

■

A.3 AXIOMATIC SEMANTICS

In the *axiomatic approach* (Floyd, 1967; Hoare, 1969; Dijkstra, 1976; Gries, 1981) the meanings of syntactic entities are specified in terms of *formulas* in some logical (deductive) system. The basic formulas of interest in *Hoare logic* are *correctness formulas* of the form

{P} S {Q}

where P, Q are predicates or *assertions* and S is some legal program statement. This formula is to be read as: If the state (of the set of program variables) is such that the assertion P is true before S begins execution, then the execution of S leads to a state such that the assertion Q is true when (and if) S terminates. P and Q are also called the *precondition* and *postcondition,* respectively, of the statement S.

Correctness formulas are of interest because they allow us to prove the correctness of programs. Consider, as a simple example, a program

PR1 : **begin** S_1 ; S_2 ; S_3 **end**

Suppose, further, that (1) the state of the program variables at the onset of PRI's execution is such that it always satisfies an assertion P_0; and (2) the functional requirements that PR1 is intended to meet are captured by an assertion P_3. We can thus construct a correctness formula

{P_0} **begin** S_1 ; S_2 ; S_3 **end** {P_3}

that we wish to make a *valid* formula—that is, elevate to the rank of a theorem by showing that for all possible states in which PR1 begins execution this formula will always be true.

To do this, we need to construct additional assertions P_1 and P_2, show that the formulas

{P_0} S_1 {P_1}
{P_1} S_2 {P_2}
{P_2} S_3 {P_3}

are valid, and try to infer that {P_0} **begin** S_1; S_2; S_3 **end** {P_3} is also valid. Proving the validity of correctness formulas in this fashion requires a logical (or deductive, or axiomatic) system.

Logical systems collectively termed *Hoare logics* were invented with precisely this objective in mind. A Hoare logic essentially consists of *axioms* that characterize the semantics of the atomic constituents of a programming (or microprogramming or hardware description) language, and a collection of *rules of inference* (also called *proof rules*) that characterize the semantics of the language's composite statements. Such rules of inference are usually expressed in the notation

$$\frac{F_1, F_2, \ldots , F_n}{F}$$

which states that if the "premises" $F_1, F_2, \ldots, F_n$ are valid then the "conclusion" F is also valid. Here, $F_1, F_2, \ldots, F_n$ are either correctness formulas or assertions whereas F is a correctness formula.

Example A.4

As an example of axiomatic semantics, we show first the "standard" axiom of assignment. Let P be an assertion and let P[x/E] denote P with all free occurrences of x in P replaced by E. Then the axiom of assignment is given by

$\{P[x/E]\} x := E \{P\}$

This simply states that if P is the postcondition of an assignment then its precondition will be P[x/E]. We can, thus, use this axiom to prove that the formula "$\{x \geq 0\} x := x + 1 \{x \geq 1\}$" is valid.

Note that the axiom of assignment as given here is useful in proofs of correctness when it is applied as a *backward rule:* For some postcondition P and assignment $x := E$ it gives the *weakest* (i.e., best possible) *precondition* (Dijkstra, 1976) $R = P[x/E]$ such that

$\{R\} x := E \{P\}$

is valid.

Example A.5

An alternative axiom of assignment that may be applied as a *forward rule* in proofs of correctness may be formulated as follows (de Bakker, 1980, Chapter 2): Let the notation

thereis y [p]

be read as "there exists some y such that the predicate p is true." Also, let the notation

E[x/E']

denote the expression E with all occurrences of x in E being replaced by a (type compatible) expression E'. Then we have

$\{P\} x := E \{\text{\textbf{thereis}} \ Y[P[x/Y] \wedge x = E[x/Y]]\}$

where Y is not x, and Y is not in the sets of variables appearing either in P or in E.

Intuitively, this rule states that if P is true before the assignment then (1) P[x/Y] holds after the assignment, where Y is a new variable that has the *old* value of x as its current value; and (2) for this same value of Y, x = E[x/Y].

Applying this axiom we see that given a precondition $\{x = 1\}$ and an assignment statement, the formula

$\{x = 1\} \ x := x + 1 \ \{\text{\textbf{thereis}} \ Y[Y = 1 \wedge x = Y + 1]$

is true; that is

$\{x = 1\} \, x := x + 1 \, \{x = 2\}$

is valid.

The postcondition given by this axiom is, then, the *strongest postcondition* Q such that given P and x := E

$\{P\} \, x := E \, \{Q\}$

is true. ∎

Example A.6

Proof rules for two composite statements in typical Algol-like languages are

(PR1):
$$\frac{\{P_1\}S_1\{P_2\}, \ \{P_2\}S_2\{P_3\}}{\{P_1\}S_1; \ S_2\{P_3\}}$$

(PR2):
$$\frac{\{P \wedge B\}S_1\{Q\}, \ \{P \wedge \neg B\}S_2\{Q\}}{\{P\} \ \textbf{if B then } S_1 \textbf{ else} S_2\{Q_2\}}$$

PR1 is the proof rule for sequential composition; it states that if the premises $\{P_1\}S_1\{P_2\}$ and $\{P_2\}S_2\{P_3\}$ are valid — that is, can be shown to be true — then the formula $\{P_1\}S_1; S_2\{P_3\}$ is valid. PR2 gives the rule for the **if then else** statement. According to this rule, if the assertion P holds on entry to an **if** statement, and if the formulas $\{P \wedge B\}S_1\{Q\}$ and $\{P \wedge \neg B\}S_2\{Q\}$ are valid, then the formula $\{P\}$ **if B then** S_1 **else** S_2 $\{Q\}$ will also be valid.

As a trivial example of how axiomatic semantics may be applied to verification, consider the correctness formula D1.

D1: $\{\text{PRE} : x \geq 0 \wedge y \geq 0\}$
  if $x \geq y$ **then** $z := x$ **else** $z := y$
  $\{\text{POST}: z \geq x \wedge z \geq y \wedge (z = x \lor z = y)\}$

To prove D1 we have to show that the formulas

F1: $\{\text{PRE} \wedge x \geq y\} \, z := x \, \{\text{POST}\}$
F2: $\{\text{PRE} \wedge x < y\} \, z := y \, \{\text{POST}\}$

are valid. Now, given z: = x and the postcondition POST, applying the axiom of assignment of Example A.4 backwards we obtain as the weakest precondition, $x \geq y$; that is, the following valid formula:

$\{x \geq y\} \, z := x \, \{\text{POST}\}$

Since PRE $\wedge \, x \geq y$ implies $x \geq y$, it follows that F1 is valid. Similarly, given z: = y and POST, applying the backward assignment axiom yields the weakest precondition $x \leq y$; that is,

$\{x \leq y\} \, z := y \, \{\text{POST}\}$

is valid. Since PRE $\wedge \, x < y$ implies $x \leq y$, it follows that F2 is valid. Hence, by proof rule PR1, D1 is also valid. ∎

A.4 COMPARISONS OF SEMANTIC MODELS

Some authors, notably Donahue (1976) and Ashcroft and Wadge (1982), have pointed out that these different modes of defining the semantics of a language are complementary rather than conflicting in the sense that

1. They define language semantics at different levels of abstractions and, consequently.
2. Each approach may serve distinct roles.

We observe, for example, that operational semantics are strongly suggestive of how the language may be *implemented* by prescribing sequences of state transformations that result from the interpretation of a syntactic entity. The denotational approach abstracts from state transformation sequences but retains the concept of states and defines meanings of language entities using mathematical functions. The axiomatic model also retains the concept of states; however, the meanings of language constructs are defined in terms of formulas and inference rules. Furthermore, axiomatic semantics is, by design, more conducive to the activities of design and verification than other forms of semantics.

The relationship between denotational and axiomatic semantics has been particularly well enunciated by de Bakker (1980). It is well worth considering, at least briefly, his treatment of this relationship.

1. He first defines the syntax of a *programming language* and then specifies the denotational semantics of this language.
2. A language for expressing *assertions* is introduced along with a denotational definition of its semantics.
3. The *correctness formula* is then introduced and the meaning or semantics of such formulas is defined denotationally.
4. Just what constitutes a *valid formula* is defined in denotational terms.
5. De Bakker next considers the assignment statement and proposes as *theorems* the formulas I have stated in Examples A.4 and A.5 as "axioms." Using the denotational semantics of the programming language, the assertion language and correctness formulas, he *proves* the "axioms" of assignments.
6. Proof rules for the composite statements (e.g., sequential composition, **if then** statement) are introduced and then *proved* to be sound, again based on the underlying denotational semantics.
7. At this stage, an *axiomatic proof theory* (consisting of axioms and proof rules) has been constructed in terms of the denotational semantics of the relevant languages. This proof theory can now be applied to the proofs of correctness formulas. The notion of a *proof* of a correctness formula within the axiomatic system is defined.
8. Finally, the soundness and completeness of the proof theory is itself proved. A proof system is *sound* when no invalid formula is provable within the system—that is, every provable formula is also a valid formula. A proof system is *complete* when every valid formula is provable within the system.

Because our concern here and in Chapter 5 is with correctness rather than meaning *per se,* we will not consider, or elaborate any further, denotational semantics. Almost all of our discussion of verification will rely on axiomatic semantics and the notion of an axiomatic proof theory.

A.5 PROOFS OF SEQUENTIAL SYSTEMS

Table A.1 lists the axiom of assignment and a set of proof rules for the (sequential) programming language Pascal (Hoare and Wirth, 1973). Several new proof rules will be observed.

The first rule of consequence states that if the execution of a statement S ensures the truth of the assertion R then it also ensures the truth of any assertion implied by R. The second rule of consequence states that if an assertion P implies an assertion R such that R is a precondition of a valid correctness formula involving statement S and postcondition Q, then the formula $\{P\}S\{Q\}$ is also valid. In the first iteration rule, the assertion P is called a *loop invariant* since it remains unchanged regardless of how many times the loop body S is executed.

Consider now the application of these rules to proof of correctness of a sequential program

TABLE A.1   The Basic Axiom and Proof Rules for Pascal

Assignment Axiom:	$\{P[x/E/\}x:=E\ \{P\}$

Rules of Consequence: 1. $\dfrac{\{P\}S\{R\},\ R \supset Q}{\{P\}S\{Q\}}$

2. $\dfrac{P \supset R,\ \{R\}S\{Q\}}{\{P\}S\{Q\}}$

Rule of Sequential Composition: $\dfrac{\{P_1\}S_1\{P_2\},\ \{P_2\}S_2\{P_3\},\ \ldots,\ \{P_n\}S_n\{P_{n+1}\}}{\{P_1\}\ \textbf{begin}\ S_1;S_2;\ldots;S_n\ \textbf{end}\ \{P_{n+1}\}}$

Condition Rules: 1. $\dfrac{\{P \wedge B\}S_1\{Q\},\ \{P \wedge \neg B\}S_2\{Q\}}{\{P\}\ \textbf{if B then } S_1\ \textbf{ else } S_2\{Q\}}$

2. $\dfrac{\{P \wedge B\}S\{Q\},\ P \wedge \neg B \supset Q}{\{P\}\ \textbf{if B then } S\{Q\}}$

Iteration Rules: 1. $\dfrac{\{P \wedge B\}S\{P\}}{\{P\}\ \textbf{while B do } S\ \{P \wedge \neg B\}}$

2. $\dfrac{\{P\}S\{Q\},\ Q \wedge \neg B \supset P}{\{P\}\ \textbf{repeat } S\ \textbf{until B}\ \{Q \wedge B\}}$

$\{P\}$ **begin** $S_1; S_2; \ldots ; S_n$ **end** $\{Q\}$

For example, suppose we have a program that performs multiplication of two positive integers by repeated additions. Inserting the desired pre- and postconditions, the correctness formula, the validity of which we seek to show, might be as follows:

$\{x > 0 \wedge y > 0\}$

```
begin
  z: = 0;
  u: = x;
  repeat
    z: = z + y;
    u: = u − 1
  until u = 0
end
```
(Pr1)

$\{z = x^*y\}$

To prove that Pr1 is correct, the rule of sequential composition must eventually be applied: Pr1 is the formula that will appear in the form of a consequence of that rule. Hence, we must invent assertions as postconditions for statements appearing inside the program such that from the resulting set of antecedent formulas, the application of the sequential composition rule will allow us to infer the correctness of Pr1.

The result of inserting such appropriate assertions into the program is a *proof outline* of the form shown in Figure A1. Note that, now, if we can prove that

$\{x > 0 \wedge y > 0\}$

```
z: = 0;
u: = x
```
(Pr2)

$\{(z + u^*y = x^*y) \wedge (u > 0)\}$

and

$\{(z + u^*y = x^*y) \wedge (u > 0)\}$

```
repeat
  z: = z + y
  u: = u − 1
until u = 0
```
(Pr3)

$\{(z + u^*y = x^*y) \wedge u = 0\}$

then the rule of sequential composition will give us that Pr1 is valid.

It can easily be shown by using the axiom of assignment and the rule of sequential composition that Pr2 is a valid formula. To prove Pr3, consider the relevant segment of Figure A1. Applying the axiom of assignment and the composition rule once more, it can be shown that

$\{(z + u*y = x*y) \wedge (u > 0)\}$

(Pr4)

```
z: = z + y;
u: = u − 1
```

$\{(z + u*y = x*y) \wedge (u \geq 0)\}$

and clearly

$(z + u*y = x*y) \wedge (u \geq 0) \wedge \neg(u = 0)$
$\quad \supset (z + u*y = x*y) \wedge (u > 0)$

(Pr5)

Hence, using Pr4 and Pr5 as antecedents, the proof rule for the *repeat* statement tells us that

$\{(z + u*y = x*y) \wedge (u > 0)\}$

```
repeat
    z: = z + y;
    u: = u − 1
until u = 0
```

(Pr6)

$\{(z + u*y = x*y) \wedge (u = 0)\}$

$\{x > 0 \wedge y > 0\}$

```
begin
    (x > 0 ∧ y > 0}

        z: = 0;
        u: = x

    {(z + u*y = x*y) ∧ (u > 0)}

        repeat
            {(z + u*y = x*y) ∧ (u > 0)}

                z: = z + y;
                u: = u − 1

            {(z + u*y = x*y) ∧ (u ≥ 0)}

        until u = 0

    {(z + u*y = x*y) ∧ (u = 0)}

end
```

$\{z = x*y\}$

FIGURE A.1 **Proof outline of the multiplication program.**

Hence, applying the sequential composition rule, Pr1 is correct.

You will note that once the desired assertions are identified the application of the proof theory is straightforward. Most of the intellectual content in developing provably correct designs or in actually verifying designs lies in the development of assertions, particularly in the construction of *loop invariants*. An extensive discussion of how invariants may be developed is given in Gries (1981). It is important to note at this point that the proof of the correctness of formula Pr1 is a proof of *partial* correctness in that it *assumes* that the program terminates. Proof of termination must be demonstrated separately. In that case we will have shown that the program is *totally* correct.

A.6 PROOFS OF PARALLEL SYSTEMS

Generally speaking, information processing systems may involve concurrently active components; I will call these *parallel systems* and, clearly, any comprehensive proof theory must allow for the verification of parallel system designs.

Let us denote a parallel system by the notation

cobegin $S_1 \parallel S_2 \parallel \ldots \parallel S_n$ **coend**

where each S_i is a component of the system. The *cobegin* statement denotes a design in which $S_1, \ldots, S_n$ can be active in parallel. That is, at any given time two or more of the S_i's may be active. A *cobegin* statement terminates only when the components $S_1, \ldots, S_n$ have *all* terminated.

The precise semantics of a *cobegin* statement will depend on a number of factors, the most important of which are:

1. The *kind of system* under consideration. For example, we may be dealing with horizontal microprograms in which case the S_i's may represent indivisible micro-operations and the *cobegin* statement denotes the execution of a collection of micro-operations to be executed from a single control store word. Alternatively, we may be concerned with a multiprocess program in which the S_i's denote sequential processes of arbitrary complexity.
2. The basic *model of parallel processing*. For example, the S_i's may be communicating with one another through shared variables or memory; alternatively, they may communicate by passing messages between one another.
3. The underlying *timing* assumptions. For example, no assumption at all may have been made about the relative speeds of the individual S_i's; alternatively, each S_i may require a specific amount of time as determined by a single global clock or by individual clocks.

Thus, we cannot, in this discussion, give the kind of proof rule that has been given for sequential systems. What we can give here is the general form of the proof rule for the *cobegin* statement.

Informally stated, let the binary predicate

interference-free (S_i, S_j)

mean that the components S_i, S_j do not interfere with one another. That is, the correctness of S_i with respect to its pre-/postcondition will not be affected by the concurrent activation of S_j and vice versa. Then, we have

$$\frac{\{P_1\}S_1\{Q_1\}, \ldots, \{P_n\}S_n\{Q_n\}, \text{ for all } <S_i,S_j> (i \neq j):\text{interference-free } (S_i, S_j)}{\{P_1 \wedge \ldots \wedge P_n\} \text{ cobegin } S_1 \parallel \ldots \parallel S_n \text{ coend } \{Q_1 \wedge \ldots \wedge Q_n\}}$$

In Chapter 5, Section 5.5, where we consider a specific instance of parallel systems, a formal definition of "interference-free" is given. For the present it is sufficient to note how one may go about proving that the design of a parallel system is correct.

1. First, prove that each of the antecedent formulas $\{P_i\}S_i\{Q_i\}$ are correct using the theory of sequential system verification.
2. Next show that every pair of components $<S_i,S_j>$ is interference free.
3. By the proof rule for parallel composition, the correctness formula $\{P_1 \wedge \ldots \wedge P_n\}$ **cobegin** $\ldots$ **coend** $\{Q_1 \wedge \ldots \wedge Q_n\}$ is established.

REFERENCES

Ackerman, W. B. (1982) "Data Flow Languages." *Computer* 15(2), 15–25.

Adams, D. A. (1968) "A Computational Model with Data Flow Sequencing." Technical Report TR-CS 117, Department of Computer Science, Stanford University, Stanford, Calif.

Advanced Micro Devices (1983) *Bipolar Microprocessor Logic and Interface Data Book.* Advanced Micro Devices, Sunnyvale, Calif.

Agerwala, T., and Arvind (1982) "Data Flow Systems: Guest Editors' Introduction." *Computer* 15(2), 10–14.

Agrawala, A. K., and Rauscher, T. G. (1976) *Foundations of Microprogramming.* Academic Press, New York.

Agüero, U. (1978) "A Theory of Plausibility for Computer Architecture Designs." Ph.D. Dissertation, Center for Advanced Computer Studies, University of Southwestern Louisiana, Lafayette.

Agüero, U., and Dasgupta, S. (1978) "A Plausibility-Driven Approach to Computer Architecture Design." *Comm ACM* 30(11), 922–932.

Aho, A. V., Hopcroft, J. E., and Ullman, J. D. (1974) *The Design and Analysis of Algorithms.* Addison–Wesley, Reading, Mass.

Aho, A. V., and Ullman, J. D. (1973) *The Theory of Parsing, Translation and Compiling, Vol. 1: Parsing.* Prentice–Hall, Englewood-Cliffs, N.J.

Aho, A. V., and Ullman, J. D. (1977) *Principles of Compiler Design.* Addison–Wesley, Reading, Mass.

Alagic, S., and Arbib, M. A. (1978) *The Design of Well-Structured and Correct Programs.* Springer-Verlag, Berlin.

Alexander, C. (1964) *Notes on the Synthesis of Form.* Harvard University Press, Cambridge, Mass.

Alexander, W. G., and Wortman, D. B. (1975) "Static and Dynamic Characteristics of XPL Programs." *IEEE Computer* 8(11), 41–46.

Allan, V. (1986) "A Critical Analysis of the Global Optimization Problem for Horizontal Microcode." Technical Report MAD.86.20, Department of Computer Science, Colorado State University, Fort Collins, Colo.

Amamiya, M., Hakozaki, K., Yokoi, T., *et al.* (1982) "New Architecture for Knowledge Base Mechanisms." in Moto-oka (1982), 179–188.

Amamiya, M., Takesue, M., Hasegawa, R., *et al.* (1986) "Implementation and Evaluation of a List-Processing-Oriented Data Flow Machine," *Proceedings of the 13th International Symposium on Computer Architecture,* IEEE Computer Society Press, Los Alamitos, Calif., 10–19.

Amdahl, G. M., Blaauw, G. A., and Brooks, F. P. Jr. (1964) "Architecture of the IBM System/360." *IBM J Res Dev* 8(2), 87–101.

Anderson, D. W., Sparacio, F. J., and Tomasulo, R. M. (1976) "IBM System 360 Model 91, Machine Philosophy and Instruction Handling." *IBM J Res Develop* 11(1), 8–24.

Anderson, G. A., and Jensen, E. D. (1975) "Computer Interconnection Structures: Taxonomy, Characteristics and Examples." *ACM Comp Surv* 9(4), 197–214.

Andrews, G. R., and Schneider, F. B. (1983) "Concepts and Notations for Concurrent Programming," *ACM Comp Surv* 15(1), 3–44.

Andrews, M. (1980) *Principles of Firmware Engineering in Microprogram Control.* Computer Science Press, Potomac, Md.

Apt, K. R. (1981) "Ten Years of Hoare Logics. Part I." *ACM Trans Prog Lang Systems* 3(4), 431–483.

Ardoin, C. D. (1988) "Phase Coupled Resource Allocation in Instruction Pipelines." Ph.D. Dissertation, Center for Advanced Computer Studies, University of Southwestern Louisiana, Lafayette.

Ardoin, C. D., Linn, J. L., and Reynolds, B. W. (1984) "The Implementation of the Attributed Recursive Descent Architecture in VAX-11/780 Microcode." *Proceedings of the 17th Annual Workshop on Microprogramming* IEEE Computer Society Press, Silver Spring, Md. 179–190.

Armstrong, R. A. (1981) "Applying CAD to Gate Arrays Speeds 32-bit Minicomputer Design." *Electronics* (Jan. 13), 167–173.

Arvind, and Culler, D. E. (1986) "Dataflow Architectures." Laboratory for Computer Science, MIT, Cambridge, Mass., LCS/TM-294 (Feb.).

Arvind, and Gostelow, K. P. (1982) "The U-Interpreter," *Computer* 15(2), 42–50.

Arvind, Gostelow, K. P., and Plouffe, W. (1978) "An Asynchronous Programming Language and Computing Machine." Department of Information and Computer Science, University of California, Irvine, Technical Report 114a (Feb.).

Arvind, and Ianucci, R. A. (1983) "A Critique of Multiprocessing von Neumann Style." *Proceedings of the 10th International Symposium on Computer Architecture.* IEEE Computer Society Press, Los Alamitos, Calif., 426–436.

Arvind, and Ianucci, R. A. (1986) "Two Fundamental Issues in Multiprocessing." Laboratory for Computer Science MIT, Cambridge, Mass., CSG Memo 226-5.

Arvind, and Thomas, R. E. (1981) "I-Structures: An Efficient Data Structure for Functional Languages." Laboratory for Computer Science, MIT, Cambridge, Mass. LCS/TM-178 (Oct.).

Ashcroft, E. A., and Wadge, W. W. (1982) "Rx for Semantics." *ACM Trans Prog Lang Systems* 4(2), 283–294.

Avizienis, A. (1983) "A Framework for a Taxonomy of Fault Tolerant Attributes in Computer Systems." *Proceedings of the 10th Annual International Symposium on Computer Architecture.* IEEE Computer Society Press, New York, 16–21.

Ayres, R. F. (1983) *VLSI Silicon Compilation and the Art of Automatic Microchip Design,* Prentice–Hall, Englewood-Cliffs, N.J.

Baba, T., and Hagiwara, H. (1981) "The MPG System: A Machine Independent Efficient Microprogram Generator." *IEEE Trans Comput*, C-30(6), 373–395.

Backus, J. (1978) "Can Programming be Liberated from the von Neumann Style? A Functional Style and its Algebra of Programs." *Comm ACM* 21(8), 613–641.

Baer, J.-L. (1973) "A Survey of Some Theoretical Aspects of Multiprocessing." *ACM Comp Surv* 5(1), 31–80.

Baer, J.-L. (1980) *Computer Systems Architecture.* Computer Science Press, Potomac, Md.

Baer, J.-L. (1983) "Wither a Taxonomy of Computer Architecture?" *Proceedings of the IEEE International Workshop on Computer System Organization,* IEEE Computer Society Press, New York, 3–9.

Balzer, R., and Goldman, N. (1979) "Principles of Good Software Specification and their Implications for Specification Languages." *Proceedings of the IEEE Conference on Specifications of Reliable Software.* 58–67. Reprinted in Gehani and McGettrick (1986).

Banerjee, U., Chen, S.-C., Kuck, D. J., *et al.* (1979) "Time and Parallel Processor Bounds for Fortran-like Loops." *IEEE Trans Comput,* C-28(9), 660–670.

Banerji D. K., and Raymond, J. (1982) *Elements of Microprogramming.* Prentice–Hall, Englewood-Cliffs, N.J.

Banham, R. (1982) *Theory and Design in the First Machine Age.* MIT Press, Cambridge, Mass.

Barahona, P. M., and Gurd, J. R. (1986) "Processor Allocation in a Multi-ring Dataflow Machine." *J. Parall Dist Comp* 3(3), 305–327.

Barbacci, M. R. (1981) "Instruction Set Processor Specification (ISPS): The Notation and its Application." *IEEE Trans Comput* C-30(1), 26–40.

Barbacci, M. R., Barnes, G. E., Cattell, R. G., *et al.* (1978) "The ISPS Computer Description Language." Department of Computer Science, Carnegie Mellon University, Pittsburgh, Pa.

Barbacci, M. R., Grout, S., Lindstrom, G., *et al.* (1985) "Ada as a Hardware Description Language." In C. J. Koomen and T. Moto-oka (Eds), *Computer Hardware Description Languages and their Applications,* North-Holland, Amsterdam, 272–302.

Barbacci, M. R., and Northcutt, J. D. (1980) "Application of ISPS, An Architecture Description Language." *J Digital Systems* 4(3), 221–239.

Barbacci, M. R., and Parker, A. (1980) "Using Emulation to Verify Formal Architecture Descriptions." *Computer* 13(5), 51–56.

Barbacci, M. R., and Siewiorek, D. P. (1982) *The Design and Analysis of Instruction Set Processors.* McGraw–Hill, New York.

Barbacci, M. R., and Uehara, T. (1985) "Computer Hardware Description Languages: The Bridge Between Software and Hardware." *Computer* 18(2), 6–8.

Barnes, G. H., Brown, R. M., Kato, M., *et al.* (1968) "The ILLIAC IV Computer." *IEEE Trans Comput* 18(8), 746–757.

Barton, R. S. (1961) "A New Approach to the Functional Design of a Digital

Computer." *Proceedings of the Westerns Joint Computer Conference.* AFIPS Press, Montvale, N.J., 393–396.

Barton, R. S. (1970) "Ideas for Computer Systems Organization—A Personal Survey." J. T. Tou, (Ed.). *In Software Engineering.* Academic Press, New York, 7–16.

Baskett, F., and Keller, T. W. (1977) "An Evaluation of the CRAY-1 Computer." In Kuck, Lawrie, and Sameh (1977), 71–84.

Baskett, F., and Smith, A. (1976) "Interference in Multiprocessor Computer Systems with Interleaved Memory." *Comm ACM,* 19(6), 327–334.

Batcher, K. E. (1974) "STARAN Parallel Processor System Hardware." *Proceedings of the National Computer Conference,* Vol. 43, AFIPS Press, Montvale, N.J., 405–410.

Batcher, K. E. (1977) "The Multidimensional Access Memory in STARAN." *IEEE Trans Comput* C-26(2), 174–177.

Batcher, K. E. (1980) "Design of a Massively Parallel Processor." *IEEE Trans Comput* C-29(9), 836–840.

Batson, A. P., and Brundage, R. E. (1977) "Segment Sizes and Lifetimes in Algol 60 Programs." *Comm ACM* 20(1), 36–44.

Belady, L. A. (1966) "A Study of Replacement Algorithms for Virtual Storage Computers." *IBM Sys J* 5(2), 78–101.

Belady, L., and Lehman, M. M. (1976) "A Model of Large Program Developments." *IBM Sys J* 15(3), 225–252.

Belady, L., and Lehman, M. M. (1979) "The Characteristics of Large Systems." In Wegner (1979), 106–141.

Belady, L. A., Nelson, R. A., and Shedler, G. S. (1969) "An Anomaly in the Space Time Characteristics of Certain Programs Running in Paging Machines." *Comm ACM* 12(6), 349–353.

Bell, C. G. (1977) "What Have We Learned from the PDP-11?" In G. G. Boulaye and D. W. Lewin (Eds.) *Computer Architecture.* D. Reidel, Boston, Mass., 1–38.

Bell, C. G. (1985) "Multis: A New Class of Multiprocessor Computers." *Science* 228 (April 26), 462–467.

Bell, C. G., and Mudge, J. C. (1978) "The Evolution of the PDP-11." In Bell, Mudge, and McNamara (1978), 379–408.

Bell, C. G., Mudge, J. C. and McNamara, J. E. (Eds.) (1978) *Computer Engineering: A DEC View of Hardware Systems Designs.* Digital Press, Bedford, Mass.

Bell, C. G., and Newell, A. (1971) *Computer Structures: Readings and Examples.* McGraw–Hill, New York.

Bell, C. G., Newell, A., Reich, M., *et al.* (1982) "The IBM System/360, System/370, 3030 and 4300: A Series of Planned Machines that Span a Wide Performance Range." In Siewiorek, Bell, and Newell (1982), 856–892.

Bell, C. G., and Strecker, W. D. (1976) "Computer Structures: What Have We Learned from the PDP-11?" *Proceedings of the 3rd Annual Symposium on Computer Architecture.* ACM/IEEE, New York, 1–14.

Benes, V. E. (1965) *Mathematical Theory of Connecting Networks and Telephone Traffic.* Academic Press, New York.

Berg, H. K., Boebert, W. E., Franta, W. R., and Moher, T. G. (1982) *Formal Methods of Program Verification and Specification.* Prentice–Hall, Englewood-Cliffs, N.J.

Bertsis, V. (1980) "Security and Protection of Data in the IBM System/38." *Proceedings of the 7th Annual Symposium on Computer Architecture* ACM/IEEE, New York, 245–252.

Bhandarkar, D. P. (1975) "Analysis of Memory Interference in Multiprocessors." *IEEE Trans Comput* C-24(9), 897–908.

Bhandarkar, D. P. (1982) "Architecture Management for Ensuring Software Compatibility in the VAX Family of Computers" *Computer,* 15(2), 87–93.

Bhuyan L. N. (1987) "Guest Editor's Introduction: Interconnection Networks for Parallel and Distributed Processing." *Computer* 20(6), 9–13.

Bhuyan, L. N., Agrawal, D. P. (1983) "Design and Performance of Generalized Interconnection Networks." *IEEE Trans Comput* C-32(12), 1081–1090.

Bilardi, G., Pracchi, M., and Preparata, F. P. (1981) "A Critique and an Appraisal of VLSI Models of Computation." In Kung, Sproull, and Steele (1981).

Birkhoff, G., and Bartee, T. C. (1970) *Modern Applied Algebra,* McGraw–Hill, New York.

Blaauw, G. A. (1976) *Digital System Implementation.* Prentice–Hall, Englewood-Cliffs, N.J.

Blaauw, G. A., and Brooks, F. P. (1964) "The Structure of System/360 Part I: Outline of Logical Structure." *IBM Syst J* 3(2 & 3), 119–135.

Blaauw, G. A., and Händler, W. (Eds.) (1981) *Workshop on Taxonomy in Computer Architecture.* Friedrich Alexander Universität Erlangen-Nürnberg, Nuremberg, West Germany.

Blakeslee, T. R. (1979) *Digital Design with Standard MSI and LSI,* 2nd ed. Wiley, New York.

Borgerson, B. R., Tjaden, G. S., and Hanson, M. L. (1978) "Mainframe Implementation with Off-the-Shelf LSI Modules." *Computer* 11(7) 42–48.

Bouknight, W. Denenberg, S. A., McIntyre, D. E., *et al.* (1972) "The ILLIAC IV System." *Proc IEEE* 60(4), 369–388.

Boyer, R. S., and Moore, J. S. (Eds.) (1981a) *The Correctness Problem in Computer Science.* Academic Press, New York.

Boyer, R. S., and Moore, J. S. (1981b) "A Verification Condition Generator for FORTRAN." In Boyer and Moore (1981a) 9–102.

Breuer, M. A. (Ed.) (1975) *Digital System Design Automation.* Computer Science Press, Potomac, Md.

Bridgeman, P. W. (1927) *The Logic of Modern Physics.* Macmillan, New York.

Brinch Hansen, P. (1973) *Operating Systems Principles.* Prentice–Hall, Englewood-Cliffs, N.J.

Brinch Hansen, P. (1977) *The Architecture of Concurrent Programs.* Prentice–Hall, Englewood-Cliffs, N.J.

Broadbent, G. (1973) *Design in Architecture.* Wiley, New York.

Brown, J. F., III, and Sites, R. L. (1984) "A Chip Set Microarchitecture for a High Performance VAX Implementation." *Proceedings of the 14th Annual Microprogramming Workshop.* IEEE Computer Society Press, New York, 48–54.

Buckle, J. K. (1978) *The ICL 2900 Series.* Macmillan, London.

Budnick, P. P., and Kuck, D. J. (1971) "The Organization and Use of Parallel Memories." *IEEE Trans Comput* 20(12), 1566–1569.

Burger, R. M., Calvin, R. K., Holton, W. C. *et al.* (1984) "The Impact of ICs on Computer Technology." *Computer* 17(10), 88–96.

Burks, A. W., Goldstine, H. H., and von Neumann, J. (1946) "Preliminary Discussion of the Logical Design of a Electronic Computing Instrument." Institute for Advanced Study, Princeton, N.J. Reprinted in Bell and Newell (1971), 92–119.

Burnett, G. J., and Coffman, E. G. (1970) "A Study of Interleaved Memory Systems." *Proceedings of the Spring Joint Computer Conference,* Vol. 36, AFIPS Press, Montvale, N.J., 467–474.

Burnett, G. J., and Coffman, E. G. (1973) "A Combinatorial Problem Related to Interleaved Memory Systems." *J ACM* 20 (Jan.), 39–45.

Burnett, G. J., and Coffman, E. G. (1975) "Analysis of Interleaved Memory Systems Using Blockage Buffers." *Comm ACM* 18(2), 91–95.

Burstall, R., and Goguen, J. A. (1981) "An Informal Introduction to Specifications Using CLEAR." In Boyer and Moore (1981a) 185–213.

Case R. P., and Padegs, A. (1978) "Architecture of the IBM System/370." *Comm ACM* 21(1), 73–95.

Cattell, R. G. G. (1980) "Automatic Derivation of Code Generators from Machine Description." *ACM Trans. Prog Lang* 2(2), 173–190.

Censier, L. M., and Feautrier, P. (1978) "A New Solution to the Coherence Problems in Multicache Systems." *IEEE Trans Comput* C-27(12), 1112–1118.

Chang D., Kuck, D. J., and Lawrie, D. H. (1977) "On the Effective Bandwidth of Parallel Memories." *IEEE Trans Comput* C-26(5), 480–490.

Charlesworth, A. E. (1981) "An Approach to Scientific Array Processing: The Architectural Design of the AP-120B/FPS-164 Family." *Computer* 14(9), 18–27.

Chen, T. C. (1971) "Parallelism, Pipelining and Computer Efficiency." *Computer Design* (Jan.), 69–74.

Chu, W. W., and Opderbeck, H. (1976). "Program Behavior and the Page Fault Frequency Algorithm." *Computer* 9(11), 29–38.

Chu, Y. (1965) "An Algol-like Computer Design Language." *Comm ACM* 8, 607–615.

Chu, Y. (1972) *Computer Organization and Microprogramming.* Prentice–Hall, Englewood-Cliffs, N.J.

Clark, W. A. (1980) "From Electron Mobility to Logical Structure: A View of Integrated Circuits." *ACM Comp Surv* 12(3), 325–356.

Coffman, E. G., and Denning, P. J. (1973) *Operating Systems Theory,* Prentice–Hall, Englewood-Cliffs, N.J.

Cohen, E., and Jefferson D. (1975). "Protection in the Hydra Operating System." *Proceedings of the 5th Symposium on Operating System Principles.* ACM, New York, 141–160.

Colclaser, R. A. (1980) *Microtelectronics: Processing and Device Design.* Wiley, New York.

Colwell, R. P., Hitchcock, C. Y., Jensen, E. D. *et al.* (1985) "Computers, Complexity, and Controversy." *Computer,* 18(9), 8–20.

Conti, C. J., Gibson, D. H., and Pitkowski, S. H. (1968) "Structural Aspects of the System 360/85: General Organization." *IBM Sys J* 7, 2–14.

Conway, R. W., Gries, D. G., and Wortman, D. B. (1977) *Introduction to Structured Programming.* Winthrop, Cambridge, Mass.

Conway, R. W., Maxwell, W. L., and Miller L. W. (1967) *Theory of Scheduling.* Addison–Wesley, Reading, Mass.

Cook, R. W., and Flynn, M. J. (1970) "System Design of a Dynamic Microprocessor." *IEEE Trans Comput,* C-19(3), 213–222.

Courtois, P. J. (1977) *Decomposability.* Academic Press, New York.

Cragon, H. G. (1980) "The Elements of Single Chip Microcomputer Architecture." *Computer* 13(10), 24–41.

Cray (1984) *CRAY X-MP Series Model 48 Mainframe Reference Manual.* HR-0097, Cray Research, Inc., Mendota Heights, Minn.

Cray (1986) *CRAY-2 Computer System Functional Description.* HR-2000, Cray Research Inc., Mendota Heights, Minn.

Crocker, S. D., Marcus, L., and van Mierop, D. (1980) "The ISI Microcode Verification System." In G. Chroust and J. Mulbacher (Eds.) *Firmware, Microprogramming and Restructurable Hardware.* North-Holland, Amsterdam.

Damm, W. (1984) "A Microprogramming Logic," Ber. No. 94, Schriften Zur Informatik und Angewandten Mathematik, Technische Hochschule Aachen, Aachen, West Germany.

Damm, W. (1985) "Design and Specification of Microprogrammed Computer Architectures." *Proceeding of the 18th Annual Workshop on Microprogramming* IEEE Computer Society Press, Los Alamitos, Calif., 3–10.

Damm, W., and Doehmen, G. (1985) "Verification of Microprogrammed Computer Architectures in the S*-System: A Case Study," *Proceedings at the 18th Annual Microprogramming Workshop.* IEEE Computer Society Press, Los Alamitos, Calif., 61–73.

Damm, W., Doehmen, G., Merkel, K., *et al.* (1986) "The AADL/S* Approach to Firmware Design Verification," *IEEE Software.* 3(4), 27–37.

Darringer, J., Brand, D., Joyner, W. H., *et al.* (1984) "LSS: A System for Production Logic Synthesis," *IBM J. Res. Dev* 28(4), 537–545.

Darringer, J. (1985) "Production Logic Synthesis." *Proceedings of the 13th Annual ACM Computer Science Conference.* ACM, New York, 13–16.

Das, C. R., and Bhuyan, L. N. (1985) "Bandwidth Availability of Multiple-Bus Multiprocessors," *IEEE Trans Comput,* C-34(10), 918–926.

Dasgupta, S. (1977) "Parallelism in Loop Free Microprograms." In B. Gilchrist (Ed.), *Information Processing 77* (Proc. IFIP Congress), North-Holland, Amsterdam, 745–750.

Dasgupta, S. (1979) "The Organization of Microprogram Stores." *ACM Comp Surv* 11(1), 39–66.

Dasgupta, S. (1980) "Some Aspects of High Level Microprogramming." *ACM Comp Surv* 12(3), 295–324.

Dasgupta, S. (1981) "S*A: A Language for Describing Computer Architectures." In M. A. Breuer and R. Hartenstein (Eds.), *Proceedings of the 5th International Symposium on Computer Hardware Description Languages and their Applications.* North-Holland, Amsterdam, 65–78.

Dasgupta, S. (1982) "Computer Design and Description Languages." In M. C. Yovits (Ed.) *Advances in Computers,* Vol. 21. Academic Press, New York, 91–155.

Dasgupta, S. (1983) "An Early Paper on Program Verification by Alan Turing." Unpublished manuscript, Center for Advanced Computer Studies, University of Southwestern Louisiana, Lafayette, La.

Dasgupta, S. (1984) *The Design and Description of Computer Architectures.* Wiley, New York.

Dasgupta, S. (1985) "Hardware Description Languages in Microprogramming Systems." *Computer* 18(2), 67–76.

Dasgupta, S. (1987) "Principles of Firmware Verification." In Habib (1988).

Dasgupta, S., and Mueller, R. A. (1986) "Firmware Engineering: The Interaction of Microprogramming and Software Technology." *IEEE Software,* 3(4), 4–5.

Dasgupta, S., and Olafsson, M. (1982) "Towards a Family of Languages for the Design and Implementation of Machine Architectures." *Proceedings of the 9th Annual International Symposium on Computer Architecture,* IEEE Computer Society Press, New York, 158–167.

Dasgupta, S., and Shriver, B. D. (1985) "Developments in Firmware Engineering." In M. C. Yovits, (Ed.) *Advances in Computers,* Vol. 24. Academic Press, New York, 101–176.

Dasgupta, S., and Tartar, J. (1976) "The Identification of Maximal Parallelism in Straight Line Microprograms." *IEEE Trans Comput.* C-25(10), 986–992.

Dasgupta, S., and Wagner, A. (1984) "The Use of Hoare Logic in the Verification of Horizontal Microprograms." *Int J Comp Info Sc* 13(6), 461–490.

Dasgupta S., Wilsey, P. A., and Heinanen, J. (1986) "Axiomatic Specifications in Firmware Development Systems." *IEEE Software,* 3(4), 49–58.

Davidson, E. S. (1971) "The Design and Control of Pipelined Function Generators." *Proceedings of the IEEE International Conference on Systems, Networks and Computers,* 19–21.

Davidson, S. (1986) "Progress in High Level Microprogramming." *IEEE Software* 3(4), 18–26.

Davidson, S., Landskov, D., Shriver, B. D., *et al.* (1981) "Some Experiments in Local Microcode Compaction for Horizontal Machines." *IEEE Trans Comput* C-30(7), 460–477.

Davidson, S., and Shriver, B. D. (1978) "Firmware Engineering: A Survey," *Computer* 11(5), 21–33.

Davidson, S., and Shriver, B. D. (1980) "MARBLE: A High-Level Machine-Independent Language for Microprogramming." In G. Chroust and J. Mulbacher (Eds.) *Firmware, Microprogramming and Restructurable Hardware.* North-Holland, Amsterdam, 1–40.

Davis, A. L. (1978) "The Architecture and System Method of DDM1: A Recursively Structured Data Driven Machine." *Proceedings of the 5th Annual Symposium on Computer Architecture.* ACM/IEEE, New York, 210–215.

Davis, C., Maley, G., Simmons, R., *et al.* (1980) "Gate Array Embodies System/370 Processor." *Electronics* (October 9), 140–143.

de Bakker, J. (1980) *Mathematical Theory of Program Correctness.* Prentice–Hall International, Englewood-Cliffs, N.J.

Demco, J., and Marsland, T. A. (1976) "An Insight into PDP-11 Emulation." *Proceedings of the 9th Annual Workshop on Microprogramming.* ACM/IEEE, New York, 20–26.

de Millo, R., Lipton, R. J., and Perlis, A. (1979) "Social Processes and Proofs of Theorems and Programs." *Comm ACM* 22(5), 271–280.

Denning, P. J. (1968a) "The Working Set Model for Program Behavior." *Comm ACM* 11(5), 323–333.

Denning, P. J. (1968b) "Thrashing: Its Causes and Prevention," *Proceedings of the Fall Joint Computer Conference,* Vol. 33, AFIPS Press, Montvale, N.J., 915–922.

Denning, P. J. (1970) "Virtual Memory." *ACM Comp Surv* 2 (Sept.), 153–189.

Denning, P. J. (1978) "A Question of Semantics." *Comp Arch News* (SIGARCH) 6(8), 16–18.

Denning, P. J. (1980) "Working Sets Past and Present." *IEEE Trans Soft Eng* SE-6(1), 64–84.

Dennis, J. B. (1974) "First Version of a Data Flow Procedural Language." *Proc Colloque sur la Programmation* (Lecture Notes in Computer Science Vol. 19), Springer-Verlag, Berlin, 362–376.

Dennis, J. B. (1980) "Dataflow Supercomputers." *Computer* 13(11), 48–56.

Dennis, J. B., Fuller, S. H., Ackerman, W. B., *et al.* (1979) "Research Directions in Computer Architecture." In Wegner (1979), 514–556.

Dennis, J. B., and Misunas, D. P. (1974) "A Preliminary Architecture for a Basic Data Flow Processor." Laboratory for Computer Science, MIT, Cambridge, Mass., CSG Memo 102.

Dennis, J. B., and Misunas, D. P. (1975) "A Preliminary Architecture for a Basic Data Flow Processor." *Proceedings of the 2nd Annual Symposium on Computer Architecture.* ACM/IEEE, New York, 126–132.

Dennis, J. B., and Van Horn, E. C. (1966) "Programming Semantics for Multiprogrammed Computations." *Comm ACM* 9(3), 143–155.

DeWitt, D. J. (1976) "A Machine Independent Approach to the Production of Horizontal Microcode." Ph.D. Thesis, Department of Computer and Communication Science, University of Michigan, Ann Arbor.

Dietmeyer, D. L., and Duley, J. R. (1975) "Register-Transfer Languages and Their Translations." In Breuer (1975), 117–218.

Digital (1978) *The PDP-11 Processor Handbook.* Digital Equipment Corporation, Maynard, Mass.

Digital (1979) *The KA780 Central Processor Technical Description.* Digital Equipment Corporation, Maynard, Mass.

Digital (1981a) *The VAX Architecture Handbook;.* Digital Equipment Corporation, Maynard, Mass.

Digital (1981b) *The VAX Hardware Handbook.* Digital Equipment Corporation, Maynard, Mass.

Digital (1985) "The VAX 8600 Processor." *Digital Technical Journal.* Digital Equipment Corporation, Hudson, Mass.

Dijkstra, E. W. (1960) "Recursive Programming." *Num Math* 2(5), 312–318.

Dijkstra, E. W. (1968) "Cooperating Sequential Processes." In F. Genuys (Ed.), *Programming Languages.* Academic Press, New York, 43–112.

Dijkstra, E. W. (1972) "Notes on Structured Programming." In O. J. Dahl, E. W. Dijkstra, and C. A. R. Hoare. *Structured Programming.* Academic Press, New York, 1–82.

Dijkstra. E. W. (1976) *A Discipline of Programming.* Prentice–Hall, Englewood Cliffs, N.J.

Director, S., Parker, A. C., Siewiorek, D. P., *et al.* (1981) "A Design Methodology and Computer Aids for Digital VLSI Systems." *IEEE Trans Circuits Systems* CAS-28(7), 634–645.

Ditzel, D. R. (1980) "Program Measurements on a High Level Language Computer." *Computer* 13(8), 62–72.

Ditzel, D. R., and Patterson, D. A. (1980) "Retrospective on High Level Language Computer Architecture." *Proceedings of the 7th Annual Symposium on Computer Architecture.* ACM/IEEE, New York, 97–104.

Djordjevic, J., Ibbett, R. N., and Barbacci, M. R. (1980) "Evaluation of Computer Architecture Using ISPS," *Proc IEE*(U.K.) 127(4), Part E, 126–135.

Doehmen, G. (1985) "Verifikation eines Emulators: Eine Fallstudie zur Verifikation Mikroprogrammierter Rechnerarchitekturen." Schriften zur Informatik und Angewandten Mathematik, Technische Hochschule Aachen, Aachen, West Germany.

Donahue, J. E. (1976) *Complementary Definitions of Programming Language Semantics.* Springer-Verlag, Berlin.

Doran, R. W. (1979) *Computer Architecture: A Structured Approach.* Academic Press, New York.

Dubois, M., and Briggs, F. A. (1982) "Effects of Cache Coherency in Multiprocessors." *IEEE Trans Comput* C-31(11), 1083–1099.

Duda, M. R., and Mueller, R. A. (1984) "μ-C Microprogramming Language Specification." Technical Report CS-84-11, Department of Computer Science, Colorado State University, Fort Collins, Colo.

Dudani, S., and Stabler, E. (1983) "Types of Hardware Description." In T. Uehara and M. R. Barbacci (Eds.) *Computer Hardware Description Languages and Their Applications* (Proceedings of the 6th International Symposium), North-Holland, Amsterdam, 127–136.

Duley, J. R., and Dietmeyer, D. L. (1968) "A Digital System Design Language (DDL)." *IEEE Trans Comput* C-17(9), 850–861.

Dunn, G., and Everitt, B. S. (1982) *An Introduction to Mathematical Taxonomy,* Cambridge University Press, Cambridge, England.

Eckhouse, R. H. Jr. (1971) "A High Level Microprogramming Language (MPL)." Ph.D. Thesis, Department of Computer Science, State University of New York, Buffalo.

Elshoff, J. L. (1976) "An Analysis of Some Commercial PL/1 Programs." *IEEE Trans Soft Eng* (June), 113–120.

Emer, J. S. and Clark, D. W. (1984), "A Characterization of Processor Performance in the VAX-II/780," *Proc. 11th Annual Symposium on Computer Architecture,* IEEE Comp. Soc. Press, Los Angeles, CA, 301–310.

Encore (1986) *Multimax Technical Summary.* Encore Computer Corp., Marlboro, Mass.

England, D. M. (1972) "Architectural Features of System 250." *Infotech State of The Art Report on Operating Systems.* Infotech, Maidenhead, U.K.

Enslow, P. H. (1977) "Multiprocessor Organization." *ACM Comp Surv* 9(1), 103–129.

Ercegovac, M. D., and Lang, T. (1985) *Digital Systems and Hardware/Firmware Algorithms.* Wiley, New York

Estrin, G. (1978) "A Methodology for Design of Digital Systems—Supported by SARA at the Age of One." *Proceedings of the AFIPS National Computer Conference.* Vol. 47, AFIPS Press, Arlington, Va., 313–324.

Estrin, G. (1985a) "SARA in the Design Room." *Proceedings of the 13th Annual ACM Computer Science Conference.* ACM, New York, 1–12.

Estrin, G. (1985b) "The Story of SARA." In Giloi and Shriver (1985), 29–46.

Falkoff, A. D., Iverson, K. E., and Sussenguth, E. H. (1964) "A Formal Description of the System/360." *IBM Sys J* 3, 198–262.

Feng, T. Y. (1981) "A Survey of Interconnection Networks." *Computer* (Dec) 12–27.

Feuer, M., Khokhani, K. H., and Mehta, D. (1980) "Computer Aided Design Wires 5000-Circuit Chip." *Electronics* (October 9), 144–145.

Filman, R. E., and Friedman, D. P. (1984) *Coordinated Computing.* McGraw-Hill, New York.

Fisher, A. L., and Kung, H. T. (1983) "Synchronizing Large VLSI Processor Arrays." *Proceedings of the 10th Symposium on Computer Architecture,* IEEE Computer Society Press, Los Alamitos, Calif., 59–66.

Fisher, J. A. (1981) "Trace Scheduling: A Technique for Global Microcode Compaction." *IEEE Trans Comput* C-30(7), 478–490.

Fisher, J. A. (1983) "Very Long Instruction Word Architectures and the ELI-512." *Proceedings of the 10th Annual International Symposium on Computer Architecture* IEEE Computer Society Press, 140–150.

Fisher, J. A., Landskov, D., and Shriver, B. D. (1981) "Microcode Compaction: Looking Backward and Looking Forward." *Proceedings of the National Computer Conference* AFIPS Press, Montvale, N.J., 95–102.

Fitzpatrick, D., Foderaro, J. K., Katevenis, M. G. H., *et al.* (1981) "VLSI Implementations of a Reduced Instruction Set Computer." In Kung, Sproull, and Steele (1981), 327–336.

Floyd, R. W. (1967) "Assigning Meanings to Programs." *Mathematical Aspects of Computer Science,* 19. American Mathematical Society, Providence, R.I.

Floyd, R. W. (1979) "The Paradigms of Programming." (ACM Turing Award Lecture). *Comm ACM* 22(8), 455–460.

Flynn, M. J. (1966) "Very High Speed Computing Systems." *Proc IEEE* 54 (Dec.), 1901–1909.

Flynn, M. J. (1974) "Trends and Problems in Computer Organization." *Information Processing 74* (Proceeding of the 1974 IFIP Congress) North-Holland, Amsterdam, 3–10.

Flynn, M. J. (1977) "The Interpretive Interface: Resources and Program Representation in Computer Organization." In Kuck, Lawrie, and Sameh (1977), 41–70.

Flynn, M. J. (1980) "Directions and Issues in Architecture and Language." *Computer,* 13(10), 5–22.

Flynn, M. J. (1981) "Customized Microcomputers." In M. J. Flynn, N. R. Harris, and D. P. McCarthy (Eds.) *Microcomputer System Design,* Lecture Notes in Computer Science 126, Springer-Verlag, Berlin, 182–222.

Flynn, M. J., and Hoevel, L. W. (1983) "Execution Architecture: The DELTRAN Experiment." *IEEE Trans Comput* C-32(2), 156–174.

Flynn M. J., and Huck, J. C. (1984) "Emulation." In C. R. Vick and C. V. Ramamoorthy (Eds.) *Handbook of Software Engineering.* Van Nostrand–Rheinhold, New York, 134–148.

Flynn, M. J., and MacLaren, M. D. (1967) "Microprogramming Revisited." *Proceedings of the ACM 22nd National Conference* ACM, New York, 457–464.

Flynn, M. J., and Rosin, R. F. (1971) "Microprogramming: An Introduction and Viewpoint." *IEEE Trans Comp.* C-20(7), 727–731.

Foderaro, J., van Dyke, K., and Patterson, D. A. (1982) "Running RISCs." *VLSI Design,* 3(5), 27–32.

Fossum, T., McElroy, J. B., and English, W. (1985) "An Overview of the VAX 8600 System." *Digital Tech J.* Digital Equipment Corporation, Hudson, Mass, 8–23.

Foster, C. C., and Iberall, T. (1985) *Computer Architecture,* 3rd ed. Van Nostrand–Rheinhold, New York.

Foster, M. J., and Kung, H. T. (1980) "The Design of Special Purpose VLSI Chips." *Computer* 13(1), 26–40.

Frank, E. H., and Sproull, R. F. (1981) "Testing and Debugging Custom Integrated Circuits." *ACM Comp Surv* 13(4), 425–451.

Franklin, M. A., Graham, G. S., and Gupta, R. K. (1978) "Anomalies with Variable Partition Paging Algorithms." *Comm ACM* 21(3), 232–236.

Freeman, P. (1980a) "The Context of Design." In Freeman and Wasserman (1980), 2–4.

Freeman P. (1980b) "The Central Role of Design in Software Engineering: Implications for Research." In H. Freeman and P. M. Lewis (Eds.) *Software Engineering.* Academic Press, New York, 121–132.

Freeman, P., and Wasserman, A. (1980) *Tutorial on Software Design Techniques,* IEEE Computer Society Press, Los Alamitos, Calif.

Fuller, S. H., Ousterhout, J. K., Raskin, L., *et al.* (1977a) "Multi-Microprocessors: An Overview and Working Example," *Proc IEEE* 61(2), 216–228.

Fuller, S. H. Shamon, P., Lamb, D., *et al.* (1977b) "Evaluation of Computer Architectures via Test Programs." *Proc AFIPS Nat Comp Conf* Vol. 46, 147–160.

Fuller, S. H., Stone, H. S., and Burr, W. E. (1977c). "Initial Selection and Screening of the CFA Candidate Computer Architectures." *Proc. AFIPS Nat Comp Conf,* 46, 139–146.

Gajski, D. D. *et al.* (1982) "A Second Opinion on Dataflow Machines and Languages." *Computer* 15(2), 58–70.

Gajski, D. D., and Peir, J-K. (1985) "Essential Issues in Multiprocessor Systems." *Computer* 18(6), 9–28.

Ganapathi, M., Fischer, C. N., and Hennessy, J. (1982) "Retargetable Compiler Code Generation." *ACM Comp Surv* 14(4), 573–592.

Gehani, N., and McGettrick, A. D. (Eds.) (1986) *Software Specification Techniques,* Addison–Wesley, Reading, Mass.

German, S. M., and Leiberherr, K. J. (1985) "Zeus: A Language for Expressing Algorithms in Hardware." *Computer* 18(2), 55–65.

Ghoshal, D., and Bhuyan, L. N. (1987) "Analytical Modeling and Architectural Modifications of a Dataflow Computer." *Proceedings of the 14th International Symposium on Computer Architecture,* IEEE Computer Society Press, Los Alamitos, Calif., 81–89

Giloi, W. K. (1981) "A Complete Taxonomy of Computer Architecture Based on the Abstract Data Type View." In Blaauw and Händler (1981), 19–38.

Giloi, W. K. (1983) "Towards a Taxonomy of Computer Architecture Based on the Machine Data Type View." *Proceedings of the 10th Annual International Symposium on Computer Architecture.* IEEE Computer Society Press, New York, pp 6–15.

Giloi, W. K., and Gueth, R. (1982) "Concepts and Realization of a High Performance Data Type Architecture." *Int J Comp Info Sc* 11(1), 25–54.

Giloi, W. K., and Shriver, B. D. (Eds.) (1985) *Methodologies for Computer System Design.* North-Holland, Amsterdam.

Goke, R., and Lipovski, G. J. (1973) "Banyon Networks for Partitioning on Multiprocessor Systems." *Proceedings of the 1st Annual Symposium on Computer Architecture* ACM/IEEE, New York, 21–30.

Goldstine, H. H. (1972) *The Computer from Pascal to von Neuman,* Princeton University Press, Princeton, N.J.

Gonzalez, M. J. (1977) "Deterministic Processor Scheduling." *ACM Comp Surv* 9(3), 173–204.

Gordon, M. J. (1979) *The Denotational Description of Programming Languages.* Springer-Verlag, Berlin.

Gottlieb, A., *et al.* (1983) "The NYU Ultracomputer—Designing an MIMD Shared Memory Parallel Computer." *IEEE Trans Comput* C-32(2), 175–189.

Gottlieb, A. (1986) "The New York University Ultracomputer." In Metropolis *et al.* (1986), 66–77.

Gottlieb, A., Lubachevsky, B., Rudolph, L. (1983) "Basic Techniques for the Efficient Coordination of Large Numbers of Cooperating Sequential Processors," *ACM Trans Prog Lang Sys* April (5) 2.

Gould, S. J. (1977) *Ontogeny and Phylogeny.* The Belknap Press of the Harvard University Press, Cambridge, Mass.

Grasselli, A. (1962) "The Design of Program-Modifiable Microprogrammed Control Units." *IRE Trans Elect Comp* (June), 336–339.

Gries, D. G. (1971) *Compiler Construction for Digital Computers.* Wiley, New York.

Gries, D. G. (Ed.) (1978) *Programming Methodology.* Springer-Verlag, New York.

Gries, D. G. (1981) *The Science of Programming.* Springer-Verlag, New York.

Gries, R., and Woodward, J. A. (1984) "Software Tools Used in the Development of a VLSI VAX Microcomputer." *Proceedings of the 17th Annual Workshop on Microprogramming.* IEEE Computer Society Press, Silver Spring, Md., 55–58.

Grishman, R., and Su, B. (1983) "A Preliminary Evaluation of Trace Scheduling for Global Microcode Compaction." *IEEE Trans Comput* C-32(12), 1191–1193.

Gross, T. R., and Hennessy, J. L. (1982) "Optimizing Delayed Branches." *Proceedings of the 15th Annual Workshop on Microprogramming.* IEEE Computer Society Press, Los Angeles, Calif., 114–120.

Guffin, R. M. (1982) "A Microprogramming-Language-Directed Microarchitecture." *Proceedings of the 15th Annual Workshop on Microprogramming.* IEEE Computer Society Press, Los Angeles, Calif., 42–49.

Guha, R. K. (1977) "Dynamic Microprogramming in a Time Sharing Environment." *Proceedings of the 10th Annual Workshop on Microprogramming.* ACM/IEEE, New York, 55–60.

Gupta, A., and Toong, H. D. (1983) "An Architectural Comparison of 32-bit Microprocessors." *IEEE Micro* (Feb.), 9–22.

Gurd, J., and Bohm, W. (1986) "Implicit Parallel Processing: SISAL on the Manchester Dataflow Computer." *Proceedings of the IBM Europe Institute on Parallel Processing.* Oberlach, Austria.

Gurd, J., and Kirkham, C. C. (1986) "Data Flow: Achievements and Prospects." In H.-J. Kugler (ED.), *Information Processing 86* (Proceedings of the IFIP Congress, 1986). North-Holland, Amsterdam, 61–68.

Gurd, J., Kirkham, C. C., and Watson, I. (1985) "The Manchester Prototype Dataflow Computer." *Comm ACM* 28(1), 34–52.

Gurd, J., and Watson, I. (1983) "Preliminary Evaluation of a Prototype Dataflow Computer." In R. E. A. Mason (Ed.) *Information Processing 83* (Proceedings of the IFIP Congress, 1983). Elsevier North-Holland, Amsterdam, 545–551.

Gurd, J. R., Watson, I., and Glauert, J. R. (1978) "A Multilayered Data Flow Computer Architecture." Internal Report of the Department of Computer Science, University of Manchester, U.K.

Gurd, R. P. (1983) "Experience Developing Microcode Using a High Level Language," *Proceedings of the 16th Annual Workshop on Microprogramming.* IEEE Computer Society Press, Los Angeles, Calif., 179–184.

Guttag, J. V. (1979) "Notes on Type Abstraction." *Proceedings of the Conference on Specification of Reliable Software* 36–46. Reprinted in Gehani and McGettrick (1986).

Guttag, J. V., and Horning, J. J. (1980) "Formal Specification as a Design Tool." *Proceedings of the 7th Annual ACM Symposium on Principles of Programming Languages.* 251–261. Reprinted in Gehani and McGettrick (1986).

Guttag, J. V., Horning, J. J., and Wing, J. M. (1982) "Some Notes on Putting Formal Specifications to Productive Use." *Sc Comp Prog* 2 (Dec.), 53–68.

Guttag, J. V., Horning, J. J., and Wing, J. M. (1985) "The Larch Family of Specification Languages." *IEEE Software* 2(5), 24–36.

Habermann, N. (1976) *Introduction to Operating System Design.* SRA, Chicago.

Habib, S. (Ed.) (1988) *Microprogramming and Firmware Engineering,* Van Nostrand-Rheinhold, New York.

Hack, J. J. (1986) "Peak vs. Sustained Performance in Highly Concurrent Vector Machines." *Computer,* 19(9), 11–19.

Hagiwara, H., Tomita, S., Oyanagi, S., *et al.* (1980) "A Dynamically Microprogrammable Computer with Low-Level Parallelism." *IEEE Trans Comput* C-29(7), 577–595.

Haken, W., Appel, K., and Koch, J. (1977) "Every Planar Map is Four Colorable." *Illinois J Math* 21(84), 429–567.

Halbert, D., and Kessler, P. (1980) "Windows of Overlapping Register Frames." Computer Science Division, Department of Electrical Engineering and Computer Science, University of California, Berkeley.

Hamacher, V. C., Vranesic, Z. G., and Zaky, S. G. (1984) *Computer Organization,* 2nd ed. McGraw–Hill, New York.

Hammerstrom, D. (1983) "The Migration of Functions into Silicon." Tutorial presented at the 10th International Symposium on Computer Architecture, Stockholm (June).

Händler, W. (1977) "The Impact of Classification Schemes on Computer Architecture." *Proceedings of the 1977 International Conference on Parallel Processing.* 7–15.

Händler, W. (1981) "Standards, Classification and Taxonomy: Experiences with ECS." In Blaauw and Händler (1981), 39–75.

Hayes, J. P. (1978) *Computer Architecture and Organization.* McGraw–Hill, New York.

Hayes, J. P. (1984) *Digital Systems and Microprocessors.* McGraw–Hill, New York.

Hellerman, H. (1967) *Digital Computer System Principles.* McGraw–Hill, New York.

Hennessy, J. L. (1984) "VLSI Processor Architecture." *IEEE Trans Comput* C-33(12), 1221–1246.

Hennessy, J. L., and Gross, T. (1983) "Postpass Code Optimization of Pipeline Constraints." *ACM Trans Prog Lang System* 5(3), 422–448.

Hennessy, J. L., Jouppi, N., Przybylski, S., *et al.* (1982) "MIPS: A Microprocessor Architecture." *Proceedings of the 15th Annual Workshop on Microprogramming.* IEEE Computer Society Press, Los Angeles, Calif., 17–22.

Hennessy, J. L., Jouppi, N., Przybylski, S., *et al.* (1983) "Design of a High Performance VLSI Processor." *Proceedings of the 3rd Caltech Conference on VLSI,* California Institute of Technology, Pasadena, Calif., 33–54.

Hill, F. J., and Peterson, G. R. (1978) *Digital Systems: Hardware Organization and Design.* Wiley, New York.

Hillis, D. (1985) *The Connection Machine.* MIT Press, Cambridge, Mass.

Hitchcock, C. Y., and Sprunt, H. M. B. (1985) "Analyzing Multiple Register Sets." *Proceedings of the 12th Annual International Symposium on Computer Architecture.* IEEE Computer Society Press, Silver Spring, Md., 55–63.

Hoare, C. A. R. (1969) "An Axiomatic Approach to Computer Programming." *Comm ACM* 12(10), 576–580, 583.

Hoare, C. A. R. (1972) "Towards a Theory of Parallel Programming" in C. A. R. Hoare, R. H. Perrot (Eds.) *Operating Systems Techniques,* Academic Press, New York, 61–71.

Hoare, C. A. R. (1978) "Communicating Sequential Processes." *Comm ACM* 21(8), 666–677.

Hoare, C. A. R. (1985) *Communicating Sequential Processes.* Prentice–Hall, Englewood-Cliffs, N.J.

Hoare, C. A. R., and Shepherdson, J. C. (Eds.) (1985) *Mathematical Logic and Programming Languages.* Prentice–Hall, Englewood-Cliffs, N.J.

Hoare, C. A. R., and Wirth, N. (1973) "An Axiomatic Definition of the Programming Language Pascal." *Acta Inf* 2, 335–355.

Hockney, R. W. (1981) "A Structural Taxonomy of Computers." In Blaauw and Händler (1981), 77–92.

Hoevel, L. W. (1974) "Ideal Directly Executed Languages: An Analytical Argument for Emulation." *IEEE Trans Comput* C-23(8), 759–767.

Hoevel, L. W., and Wallach, W. A. (1975) "A Tale of Three Emulators." Computer Systems Laboratory, Technical Report TR-98, Stanford University, Stanford, Calif.

Hopcroft, J. E., and Ullman, J. D. (1969) *Formal Languages and their Relation to Automata.* Addison–Wesley, Reading, Mass.

Hopkins, M. (1983). "A Perspective on Microcode." *Proceedings of COMPCON 83* (Spring), IEEE, New York, 108–110.

Hopkins, W. C., Horton, M. J., and Arnold, C. S. (1985) "Target-Independent High-Level Microprogramming." *Proceedings of the 18th Annual Workshop on Microprogramming.* IEEE Computer Society Press, Los Angeles, 137–144.

Hord, R. M. (1982) *ILLIAC IV: The First Supercomputer.* Computer Science Press, Rockville, Md.

Horning, J. J., and Randell, B. (1973) "Process Structuring," *ACM Comp Surv* 5(1), 5–30.

Horowitz, E., and Sahni, S. (1978) *Fundamentals of Computer Algorithms.* Computer Science Press, Rockville, Md.

Huffman, D. A. (1952) "A Method for the Construction of Minimum Redundancy Codes." *Proc IRE* 40 (Sept.), 1098–1101.

Husson, S. S. (1970) *Microprogramming: Principles and Practices.* Prentice–Hall, Englewood-Cliffs, N.J.

Hwang, K. (Ed.) (1984) *Tutorial on Supercomputers: Design and Applications.* IEEE Computer Society Press, Los Alamitos, Calif.

Hwang, K., and Briggs, F. (1984) *Computer Architecture and Parallel Processing.* McGraw–Hill, New York.

Hwang, K., Su, S.-P., and Ni, L. M. (1981) "Vector Computer Architecture and Processing Techniques." In M. C. Yovits (Ed.) *Advances in Computers,* Vol. 20, Academic Press, New York, 116–199.

Ibbett, R. (1982) *High Performance Computer Systems.* Springer-Verlag, Heidelberg.

IBM (1981) *IBM System/370 Principles of Operation.* GA 22-7000-8, IBM Corp., White Plains, N.Y.

Iliffe, J. K. (1968) *Basic Machine Principles,* McDonald/American Elsevier, London, (2nd edition, 1972).

INMOS Ltd. (1984) *Occam Programming Manual.* Prentice–Hall, Englewood-Cliffs, N.J.

Intel Corporation (1981) *The iAPX-432 GDP Architecture Reference Manual.* Santa Clara, Calif.

Intermetrics (1984a) *VHDL Language Requirements.* Technical Report IR-MD-020-1, Intermetrics, Bethesda, Md.

Intermetrics (1984b) *VHDL User's Manual.* Vols. 1–3. Technical Report IR-MD-029, Intermetrics, Bethesda, Md.

Intermetrics (1984c) *VHDL Language Reference Manual.* Technical Report IR-MD-025-1, Intermetrics, Bethesda, Md.

Isoda, S., Kobayashi, Y., and Ishida, T. (1983) "Global Compaction of Horizontal Microprograms Based on the Generalized Data Dependency Graph." *IEEE Trans Comput* C-32(10), 922–931.

Iverson, K. E. (1962) *A Programming Language.* Wiley, New York.

Jensen, K., and Wirth, N. (1975) *Pascal: User Manual and Report,* 2nd ed. Springer-Verlag, Berlin.

Johnson, D., *et al.* (1980) "Automatic Partitioning of Programs in Multiprocessor Systems." *Proceedings of IEEE COMPCON,* IEEE Press, New York, 175–178.

Johnson, P. M. (1978) "An Introduction to Vector Processing." *Computer Design* (Feb.), 89–97.

Johnson, S. C. (1978) "A Portable C Compiler: Theory and Practice." *Proceed-*

ings of the 5th Annual Symposium on Programming Language, ACM, New York, 97–104.

Jones, A. K., and Schwarz, P. (1980) "Experience Using Multiprocessor Systems—A Status Report." *ACM Comp Surv* 12(2), 121–165.

Jones, C. B. (1980) *Software Development: A Rigorous Approach.* Prentice–Hall, Englewood-Cliffs, N.J.

Jones, J. C. (1980) *Design Methods: Seeds of Human Future,* 2nd ed. Wiley, New York.

Jones, J. C. (1984) *Essays in Design.* Wiley, New York.

Jordan, H. F. (1985) "HEP Architecture, Programming and Performance." In Kowalik (1985) 1–40.

Jordan, T. L. (1982) "A Guide to Parallel Computation and Some Cray-1 Experiences." In Rodrigue (1982) 1–50.

Karp, R. M., and Miller, R. E. (1966) "Properties of a Model for Parallel Computations: Determinacy, Termination, Queueing," *SIAM J Appl Math* 14(6), 1390–1411.

Katevenis, M. G. H. (1985) *Reduced Instruction Set Computer Architectures for VLSI.* MIT Press, Cambridge, Mass.

Katz, D. (1983) "VLSI Gate Arrays and CAD Methods." In Rabbat (1983) 139–151.

Katzman, J. A. (1977) "The Tandem 16: A Fault Tolerant Computing System." Tandem Computers Inc., Cupertino, Calif. Reprinted in Siewiorek, Bell, and Newell (1982) 470–480.

Kautz, W. H. (1971) "Programmable Cellular Logic." In Mukhopadhay (1971), 369–421.

Kavi, K., and Cragon, H. G. (1983) "A Conceptual Framework for the Description and Classification of Computer Architectures." *Proceedings of the IEEE International Workshop on Computer Systems Organization* IEEE Computer Society Press, New York, 10–19.

Kawakami, K., and Gurd, J. R. (1986) "A Scalable Dataflow Storage." *Proceedings of the 13th International Symposium on Computer Architectural.* IEEE Computer Society Press, Los Alamitos, Calif., 243–250.

Keedy, J. L. (1978a) "On the Use of Stacks in the Evaluation of Expressions." *SIGARCH Comp Arch News* 6(6), 22–28.

Keedy, J. L. (1978b) "On the Evaluation of Expressions Using Accumulators, Stacks, and Store-Store Instructions." *SIGARCH Comp Arch News* 7(4), 24–28.

Keedy, J. L. (1979) "More on the Use of Stacks in the Evaluation of Expressions." *SIGARCH Comp Arch News* 7(8), 18–23.

Keller, R. M. (1975) "Lookahead Processors." *ACM Comp Surv* 7(4), 177–196.

Kernighan, B. W., and Ritchie, D. M. (1978) *The C Programming Language.* Prentice–Hall, Englewood-Cliffs, N.J.

Kershew, D. (1982) "Solution of Single Tridiagonal Linear Systems and Vectorization of the ICCG Algorithm on the CRAY-1." In Rodrigue (1982) 85–100.

Kilburn, T., Edwards, D. B. G., Lanigan, M. J., *et al.* (1962) "One Level Storage System." *Trans IRE* EC-11(2), 223–235. Reprinted in Bell and Newell (1971) 276–290.

Kilburn, T., Morris, D., Rohl, J. S., and Summer, F. H. (1969) "A System Design Proposal." *Information Processing 68* (Proceedings of the IFIP Congress, 1968), North-Holland, Amsterdam, 806–811.

Klassen, A., and Dasgupta, S. (1981) "S*(QM-1): An Instantiation of the High Level Language Schema S* for the Nanodata QM-1." *Proceedings of the 14th Annual Workshop on Microprogramming.* ACM/IEEE, New York, 126–130.

Kleir, R. L., and Ramamoorthy, C. V. (1971) "Optimization Strategies for Microprograms." *IEEE Trans Comput* C-20(7), 783–795.

Knuth, D. E. (1968) *The Art of Computer Programming: Volume 1: Fundamental Algorithms.* Addison–Wesley, Reading, Mass.

Knuth, D. E. (1971) "An Empirical Study of FORTRAN Programs." *Software —Practice and Experience.* 1, 105–133.

Knuth, D. E., and Rao, G. S. (1975) "Activity in Interleaved Memory." *IEEE Trans Comput* C-24(9), 943–944.

Kogge, P. M. (1981) *The Architecture of Pipelined Computers.* McGraw–Hill, New York.

Kohavi, Z. (1982) *Switching and Finite Automata Theory,* 2nd ed. McGraw–Hill, New York.

Kornerup, P., and Shriver, B. D. (1975) "An Overview of the MATHILDA System." *ACM SIGMICRO Newsletter,* 5(4), 25–53.

Kowalik, J. S. (Ed.) (1985) *Parallel MIMD Computations: HEP Supercomputer and Its Applications.* MIT Press, Cambridge, Mass.

Kuck, D. J. (1968) "ILLIAC IV Software and Application Programming." *IEEE Trans Comput* C-17, 758–770.

Kuck, D. J. (1976) "Parallel Processing of Ordinary Programs." In M. Rubinoff and M. C. Yovits (Eds.) *Advances in Computers,* Vol. 15. Academic Press, New York, 119–179.

Kuck, D. J. (1977) "A Survey of Parallel Machine Organization and Programming." *ACM Comp Surv* 9(1), 29–60.

Kuck, D. J. (1978) *The Structure of Computers and Computation,* Vol. 1. Wiley, New York.

Kuck, D. J., Kuhn, R. H., Leasure, B., *et al.* (1980) "The Structure of an Advanced Retargetable Vectorizer." *Proceedings of COMPSAC 80.,* IEEE Computer Society.

Kuck, D. J., Kuhn, R. H., Padua, D., *et al.* (1981) "Dependence Graphs and Compiler Organization." *Proceedings of the 8th Annual ACM Symposium on Principles of Programming Languages.* Williamsburg, Va., 207–218.

Kuck, D. J., Lawrie, D., Cytron, R., *et al.* (1986) "Cedar Project." In Metropolis *et al.* (1986) 97–123.

Kuck, D. J., Lawrie, D. H., and Sameh, A. (Eds.) (1977) *High Speed Computer and Algorithm Organization.* Academic Press, New York.

Kuck, D. J. and Stokes, R. A. (1982) "The Burroughs Scientific Processor (BSP)." *IEEE Trans Comput* C-31(5), 363–376.

Kuhn, T. S. (1970) *The Structure of Scientific Revolutions,* 2nd ed. University of Chicago Press, Chicago.

Kung, H. T. (1979) "Let's Design Algorithms for VLSI Systems." Technical Report, Department of Computer Science, Carnegie-Mellon University, Pittsburgh.

Kung, H. T. (1982) "Why Systolic Architectures?" *Computer* 15(1), 37–46.

Kung, H. T., and Leiserson, C. E. (1980) "Highly Concurrent Systems." Mead and Conway (1980) Chapter 8.

Kung, H. T., Sproull, R., and Steele, G. (1981) *VLSI Systems and Computations.* Computer Science Press, Rockville, Md.

Kunkel, S. R., and Smith, J. E. (1986) "Optimal Pipelining in Supercomputers." *Proceedings of the 13th International Symposium on Computer Architecture* IEEE Computer Society Press, Washington, D.C. 404–411.

Lah, J., and Atkins, D. E. (1983) "Tree Compaction of Microprograms." *Proceedings of the 16th Annual Workshop on Microprogramming.* IEEE Computer Society Press, Los Angeles, Calif. 23–33.

Landskov, D., Davidson, S., Shriver, B. D., *et al.* (1980) "Local Microcode Compaction Techniques." *ACM Comp Surv* 12(3), 261–294.

Lang, T., Valero, M., and Alegre, J. (1982) "Bandwidth of Crossbar and Multiple-Bus Connections for Multiprocessors." *IEEE Trans Comput* C-31(12), 1227–1233.

Lattin, W. W., Bayliss, J. A., Budde, D. L., *et al.* (1981) "A 32b VLSI Micromainframe Computer System." *Proceedings of the 1981 IEEE International Solid State Circuits Conference,* 110–111.

Lavington, S. H. (1978) "The Manchester Mark I and Atlas: A Historical Perspective." *Comm ACM* 21(1), 4–12.

Lawrie, D. H. (1975) "Access and Alignment of Data in an Array Processor." *IEEE Trans Comput* C-24(12), 1145–1155.

Lawrie, D. H., Layman, T., Baer, D., *et al.* (1975) "Glypnir—A Programming Language for ILLIAC IV." *Comm ACM* 18(3), 157–164.

Lawson, B. (1980) *How Designers Think: The Design Process Demystified.* Architectural Press, London.

Lawson, H. W. (1968) "Programming Language Oriented Instruction Streams." *IEEE Trans Comput* C-17, 476–485.

Lawson, H. W., and Malm, B. (1973) "A Flexible Asynchronous Microprocessor." *BIT* 13, 165–176.

Lawson, H. W., and Smith, B. K. (1971) "Functional Characteristics of a Multilingual Processor." *IEEE Trans Comput* C-20(7), 732–742.

Lee, F. S., Long, S. I., Zucca, R., *et al.* (1983) "VLSI Gallium Arsenide Technology." In Rabbat (1983) 257–295.

Lehman, M. M. (1974) "Programs, Cities, Students—Limits to Growth." Inaugural Lecture Series, Vol. 9., Imperial College of Science and Technology, London. Also in D. G. Gries (1978), 42–69.

Lehman, M. M. (1984) "Program Evolution." *Info Proc Mgmt* 20(1–2, 19–36.

Leiserson, C. E. (1983) *Area-Efficient VLSI Computation.* MIT Press, Cambridge, Mass.

Leung, C. K. C. (1979) "ADL: An Architecture Description Language for Packet Communication Systems." *Proceedings of the 4th International Symposium on Computer Hardware Description Languages.* IEEE Computer Society, New York, 6–13.

Leung, C. K. C. (1981) "On a Topdown Design Methodology for Packet Systems." In M. A. Breuer and R. Hartenstein (Eds.) *Computer Hardware Description Languages and their Applications.* North Holland, Amsterdam, 171–184.

Levitt, K., Robinson, L., and Silverberg, B. A. (1979) *The HDM Handbook,* SRI International, Menlo Park, Calif.

Levy, H. M. (1984) *Capability-Based Computer Systems.* Digital Press, Bedford, Mass.

Lewis, T. G., Malik, K., and Ma, P.-Y. (1980) "Firmware Engineering Using a High Level Microprogramming System to Implement Virtual Instruction Set Processors." In G. Chroust and J. Mulbacher (Eds.) *Firmware, Microprogramming, and Restructurable Hardware,* North-Holland, Amsterdam, 65–88.

Lieberherr, K. J. (1984) "Towards a Standard Hardware Description Language." *Proceedings of the 21st ACM/IEEE Design Automation Conference.* Albuquerque, N.M., (June), 265–272.

Lim, W. Y-P. (1982) "HISDL—A Structure Description Language." *Comm ACM* 25(11), 823–830.

Lim, Y-P., and Leung, C. K. C. (1983) "PADL—A Packet Architecture Description Language," In T. Uehara and M. R. Barbacci (eds.) *Computer Hardware Description Languages and their Applications* (Proceedings of the 6th International Symposium). North-Holland, Amsterdam, 233–242.

Lincoln, N. R. (1986) "Great Gigaflops and Giddy Guarantees." In Metropolis, *et al.* (1986) 16–24.

Linger, R. C., Mills, H. D., and Witt, B. I. (1979) *Structured Programming.* Addison–Wesley, Reading, Mass.

Linn, J. L. (1983) "SRDAG Compaction: A Generalization of Trace Scheduling." *Proceedings of the 16th Annual Workshop on Microprogramming.* IEEE Computer Society Press, Los Angeles, Calif., 11–22.

Liptay, J. S. (1968) "Structural Aspects of System 360/85: The Cache." *IBM Sys J* 7, 15–21.

Liskov, B. (1980) "Modular Program Construction Using Abstractions." In D. Bjorner (Ed.) *Abstract Software Specifications.* Springer-Verlag, Berlin, 354–389.

Liskov, B., and Berzins, V. (1979) "An Appraisal of Program Specifications." In Wegner (1979) 276–301.

Lonergan, W., and King, P. (1961) "Design of the B5000 System." *Datamation* 7(5), 28–32.

Lubeck, O., Moore, J., and Mendez, R. (1985) "A Benchmark Comparison of Three Supercomputers: Fujitsu VP-2000, Hitachi 5810/20, CRAY X-MP/2." *Computer* 18(12), 10–24.

Lucas, P., and Walk, K. (1969) "On the Formal Description of PL/1." *Ann Rev Autom Prog* 6(3), 105–181.

Lunde, A. (1977) "Empirical Evaluation of Some Features of Instruction Set Processor Architectures." *Comm ACM* 20(3), 143–152.

Ma, P.-Y., and Lewis, T. G. (1980) "Design of a Machine Independent Optimizing System for Emulator Development." *ACM Trans Prog Lang Syst* 2(2), 239–262.

Ma, P.-Y., and Lewis, T. G. (1981) "On the Design of a Microcode Compiler for a Machine Independent High Level Language." *IEEE Trans Soft Eng* (May), 261–274.

Madnick, S. E., and Donovan, J. J. (1974) *Operating Systems.* McGraw–Hill, New York.

Mallach, E. (1975) "Emulation Architecture." *Computer* 8(8), 24–32.

Mallach, E., and Sondak, N. (Eds.) (1983) *Advances in Microprogramming.* Artech House, Dedham, Mass.

Manville, W. D. (1973) "Microprogramming Support for Programming Languages." Ph.D. Thesis, Computer Laboratory, University of Cambridge, U.K.

Marathe, M. (1977) "Performance Evaluation at the Hardware Architecture Level and the Operating System Kernel Design Level." Ph.D. Dissertation, Department of Computer Science, Carnegie-Mellon University, Pittsburgh, Pa.

March, L. (Ed.) (1976) *The Architecture of Form.* Cambridge University Press, Cambridge, England.

Marcus, L., Crocker, S. D. and Landauer, J. R. (1984) "SDVS: A System for Verifying Microcode Correctness." *Proceedings of the 17th Annual Microprogramming Workshop.* IEEE Computer Society Press, Los Alamitos, Calif. 246–256.

Marsland, T. A., and Demco, J. (1978) "A Case Study of Computer Emulation." *INFOR* (Canada) 16(2), 112–131.

Maruyama, F., and Fujita, M. (1985) "Hardware Verification." *Computer* 18(2), 22–32.

Marwedel, P. (1984) "A Retargetable Compiler for a High Level Microprogramming Language." *Proceedings of the 17th Annual Microprogramming Workshop.* IEEE Computer Society Press, Los Alamitos, Calif. 267–274.

Marwedel, P. (1985) "The MIMOLA Design System: A System Which Spans Several Levels." In Giloi and Shriver (1985) 223–238.

Masson, G. M., Gingher, G. C., and Nakamura, S. (1979) "A Sampler of Circuit Switching Networks." *Computer* 12(6), 32–48.

Matick, R. E. (1977) *Computer Storage Systems and Technology.* Wiley, New York.

Matick, R. E. (1980) "Memory and Storage." In Stone (1980) 205–274.

Mattson, R. L., Gecsei, J., Slutz, D. L., *et al.* (1970) "Evaluation Techniques for Storage Hierarchies." *IBM Sys J* 9(2), 78–117.

Mayr, E. (1969) *Principles of Systematic Zoology.* McGraw–Hill, New York.

Mayr, E. (1982) *The Growth of Biological Thought: Diversity, Evolution, and Inheritance.* Harvard University Press, Cambridge, Mass.

McGraw, J. R. (1982) "The VAL Language: Description and Analysis." *ACM Trans Prog Lang Syst* 4(1), 44–82.

McGraw, J. R., *et al.* (1983) "SISAL—Streams and Iterations in a Single

Assignment Language: Language Reference Manual." Lawrence Livermore National Laboratory, Livermore, Calif.

Mead, C. A., and Conway, L. (1980) *Introduction to VLSI Systems.* Addison–Wesley, Reading, Mass.

Melliar-Smith, P. M. (1979) "System Specification." In T. Anderson and B. Randell (Eds.) *Computing Systems Reliability.* Cambridge University Press, Cambridge, U.K.

Mendez, R. (1984) "Benchmarks on Japanese and American Supercomputers —Preliminary Results." *IEEE Trans Comput* C-33(4), 374.

Merrifield, C. W. (1879) "Report of the Committee Appointed to Consider the Advisability and to Estimate the Expense of Constructing Mr. Babbage's Analytical Machine and of Printing Tables by its Means." Reprinted in Randell (1975).

Metropolis, N., Sharp, D. H., Worlton, W. J., *et al.* (Eds.) (1986) *Frontiers of Supercomputing.* University of California Press, Berkeley, Calif.

Metropolis, N., and Worlton, J. (1980) "A Trilogy on Errors in the History of Computing" *Annals Hist Comp* 2(1), 49–59

Microdata (1970) *Microprogramming Handbook,* 2nd ed. Microdata Corporation, Santa Ana, Calif.

Millman, J., and Halkias, C. C. (1972) *Integrated Electronics.* McGraw–Hill, New York.

Mills, H. D. (1972) "Mathematical Foundations for Structured Programming." Internal Report, IBM Corporation. Reprinted in H. D. Mills, *Software Productivity.* Little, Brown & Co., Boston, 1983.

Millstein, R. E. (1973) "Control Structures in ILLIAC IV FORTRAN." *Comm ACM* 16(10), 622–627.

Minnick, R. C. (1967) "A Survey of Microcellular Research." *J ACM* 14, 203–241.

Monolithic Memories (1982) *Bipolar LSI Data Book,* 4th ed. Monolithic Memories, Sunnyvale, Calif.

Moore, G. E. (1979) "VLSI: Some Fundamental Challenges." *IEEE Spectrum* (April), 30–37.

Morris, D., and Ibbett, R. (1979) *The MU5 Computer Systems.* Macmillan, London.

Morris, F. L., and Jones, C. B. (1984) "An Early Program Proof by Alan Turing." *Annals Hist Comp* 6(2), 139–143.

Morris, J. B. (1972) "Demand Paging through Utilization of Working Sets on the MANIAC II." *Comm ACM* 15(10), 867–872.

Morse, S. P., Ravenal, B. W., Mazor, S., *et al.* (1978) "Intel Microprocessors: 8008 to 8086," Intel Corporation, Aloha, Or. Reprinted in Siewiorek, Bell, and Newell (1982), 615–642.

Mostow, J. (1985) "Models of the Design Process." *AI Magazine* (Spring), 44–57.

Moszkowski, B. (1985) "A Temporal Logic for Multilevel Reasoning about Hardware." *Computer* 18(2), 10–19.

Moszkowski, B. (1986) *Executing Temporal Logic Programs,* Cambridge University Press, Cambridge, England.

Moto-oka, T. (Ed.) (1982) *Fifth Generation Computer Systems,* North-Holland, Amsterdam.

Mudge, T. N., Hayes, J. P., Buzzard, G. D., *et al.* (1984) "Analysis of Multiple-bus Interconnection Networks." *Proceedings of the International Conference on Parallel Processing.* IEEE, August, 228–232.

Mudge, T. N., Hayes, J. P., Buzzard, G. D., *et al.* (1986) "Analysis of Multiple Bus Interconnection Networks." *J Parall Dist Comp* 3(3), 328–343.

Mudge, T. N., Hayes, J. P., and Winsor, D. C. (1987) "Multiple Bus Architectures." *Computer,* 20(6), 42–48.

Mueller, R. A. (1984) *Automated Microcode Synthesis.* UMI Research Press, Ann Arbor, Mi.

Mueller, R. A., and Duda, M. R. (1986) "Formal Methods of Microcode Verification and Synthesis." *IEEE Software* 3(4), 38–48.

Mueller, R. A., and Varghese, J. (1985) "Knowledge Based Code Selection Methods in Retargetable Microcode Synthesis." *IEEE Design Test* 2(3), 44–55.

Mukhopadhay, A. (Ed.) (1971) *Recent Developments in Switching Theory.* Academic Press, New York.

Mukhopadhay, A., and Stone, H. S. (1971) "Programmable Cellular Logic." In Mukhopadhay (1971), 256–315.

Muroga, S. (1982) *VLSI System Design.* Wiley, New York.

Myers, G. J. (1977) "The Case Against Stack-Oriented Instruction Sets." *SIGARCH Comp Arch News* 6(3), 7–10.

Myers, G. J. (1978a) Letter to the Editor. *SIGARCH Comp Arch News* 6(8), 25–26.

Myers, G. J. (1978b) "The Evaluation of Expressions in a Storage-Storage Architecture." *SIGARCH Comp Arch News* 6(9), 20–23.

Myers, G. J. (1980) *Digital System Design with LSI Bit-Slice Logic.* Wiley, New York.

Myers, G. J. (1982) *Advances in Computer Architecture.* Wiley, New York.

Nagle, A., Cloutier, R., and Parker, A. C. (1982) "Synthesis of Hardware for the Control of Digital Systems." *IEEE Trans CAD,* CAD-1(4), 201–212.

Nanodata (1979) *The QM-1 Hardware Level User's Manual.* Nanodata Corporation, Williamsburg, N.Y.

Naur, P. (Ed.) (1963) "Revised Report on the Algorithmic Language Algol 60." *Numerische Mathematik* 4, 420–453.

Neuhauser, C. J. (1977) "Emmy System Processor—Principles of Operation." Computer System Laboratory Technical Note TN-114, Stanford University, Stanford, Calif.

Neuhauser, C. J. (1980) "Analysis of the PDP-11 Instruction Stream." Technical Report 183, Computer System Laboratory, Stanford University, Stanford, Calif.

Northcutt, J. D. (1980) "High Level Fault Insertion and Simulation with ISPS."

Proceedings of the 17th Design Automation Conference. ACM/IEEE, Minneapolis, June.

Noyce, R., and Hoff, M. (1981) "A History of Microprocessor Development at Intel." *IEEE Micro* 1(1), 8–22.

Oakley, J. D. (1979) "Symbolic Execution of Formal Machine Descriptions." Technical Report Department of Computer Science, Carnegie-Mellon University, Pittsburgh, Pa.

Olafsson, M. (1981) "The QM-C: A C-Oriented Instruction Set Architecture for the Nanodata QM-1." Technical Report TR81-11, Department of Computer Science University of Alberta, Edmonton, Alberta, Canada.

Opderbeck, H., and Chu, W. W. (1974) "Performance of the Page Fault Frequency Replacement Algorithm in a Multiprogramming Environment." *Information Processing 74* (Proceedings of the IFIP Congress, 1974), North-Holland, Amsterdam, 235–241.

Opler, A. (1967) "Fourth Generation Software." *Datamation* 13(1), 22–24.

Organick, E. I. (1972) *The Multics System: An Examination of Its Structure.* MIT Press, Cambridge, Mass.

Organick, E. I. (1973) *Computer Systems Organization: The B5700/B6700 Series.* Academic Press, New York.

Organick, E. I., and Hinds, J. A. (1978) *Interpreting Machines: Architecture and Programming of the B1700/B1800 Series.* North-Holland, New York.

Owicki, S., and Gries, D. G. (1976) "An Axiomatic Proof Technique for Parallel Programs." *Acta Informatica* 6, 319–340.

Papamarcos, M. S., and Patel, J. H. (1984) "A Low Overhead Solution for Multiprocessors with Private Cache Memories." *Proceedings of the 11th International Symposium on Computer Architecture,* IEEE Computer Society Press, Los Alamitos, Calif. 348–354.

Parke, F. I. (1979) "An Introduction to the N.mPC Design Environment." *Proceedings of the 16th Design Automation Conference.* (June), 513–519.

Parker, A. C. (1984) "Automated Synthesis of Digital Systems." *IEEE Design and Test of Computers.* 1(4), 75–81.

Parker, A. C., Thomas, D. E., Crocker, S. D., *et al.* (1979) "ISPS: A Retrospective View." *Proceedings of the 4th International Symposium on Computer Hardware Description Languages and Their Applications.* IEEE, New York, 21–27.

Parker, A. C., and Wallace, J. J. (1981) "An I/O Hardware Description Language." *IEEE Trans Comput* C-30(6), 423–428.

Parnas, D. L. (1972) "On the Criteria to be Used in Decomposing Systems into Modules." *Comm ACM* 5(12), 1053–1058.

Parnas, D. L. (1977) "The Use of Precise Specifications in the Development of Software." In B. Gilchrist (Ed.) *Information Processing 77* (Proceedings of the IFIP Congress). North-Holland, Amsterdam, 861–868.

Parnas, D. L., and Darringer, J. A. (1967) "SODAS and a Methodology for System Design." AFIPS Fall Joint Computer Conference. AFIPS Press, Montvale, N.J., Vol. 31, 449–474.

Patel, J. H. (1981) "Performance of Processor-Memory Interconnections for Multiprocessors." *IEEE Trans Comput* C-30(10), 771–780.

Patnaik, L. M., Govindarajan, R., and Ramadoss, N. S. (1986) "Design and Performance Evaluation of EXMAN: An Extended MANchester Data Flow Computer." *IEEE Trans Comput* C-35(3), 229–244.

Patt, Y. N., Hwu, W-M., and Shebanow, M. (1985a) "HPS: A New Microarchitecture: Rationale and Introduction." *Proceedings of the 18th Annual Workshop on Microprogramming.* IEEE Computer Society Press, Washington, D.C., 103–108.

Patt, Y. N., Melvin, S. W., Hwu, W-M., *et al.* (1985b) "Critical Issues Regarding HPS, A High Performance Microarchitecture." *Proceedings of the 18th Annual Workshop on Microprogramming.* IEEE Computer Society Press, Washington, D.C., 109–116.

Patterson, D. A. (1976) "STRUM: Structured Programming System for Correct Firmware." *IEEE Trans Comput* C-25(10), 974–985.

Patterson, D. A. (1981) "An Experiment in High Level Language Microprogramming and Verification." *Comm ACM* 24(10), 699–709.

Patterson, D. A. (1985) "Reduced Instruction Set Computers." *Comm ACM* 28(1), 8–21.

Patterson, D. A., and Dietzel, D. (1980) "The Case for the Reduced Instruction Set Computer." *Computer Architecture News (SIGARCH)* 8(6), 25–33.

Patterson, D. A., Lew, K., and Tuck, R. (1979) "Towards an Efficient Machine Independent Language for Microprogramming." *Proceedings of the 12th Annual Workshop on Microprogramming.* ACM/IEEE, New York, 22–35.

Patterson, D. A., and Piepho, R. (1982) "RISC Assessment: A High Level Language Experiment." *Proceedings of the 9th Annual Symposium on Computer Architecture* IEEE Computer Society Press, Los Angeles, Calif., 3–8.

Patterson, D. A., and Sequin, C. (1980) "Design Considerations for Single-Chip Computers of the Future." *IEEE Trans Comput* C-29(2), 108–116.

Patterson, D. A., and Sequin, C. (1981) "RISC I: A Reduced Instruction Set Computer." *Proceedings of the 8th Annual International Symposium on Computer Architecture* IEEE Computer Society Press, 443–458.

Patterson, D. A., and Sequin, C. (1982) "A VLSI RISC." *Computer* 15(9), 8–21.

Perrott, R. H. (1979) "A Language for Array and Vector Processors." *ACM Trans Prog Lang Syst* 1(2), 177–195.

Perrott, R. H., and Zarea-Aliabadi, A. (1986) "Supercomputer Languages." *ACM Comp Surv* 18(1), 5–22.

Petri, C. A. (1962) "Kommunikation mit Automaten," Ph.D. Dissertation, University of Bonn, Bonn, West Germany.

Peuto, B., and Shustek, L. J. (1977) "An Instruction Timing Model of CPU Performance." *Proceedings of the 4th Annual Symposium on Computer Architecture.* ACM/IEEE, New York, 165–178.

Pevsner, N. (1963) *An Outline of European Architecture.* Penguin Books, London.

Pfister, G. F., Brantley, W. C., George, D. A., *et al.* (1985) "The IBM Research

Parallel Processor Prototype (RP3): Introduction and Architecture." *Proceedings of the 1985 International Conference on Parallel Processing* (Aug.), 764–771.

Piloty, R., Barbacci, M. R., Borrione, D., *et al.* (1983) *CONLAN Report,* Lecture Notes in Computer Science, No. 151, Springer-Verlag, Berlin.

Pohm, A. V. (1984) "High Speed Memory Systems." *Computer* 18(10), 162–172.

Popper, K. R. (1965) *Conjectures and Refutations: The Growth of Scientific Knowledge.* Harper & Row, New York.

Popper, K. R. (1968) *The Logic of Scientific Discovery.* Harper & Row, New York.

Popper, K. R. (1972) *Objective Knowledge: An Evolutionary Approach.* Clarendon Press, Oxford, U.K.

Rabbat, G. (Ed.) (1983) *Hardware and Software Concepts in VLSI.* Van Nostrand-Rheinhold, New York.

Radin, G. (1982) "The 801 Minicomputer." *Proceedings of the ACM Symposium on Architectural Support for Programming Languages and Operating Systems.* ACM, New York, 39–47.

Rakoczi, L. L. (1969) "The Computer-Within-a-Computer, A Fourth Generation Concept." *IEEE Comp Group News.* 3(2), 14.

Ramamoorthy, C. V., and Li, H. F. (1977) "Pipeline Architecture." *ACM Comp Surv* 9(1), 61–102.

Randell, B. (1969) "A Note on Storage Fragmentation and Program Segmentation." *Comm ACM* 12(7), 365–369.

Randell, B. (Ed.) (1975) *Origins of Digital Computers.* Springer-Verlag, New York.

Randell, B., and Russell, L. J. (1964). *Algol 60 Implementation.* Academic Press, New York.

Rau, B. R. (1979) "Interleaved Memory Bandwidth in a Model of a Multiprocessor System." *IEEE Trans Comput* C-28(9), 678–681.

Rauscher, T. G., and Adams, P. N. (1980) "Microprogramming: A Tutorial and Survey of Recent Developments." *IEEE Trans Comput* C-29(1), 2–19.

Reddaway, S. F. (1973) "DAP—A Distributed Array Processor." *Proceedings of the 1st Annual Symposium on Computer Architecture.* ACM/IEEE, New York.

Redfield, S. R. (1971) "A Study in Microprogrammed Processors: A Medium Sized Microprogrammed Processor." *IEEE Trans Comput* C-20(7), 743–750.

Rennels, D. A. (1978) "Reconfigurable Modular Computer Networks for Spacecraft On-Board Processing." *Computer* 11(7), 49–59.

Rice, R. (Ed.) (1980) *VLSI: The Coming Revolution in Applications and Design.* IEEE Computer Society, New York.

Rice, R. (Ed.) (1982) *VLSI Support Technologies: Computer-Aided Design, Testing, and Packaging.* IEEE Computer Society Press, Los Alamitos, Calif.

Rideout, D. J. (1981) "Considerations for Local Compaction of Nanocode for the Nanodata QM-1." *Proceedings of the 14th Annual Workshop on Microprogramming.* ACM/IEEE, New York, 205–214.

Riganati, J. P., and Schneck, P. B. (1984) "Supercomputing." *Computer* 17(10), 97–113.

Robertson, E. L. (1979) "Microcode Bit Optimization is NP-Complete." *IEEE Trans Comp,* C-28(4), 316–319.

Robinson, L., Levitt, K. N., Neumann, P. G., *et al.* (1977) "A Formal Methodology for the Design of Operating System Software." In R. T. Yeh (Ed.) *Current Trends in Programming Methodology, Vol. I, Software Specification and Design.* Prentice–Hall, Englewood-Cliffs, N.J., 61–110.

Rodrigue, G. (Ed.) (1982) *Parallel Computations.* Academic Press, New York.

Rodriguez, J. E. (1969) "A Graph Model for Parallel Computation." Report MAC-TR-64, Project MAC, Massachusetts Institute of Technology, Cambridge, Mass.

Rose, C. W., Ordy, G. M., and Drongowski, P. (1984) "N.mPC: A Study in University-Industry Technology Transfer." *IEEE Design Test* 1(1), 44–56.

Rosenberg, A. L. (1981) "Three Dimensional Integrated Circuitry." In Kung, Sproull, and Steele (1981), 69–80.

Rosin, R. F. (1969a) "Supervisory and Monitor Systems." *ACM Comp Surv* 1(1), 37–54.

Rosin, R. F. (1969b) "Contemporary Concepts of Microprogramming and Emulation." *ACM Comp Surv* 1(4), 197–212.

Rosin, R. F. (1974) "The Significance of Microprogramming." *Proceedings of the International Computer Symposium 1973.* North-Holland, Amsterdam.

Rosin, R. F., Frieder, G., and Eckhouse, R. H. (1972) "An Environment for Research in Microprogramming and Emulation." *Comm ACM* 15(8), 748–760.

Ross, D. T. (1977) "Structured Analysis (SA): A Language for Communicating Ideas." *IEEE Trans Soft Eng,* SE-3(1), 16–34.

Ross, H. H. (1974) *Biological Systematics.* Addison–Wesley, Reading, Mass.

Rumbaugh, J. (1977) "A Dataflow Multiprocessor." *IEEE Trans Comput* C-26(2), 138–146.

Ruse, M. (1973) *The Philosophy of Biology.* Hutchinson University Library, London.

Russell, R. M. (1978) "The CRAY-1 Computer System." *Comm ACM* 21(1), 63–72.

Rutihauser, H. (1967) *Description of Algol 60.* Springer-Verlag, Berlin.

Rymarczyk, J. (1982) "Coding Guidelines for Pipelined Processors." *Proceedings of the ACM Symposium on Architectural Support for Programming Languages and Operating Systems,* ACM, New York, 12–19.

Salisbury, A. B. (1976) *Microprogrammable Computer Architectures.* Elsevier, New York.

Sameh, A. H. (1977) "Numerical Parallel Algorithms—A Survey." In Kuck, Lawrie, and Sameh (1977) 207–228.

Samelson, K., and Bauer, F. L. (1959) "Sequential Formula Translation." *Comm ACM* 3(2), 76–83.

Samudrala, S., Lo, C., Brown, J, F. III, *et al.* (1984) "Design Verification of a VLSI VAX Microcomputer." *Proceedings of the 17th Annual Workshop on Microprogramming.* IEEE Computer Society Press, Silver Spring, Md, 59–63.

Sargeant, J., and Kirkham, C. C. (1986) "Stored Data Structures on the Manchester Dataflow Machine." *Proceedings of the 13th International Symposium on Computer Architecture.* IEEE Computer Society Press, Los Alamitos, Calif., 235–242.

Satyanarayanan, M. (1980) *Multiprocessors: A Comparative Survey.* Prentice–Hall, Englewood-Cliffs, N.J.

Scherlis, W. L. and Scott, D. S. (1983) "First Steps Towards Inferential Programming." In R. E. A. Mason (Ed.) *Information Processing 83* (Proceedings of the IFIP Congress), North-Holland, Amsterdam, 199–212.

Schlaeppi, H. P. (1964) "A Formal Language for Describing Machine Logic, Timing and Sequencing (LOTIS)." *IEEE Trans Comput* C-13(8), 439–448.

Schön, D. A. (1983) *The Reflective Practitioner.* Basic Books, New York.

Schwartz, S. J. (1968) "An Algorithm for Minimizing Read-Only Memories for Machine Control." *Proceedings of the IEEE 10th Annual Symposium on Switching and Automata Theory.* IEEE, New York, 28–33.

Seewaldt, T., and Estrin, G. (1985) "A Multilevel Design Procedure to Foster Functional and Informational Strength." In Giloi and Shriver (1985), 11–28.

Seitz, C. L. (1985) "The Cosmic Cube." *Comm ACM* 28(1), 22–33.

Severn, M. J. (1976) "A Minicomputer Compatible Microcomputer System: The DEC LSI-11." *Proceedings of the IEEE,* 64(6). Reprinted in Bell, Mudge, and McNamara (1978) 301–315.

Shahdad, M., Lipsett, R., Marschner, E., *et al.* (1985) "VHSIC Hardware Description Language." *Computer* 18(2), 94–104.

Sheraga, R. J., and Gieser, J. L. (1983) "Experiments in Automatic Microcode Generation." *IEEE Trans Comput* C-32(6), 557–568.

Shibayama, K., Tomita, S., Hagiwara, H., *et al.* (1980) "Performance Evaluation and Improvement of a Dynamically Microprogrammable Computer with Low Level Parallelism." *Information Processing 80* (Proceedings of the IFIP Congress). North-Holland, Amsterdam, 181–186.

Shima, M. (1979) "Demystifying Microprocessor Design." *IEEE Spectrum* (July). Reprinted in Rice (1980) 274–282.

Shostak, R. E. (1983) "Formal Verification of VLSI Designs." *Proc COMPCON* (Spring) IEEE Computer Society Press, Silver Spring, Md.

Shriver, B. D. (1978) "Firmware: The Lessons of Software Engineering." *Computer* 11(5), 19–20.

Shriver, B. D., and Kornerup, P. (1980) "A Description of the MATHILDA Processor." Technical Report DAIMI PB-52, Computer Science Department, Aarhus University, Aarhus, Denmark.

Shustek, L. J. (1978) "Analysis and Performance of Computer Instruction Sets."

Ph.D. Dissertation, Computer Systems Laboratory, Stanford University, Stanford, Calif.

Siegel, H. J. (1979) "Interconnection Networks for SIMD Machines." *Computer* 12(6), 57–65.

Siegel, H. J. (1984) *Interconnection Networks for Large Scale Parallel Processing: Theory and Case Studies.* Lexington Books, Lexington, Mass.

Siewiorek, D. P., Bell, C. G., and Newell, A. (1982) *Computer Structures: Principles and Examples.* McGraw–Hill, New York.

Siewiorek, D. P., Thomas, D. E., and Schanfeller, D. L. (1978) "The Use of LSI Modules in Computer Structures: Trends and Limitations. *Computer* 11(7), 16–25.

Simon, H. A. (1975) "Style in Design." In C. Eastman (Ed.) *Spatial Synthesis in Computer Aided Building Design.* Wiley, New York, 287–309.

Simon, H. A. (1976) *Administrative Behavior.* Free Press, New York.

Simon, H. A. (1981) *The Sciences of the Artificial,* 2nd ed. MIT Press, Cambridge, Mass.

Simon, H. A. (1982) *Models of Bounded Rationality,* Vol. 2. MIT Press, Cambridge, Mass.

Sint, M. (1980) "A Survey of High Level Microprogramming Languages." *Proceedings of the 13th Annual Workshop on Microprogramming.* IEEE Computer Society Press, New York, 141–153.

Sint, M. (1981) "MIDL — A Microinstruction Description Language." *Proceedings of the 14th Annual Microprogramming Workshop.* IEEE Computer Society Press, Los Alamitos, Calif., 95–107.

Skinner, B. F. (1974) *About Behaviorism,* Knopf, New York.

Smith, A. J. (1982) "Cache Memories." *ACM Comp Surv* 14(3), 473–529.

Snow, E. A., and Siewiorek, D. P. (1978) "Impact of Implementation Design Tradeoffs on Performance: The PDP-11, A Case Study." In Bell, Mudge, and McNamara (1978) 327–364.

Snow, E. A., and Siewiorek, D. P. (1982) "Implementation and Performance Evaluation of the PDP-11 Family." In Siewiorek, Bell, and Newell (1982) 666–679.

Snyder, L. (1982) "An Introduction to the Configurable Highly Parallel Computer." *Computer* 15(1), 47–56.

Snyder, L. (1984) "Supercomputers and VLSI: The Effect of Large Scale Integration on Computer Architecture." In M. C. Yovits (Ed.) *Advances in Computers* Vol. 23. Academic Press, New York, 1–33.

Sokal, R. R. and Sneath, P. H. A. (1963) *Principles of Numerical Taxonomy.* Freeman, San Francisco.

Sommerville, I. (1985) *Software Engineering,* 2nd ed. Addison–Wesley, Reading, Mass.

Spirn, J. R. (1977) *Program Behavior: Models and Measurements.* Elsevier, New York.

Srini, V. P., and Asenjo, J. F. (1983) "Analysis of CRAY-1 Architecture." *Proceedings of the 10th International Symposium on Computer Architecture* IEEE Computer Society Press, Los Alamitos, Calif., 194–206.

Stankovic, J. A. (1981) "The Types and Interactions of Vertical Migrations of Functions in a Multilevel Interpretive System." *IEEE Trans Comput* C-30(7), 505–513.

Steadman, P. (1979) *The Evolution of Designs.* Cambridge University Press, Cambridge, England.

Stern, N. (1980) "John von Neumann's Influence on Electronic Digital Computing, 1944–1946." *Annals Hist Comp* 2(4), 349–362.

Stern, N. (1981) *From ENIAC to EDVAC: A Case Study in the History of Technology.* Digital Press, Bedford, Mass.

Stevens, K. (1975) "CFD—A Fortran-like Language for the ILLIAC IV." *SIGPLAN Notices* (March), 72–80.

Stone, H. S. (1971) "Parallel Processing with a Perfect Shuffle." *IEEE Trans Comp.* C-20(2), 153–161.

Stone, H. S. (Ed.) (1980) *Introduction to Computer Architecture.* SRA, Chicago.

Stoy, J. E. (1977) *Denotational Semantics: The Scott-Strachey Approach to Programming Language Theory.* MIT Press, Cambridge, Mass.

Strecker, W. D. (1976) "Cache Memories for the PDP-11 Family Computers." *Proceedings of the 3rd Annual Symposium on Computer Architecture* ACM/IEEE, New York, 155–158.

Strecker, W. D. (1978) "VAX-11/780: A Virtual Address Extension to the DEC PDP-11 Family." *Proceedings of the National Computer Conference,* AFIPS Press, Montvale, N.J., 967–980.

Strecker, W. D. and Clark, D. W. (1980) "Comments on 'The Case for the Reduced Instruction Set Computer' by Patterson and Ditzel." *Comp Arch News (SIGARCH)* 8(6), 34–38.

Stritter, S., and Tredennick, N. (1978) "Microprogrammed Implementation of a Single Chip Microprocessor." *Proceedings of the 11th Annual Workshop on Microprogramming.* ACM/IEEE, New York, 8–16.

Su, B., and Ding, S. (1985) "Some Experiments in Global Microcode Compaction." *Proceedings of the 18th Annual Workshop on Microprogramming.* IEEE Computer Society Press, Los Angeles, Calif. 175–180.

Su, B., Ding, S., and Jin, L. (1984) "An Improvement of Trace Scheduling for Global Microcode Compaction." *Proceedings of the 17th Annual Workshop on Microprogramming.* IEEE Computer Society Press, Los Angeles, Calif. 78–85.

Swan, R. J., Bechtholsheim, A., Lai, K. W., *et al.* (1977) "Implementation of the Cm* Multi-Microprocessor." *Proceedings National Computer Conference.* Vol. 46, AFIPS Press, Montvale, N.J., 645–655.

Swan, R. J., Fuller, S. H., and Siewiorek, D. P. (1977) "Cm*—A Modular Multi-Microprocessor." *Proceedings of NCC* Vol. 46, AFIPS Press, Montvale, N.J., 637–644.

Swartout, W., and Balzer, R. (1982) "On the Inevitable Intertwining of Specification and Implementation." *Comm ACM* 25(7), 438–440.

Swartzlander, E. E. (Ed.) (1976) *Computer Design Development: Principal Papers.* Hayden, Rochelle Park, N.J.

Syre, J. C., Comte, D., Durrieu, G., *et al.* (1977) "LAU System—A Parallel

Data-Driven Software/Hardware System Based on Single Assignment." In M. Feilmeier (Ed.) *Parallel Computers–Parallel Mathematics.* North-Holland, Amsterdam, 347–351.

Tanaka, H., Amamiya, M., Tanaka, Y., *et al.* (1982) "The Preliminary Research of Data Flow Machine and Data Base Machine as the Basic Architecture of Fifth Generation Computer Systems." In Moto-oka (1982) 209–219.

Tanenbaum, A. S. (1978) "Implications of Structured Programming for Machine Architectures." *Comm ACM* 21(3), 237–246.

Tanenbaum, A. S. (1984) *Structured Computer Organization.* Prentice–Hall, Englewood-Cliffs, N.J.

Teichrow, D., and Hershey, E. A. (1977) "PLS/PSA: A Computer Aided Technique for Structured Documentation and Analysis of Information Processing Systems." *IEEE Trans Soft Eng* SE-3(1), 41–48.

Tesler, L. G. and Enea, H. J. (1968) "A Language Design for Concurrent Processes." *Spring Joint Computer Conference, AFIPS Conference Proceedings,* Vol. 32, AFIPS Press, Montvale, N.J., 403–408.

Texas Instruments (1981) *The TTL Data Book.* Texas Instruments, Inc., Dallas.

Thornton, J. E. (1964) "Parallel Operation in the Control Data 6600." *Proceedings of the Fall Joint Computer Conference,* AFIPS, Vol. 24, Pt. 2, AFIPS Press, Montvale, N.J., 33–40. Reprinted in Siewiorek, Bell, and Newell (1982) 730–742.

Thurber, K. J. (1976) *Large Scale Computer Architectures.* Hayden, Rochelle Park, N.J.

Tokoro, M., Tamura, E., and Takizuka, T. (1981). "Optimization of Microprograms." *IEEE Trans Comput* C-30(7), 491–504.

Tomasulo, R. M. (1967) "An Efficient Algorithm for Exploiting Multiple Arithmetic Units." *IBM J Res Dev* (Jan.), 25–33.

Tomita, S., Shibayama, K., Kitamura, T., *et al.* (1983) "A User-Microprogrammable, Local Host Computer with Low Level Parallelism." *Proceedings of the 10th Annual International Symposium on Computer Architecture.* IEEE Computer Society Press, Los Angeles, Calif., 151–159.

Toong, H. D., and Gupta, A. (1981) "An Architectural Comparison of Contemporary 16-Bit Microprocessors." *IEEE Micro* (May), 26–37.

Touzeau, R. F. (1984) "A Fortran Compiler for the FPS-164 Scientific Computer." *Proceedings of the ACM SIGPLAN Symposium on Compiler Construction,* SIGPLAN Notices, 19(6), 48–57.

Tredennick, N. (1982) "The 'Cultures' of Microprogramming." *Proceedings of the 15th Annual Workshop on Microprogramming.* IEEE Computer Society Press, Los Angeles, Calif., 79–83.

Treleavan, P. C., Brownbridge, D. R., and Hopkins, R. P. (1982) "Data Driven and Demand Driven Computer Architecture." *ACM Comp Surv* 14(1), 93–144.

Trivedi, K. S. (1982) *Probability and Statistics with Reliability Queueing and Computer Science Applications.* Prentice–Hall, Englewood-Cliffs, N.J.

Troiani, M., Ching, S. S., Quaynor, N. N., *et al.* (1985) "The VAX 8600 I Box, A

Pipelined Implementation of the VAX Architecture." *Digital Tech J* Digital Equipment Corp., Hudson, Mass., 24–42.

Tseng, C. J., and Siewiorek, D. P. (1982) "The Modeling and Synthesis of Bus Systems." Technical Report DRC-18-42-82, Design Research Center, Carnegie-Mellon University, Pittsburgh, Pa.

Tucker, A. B., and Flynn, M. J. (1971) "Dynamic Microprogramming: Processor Organization and Programming." *Comm ACM* 14(4), 240–250.

Tucker, S. G. (1967) "Microprogram Control for System/360." *IBM Sys J* 6(4), 222–241.

Turing, A. M. (1949) "Checking a Large Routine." *Report on the Conference on High Speed Automatic Calculating Machines.* University Mathematical Laboratory, Cambridge, England, 67–68.

Uehara, T., Saito, T., Maruyama, F., *et al.* (1983) "DDL Verifier and Temporal Logic." In T. Uehara and M. R. Barbacci (Eds.) *Computer Hardware Description Languages and Their Applications* (Proceedings of the 6th International Symposium), North-Holland, Amsterdam, 91–102.

Ullman, J. D. (1984) *Computational Aspects of VLSI.* Computer Science Press, Rockville, Md.

Ungar, D., Blau, R., Foley, P., *et al.* (1984) "Architecture of SOAR: Smalltalk on a RISC." *Proceedings of the 11th Annual International Symposium on Computer Architecture.* IEEE Computer Society Press, Los Angeles, Calif., 188–197.

U.S. Department of Defense (1981) *ADA Language Reference Manual.* Springer-Verlag, Berlin.

van Cleemput, W. M., and Ofek, H. (1984) "Design Automation for Digital Systems." *Computer* 17(10), 114–125.

Varian (1975) *Varian Microprogramming Guide.* Varian Data Machines, Irvine, Calif.

Vegdahl, S. (1982a) "Local Code Generation and Compaction in Optimizing Microcode Compilers." Ph.D. Thesis, Department of Computer Science, Carnegie-Mellon University, Pittsburgh, Pa.

Vegdahl, S. (1982b). "Phase Coupling and Constant Generation in an Optimizing Microcode Compiler." *Proceedings of the 15th Annual Workshop on Microprogramming.* IEEE Computer Society Press, Los Angeles, Calif. 125–133.

Vernon, M. K., and Estrin, G. (1985) "The UCLA Graph Model of Behavior: Support for Performance-Oriented Design." In Giloi and Shriver (1985), 47–65.

von Neumann, J. (1945) "First Draft of a Report on EDVAC." Memorandum, reprinted in Randell (1975), 355–364.

Wagner, A. (1983) "Verification of S*(QM-1) Microprograms," M.S. Thesis, Department of Computer Science, University of Alberta, Edmonton, Alberta, Canada.

Wagner, A., and Dasgupta, S. (1983) "Axiomatic Proof Rules for a Machine Specific Microprogramming Language." *Proceedings of the 16th Annual*

Workshop on Microprogramming. IEEE Computer Society Press, Los Angeles, Calif. 151–158.

Wagnon, G., and Maine, D. J. (1983) "An E-Machine Workbench." *Proceedings of the 16th Annual Microprogramming Workshop.* IEEE Computer Society Press, Los Alamitos, Calif. 151–158.

Watson, I., and Gurd, J. (1982) "A Practical Data Flow Computer." *Computer* 15(2), 51–57.

Wegner, P. (1972a) "The Vienna Definition Language." *ACM Comp Surv* 4(1), 5–63.

Wegner, P. (1972b) "Programming Language Semantics." In R. Rustin (Ed.) *Formal Semantics of Programming Languages.* Prentice–Hall, Englewood-Cliffs, N.J., 149–248.

Wegner, P. (Ed.) (1979) *Research Directions in Software Technology.* MIT Press, Cambridge, Mass.

Weiss, S., and Smith, J. E. (1984) "Instruction Issue Logic for Pipelined Supercomputers." *Proceedings of the 11th International Symposium on Computer Architecture.* IEEE Computer Society Press, Los Alamitos, Calif., 110–118.

Weizenbaum, J. (1976) *Computer Power and Human Reason.* Freeman, San Francisco.

Wexelblat, R. L. (Ed.) (1981) *History of Programming Languages.* Academic Press, New York.

Whitby-Strevens, C. (1985) "The Transputer." *Proceedings of the 12th International Symposium on Computer Architecture.* IEEE Computer Society Press, Los Alamitos, Calif. 292–300.

Wilkes, M. V. (1951) "The Best Way to Design an Automatic Calculating Machine." *Report of the Manchester University Computer Inaugural Conference.* University of Manchester, Manchester, U.K. Reprinted in Swartzlander (1976) 266–270.

Wilkes, M. V. (1965) "Slave Memories and Dynamic Storage Allocation." *IEEE Trans El Comput* EC-14, 270.

Wilkes, M. V. (1968) "Computers Then and Now." 1967 Turing Lecture, *J ACM* 15(1), 1–7.

Wilkes, M. V. (1969) "The Growth of Interest in Microprogramming: A Literature Survey." *ACM Comp Surv* 1(3), 139–145.

Wilkes, M. V. (1975) *Time Sharing Computer Systems.* MacDonald/Elsevier, London.

Wilkes, M. V. (1977) "Babbage as a Computer Pioneer." *Historia Mathematica* 4, 415–440.

Wilkes, M. V. (1982) "The Processor Instruction Set." *Proceedings of the 15th Annual Workshop on Microprogramming* IEEE Computer Society Press, Los Angeles, Calif. 3–5.

Wilkes, M. V. (1983) "Size, Power, and Speed." *Proceedings of the 10th Annual International Symposium on Computer Architecture* IEEE Computer Society Press, Silver Spring, Md., 2–4.

Wilkes, M. V. (1985). *Memoirs of a Computer Pioneer.* MIT Press, Cambridge, Mass.

Wilkes, M. V. (1986) "The Genesis of Microprogramming." *Ann Hist Comp* 8(2), 116–126.

Wilkes, M. V., and Needham, R. M. (1979) *The Cambridge CAP Computer and Its Operating System.* North-Holland, New York.

Wilkes, M. V., Renwick, W., and Wheeler, D. J. (1958) "The Design of a Control Unit of an Electronic Digital Computer." *Proc. IEE* (U.K.), 105.

Wilkes, M. V., and Stringer, J. B. (1953) "Microprogramming and the Design of the Control Circuits in an Electronic Digital Computer." *Proceedings of the Cambridge Philosophical Society,* Pt. 2, 49 (April), 230–238. Reprinted in Bell and Newell (1971), 335–340.

Wilner, W. T. (1972a) "Design of the Burroughs B1700." *Proceedings of the Fall Joint Computer Conference,* AFIPS Press, Montvale, N.J., 489–497.

Wilner, W. T. (1972b) "Burroughs B1700 Memory Utilization" *Proc. FJCC* AFIPS Press, Montvale, N.J., 579–586.

Wilsey, P. A. (1985) "S*M: An Axiomatic Non-Procedural Hardware Description Language for Clocked Architectures," M.S. Thesis, Center for Advanced Computer Studies, University of Southwestern Louisiana, Lafayette.

Winner, R. I. and Carter, E. M. (1986) "Automatic Vertical Migration to Dynamic Microcode: An Overview and Example." *IEEE Software* 3(4), 6–17.

Wirth, N. (1971) "Program Development by Stepwise Refinement." *Comm ACM* 14(4), 221–227.

Wolfe, T. (1981) *From Bauhaus to Our House.* Farrar, Straus & Giroux, New York.

Wood, W. G. (1978) "On the Packing of Microoperations into Microinstruction Words." *Proceedings of the 11th Annual Workshop on Microprogramming.* ACM/IEEE, New York, 51–55.

Wood, W. G. (1979) "The Computer-Aided Design of Microprograms." Ph.D. Thesis (Technical Report CST-5-79), Department of Computer Science, University of Edinburgh, Edinburgh, Scotland.

Wulf, W. A. (1981) "Compilers and Computer Architecture." *IEEE Computer* 14(7), 41–47.

Wulf, W. A., and Bell, C. G. (1972) "C.mmp: A Multiminiprocessor." *Proceedings of the Fall Joint Computer Conference,* AFIPS, Vol. 41, Pt. 2, AFIPS Press, Montvale, N.J., 765–777.

Wulf, W. A., Levin, R., and Harbison, S. (1980) *Hydra/C.mmp: An Experimental Computer System.* McGraw–Hill, New York.

Yeh, P. C., Patel, J. H., and Davidson, E. S. (1983) "Shared Cache for Multiple Stream Computer Systems." *IEEE Trans Comput* C-32(1), 38–47.

Yourdon, E. N. (Ed.) (1979) *Classics in Software Engineering.* Yourdon Press, New York.

Yourdon, E. N. (Ed.) (1982) *Writings of the Revolution, Selected Readings on Software Engineering.* Yourdon Press, New York.

Zelkowitz, M. V., Shaw, A. C., and Gannon, J. D. (1979) *Principles of Software Engineering and Design.* Prentice – Hall, Englewood-Cliffs, N.J.

Zemanek, H. (1980) "Abstract Architecture." In D. Bjorner (Ed.) *Abstract Software Specification.* Springer-Verlag, New York, 1 – 42.

Zimmerman, G. (1980) "MDS — The Mimola Design Method." *J Digital Syst* 4(3), 337 – 369.

Zurcher, W., and Randell, B. (1968) "Iterative Multilevel Modeling: A Methodology for Computer System Design." *Information Processing 68* (Proceedings of the IFIP Congress), North-Holland, Amsterdam, D138-D142.

INDEX

Ackerman, W. B., 329, 330
Adams, D. A., 324
Agerwala, T., 344
Agrawal, D. P., 304
Aho, A. V., 154, 208, 267
Alegre, J., 304, 306, 307
Alexander, W. C., 16
Allan, V., 179, 180
Amamiya, M., 332
Amdahl, G. M., 25, 254
Amdahl's Law, 254–256, 257, 275
Analytical engine, 23
Anderson, D. W., 231
Anderson, G. A., 50
Andrews, G. R., 284, 286, 291, 293, 318
Applicative languages, 329
Apt, K. R., 351
Architecture description languages (ADL):
  applications, 93–94
  in the axiomatic style, 71–74, 99, 114
  families, 67
  for fault simulation, 82
  for formal design, 85–90
  in the functional style, 71–74, 114
  for modeling and simulation, 79–82
  multilevel types, 67, 78, 98, 111, 113
  in the operational style, 67–69
  as part of simulation testbeds, 80–81
  for retargetable code generation, 83–84
  for retargetable microcode generation, 84–85
  as subclass of hardware description
    languages, 58
  varieties, 61, 66
Arithmetic pipeline, 195–196
Arnold, C. S., 61, 144, 153, 155
Array data organization, 258–261
Array processors:
  as architectural style, 241, 244
  comparison with vector processors, 242–246

  examples, 241
  grain of parallelism in, 244
  structure, 241
Arvind, 279, 296, 325, 329, 330, 332, 341,
  342, 344
Asenjo, J. F., 246
Ashcroft, E. A., 358
Associative processing, 38
Atkins, D. E., 167
Avizienis, A., 50
Axiom of assignment, 356, 359, 360
Axiomatic description, 71–74
Axiomatic proof technique, 141–142, 171, 358
Axiomatic semantics, 72, 141, 351, 355–357,
  358, 359

Baba, T., 18, 83, 84, 155, 179
Babbage, C., 23
Backus, J., 344
Baer, J. L., 25, 50, 99, 220, 242, 279
Balzer, R., 114, 128
Bandwidth, 37
Banerjee, U., 209
Benerji, D. K., 149
Banham, R., 49
Barahona, P. M., 333, 340
Barbacci, M. R., 59, 61, 79, 81, 82, 99, 127
Barnes, G. H., 241, 246, 301, 304
Barton, R. S., 21
Basic block, 208, 263
Baskett, F., 246, 253, 254, 306
Batcher, K. E., 241, 304
Behavior, definition of, 13, 77
Behavioral description, 77–78
Behaviorism, 69
Bell, C. G., 3, 26, 33, 37, 43, 51, 79, 99, 198,
  301, 304, 305, 310
Benes, V. E., 304
Berg, H. K., 351